HIMAN HIKIGAYA MAKES A SPEECH. (PART ONE)

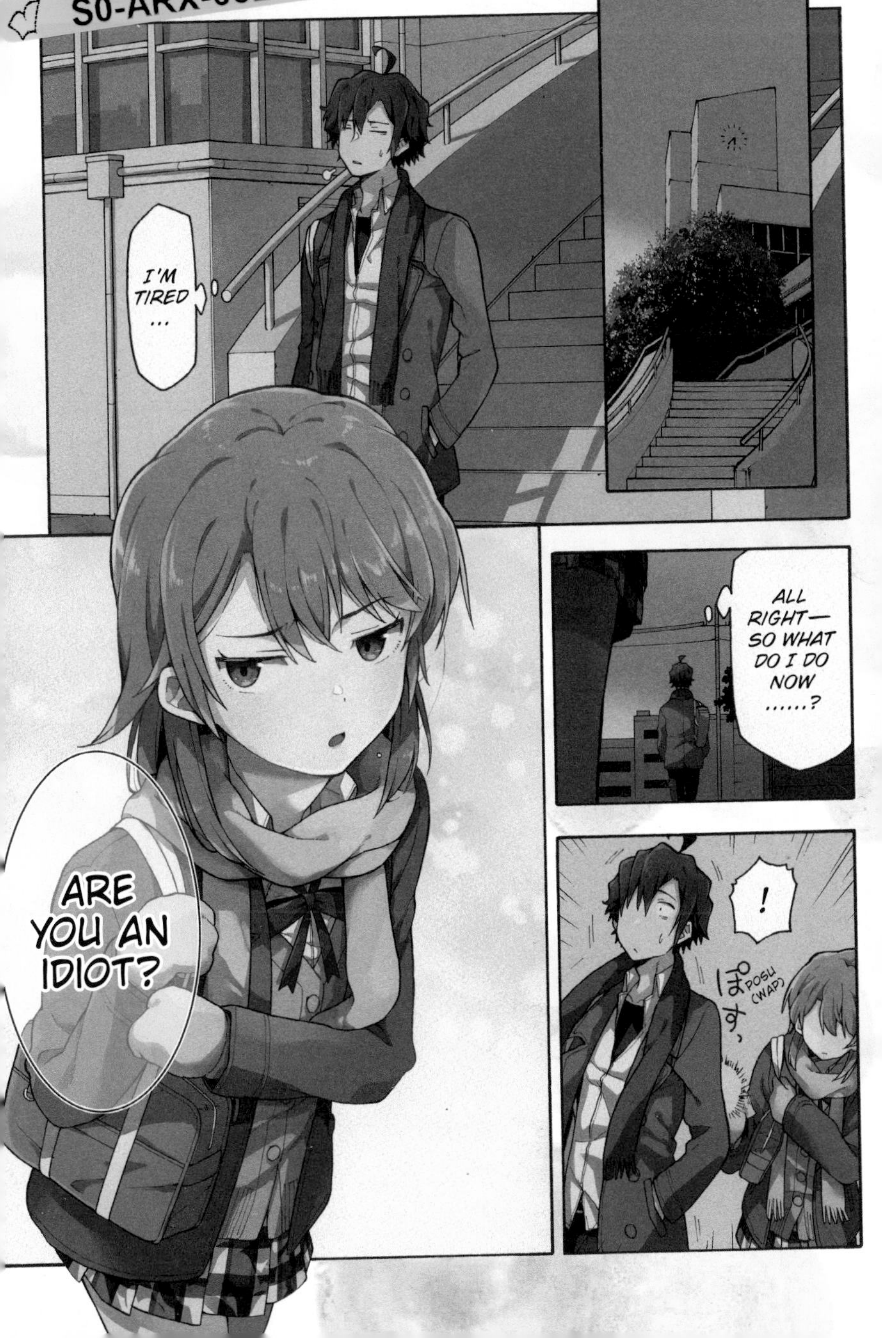
I'M TIRED ...
ALL RIGHT— SO WHAT DO I DO NOW ......?
!
ぽす、
POSU (WAP)
ARE YOU AN IDIOT?

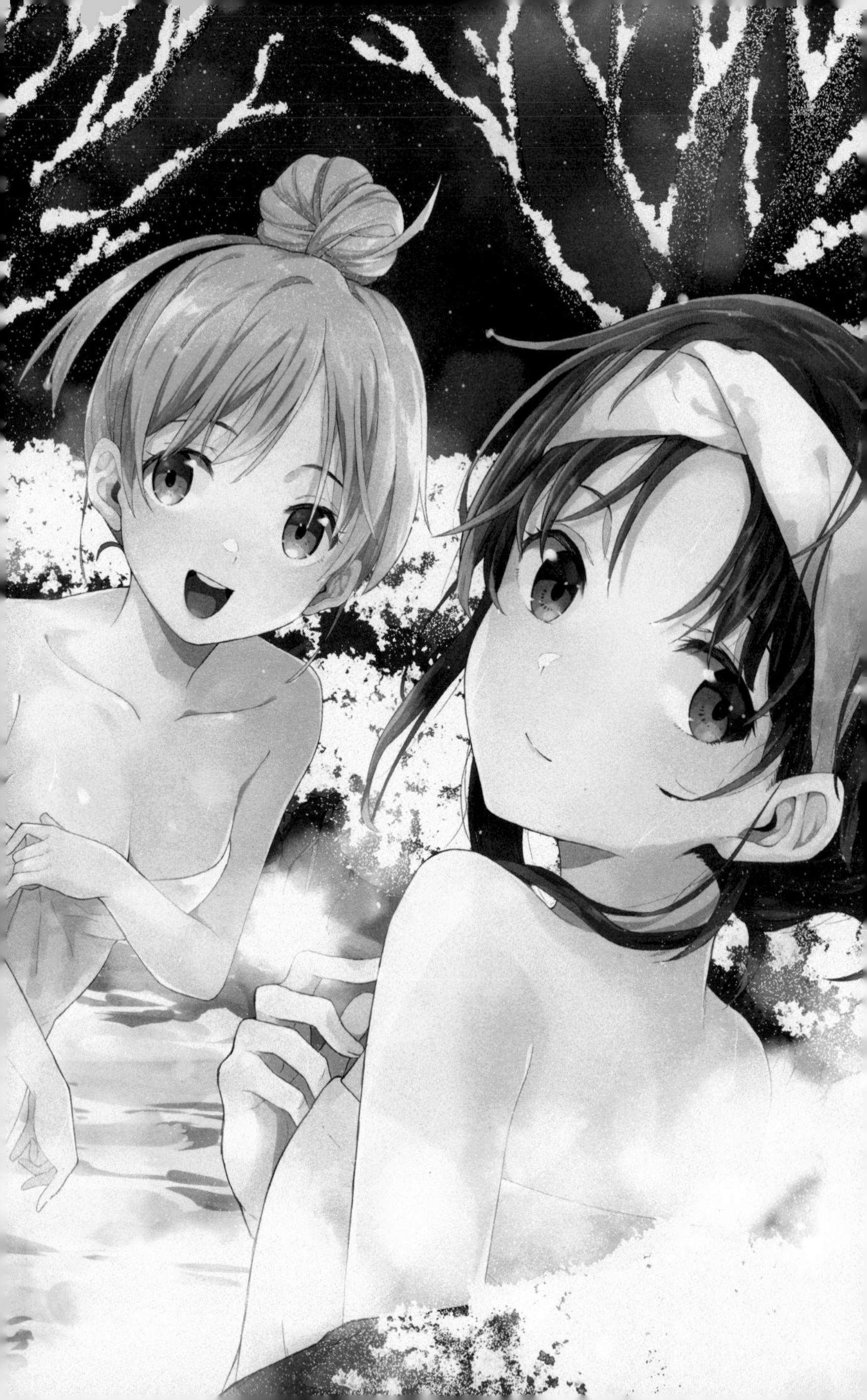

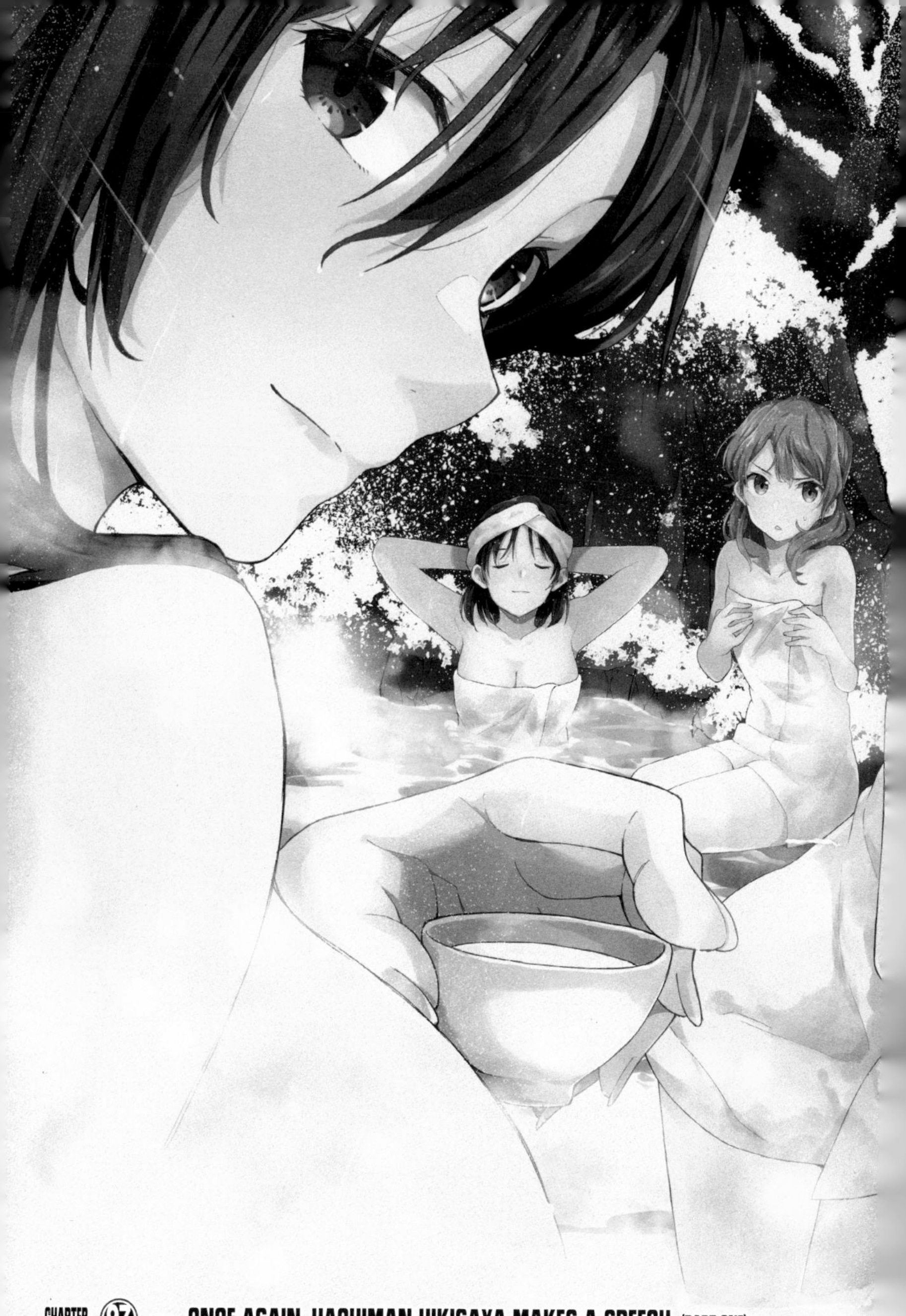

CHAPTER 97 ··· ONCE AGAIN, HACHIMAN HIKIGAYA MAKES A SPEECH. (PART ONE)

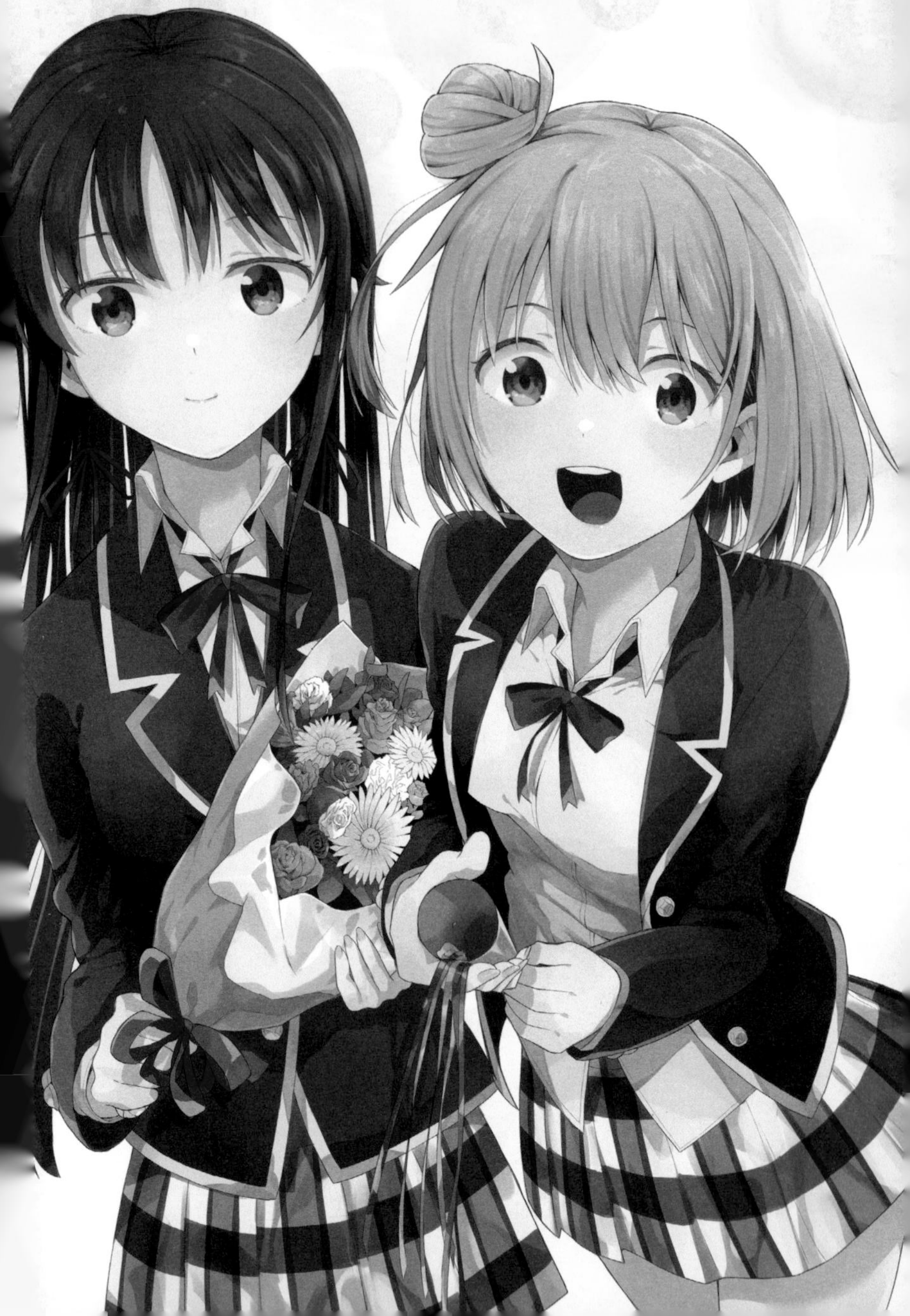

Cover illustration for *Monthly Sunday GX*, June 2021 issue

MY YOUTH ROMANTIC COMEDY iS WRONG, AS I EXPECTED @comic 18

∎Original Story
Wataru Watari
∎Art
Naomichi Io
∎Character Design
Ponkan⑧

MY YOUTH ROMANTIC COMEDY IS WRONG, AS I EXPECTED @COMIC

CHARACTERS + STORY SO FAR

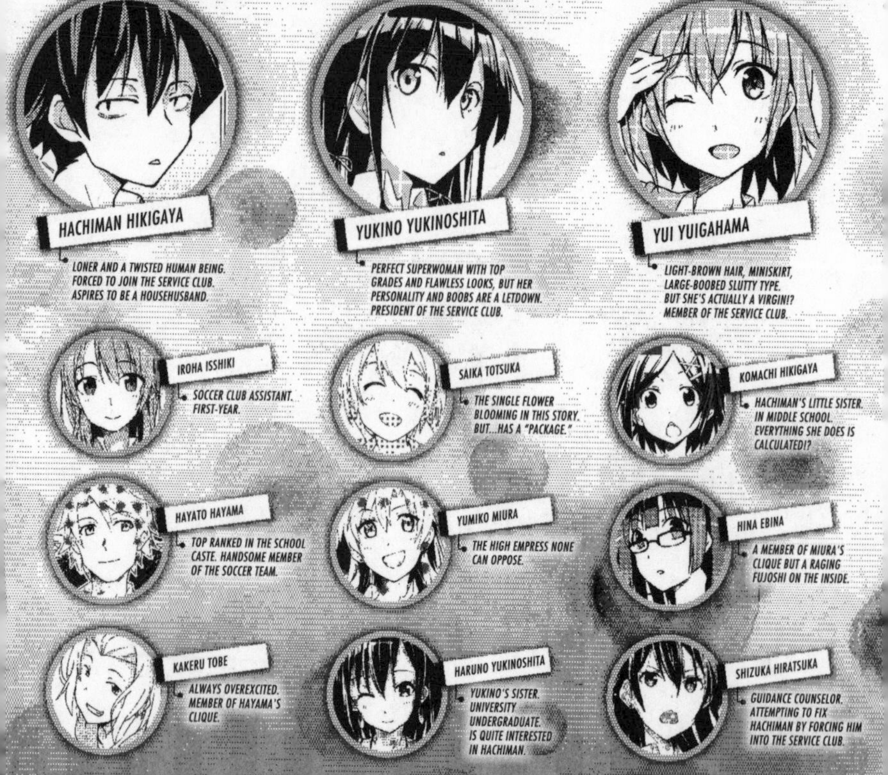
HACHIMAN HIKIGAYA
LONER AND A TWISTED HUMAN BEING. FORCED TO JOIN THE SERVICE CLUB. ASPIRES TO BE A HOUSEHUSBAND.
YUKINO YUKINOSHITA
PERFECT SUPERWOMAN WITH TOP GRADES AND FLAWLESS LOOKS, BUT HER PERSONALITY AND BOOBS ARE A LETDOWN. PRESIDENT OF THE SERVICE CLUB.
YUI YUIGAHAMA
LIGHT-BROWN HAIR, MINISKIRT, LARGE-BOOBED SLUTTY TYPE. BUT SHE'S ACTUALLY A VIRGIN!? MEMBER OF THE SERVICE CLUB.
IROHA ISSHIKI
SOCCER CLUB ASSISTANT. FIRST-YEAR.
SAIKA TOTSUKA
THE SINGLE FLOWER BLOOMING IN THIS STORY. BUT...HAS A "PACKAGE."
KOMACHI HIKIGAYA
HACHIMAN'S LITTLE SISTER. IN MIDDLE SCHOOL. EVERYTHING SHE DOES IS CALCULATED!?
HAYATO HAYAMA
TOP RANKED IN THE SCHOOL CASTE. HANDSOME MEMBER OF THE SOCCER TEAM.
YUMIKO MIURA
THE HIGH EMPRESS NONE CAN OPPOSE.
HINA EBINA
A MEMBER OF MIURA'S CLIQUE BUT A RAGING FUJOSHI ON THE INSIDE.
KAKERU TOBE
ALWAYS OVEREXCITED. MEMBER OF HAYAMA'S CLIQUE.
HARUNO YUKINOSHITA
YUKINO'S SISTER. UNIVERSITY UNDERGRADUATE. IS QUITE INTERESTED IN HACHIMAN.
SHIZUKA HIRATSUKA
GUIDANCE COUNSELOR. ATTEMPTING TO FIX HACHIMAN BY FORCING HIM INTO THE SERVICE CLUB.

SO FAR

EVERYONE IS WORKING TOWARD HOLDING A SOUBU HIGH PROM, WITH YUKINO AND IROHA IN CHARGE. BUT WHEN YUKINO'S MOTHER SUDDENLY TURNS UP AND INSISTS IT SHOULD BE CANCELED, THE PLANNING COMES TO A STANDSTILL. SEEING HOW THE GIRLS WANT THE EVENT TO PROCEED NO MATTER WHAT, HACHIMAN DECLARES HE'LL COME UP WITH A NEW PLAN—IN OTHER WORDS, HE'LL RUN THE OPPOSITION. IT REMINDS HIM OF THE CONTEST THE SERVICE CLUB ONCE HELD WHERE THE WINNER MADE THE OTHERS DO WHATEVER THEY SAID...

CONTENTS

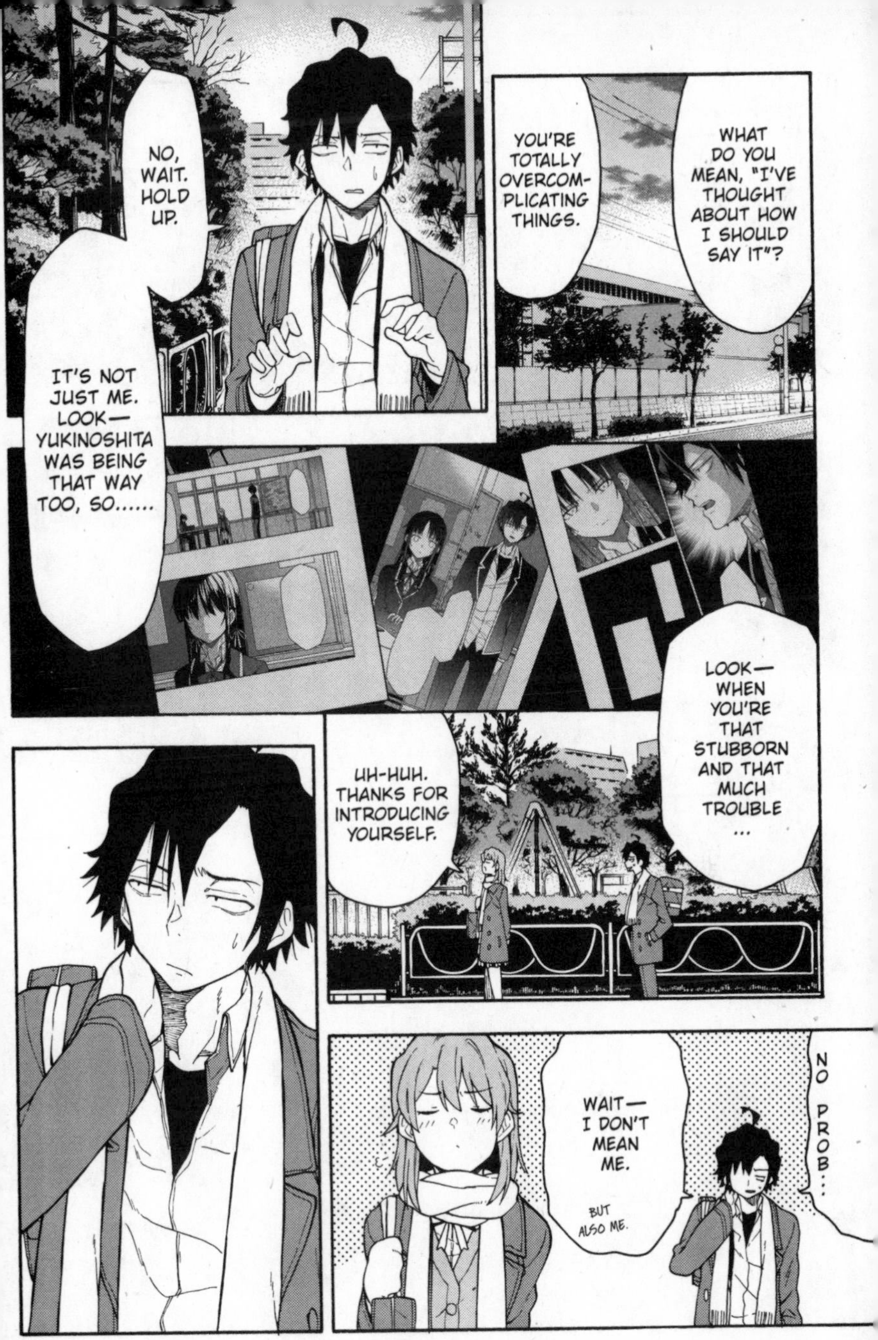
WHAT DO YOU MEAN, "I'VE THOUGHT ABOUT HOW I SHOULD SAY IT"?
YOU'RE TOTALLY OVERCOMPLICATING THINGS.
NO, WAIT. HOLD UP.
IT'S NOT JUST ME. LOOK—YUKINOSHITA WAS BEING THAT WAY TOO, SO......
LOOK—WHEN YOU'RE THAT STUBBORN AND THAT MUCH TROUBLE ...
UH-HUH. THANKS FOR INTRODUCING YOURSELF.
NO PROB...
WAIT—I DON'T MEAN ME.
BUT ALSO ME.

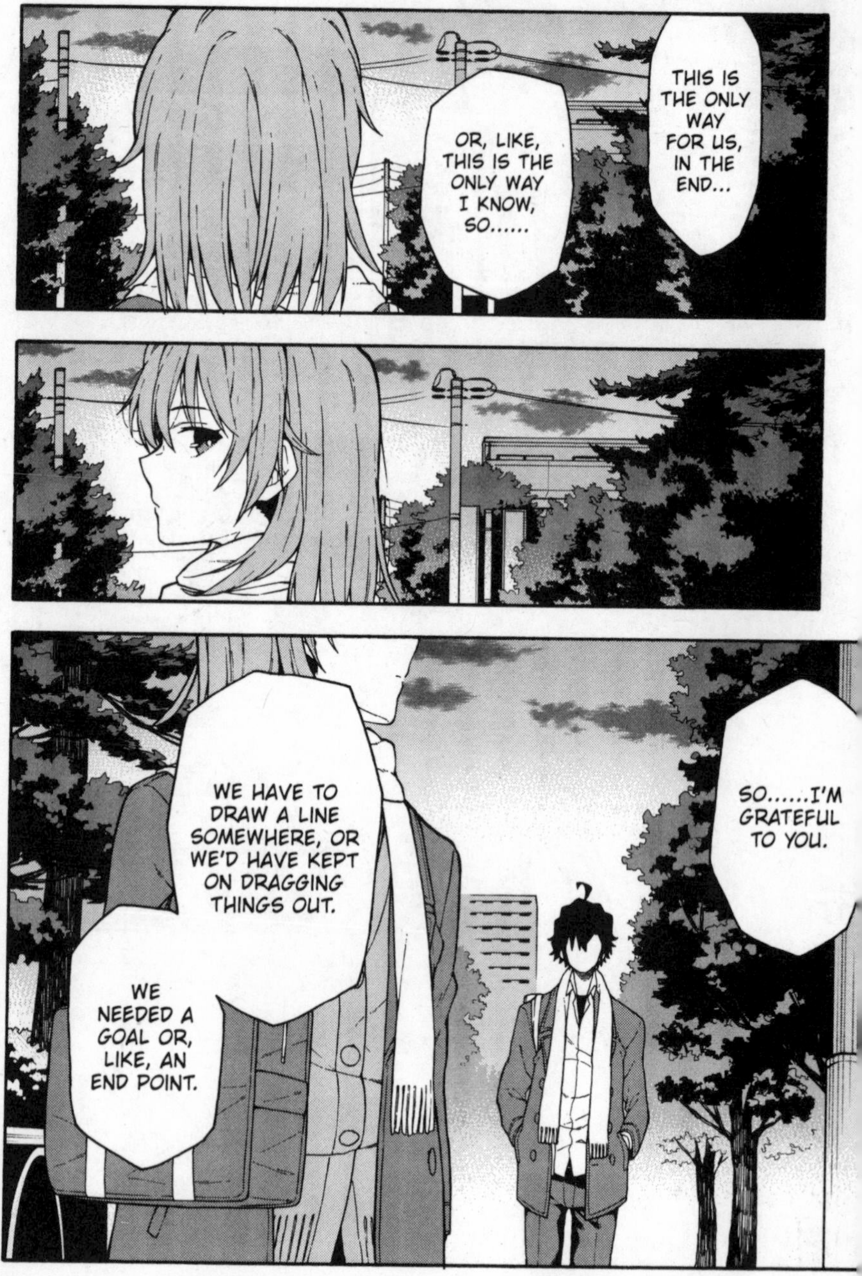
THIS IS THE ONLY WAY FOR US, IN THE END...
OR, LIKE, THIS IS THE ONLY WAY I KNOW, SO......
SO......I'M GRATEFUL TO YOU.
WE HAVE TO DRAW A LINE SOMEWHERE, OR WE'D HAVE KEPT ON DRAGGING THINGS OUT.
WE NEEDED A GOAL OR, LIKE, AN END POINT.

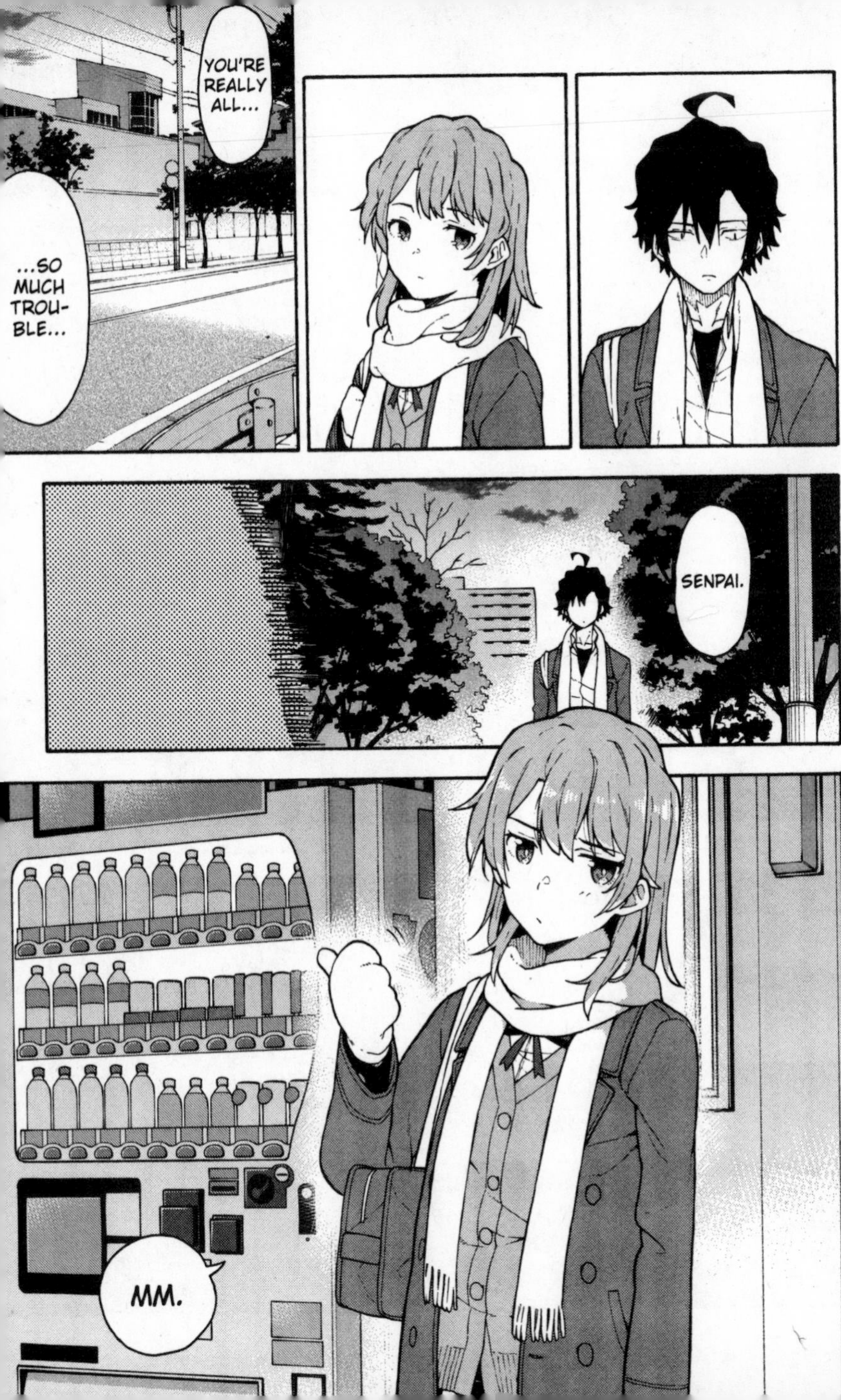
YOU'RE REALLY ALL...
...SO MUCH TROUBLE...
SENPAI.
MM.

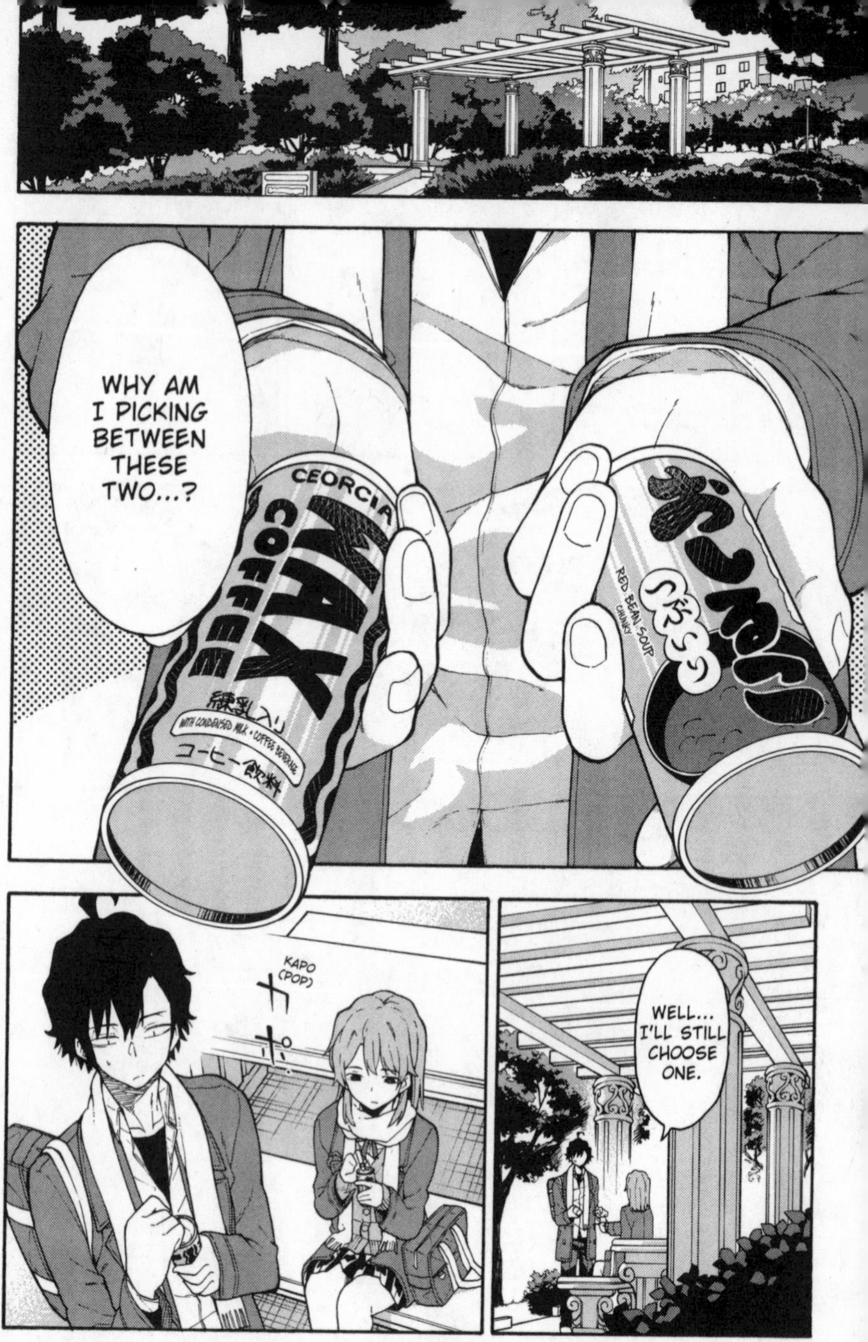
WHY AM I PICKING BETWEEN THESE TWO...?
CEORCIA
MAX COFFEE
練乳入り
WITH CONDENSED MILK • COFFEE BEVERAGE
コーヒー飲料
RED BEAN SOUP
CHUNKY
WELL... I'LL STILL CHOOSE ONE.
KAPO (POP)

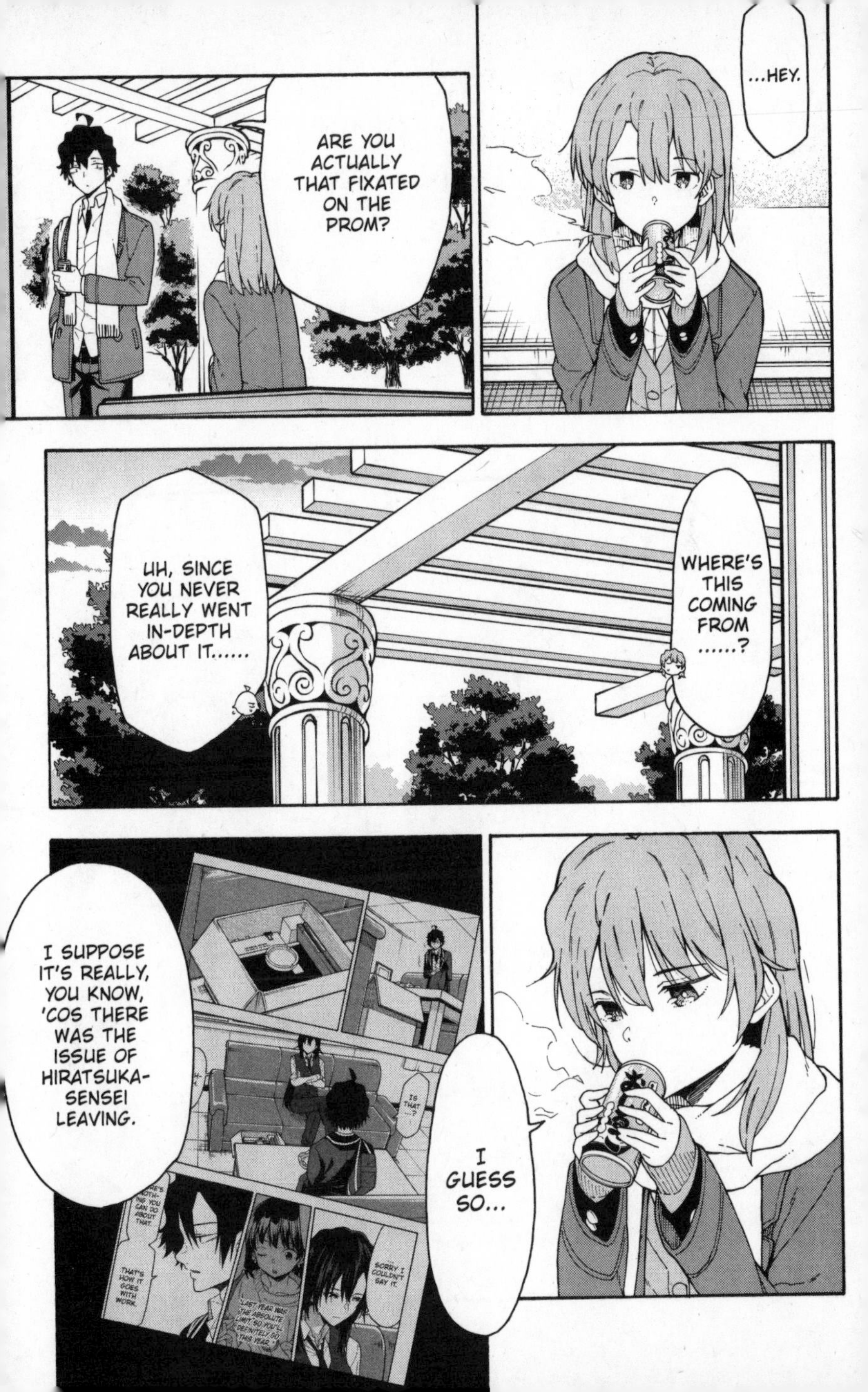
...HEY.
ARE YOU ACTUALLY THAT FIXATED ON THE PROM?
WHERE'S THIS COMING FROM ......?
UH, SINCE YOU NEVER REALLY WENT IN-DEPTH ABOUT IT......
I GUESS SO...
I SUPPOSE IT'S REALLY, YOU KNOW, 'COS THERE WAS THE ISSUE OF HIRATSUKA-SENSEI LEAVING.
IS THAT ...?
SORRY I COULDN'T SAY IT.
"LAST YEAR WAS THE ABSOLUTE LIMIT, SO YOU'LL DEFINITELY GO THIS YEAR."
THAT'S HOW IT GOES WITH WORK.

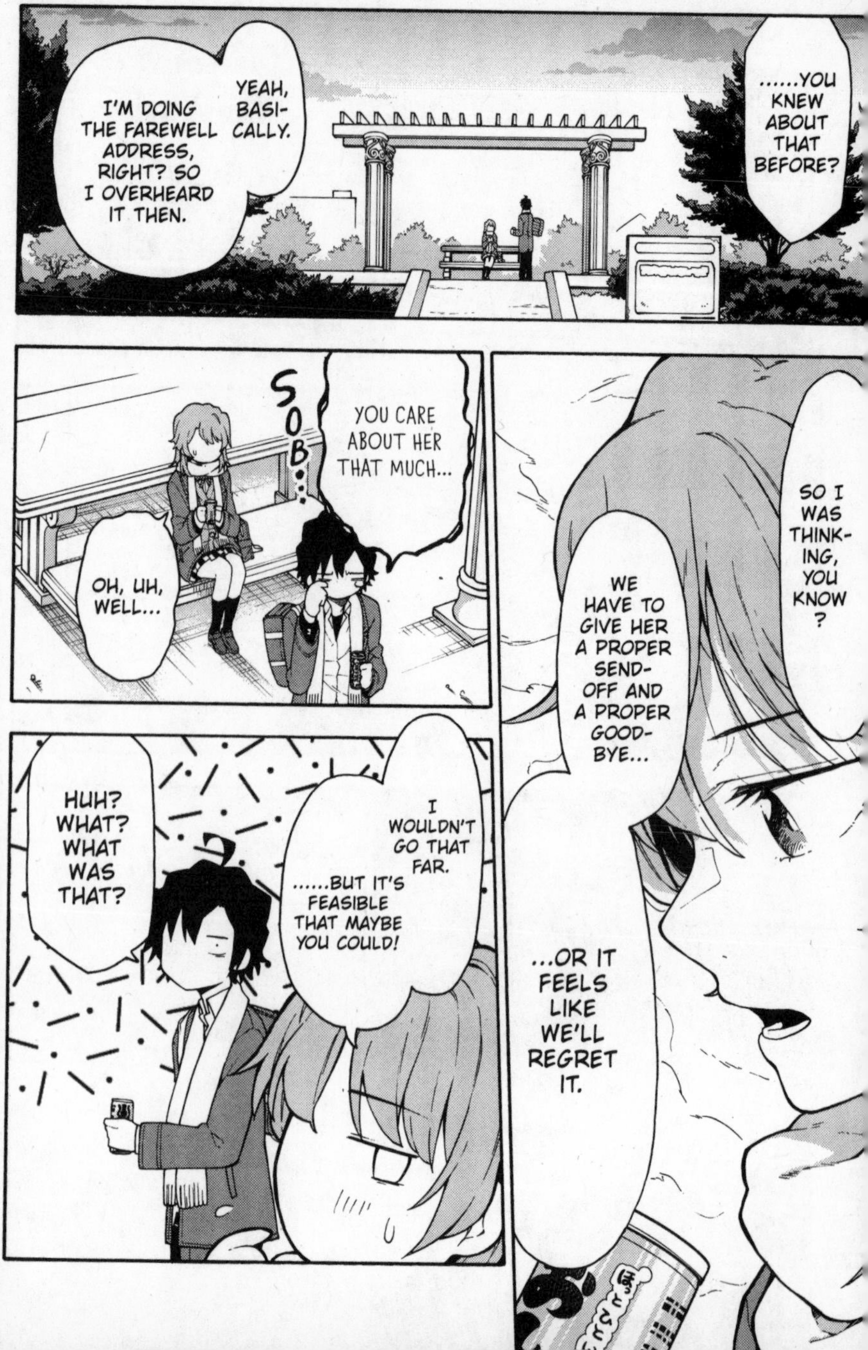

......YOU KNEW ABOUT THAT BEFORE?
YEAH, BASI-CALLY.
I'M DOING THE FAREWELL ADDRESS, RIGHT? SO I OVERHEARD IT THEN.
SO I WAS THINK-ING, YOU KNOW?
WE HAVE TO GIVE HER A PROPER SEND-OFF AND A PROPER GOOD-BYE...
...OR IT FEELS LIKE WE'LL REGRET IT.
YOU CARE ABOUT HER THAT MUCH...
SOB...
OH, UH, WELL...
I WOULDN'T GO THAT FAR.
......BUT IT'S FEASIBLE THAT MAYBE YOU COULD!
HUH? WHAT? WHAT WAS THAT?

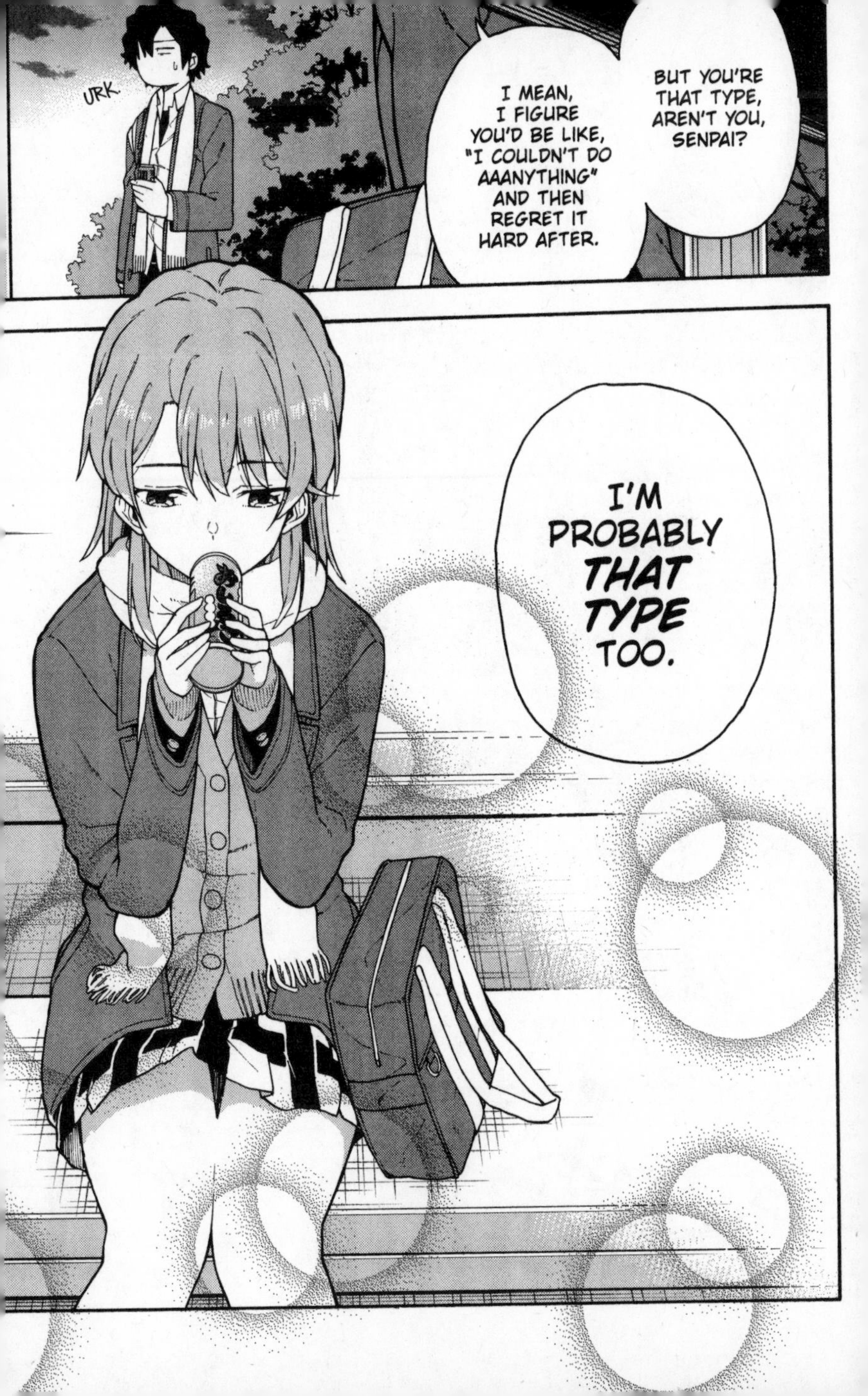
BUT YOU'RE THAT TYPE, AREN'T YOU, SENPAI?
I MEAN, I FIGURE YOU'D BE LIKE, "I COULDN'T DO AAANYTHING" AND THEN REGRET IT HARD AFTER.
URK.
I'M PROBABLY *THAT TYPE* TOO.

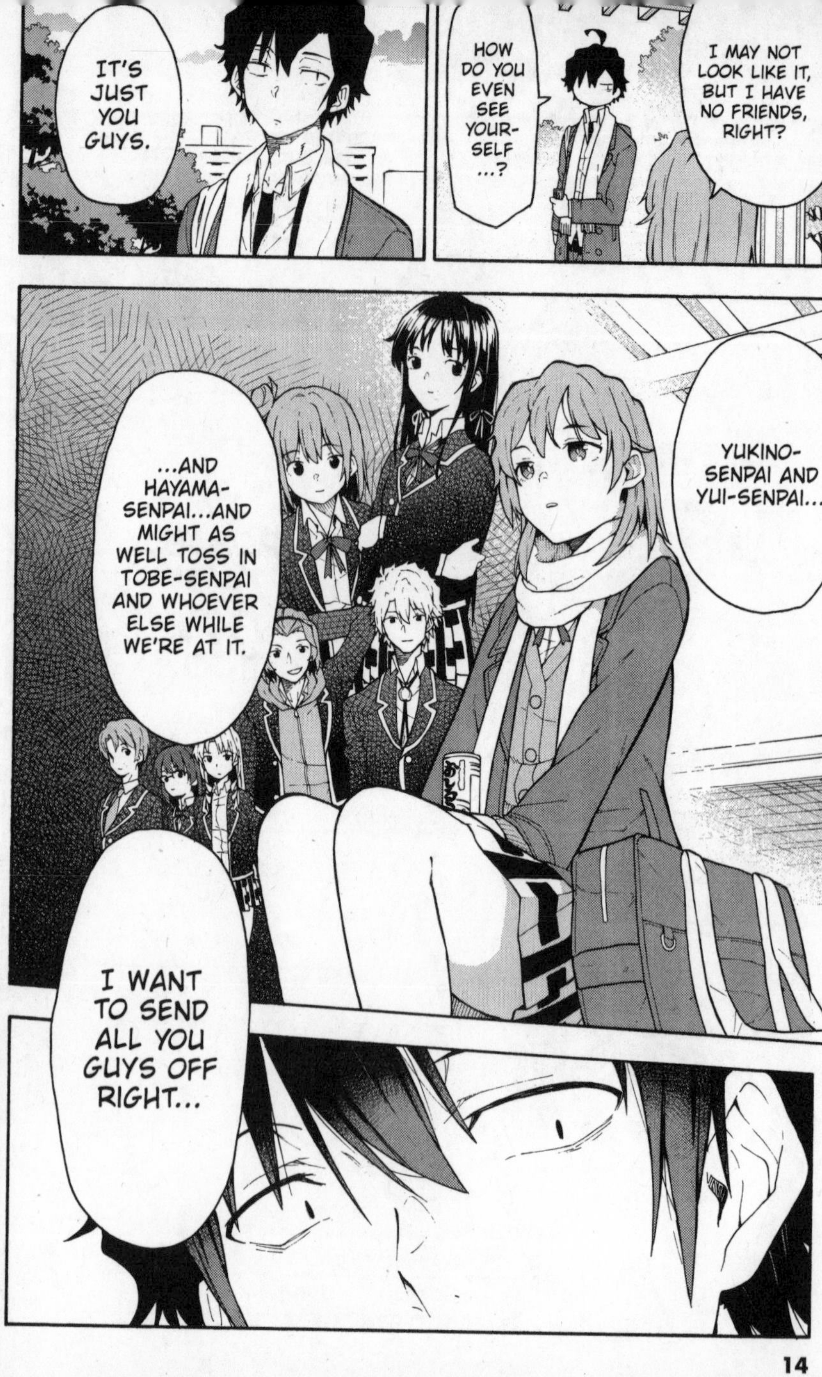
I MAY NOT LOOK LIKE IT, BUT I HAVE NO FRIENDS, RIGHT?
HOW DO YOU EVEN SEE YOURSELF...?
IT'S JUST YOU GUYS.
YUKINO-SENPAI AND YUI-SENPAI...
...AND HAYAMA-SENPAI...AND MIGHT AS WELL TOSS IN TOBE-SENPAI AND WHOEVER ELSE WHILE WE'RE AT IT.
I WANT TO SEND ALL YOU GUYS OFF RIGHT...

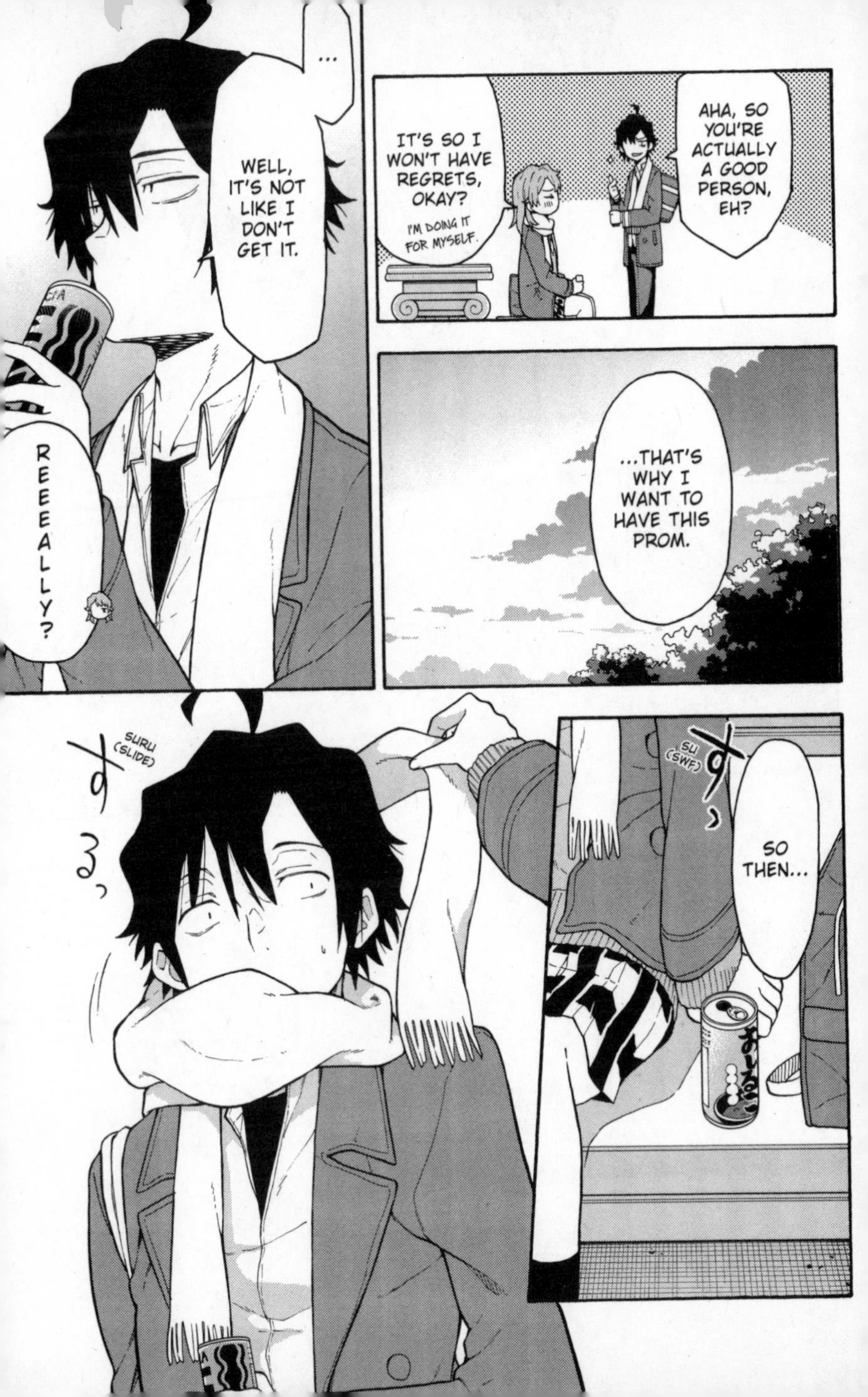
AHA, SO YOU'RE ACTUALLY A GOOD PERSON, EH?
IT'S SO I WON'T HAVE REGRETS, OKAY?
I'M DOING IT FOR MYSELF.
...THAT'S WHY I WANT TO HAVE THIS PROM.
...
WELL, IT'S NOT LIKE I DON'T GET IT.
REEEEALLY?
SU (SWF)
SO THEN...
SURU (SLIDE)

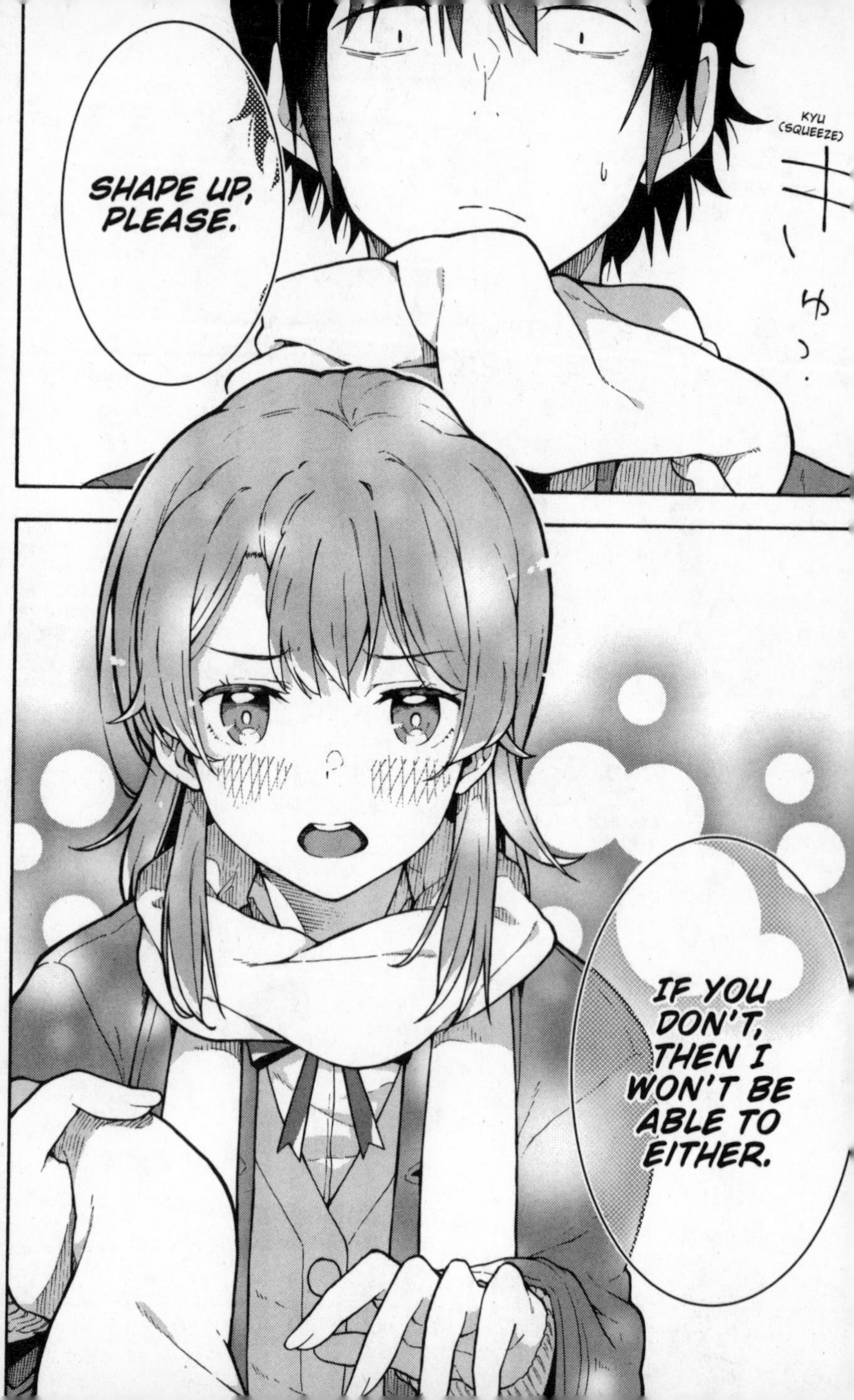
KYU (SQUEEZE)
キュッ
SHAPE UP, PLEASE.
IF YOU DON'T, THEN I WON'T BE ABLE TO EITHER.

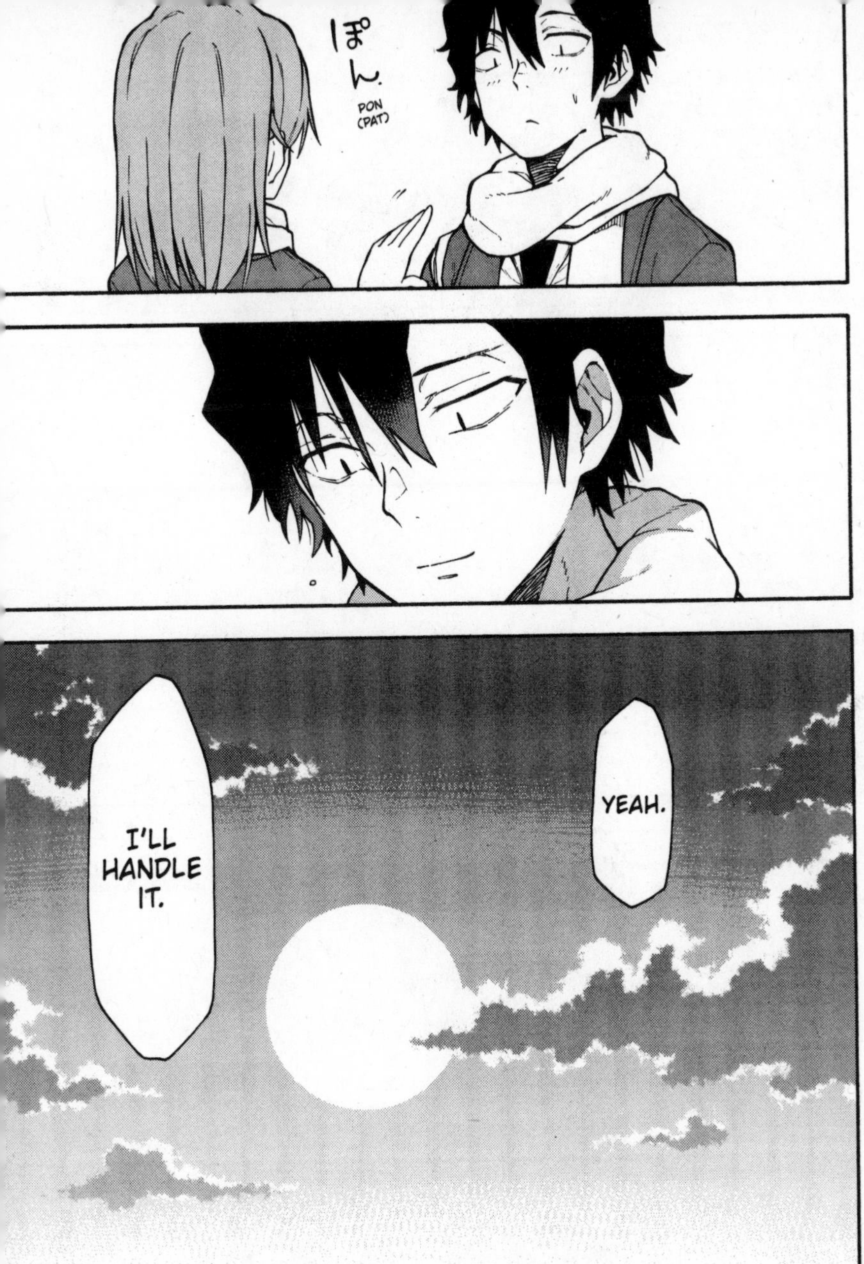
ぽん.
PON (PAT)
YEAH.
I'LL HANDLE IT.

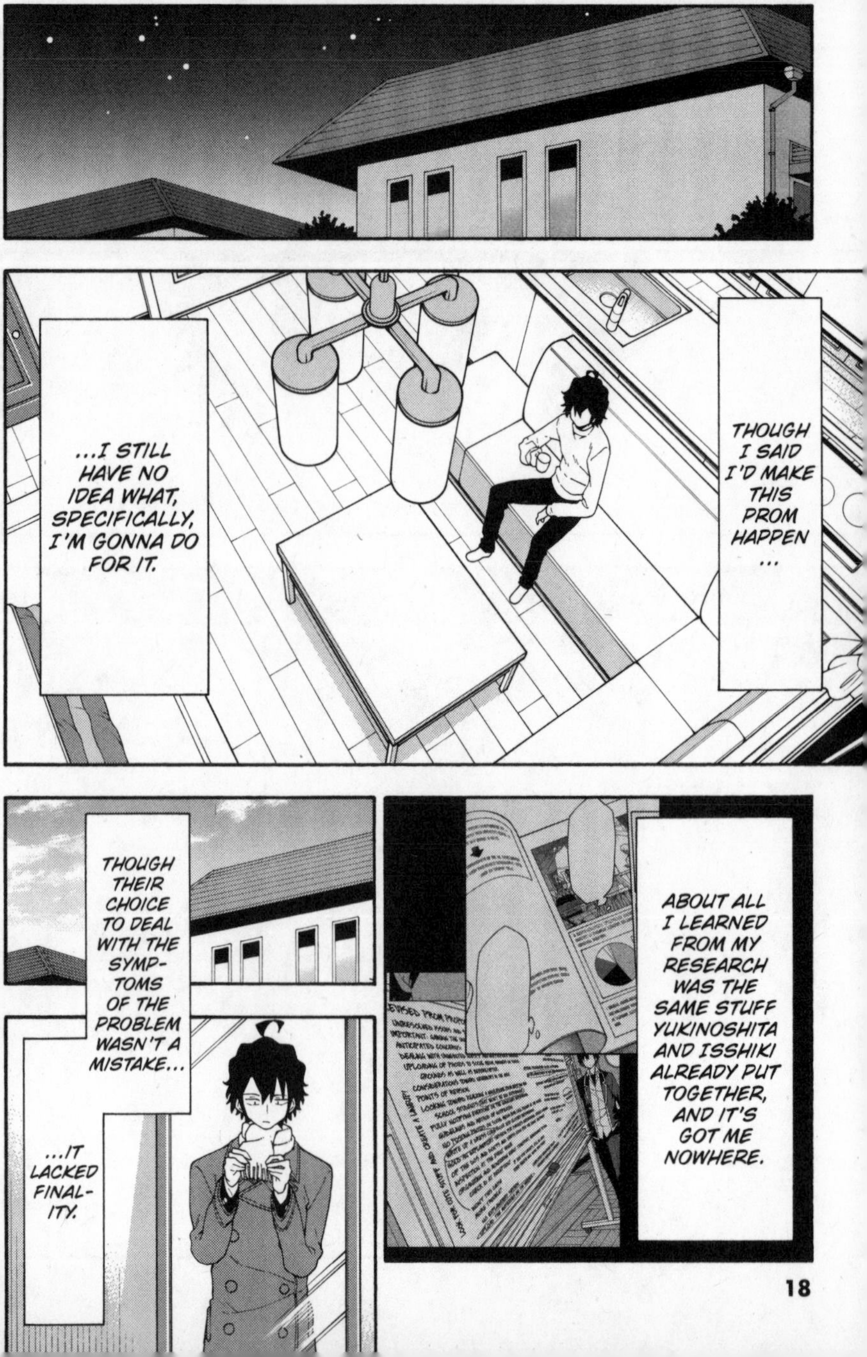
THOUGH I SAID I'D MAKE THIS PROM HAPPEN...
...I STILL HAVE NO IDEA WHAT, SPECIFICALLY, I'M GONNA DO FOR IT.
ABOUT ALL I LEARNED FROM MY RESEARCH WAS THE SAME STUFF YUKINOSHITA AND ISSHIKI ALREADY PUT TOGETHER, AND IT'S GOT ME NOWHERE.
THOUGH THEIR CHOICE TO DEAL WITH THE SYMP-TOMS OF THE PROBLEM WASN'T A MISTAKE...
...IT LACKED FINAL-ITY.

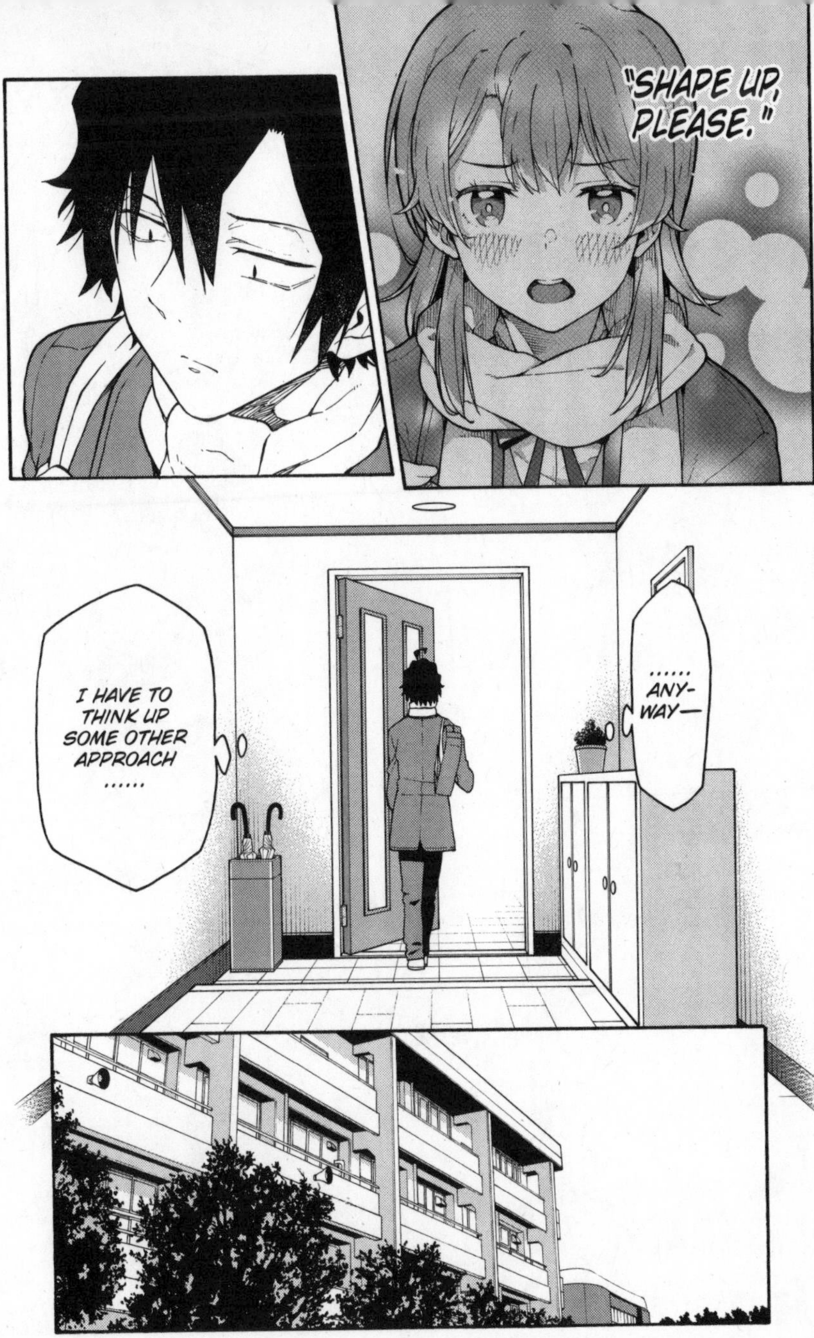
"SHAPE UP, PLEASE."
......ANY-WAY—
I HAVE TO THINK UP SOME OTHER APPROACH ......

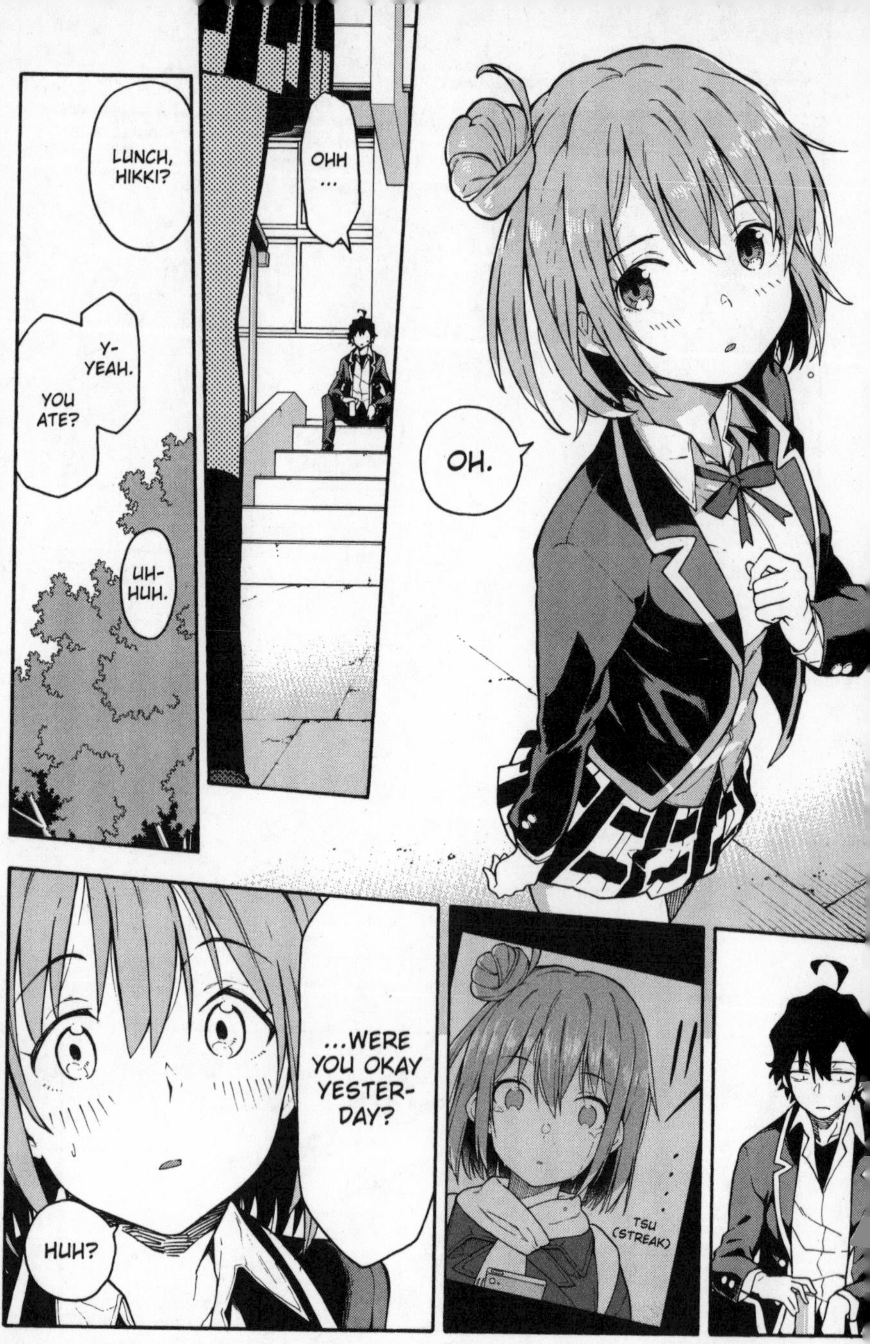
OH.
OHH ...
LUNCH, HIKKI?
Y-YEAH.
YOU ATE?
UH-HUH.
TSU (STREAK)
...WERE YOU OKAY YESTER-DAY?
HUH?

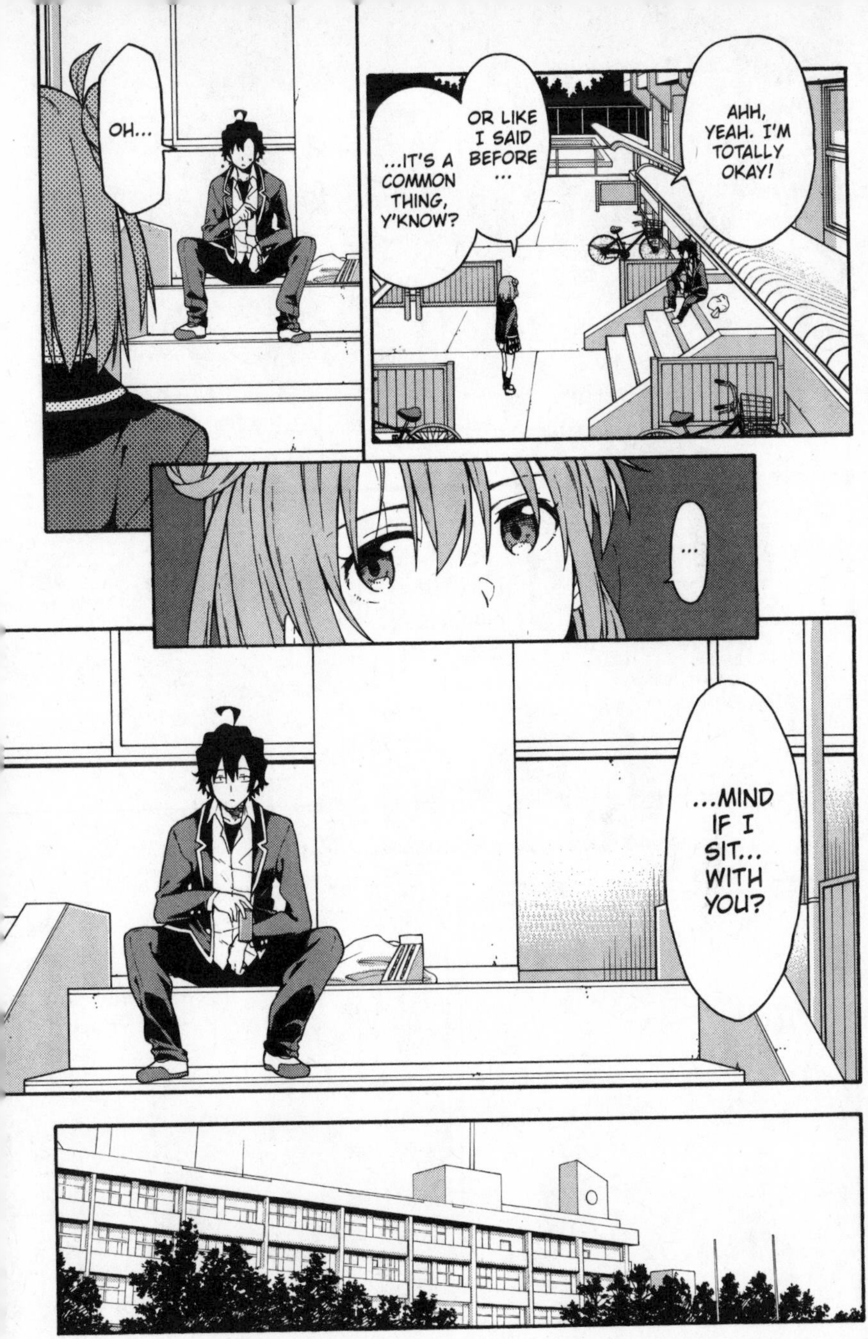
AHH, YEAH. I'M TOTALLY OKAY!
OR LIKE I SAID BEFORE ...
...IT'S A COMMON THING, Y'KNOW?
OH...
...
...MIND IF I SIT... WITH YOU?

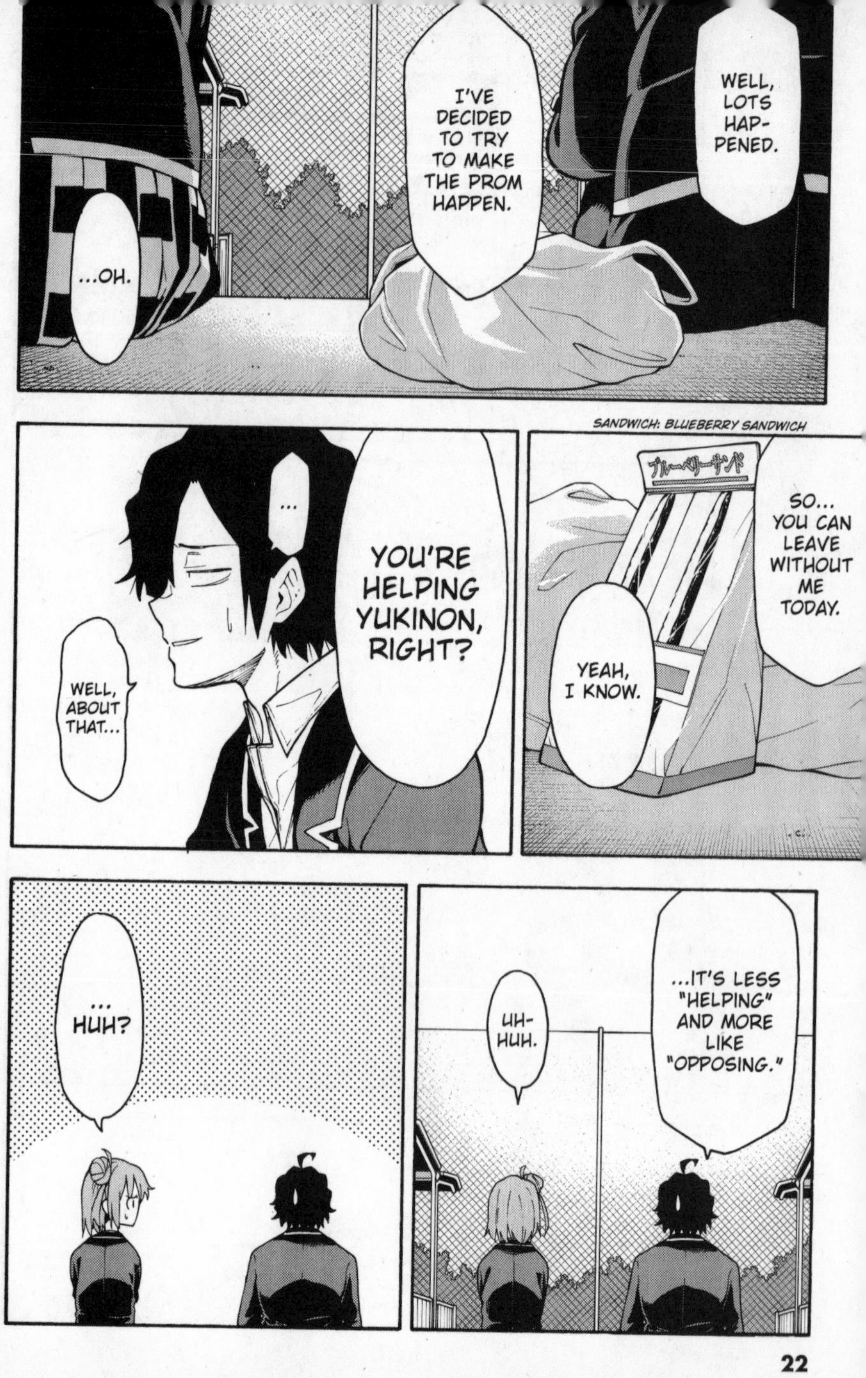
WELL, LOTS HAP-PENED.
I'VE DECIDED TO TRY TO MAKE THE PROM HAPPEN.
...OH.
SANDWICH: BLUEBERRY SANDWICH
ブルーベリーサンド
SO... YOU CAN LEAVE WITHOUT ME TODAY.
YEAH, I KNOW.
YOU'RE HELPING YUKINON, RIGHT?
...
WELL, ABOUT THAT...
...IT'S LESS "HELPING" AND MORE LIKE "OPPOSING."
UH-HUH.
... HUH?

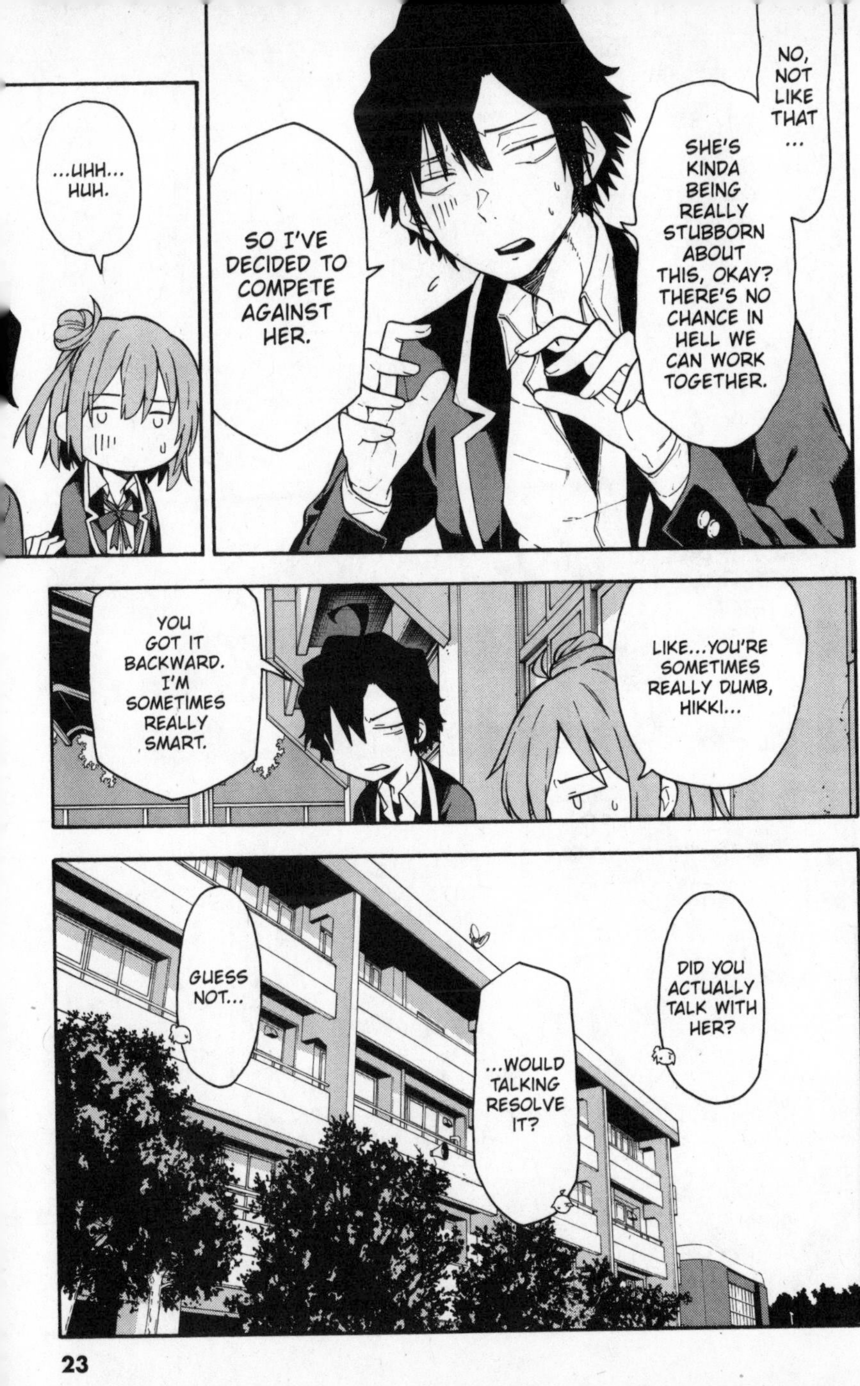
NO, NOT LIKE THAT...
SHE'S KINDA BEING REALLY STUBBORN ABOUT THIS, OKAY? THERE'S NO CHANCE IN HELL WE CAN WORK TOGETHER.
SO I'VE DECIDED TO COMPETE AGAINST HER.
...UHH... HUH.
LIKE...YOU'RE SOMETIMES REALLY DUMB, HIKKI...
YOU GOT IT BACKWARD. I'M SOMETIMES REALLY SMART.
DID YOU ACTUALLY TALK WITH HER?
...WOULD TALKING RESOLVE IT?
GUESS NOT...

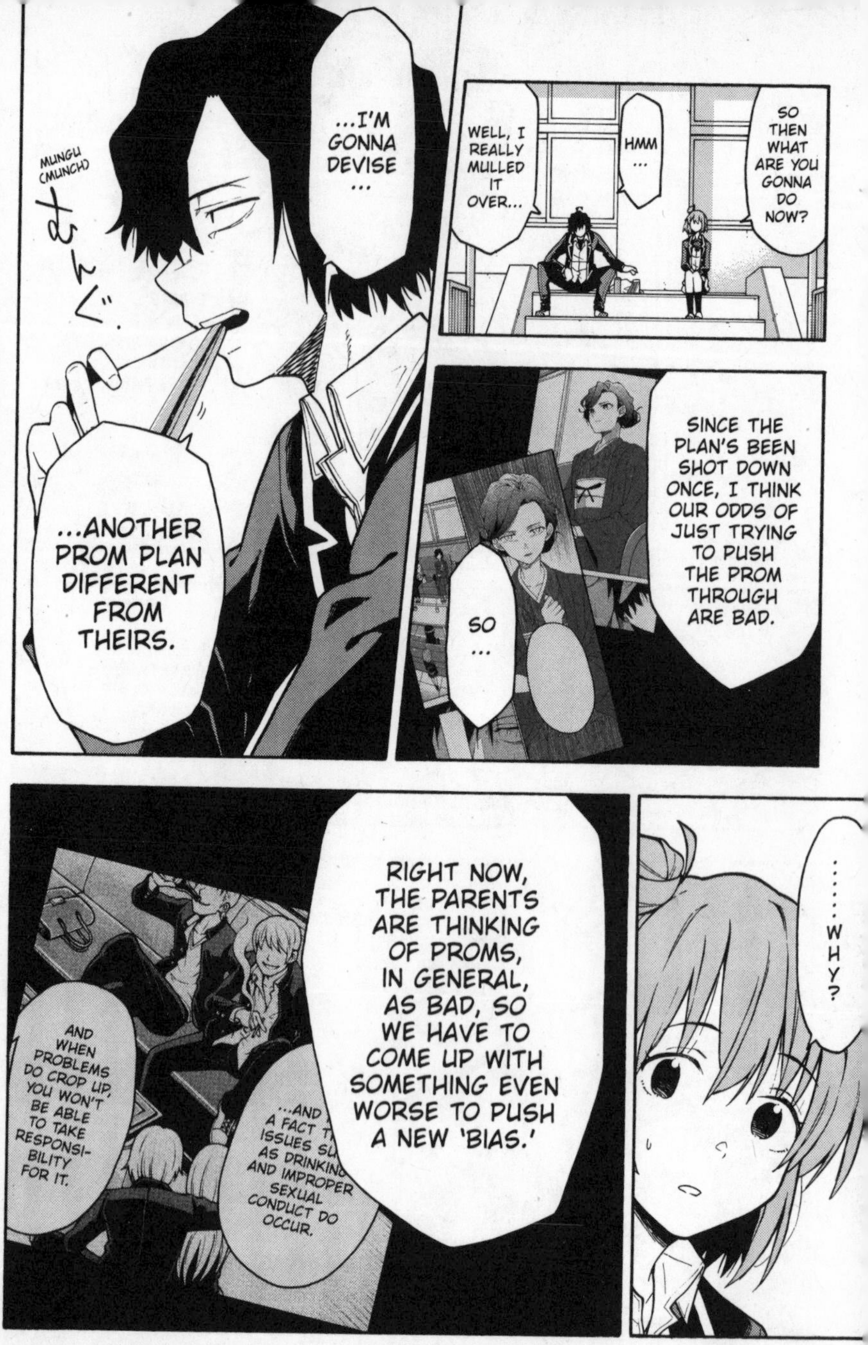
SO THEN WHAT ARE YOU GONNA DO NOW?
HMM...
WELL, I REALLY MULLED IT OVER...
SINCE THE PLAN'S BEEN SHOT DOWN ONCE, I THINK OUR ODDS OF JUST TRYING TO PUSH THE PROM THROUGH ARE BAD.
SO...
むんぐ
MUNGU (MUNCH)
...I'M GONNA DEVISE...
...ANOTHER PROM PLAN DIFFERENT FROM THEIRS.
......WHY?
RIGHT NOW, THE PARENTS ARE THINKING OF PROMS, IN GENERAL, AS BAD, SO WE HAVE TO COME UP WITH SOMETHING EVEN WORSE TO PUSH A NEW 'BIAS.'
...AND A FACT TH ISSUES SU AS DRINKIN AND IMPROPER SEXUAL CONDUCT DO OCCUR.
AND WHEN PROBLEMS DO CROP UP, YOU WON'T BE ABLE TO TAKE RESPONSIBILITY FOR IT.

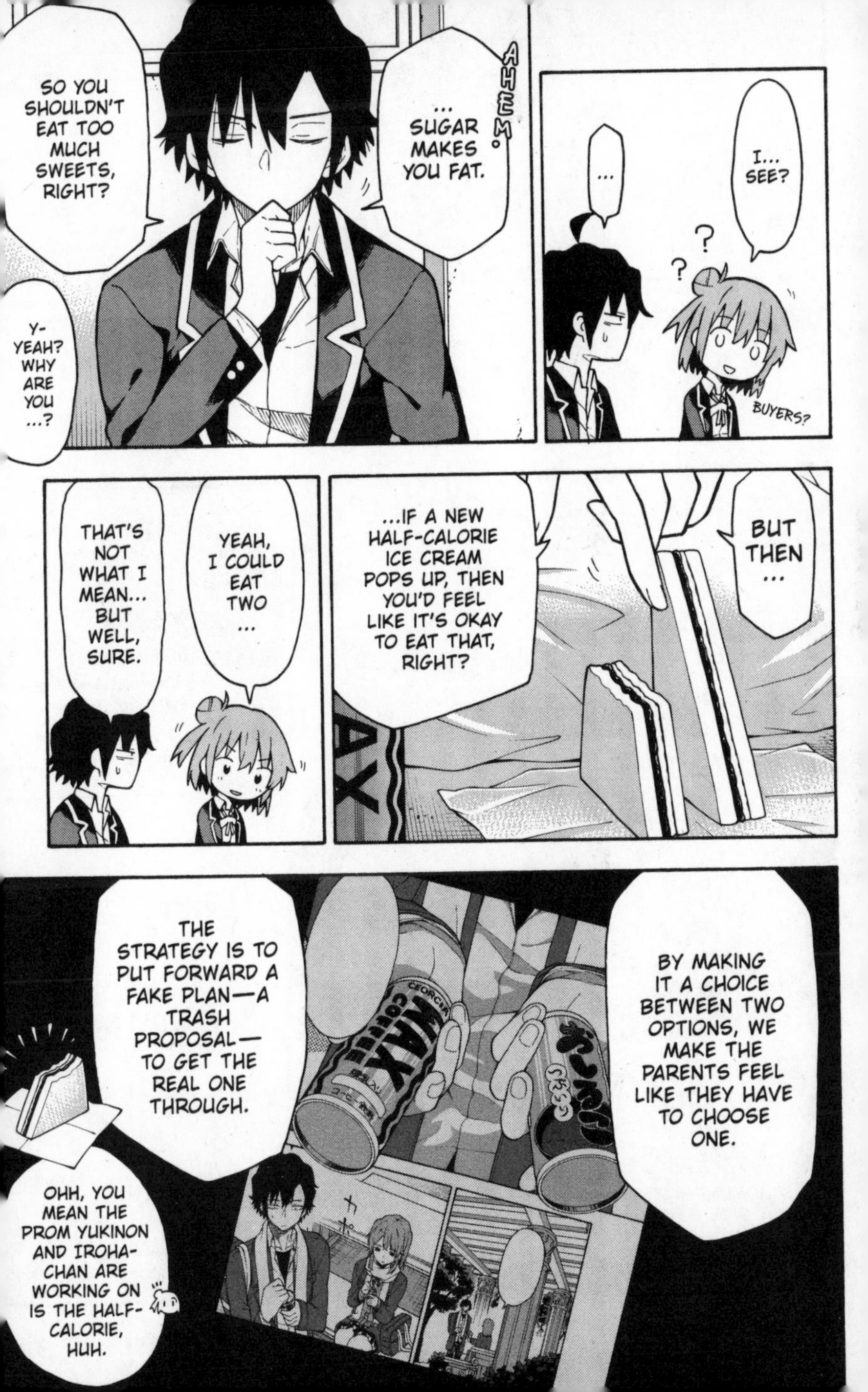
I... SEE?
...
BUYERS?
AHEM.
... SUGAR MAKES YOU FAT.
SO YOU SHOULDN'T EAT TOO MUCH SWEETS, RIGHT?
Y-YEAH? WHY ARE YOU ...?
BUT THEN ...
...IF A NEW HALF-CALORIE ICE CREAM POPS UP, THEN YOU'D FEEL LIKE IT'S OKAY TO EAT THAT, RIGHT?
YEAH, I COULD EAT TWO ...
THAT'S NOT WHAT I MEAN... BUT WELL, SURE.
BY MAKING IT A CHOICE BETWEEN TWO OPTIONS, WE MAKE THE PARENTS FEEL LIKE THEY HAVE TO CHOOSE ONE.
THE STRATEGY IS TO PUT FORWARD A FAKE PLAN—A TRASH PROPOSAL—TO GET THE REAL ONE THROUGH.
OHH, YOU MEAN THE PROM YUKINON AND IROHA-CHAN ARE WORKING ON IS THE HALF-CALORIE, HUH.

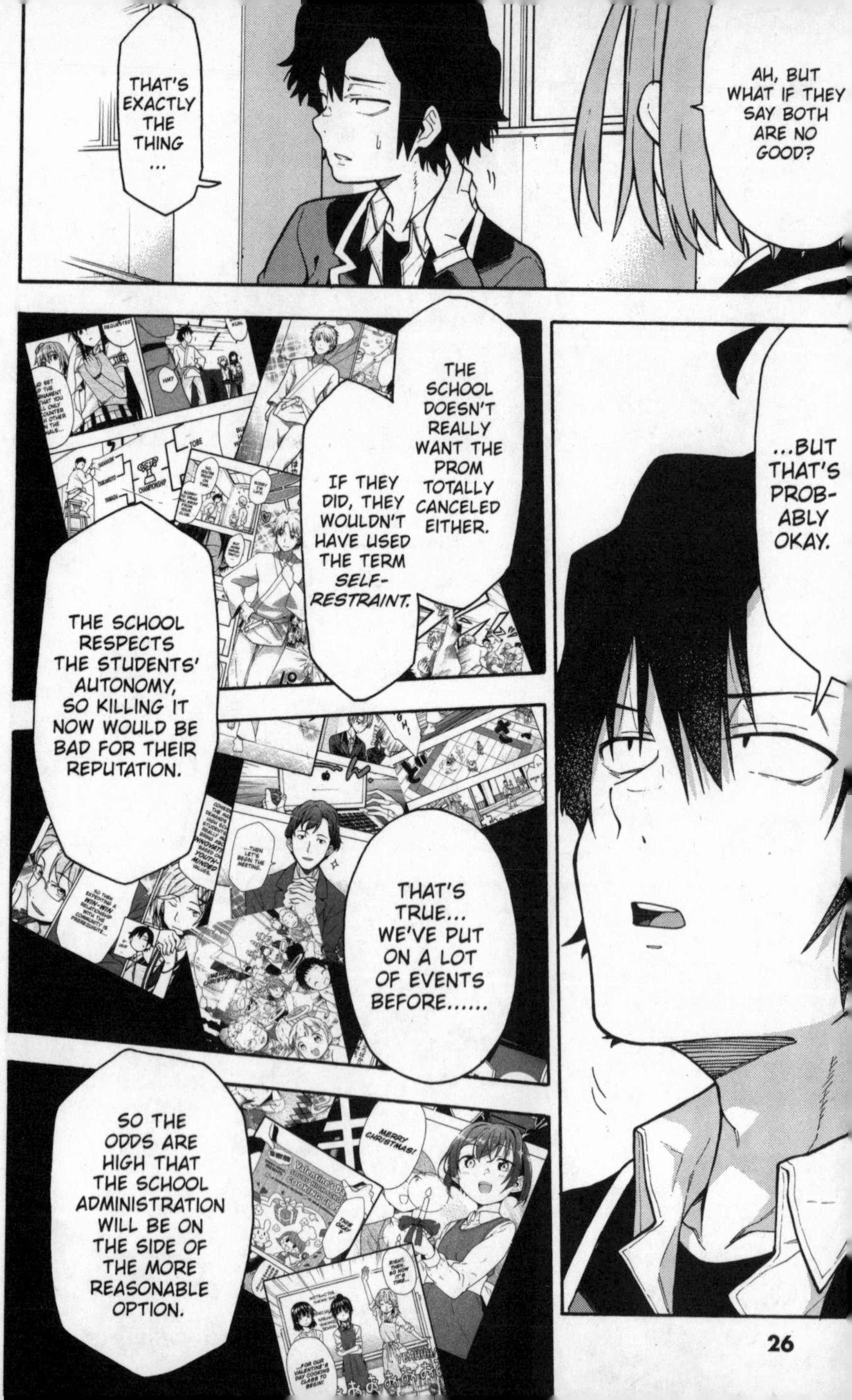
AH, BUT WHAT IF THEY SAY BOTH ARE NO GOOD?
THAT'S EXACTLY THE THING...
...BUT THAT'S PROBABLY OKAY.
THE SCHOOL DOESN'T REALLY WANT THE PROM TOTALLY CANCELED EITHER.
IF THEY DID, THEY WOULDN'T HAVE USED THE TERM *SELF-RESTRAINT.*
THE SCHOOL RESPECTS THE STUDENTS' AUTONOMY, SO KILLING IT NOW WOULD BE BAD FOR THEIR REPUTATION.
THAT'S TRUE... WE'VE PUT ON A LOT OF EVENTS BEFORE......
SO THE ODDS ARE HIGH THAT THE SCHOOL ADMINISTRATION WILL BE ON THE SIDE OF THE MORE REASONABLE OPTION.
MERRY CHRISTMAS!

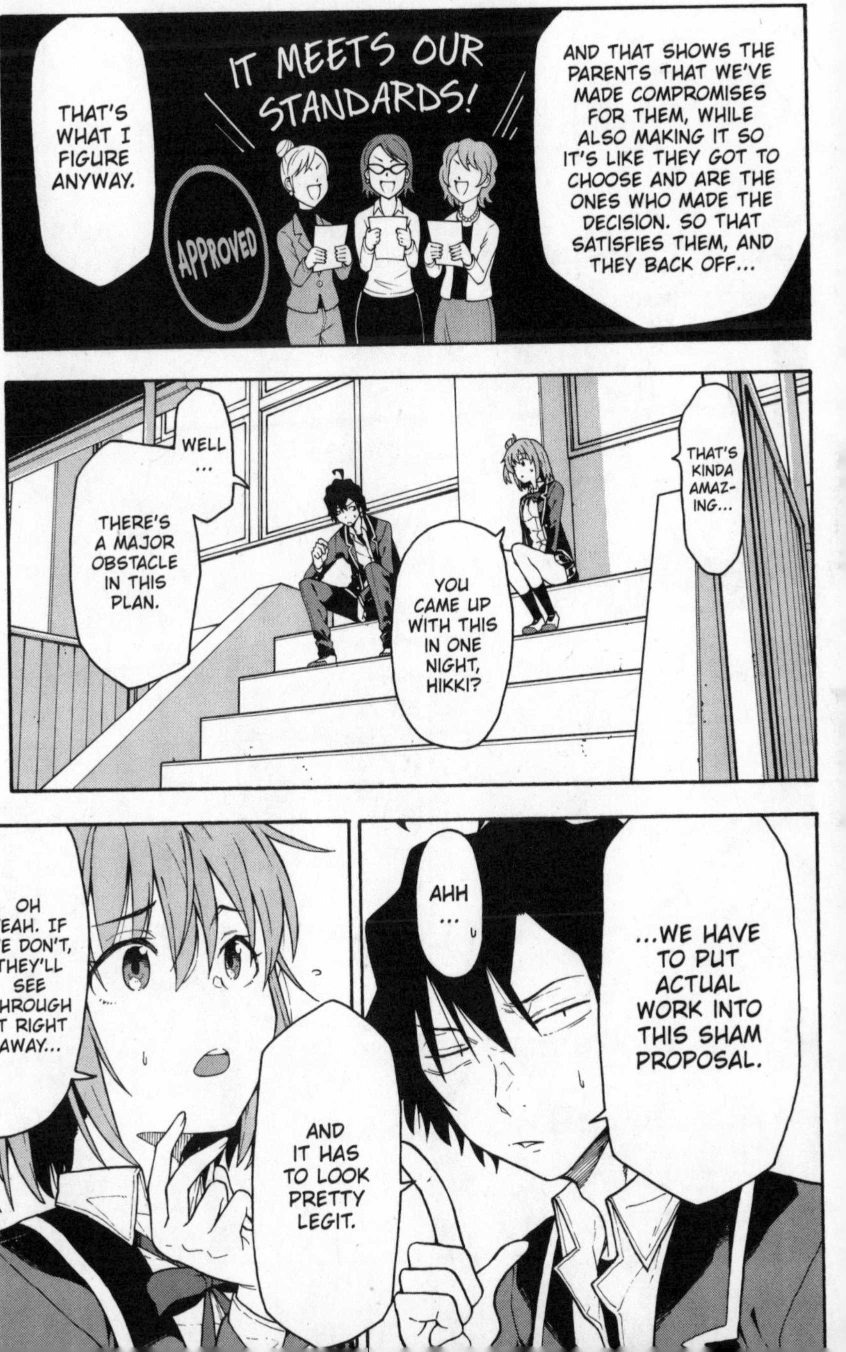
AND THAT SHOWS THE PARENTS THAT WE'VE MADE COMPROMISES FOR THEM, WHILE ALSO MAKING IT SO IT'S LIKE THEY GOT TO CHOOSE AND ARE THE ONES WHO MADE THE DECISION. SO THAT SATISFIES THEM, AND THEY BACK OFF...
IT MEETS OUR STANDARDS!
APPROVED
THAT'S WHAT I FIGURE ANYWAY.
THAT'S KINDA AMAZ-ING...
YOU CAME UP WITH THIS IN ONE NIGHT, HIKKI?
WELL ...
THERE'S A MAJOR OBSTACLE IN THIS PLAN.
...WE HAVE TO PUT ACTUAL WORK INTO THIS SHAM PROPOSAL.
AHH ...
AND IT HAS TO LOOK PRETTY LEGIT.
OH YEAH. IF WE DON'T, THEY'LL SEE THROUGH IT RIGHT AWAY...

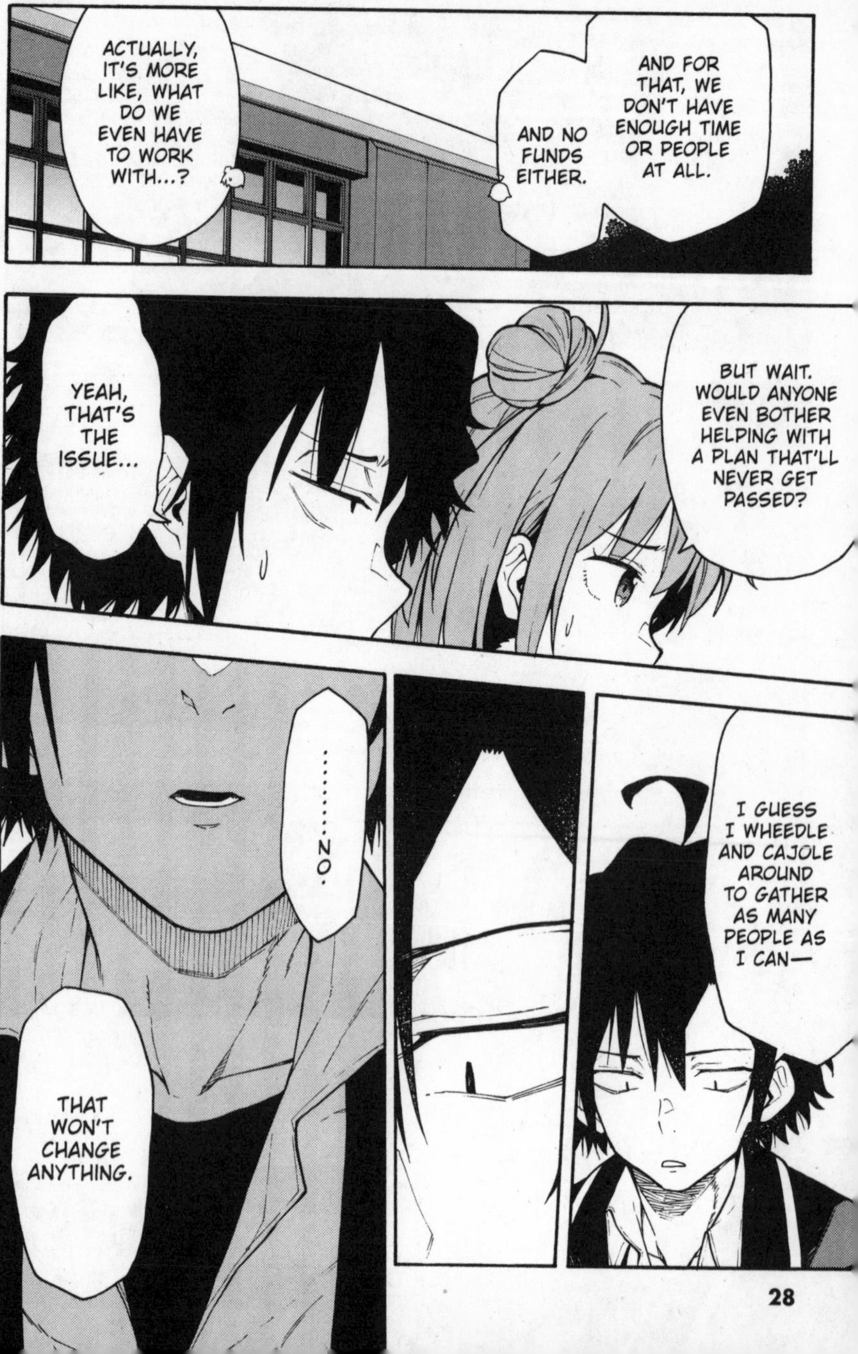
AND FOR THAT, WE DON'T HAVE ENOUGH TIME OR PEOPLE AT ALL.
AND NO FUNDS EITHER.
ACTUALLY, IT'S MORE LIKE, WHAT DO WE EVEN HAVE TO WORK WITH...?
BUT WAIT. WOULD ANYONE EVEN BOTHER HELPING WITH A PLAN THAT'LL NEVER GET PASSED?
YEAH, THAT'S THE ISSUE...
I GUESS I WHEEDLE AND CAJOLE AROUND TO GATHER AS MANY PEOPLE AS I CAN—
......NO.
THAT WON'T CHANGE ANYTHING.

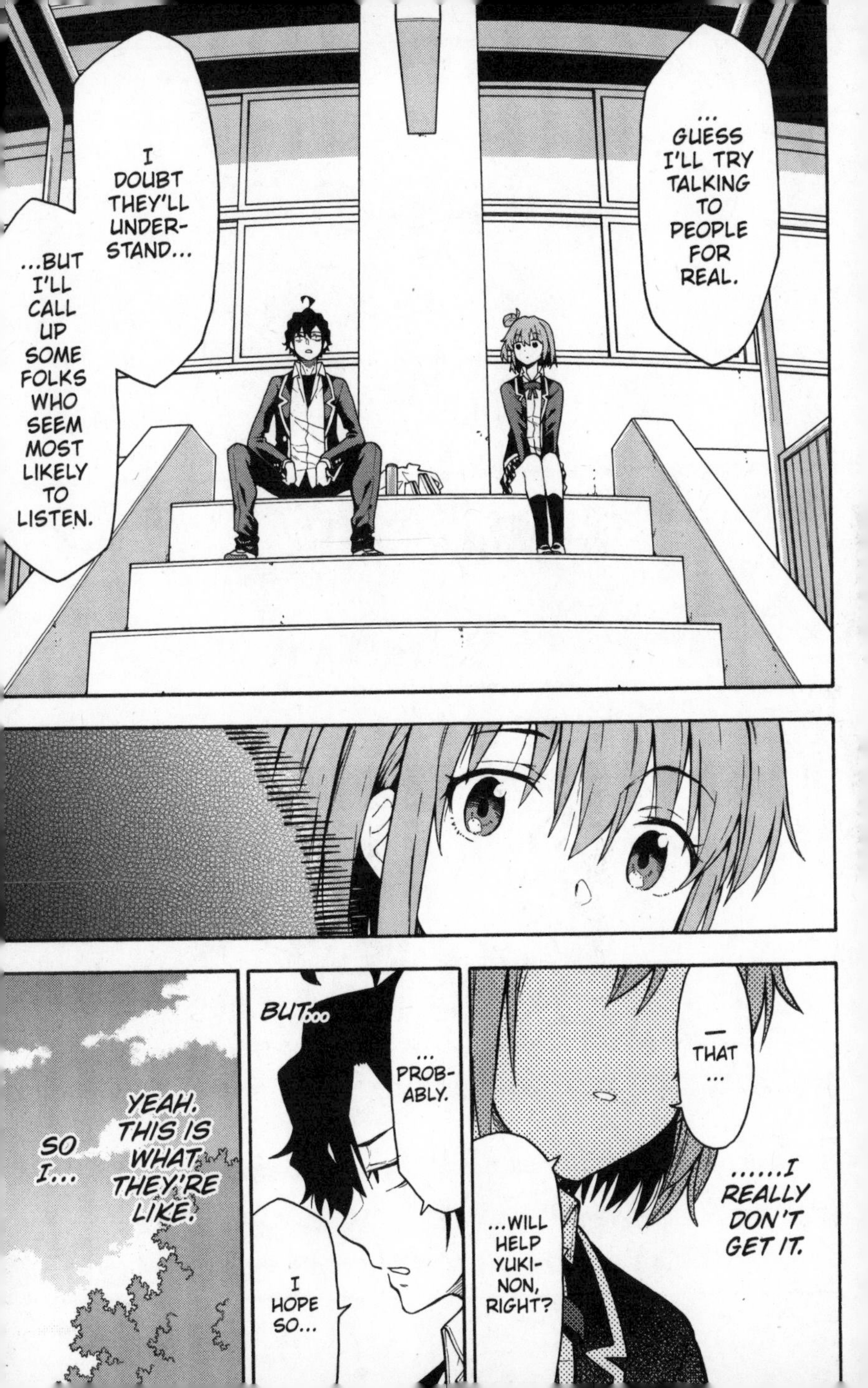
...GUESS I'LL TRY TALKING TO PEOPLE FOR REAL.
I DOUBT THEY'LL UNDER-STAND...
...BUT I'LL CALL UP SOME FOLKS WHO SEEM MOST LIKELY TO LISTEN.
—THAT...
......I REALLY DON'T GET IT.
...WILL HELP YUKI-NON, RIGHT?
...PROB-ABLY.
BUT...
I HOPE SO...
YEAH. THIS IS WHAT THEY'RE LIKE.
SO I...

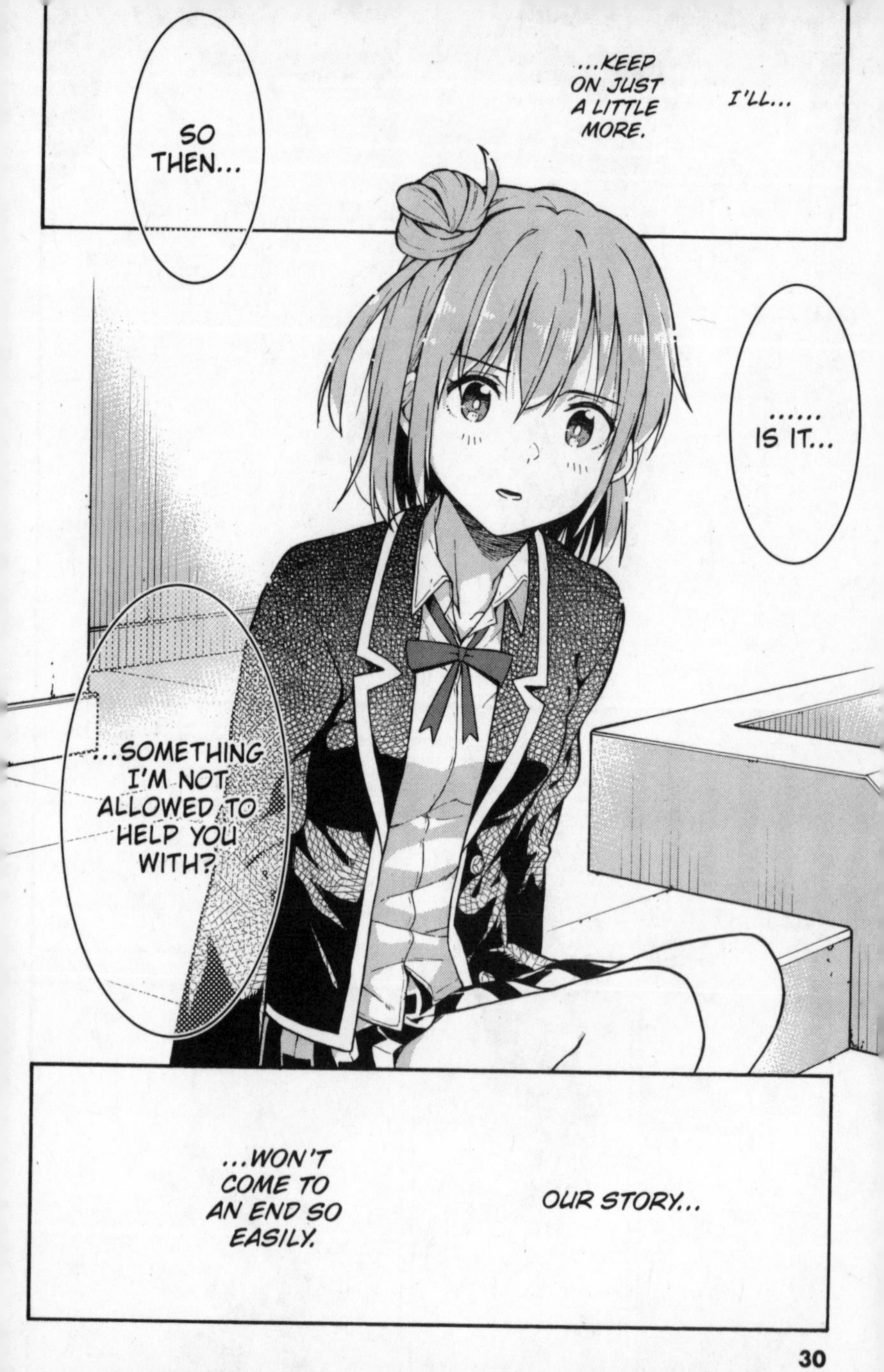
I'LL...
...KEEP ON JUST A LITTLE MORE.
SO THEN...
...... IS IT...
...SOMETHING I'M NOT ALLOWED TO HELP YOU WITH?
OUR STORY...
...WON'T COME TO AN END SO EASILY.

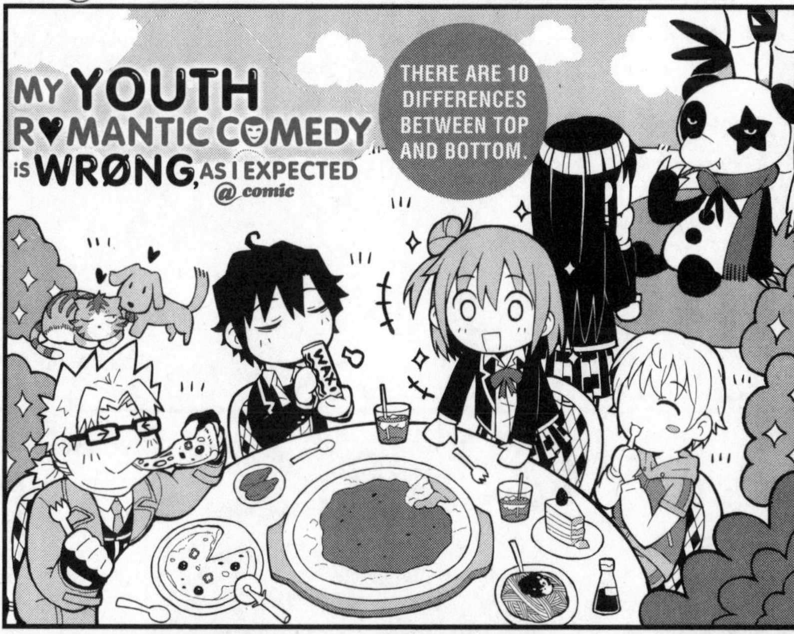
MY YOUTH ROMANTIC COMEDY IS WRONG, AS I EXPECTED @ comic
THERE ARE 10 DIFFERENCES BETWEEN TOP AND BOTTOM.
WAX

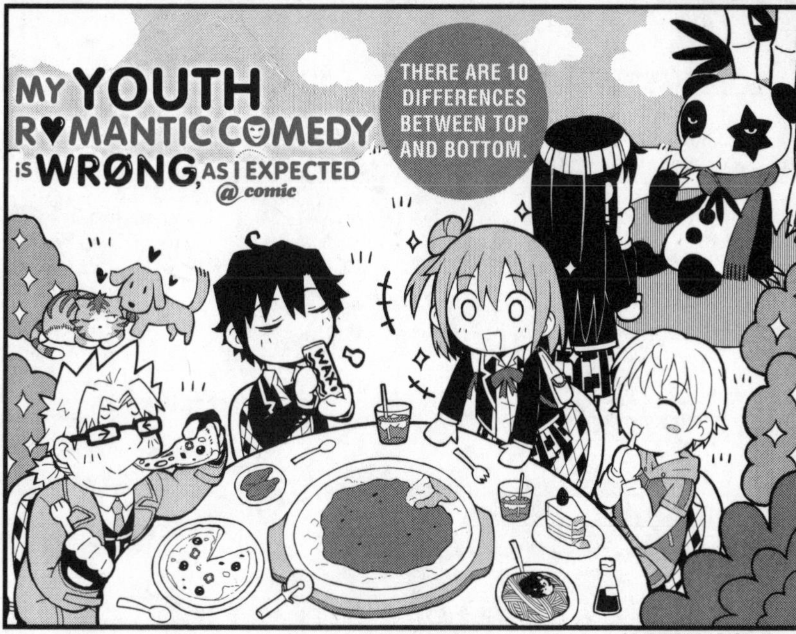
MY YOUTH ROMANTIC COMEDY IS WRONG, AS I EXPECTED @ comic
THERE ARE 10 DIFFERENCES BETWEEN TOP AND BOTTOM.
WAX

*ANSWERS ON PAGE 162

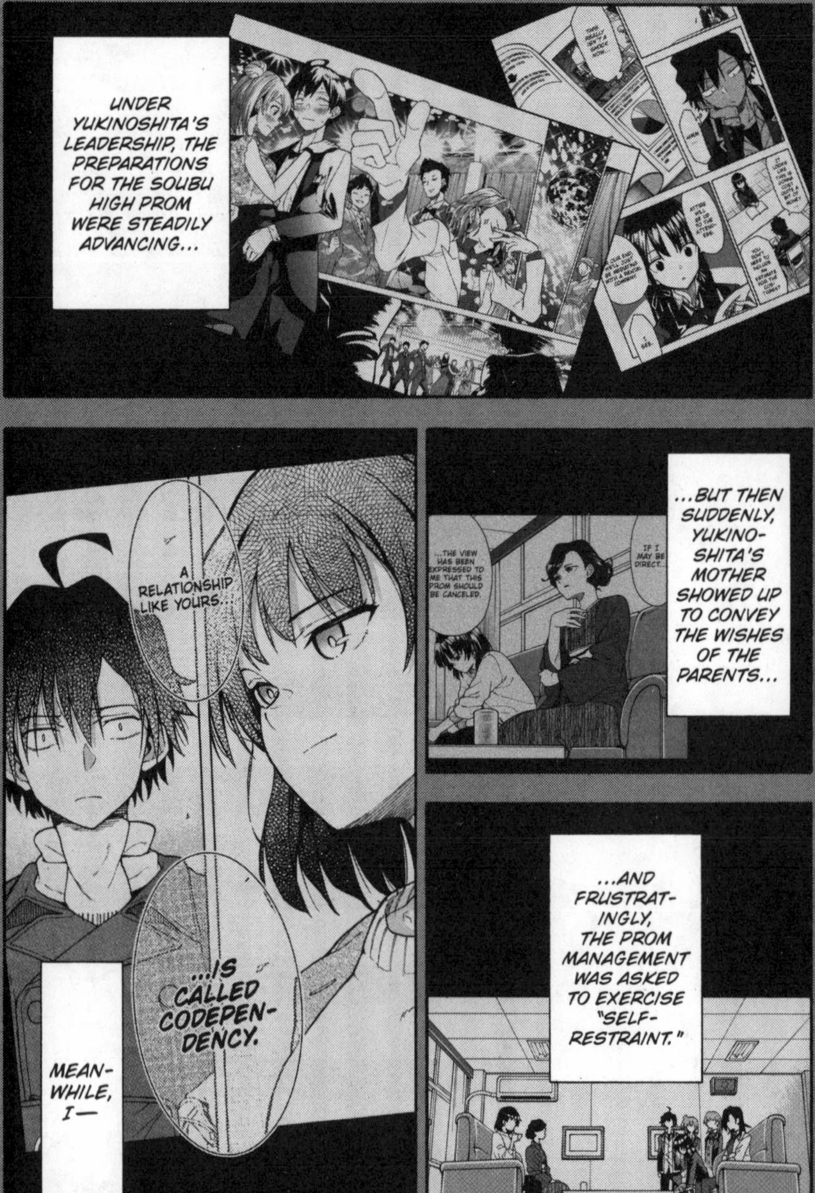
UNDER YUKINOSHITA'S LEADERSHIP, THE PREPARATIONS FOR THE SOUBU HIGH PROM WERE STEADILY ADVANCING...
...BUT THEN SUDDENLY, YUKINO-SHITA'S MOTHER SHOWED UP TO CONVEY THE WISHES OF THE PARENTS...
IF I MAY BE DIRECT...
...THE VIEW HAS BEEN EXPRESSED TO ME THAT THIS PROM SHOULD BE CANCELED.
...AND FRUSTRAT-INGLY, THE PROM MANAGEMENT WAS ASKED TO EXERCISE "SELF-RESTRAINT."
A RELATIONSHIP LIKE YOURS...
...IS CALLED CODEPEN-DENCY.
MEAN-WHILE, I—

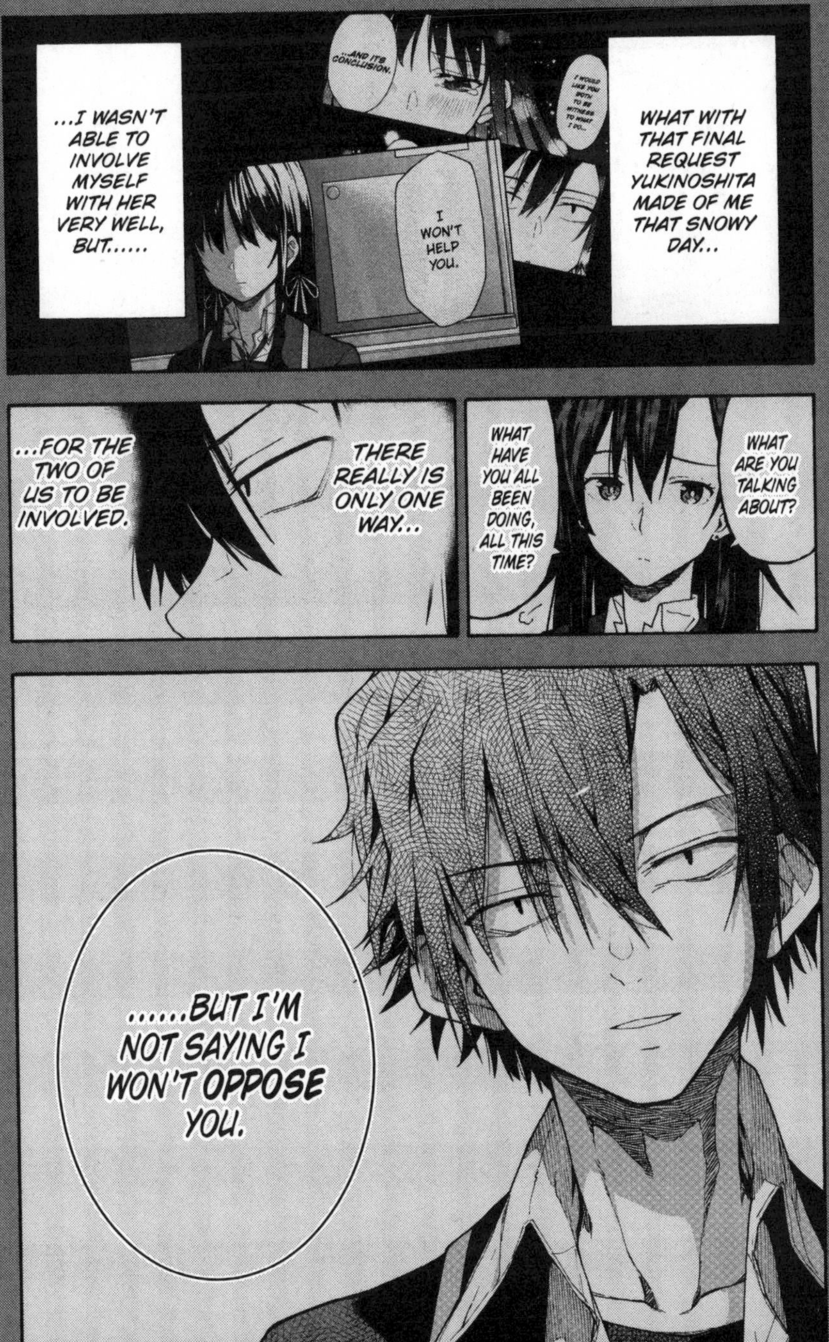
WHAT WITH THAT FINAL REQUEST YUKINOSHITA MADE OF ME THAT SNOWY DAY...
I WOULD LIKE YOU BOTH TO BE WITNESS TO WHAT I DO...
...AND IT'S CONCLUSION.
I WON'T HELP YOU.
...I WASN'T ABLE TO INVOLVE MYSELF WITH HER VERY WELL, BUT......
WHAT ARE YOU TALKING ABOUT?
WHAT HAVE YOU ALL BEEN DOING, ALL THIS TIME?
THERE REALLY IS ONLY ONE WAY...
...FOR THE TWO OF US TO BE INVOLVED.
......BUT I'M NOT SAYING I WON'T OPPOSE YOU.

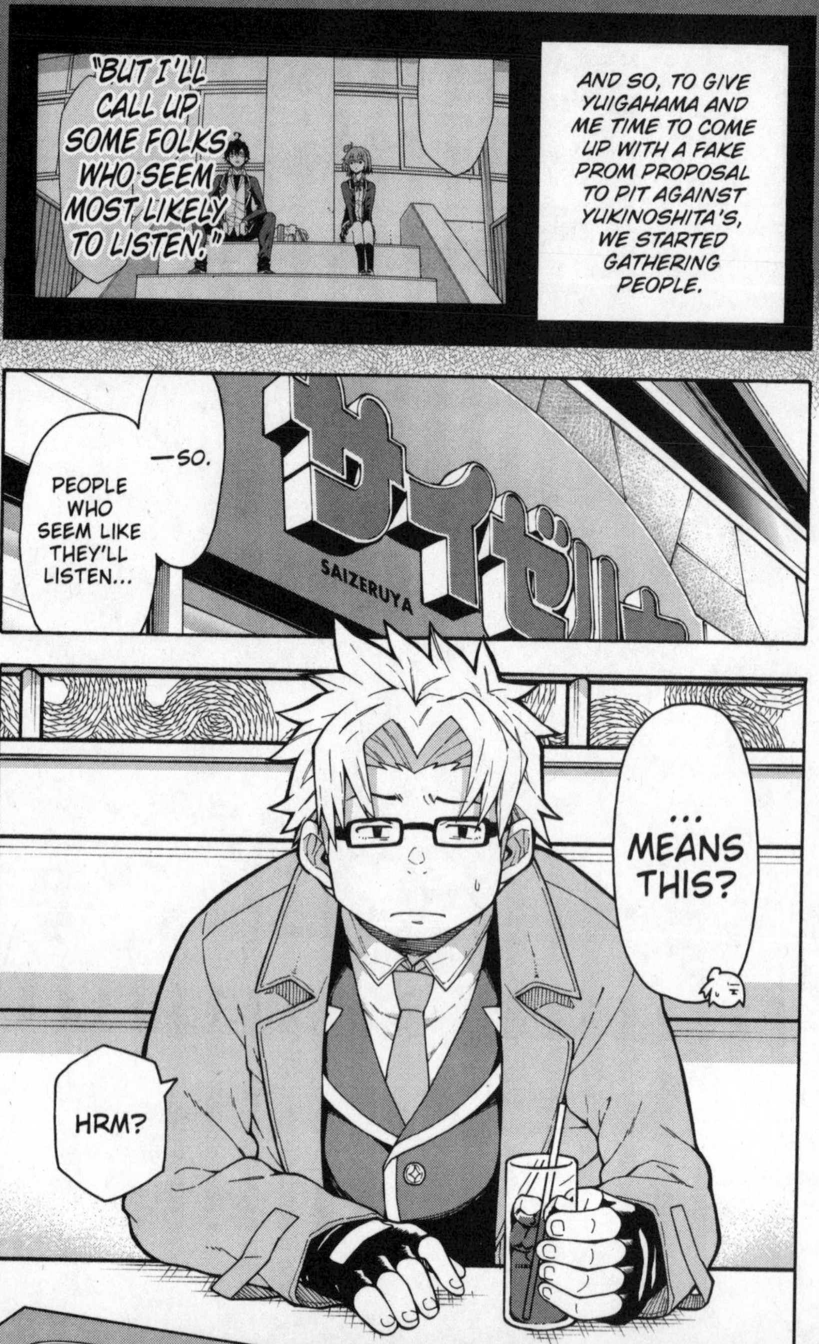
AND SO, TO GIVE YUIGAHAMA AND ME TIME TO COME UP WITH A FAKE PROM PROPOSAL TO PIT AGAINST YUKINOSHITA'S, WE STARTED GATHERING PEOPLE.
"BUT I'LL CALL UP SOME FOLKS WHO SEEM MOST LIKELY TO LISTEN."
—SO.
PEOPLE WHO SEEM LIKE THEY'LL LISTEN...
SAIZERUYA
...MEANS THIS?
HRM?

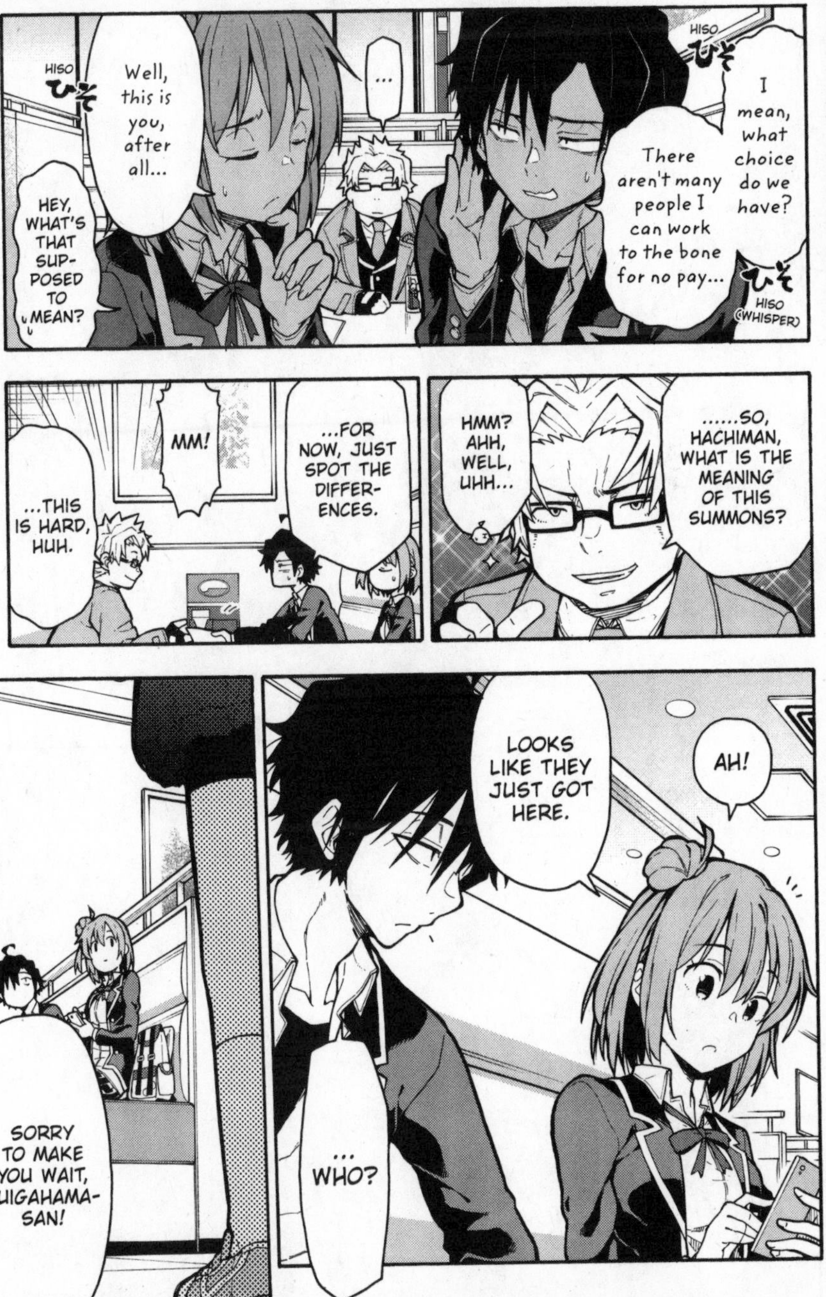
HISO
ひそ
I mean, what choice do we have?
There aren't many people I can work to the bone for no pay...
ひそ
HISO (WHISPER)
...
Well, this is you, after all...
HISO
ひそ
HEY, WHAT'S THAT SUP-POSED TO MEAN?
......SO, HACHIMAN, WHAT IS THE MEANING OF THIS SUMMONS?
HMM? AHH, WELL, UHH...
...FOR NOW, JUST SPOT THE DIFFER-ENCES.
MM!
...THIS IS HARD, HUH.
AH!
LOOKS LIKE THEY JUST GOT HERE.
... WHO?
SORRY TO MAKE YOU WAIT, YUIGAHAMA-SAN!

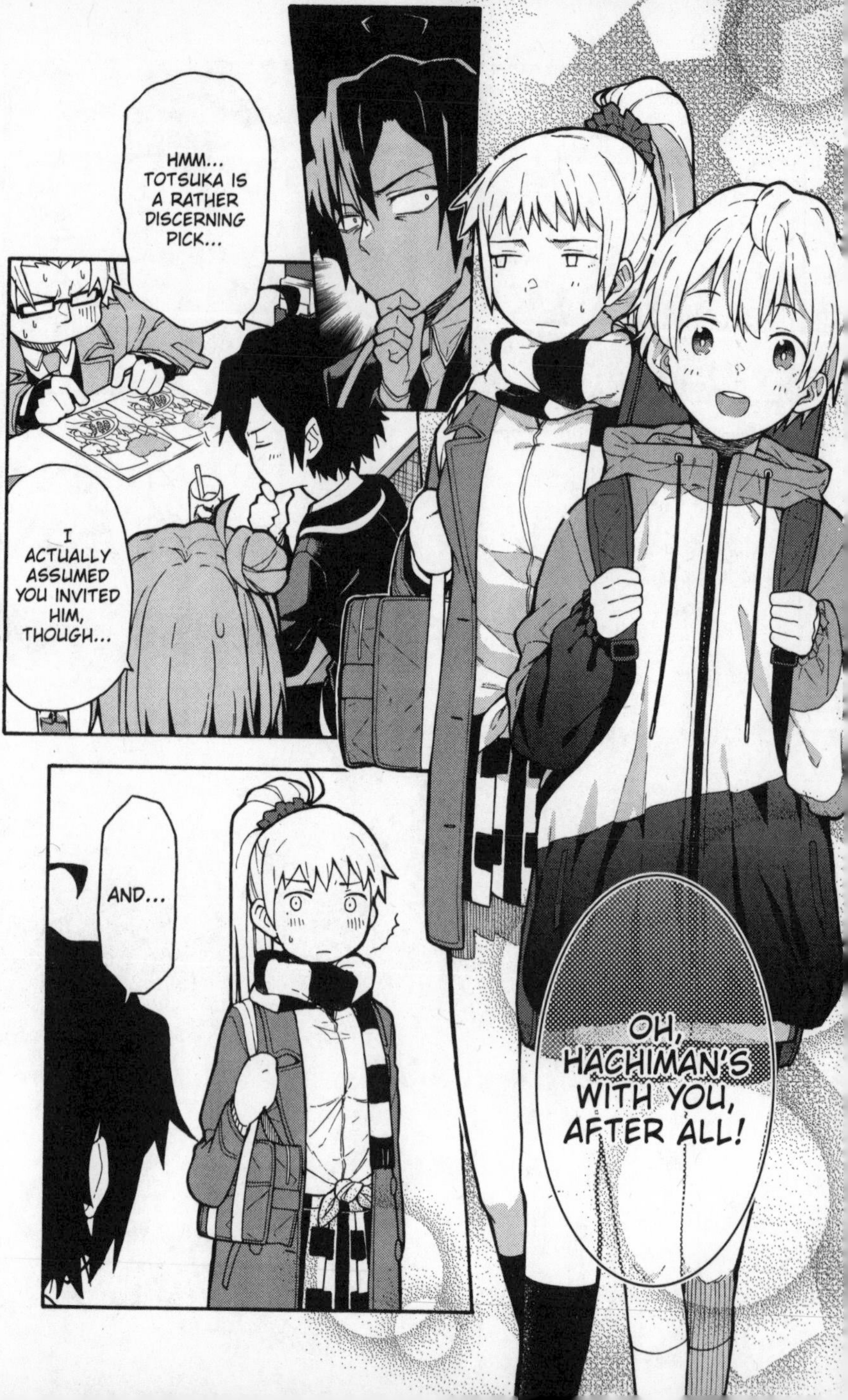
OH, HACHIMAN'S WITH YOU, AFTER ALL!
HMM... TOTSUKA IS A RATHER DISCERNING PICK...
I ACTUALLY ASSUMED YOU INVITED HIM, THOUGH...
AND...

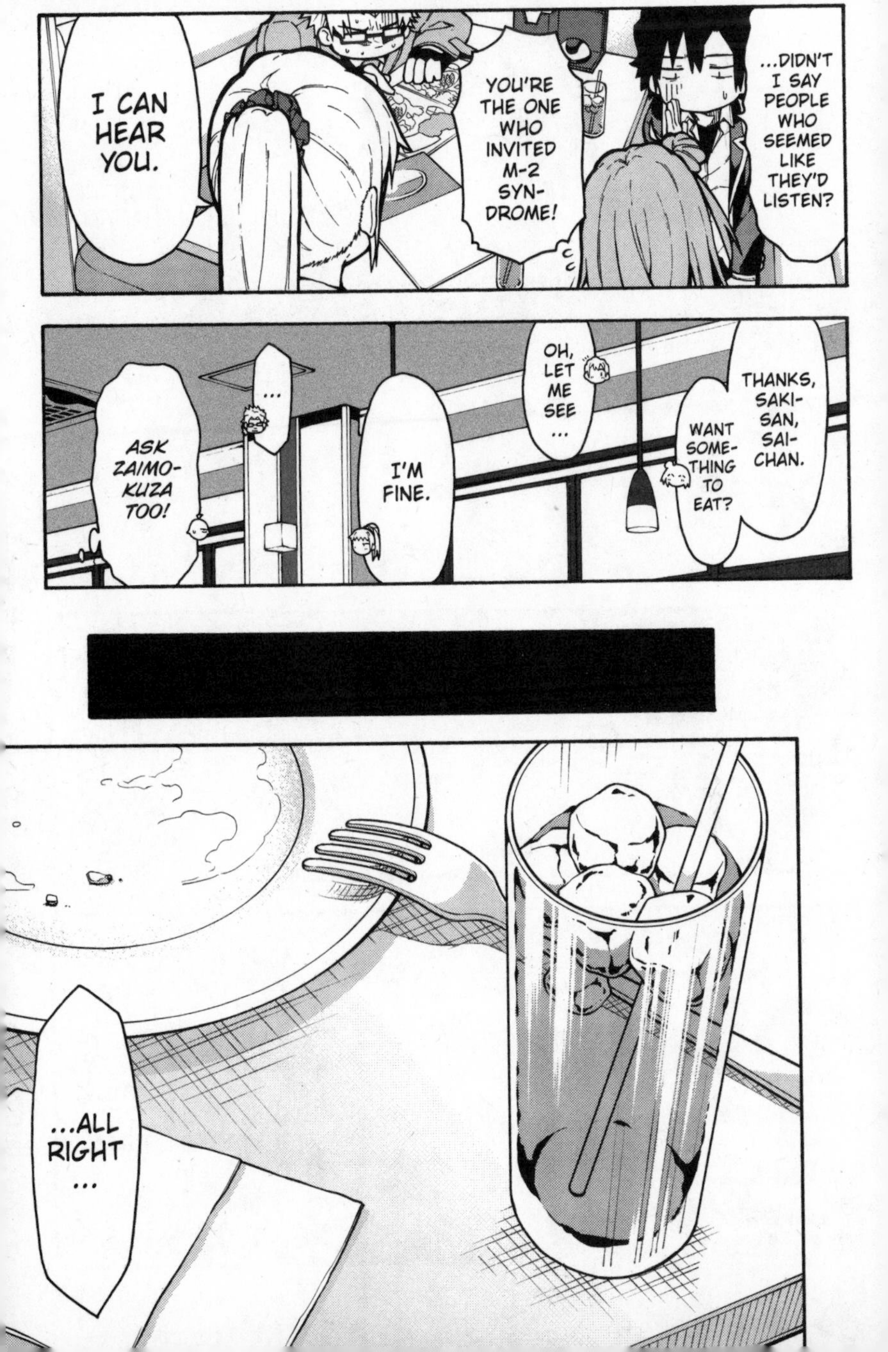
...DIDN'T I SAY PEOPLE WHO SEEMED LIKE THEY'D LISTEN?
YOU'RE THE ONE WHO INVITED M-2 SYNDROME!
I CAN HEAR YOU.
THANKS, SAKI-SAN, SAI-CHAN.
WANT SOMETHING TO EAT?
OH, LET ME SEE...
I'M FINE.
...
ASK ZAIMOKUZA TOO!
...ALL RIGHT...

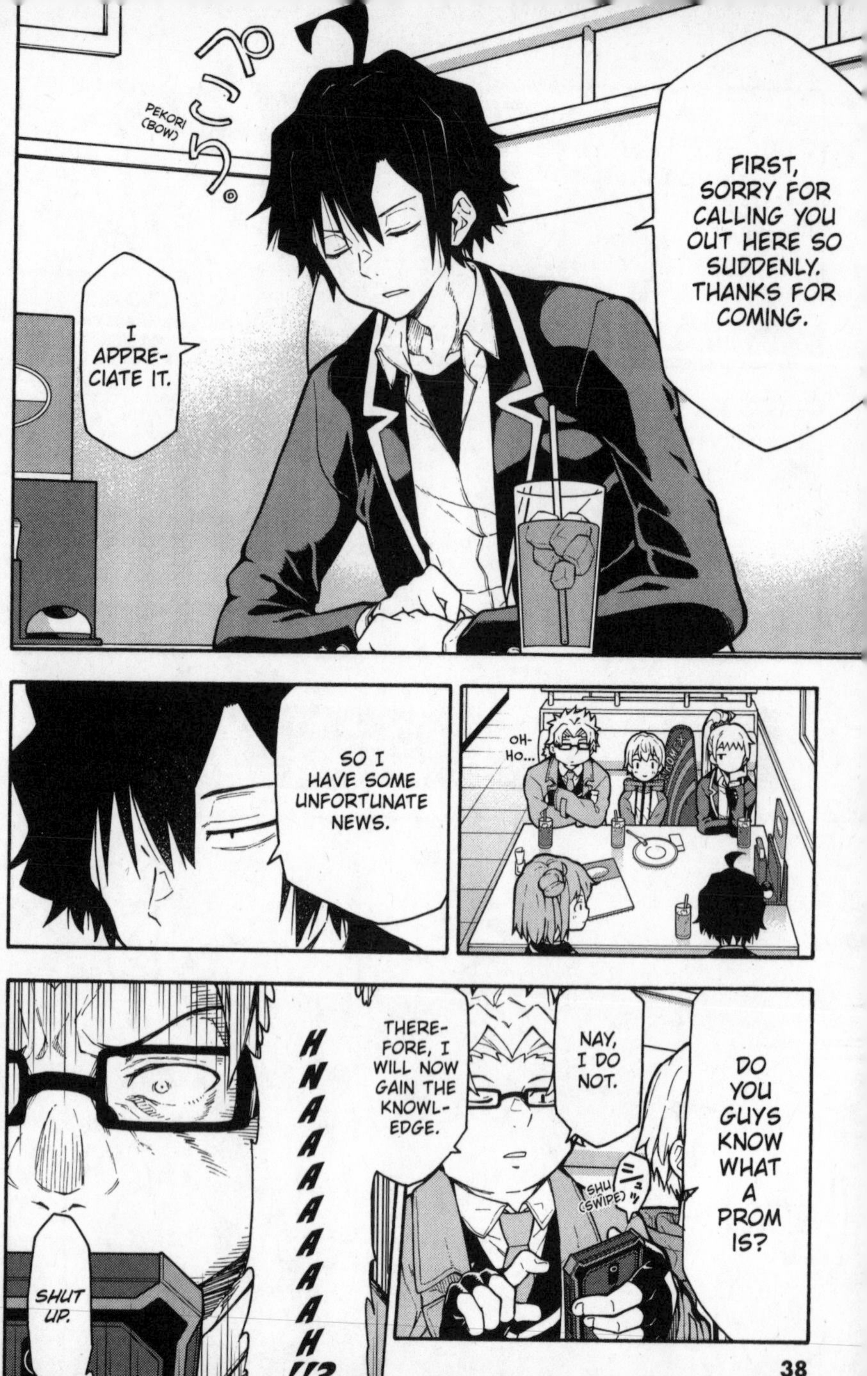
FIRST, SORRY FOR CALLING YOU OUT HERE SO SUDDENLY. THANKS FOR COMING.
PEKORI (BOW)
I APPRECIATE IT.
OH-HO...
SO I HAVE SOME UNFORTUNATE NEWS.
DO YOU GUYS KNOW WHAT A PROM IS?
NAY, I DO NOT.
SHU (SWIPE)
THEREFORE, I WILL NOW GAIN THE KNOWLEDGE.
HNAAAAAAAAH!!?
SHUT UP.

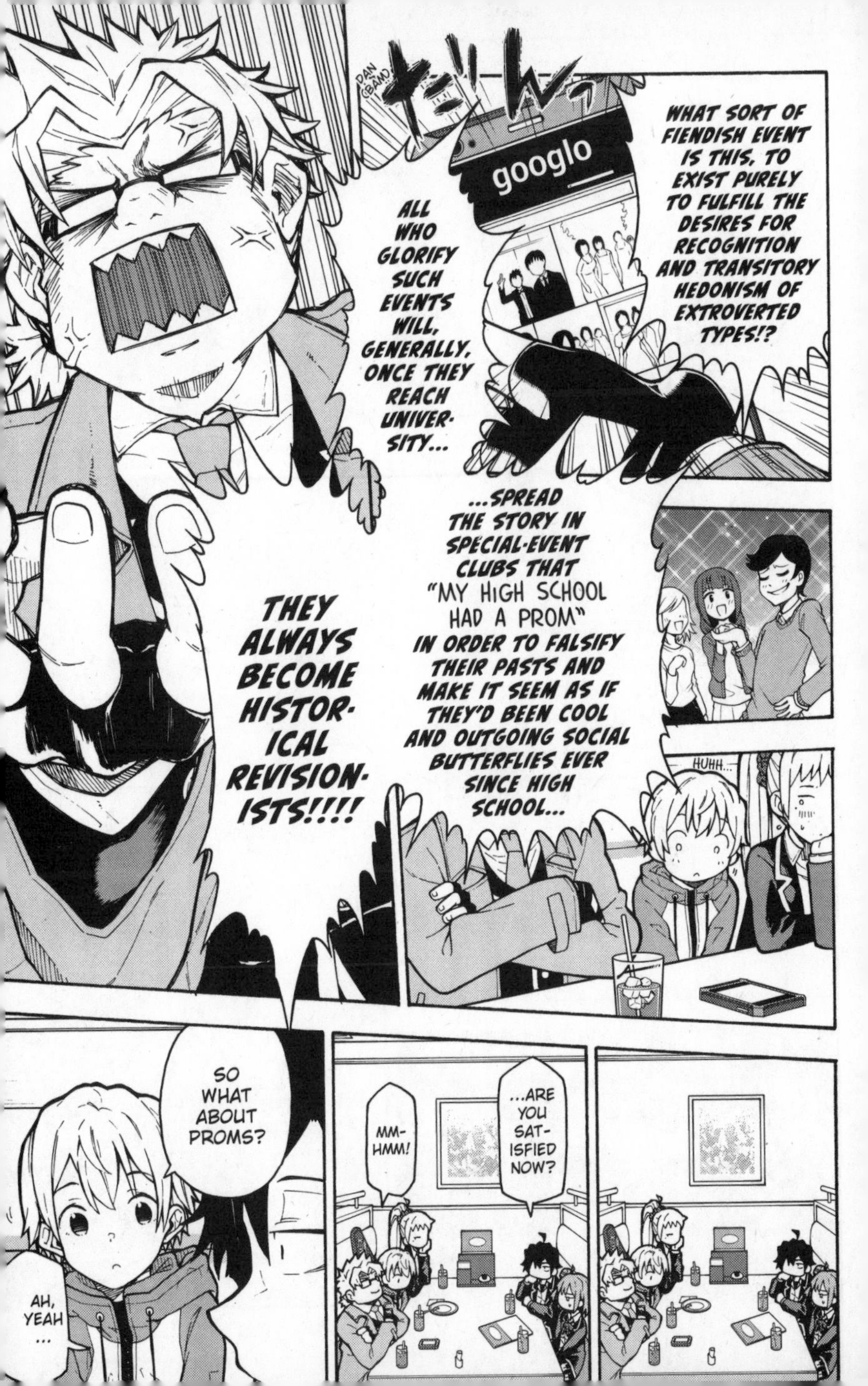
DAN (BAM)
googlo
WHAT SORT OF FIENDISH EVENT IS THIS, TO EXIST PURELY TO FULFILL THE DESIRES FOR RECOGNITION AND TRANSITORY HEDONISM OF EXTROVERTED TYPES!?
ALL WHO GLORIFY SUCH EVENTS WILL, GENERALLY, ONCE THEY REACH UNIVER-SITY...
...SPREAD THE STORY IN SPECIAL-EVENT CLUBS THAT "MY HIGH SCHOOL HAD A PROM" IN ORDER TO FALSIFY THEIR PASTS AND MAKE IT SEEM AS IF THEY'D BEEN COOL AND OUTGOING SOCIAL BUTTERFLIES EVER SINCE HIGH SCHOOL...
HUHH...
THEY ALWAYS BECOME HISTOR-ICAL REVISION-ISTS!!!!
...ARE YOU SAT-ISFIED NOW?
MM-HMM!
SO WHAT ABOUT PROMS?
AH, YEAH ...

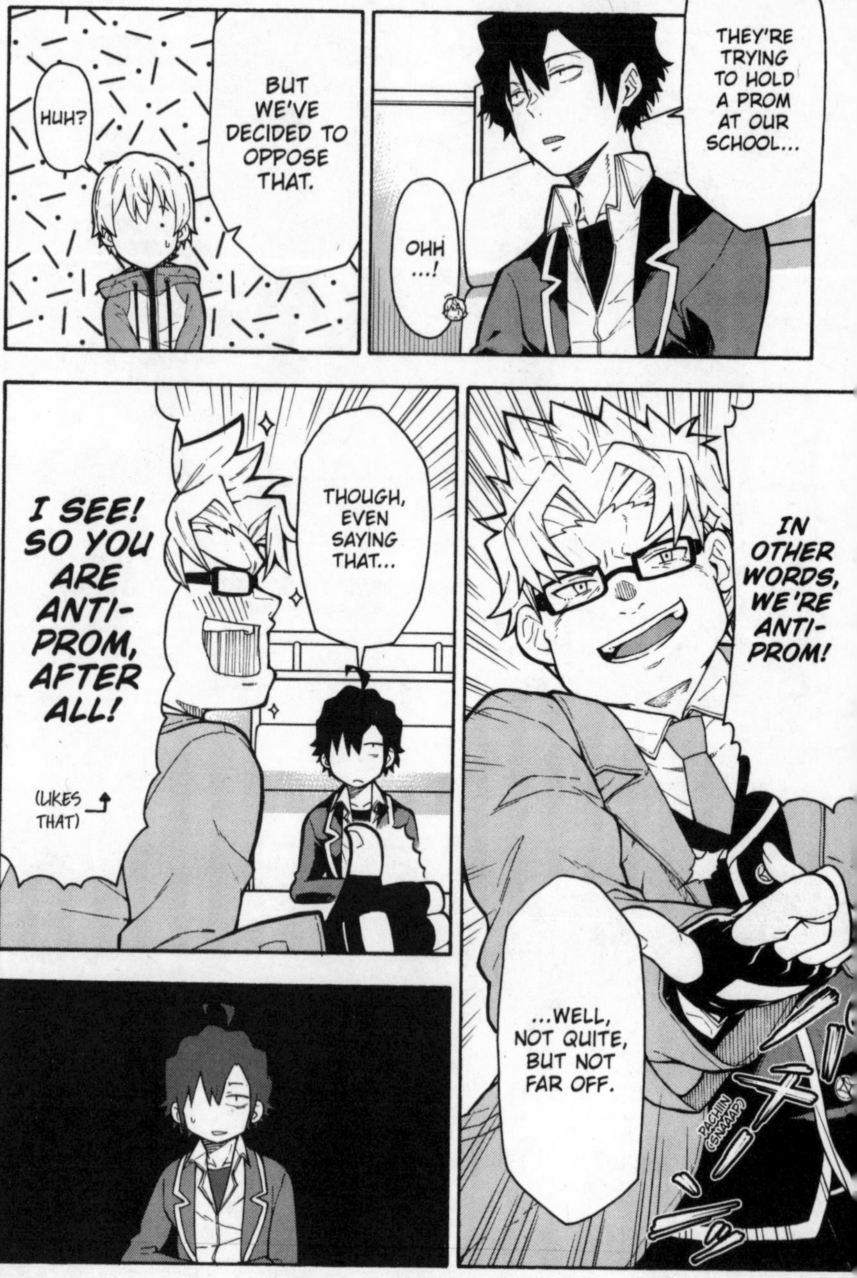
THEY'RE TRYING TO HOLD A PROM AT OUR SCHOOL...
OHH ...!
BUT WE'VE DECIDED TO OPPOSE THAT.
HUH?
IN OTHER WORDS, WE'RE ANTI-PROM!
...WELL, NOT QUITE, BUT NOT FAR OFF.
PACHIIN (SNAAAP)
THOUGH, EVEN SAYING THAT...
I SEE! SO YOU ARE ANTI-PROM, AFTER ALL!
(LIKES THAT)

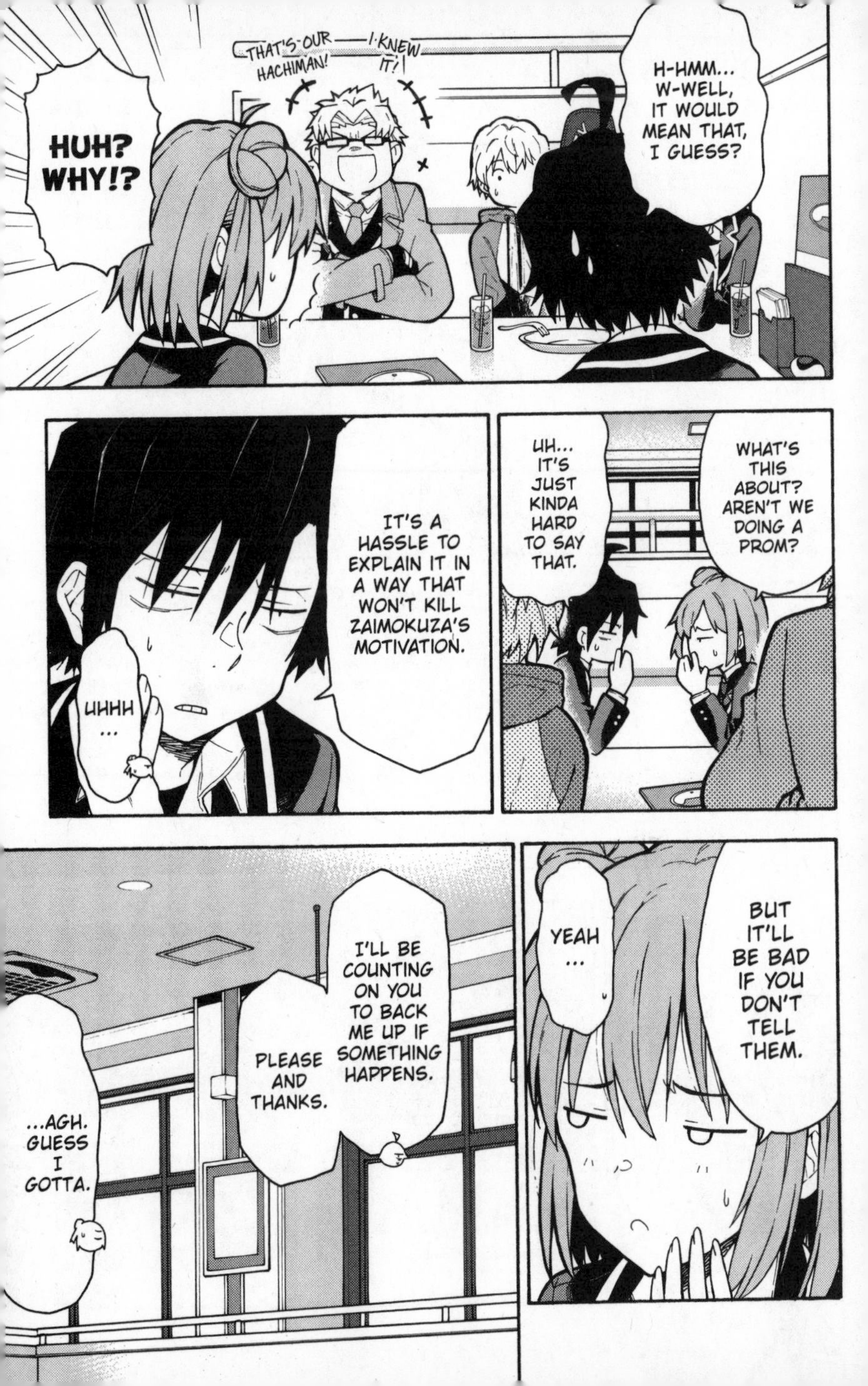
H-HMM... W-WELL, IT WOULD MEAN THAT, I GUESS?
I KNEW IT!
THAT'S OUR HACHIMAN!
HUH? WHY!?
WHAT'S THIS ABOUT? AREN'T WE DOING A PROM?
UH... IT'S JUST KINDA HARD TO SAY THAT.
IT'S A HASSLE TO EXPLAIN IT IN A WAY THAT WON'T KILL ZAIMOKUZA'S MOTIVATION.
UHHH ...
BUT IT'LL BE BAD IF YOU DON'T TELL THEM.
YEAH ...
I'LL BE COUNTING ON YOU TO BACK ME UP IF SOMETHING HAPPENS.
PLEASE AND THANKS.
...AGH. GUESS I GOTTA.

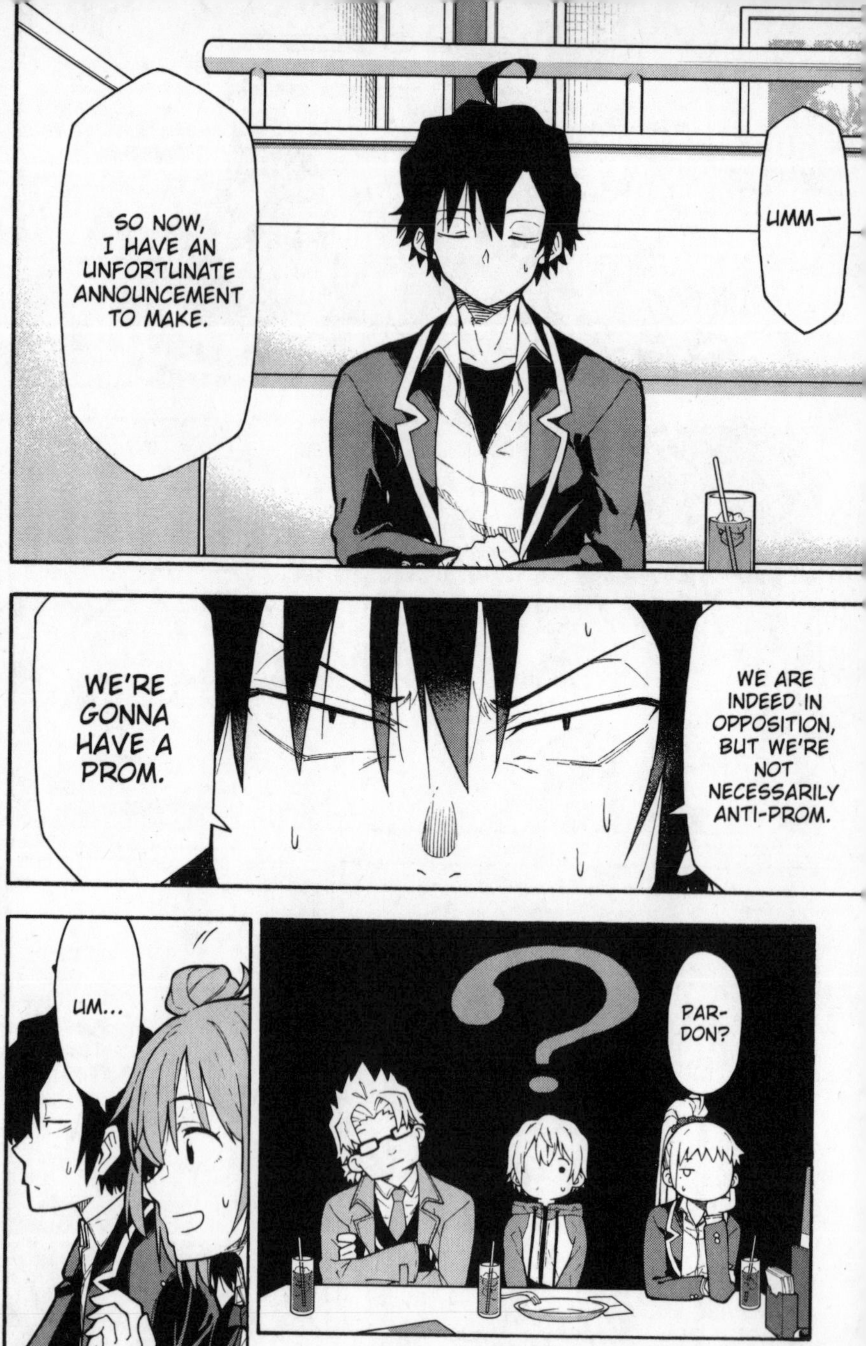
UMM—
SO NOW, I HAVE AN UNFORTUNATE ANNOUNCEMENT TO MAKE.
WE ARE INDEED IN OPPOSITION, BUT WE'RE NOT NECESSARILY ANTI-PROM.
WE'RE GONNA HAVE A PROM.
PAR-DON?
UM...

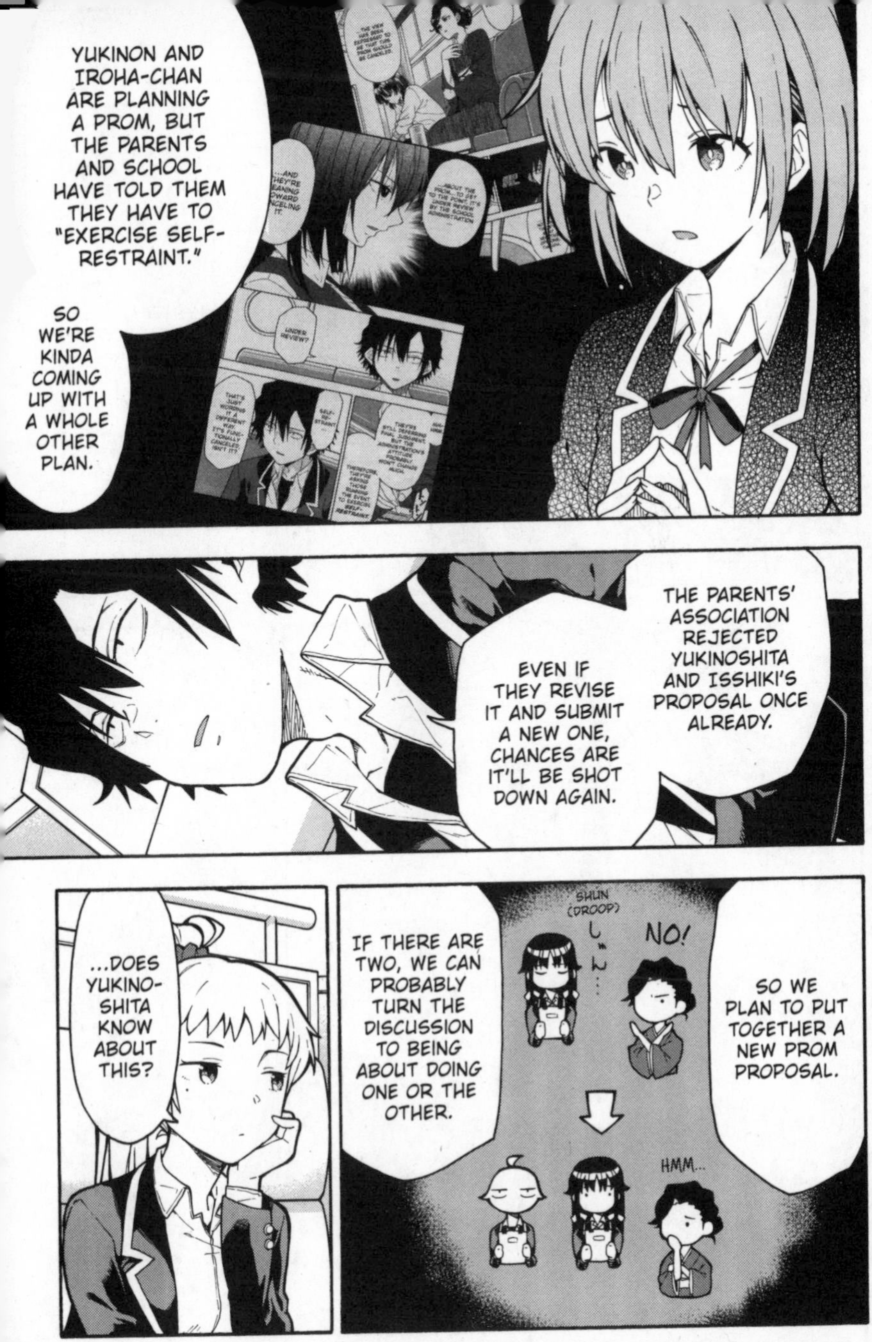
YUKINON AND IROHA-CHAN ARE PLANNING A PROM, BUT THE PARENTS AND SCHOOL HAVE TOLD THEM THEY HAVE TO "EXERCISE SELF-RESTRAINT."
SO WE'RE KINDA COMING UP WITH A WHOLE OTHER PLAN.
THE PARENTS' ASSOCIATION REJECTED YUKINOSHITA AND ISSHIKI'S PROPOSAL ONCE ALREADY.
EVEN IF THEY REVISE IT AND SUBMIT A NEW ONE, CHANCES ARE IT'LL BE SHOT DOWN AGAIN.
SO WE PLAN TO PUT TOGETHER A NEW PROM PROPOSAL.
NO!
SHUN (DROOP)
IF THERE ARE TWO, WE CAN PROBABLY TURN THE DISCUSSION TO BEING ABOUT DOING ONE OR THE OTHER.
HMM...
...DOES YUKINOSHITA KNOW ABOUT THIS?

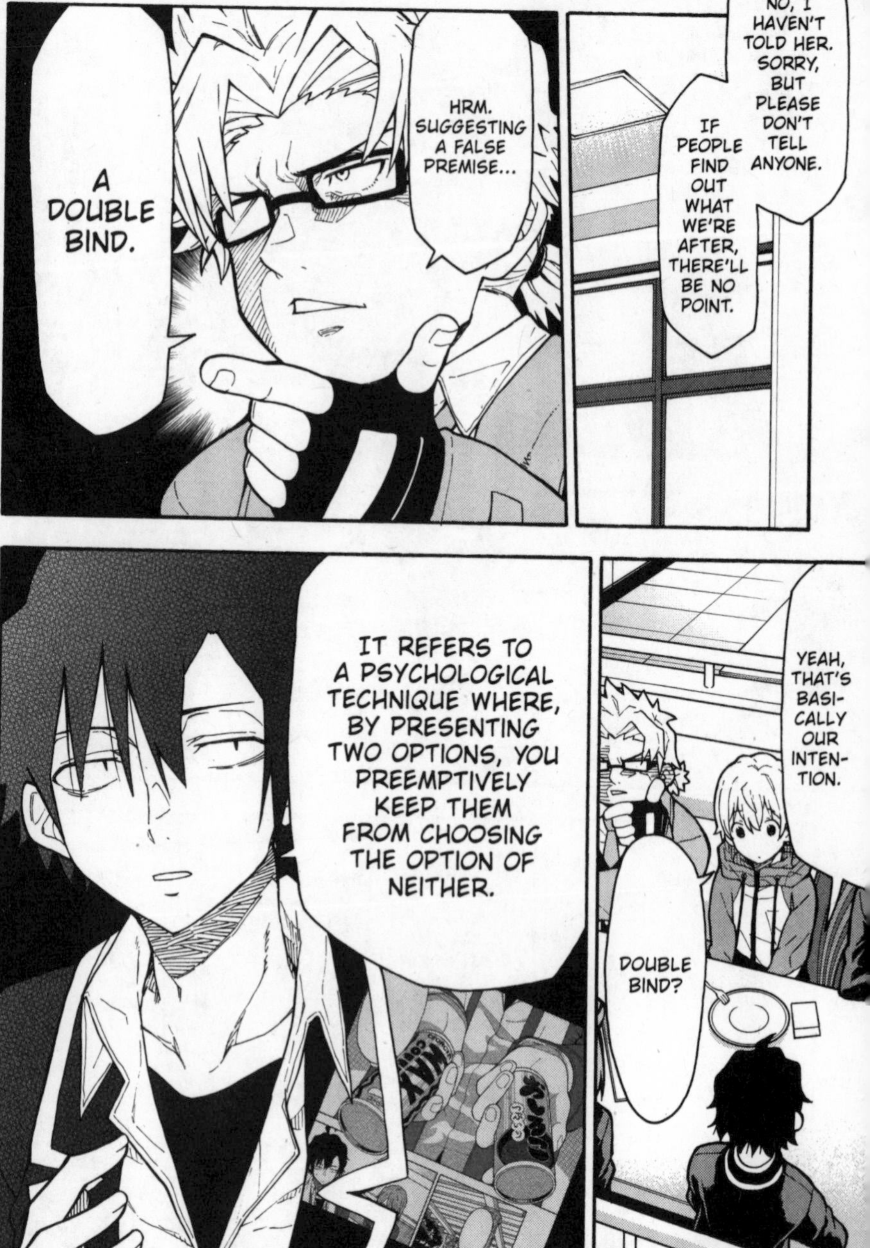
NO, I HAVEN'T TOLD HER. SORRY, BUT PLEASE DON'T TELL ANYONE.
IF PEOPLE FIND OUT WHAT WE'RE AFTER, THERE'LL BE NO POINT.
HRM. SUGGESTING A FALSE PREMISE...
A DOUBLE BIND.
YEAH, THAT'S BASI-CALLY OUR INTEN-TION.
DOUBLE BIND?
IT REFERS TO A PSYCHOLOGICAL TECHNIQUE WHERE, BY PRESENTING TWO OPTIONS, YOU PREEMPTIVELY KEEP THEM FROM CHOOSING THE OPTION OF NEITHER.

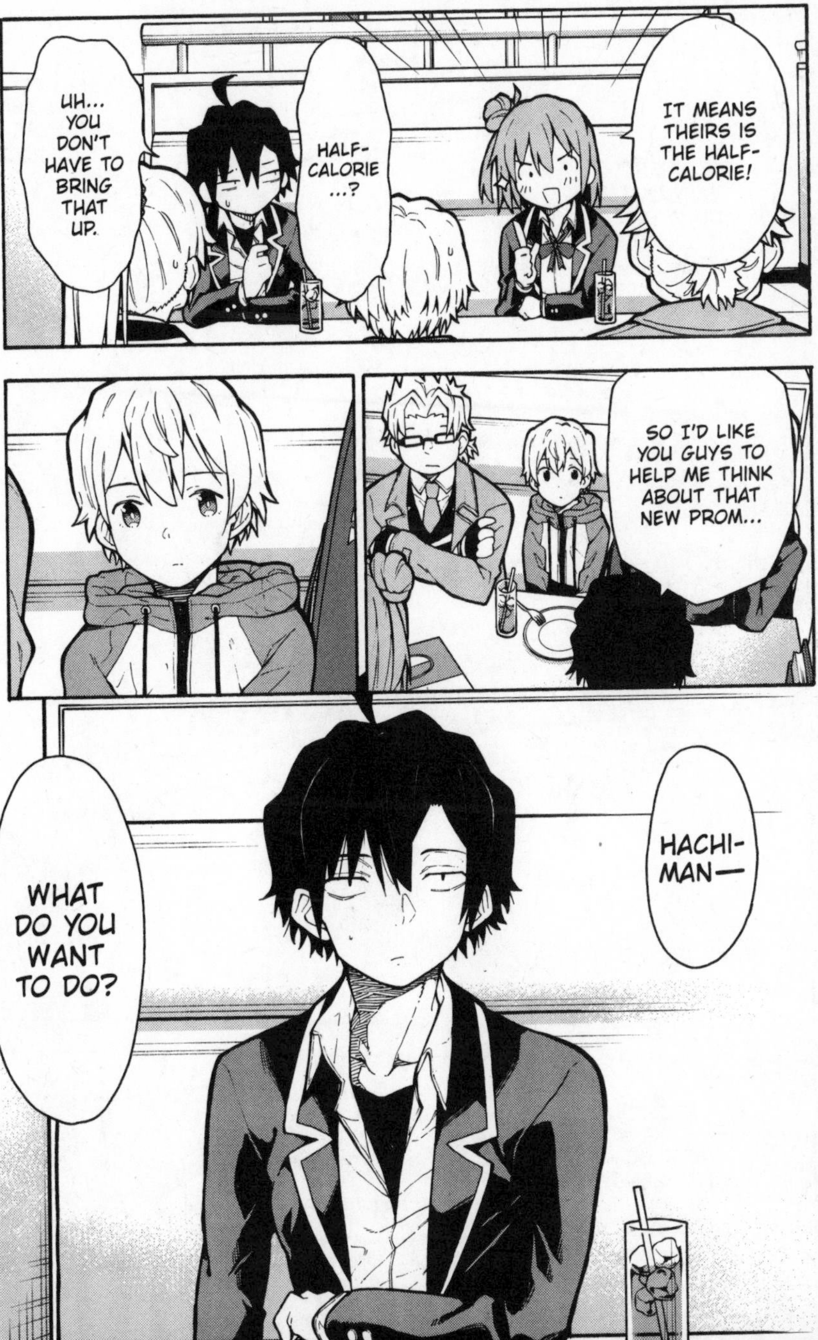
IT MEANS THEIRS IS THE HALF-CALORIE!
HALF-CALORIE ...?
UH... YOU DON'T HAVE TO BRING THAT UP.
SO I'D LIKE YOU GUYS TO HELP ME THINK ABOUT THAT NEW PROM...
HACHI-MAN—
WHAT DO YOU WANT TO DO?

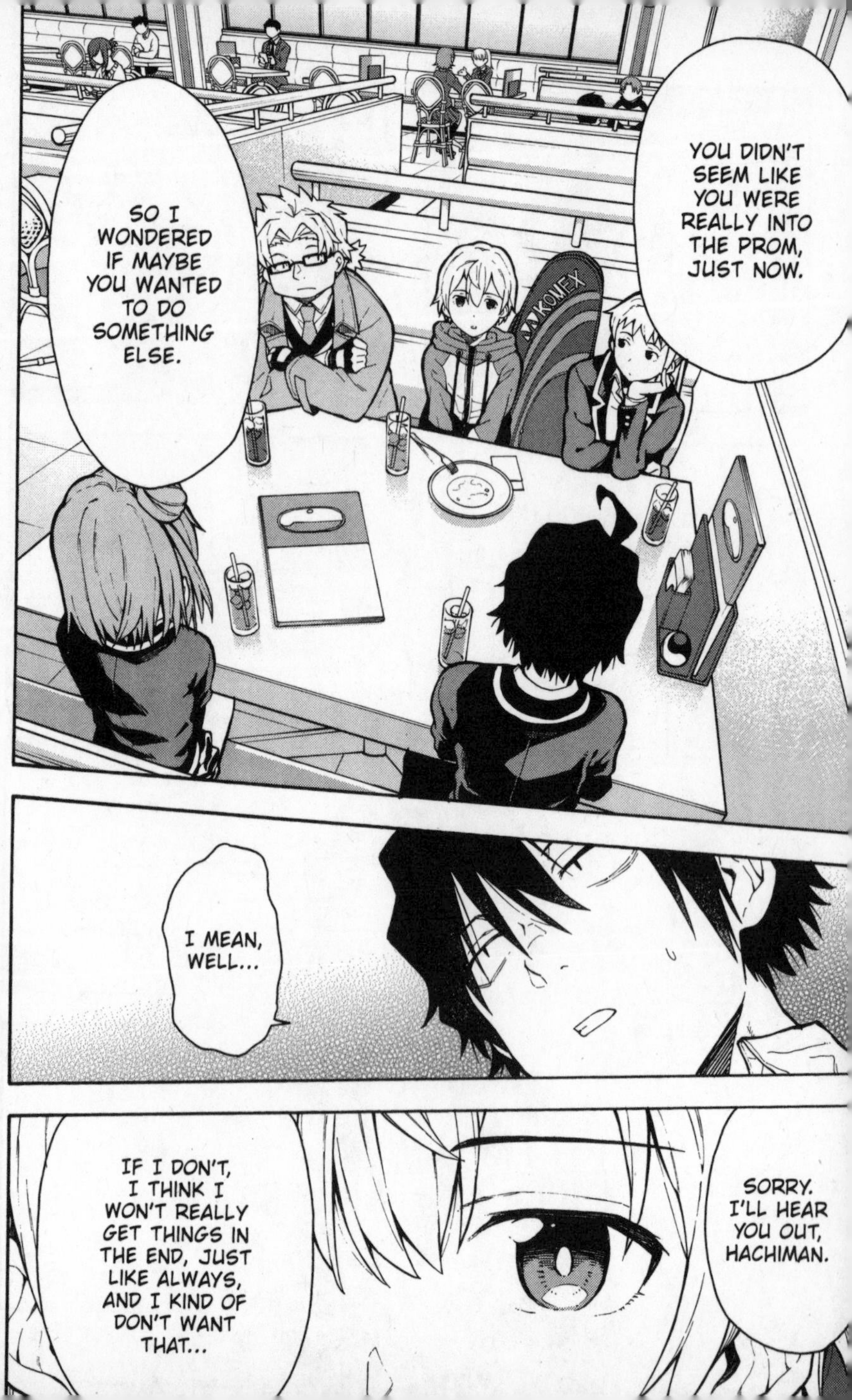
YOU DIDN'T SEEM LIKE YOU WERE REALLY INTO THE PROM, JUST NOW.
SO I WONDERED IF MAYBE YOU WANTED TO DO SOMETHING ELSE.
I MEAN, WELL...
SORRY. I'LL HEAR YOU OUT, HACHIMAN.
IF I DON'T, I THINK I WON'T REALLY GET THINGS IN THE END, JUST LIKE ALWAYS, AND I KIND OF DON'T WANT THAT...

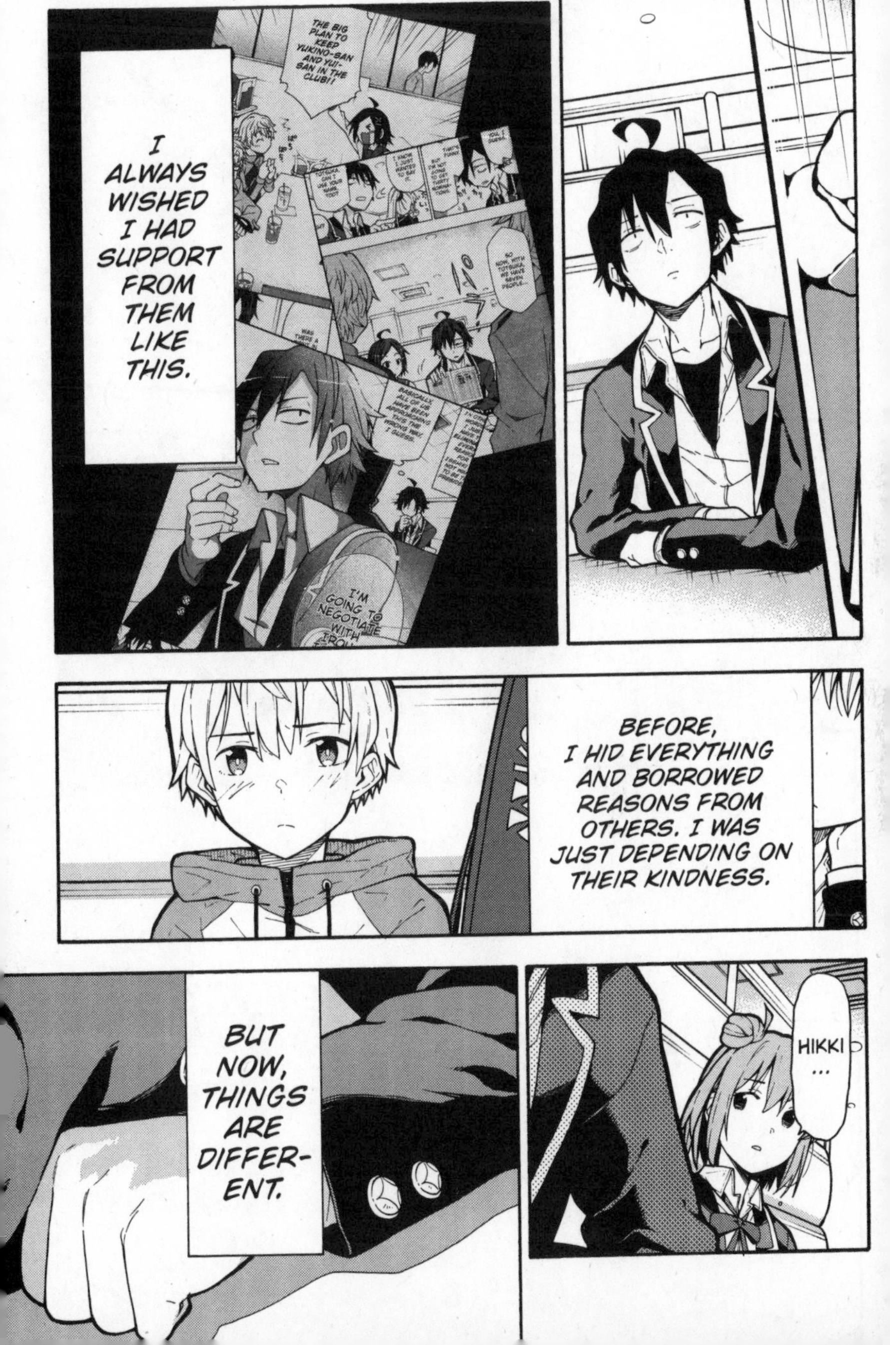
I ALWAYS WISHED I HAD SUPPORT FROM THEM LIKE THIS.
THE BIG PLAN TO KEEP YUKINO-SAN AND YUI-SAN IN THE CLUB!!
YOU, I GUESS.
THAT'S FUNNY
BUT I'M NOT GOING TO GET THIRTY NOMINATIONS.
I KNOW I JUST WANTED TO SAY IT.
TOTSUKA, CAN I USE YOUR NAME, TOO?
SO NOW, WITH TOTSUKA, WE HAVE SEVEN PEOPLE...
BASICALLY ALL OF US HAVE BEEN APPROACHING THIS THE WRONG WAY, I GUESS.
I'M GOING TO NEGOTIATE WITH
BEFORE, I HID EVERYTHING AND BORROWED REASONS FROM OTHERS. I WAS JUST DEPENDING ON THEIR KINDNESS.
HIKKI ...
BUT NOW, THINGS ARE DIFFER-ENT.

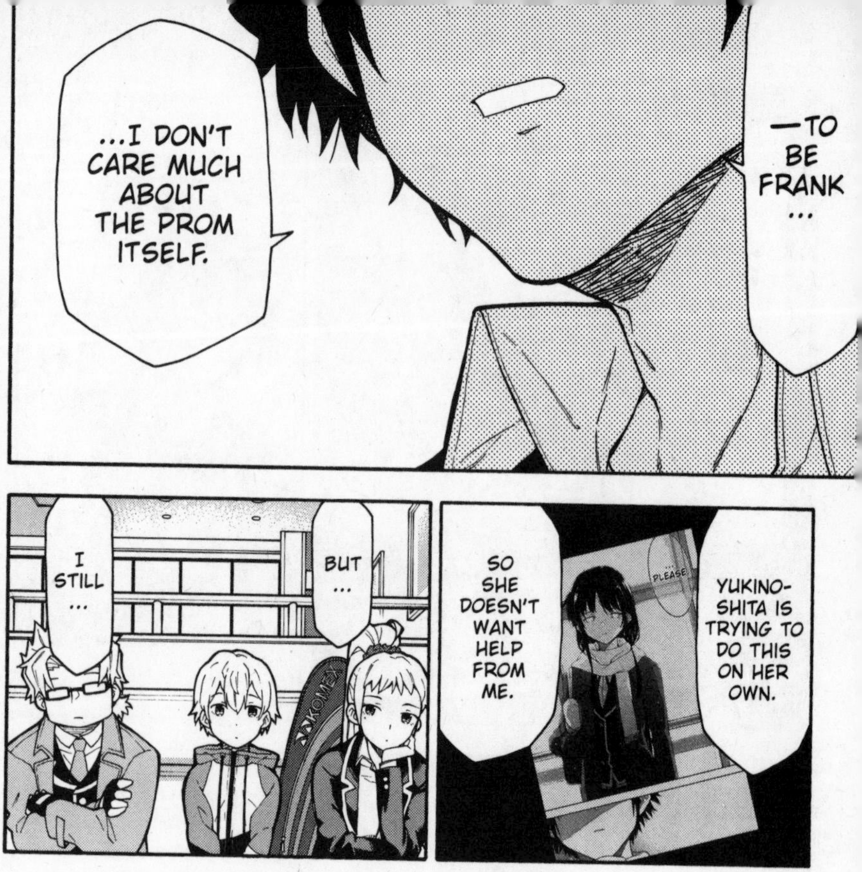
—TO BE FRANK ...
...I DON'T CARE MUCH ABOUT THE PROM ITSELF.
YUKINO-SHITA IS TRYING TO DO THIS ON HER OWN.
...PLEASE.
SO SHE DOESN'T WANT HELP FROM ME.
BUT ...
I STILL ...
KOMEX

EVEN IF IT'S PATHETIC AND SPINELESS...

...AT THE VERY LEAST, I'LL SPEAK NO LIES.

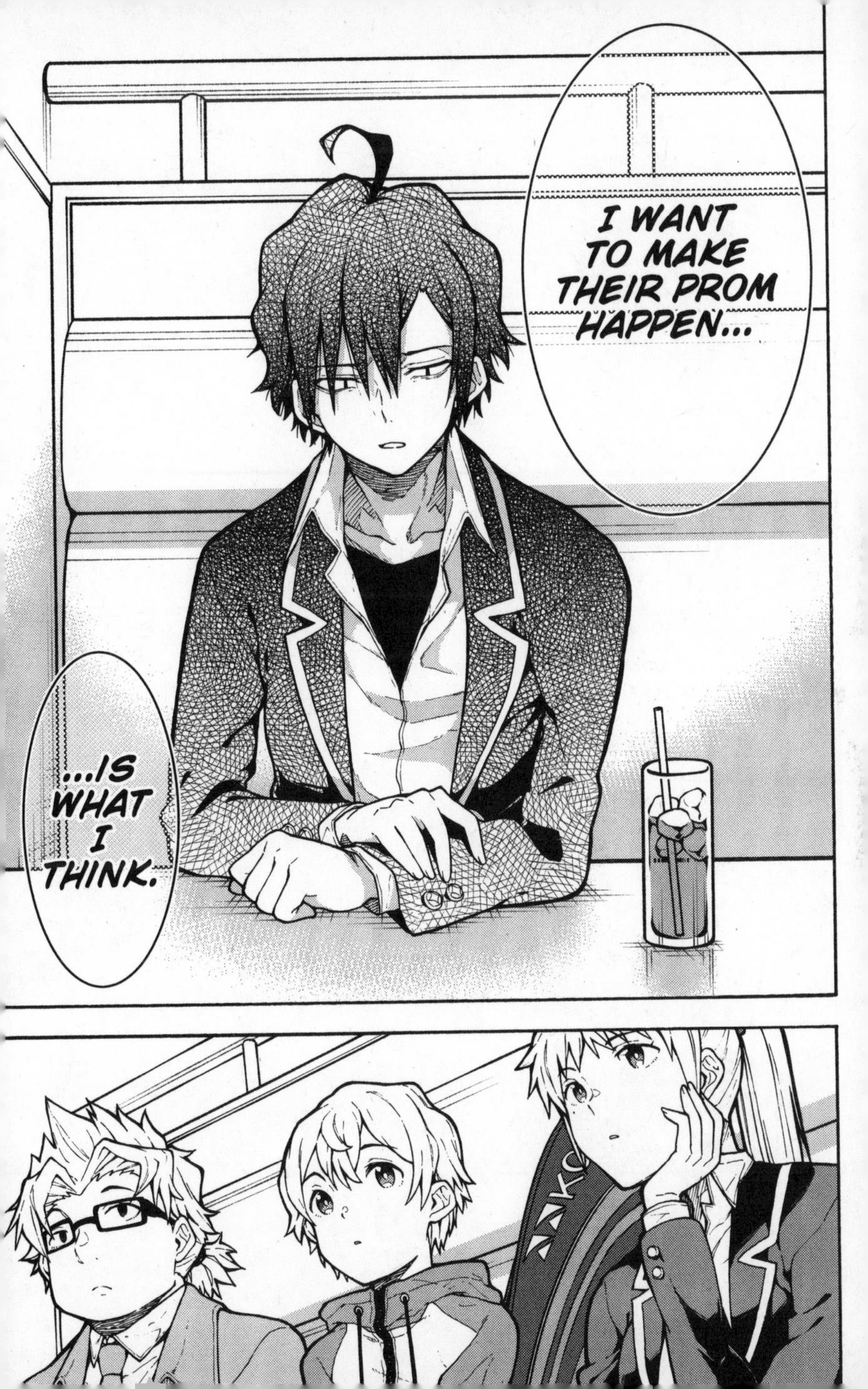
I WANT TO MAKE THEIR PROM HAPPEN...
...IS WHAT I THINK.

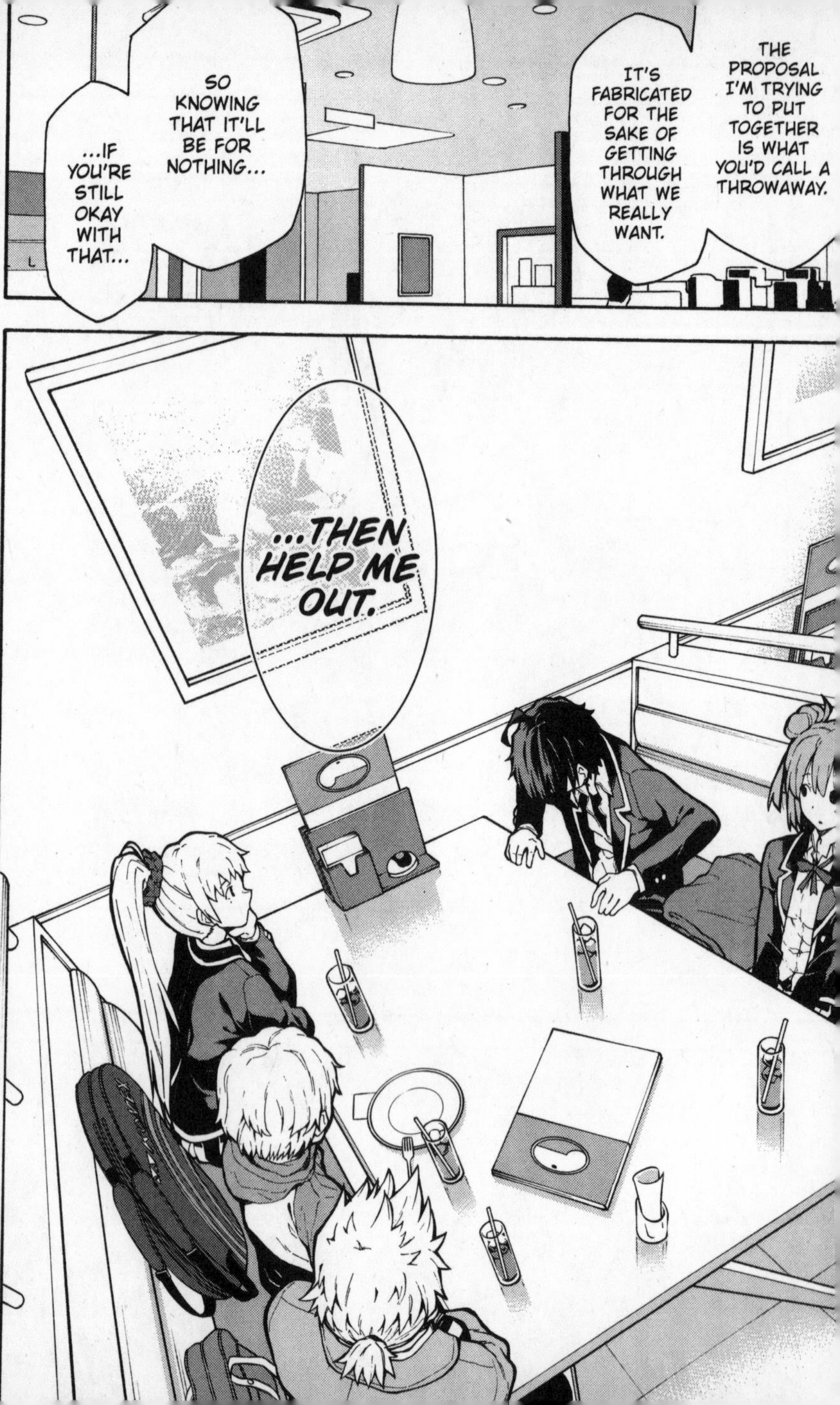
THE PROPOSAL I'M TRYING TO PUT TOGETHER IS WHAT YOU'D CALL A THROWAWAY.
IT'S FABRICATED FOR THE SAKE OF GETTING THROUGH WHAT WE REALLY WANT.
SO KNOWING THAT IT'LL BE FOR NOTHING...
...IF YOU'RE STILL OKAY WITH THAT...
...THEN HELP ME OUT.

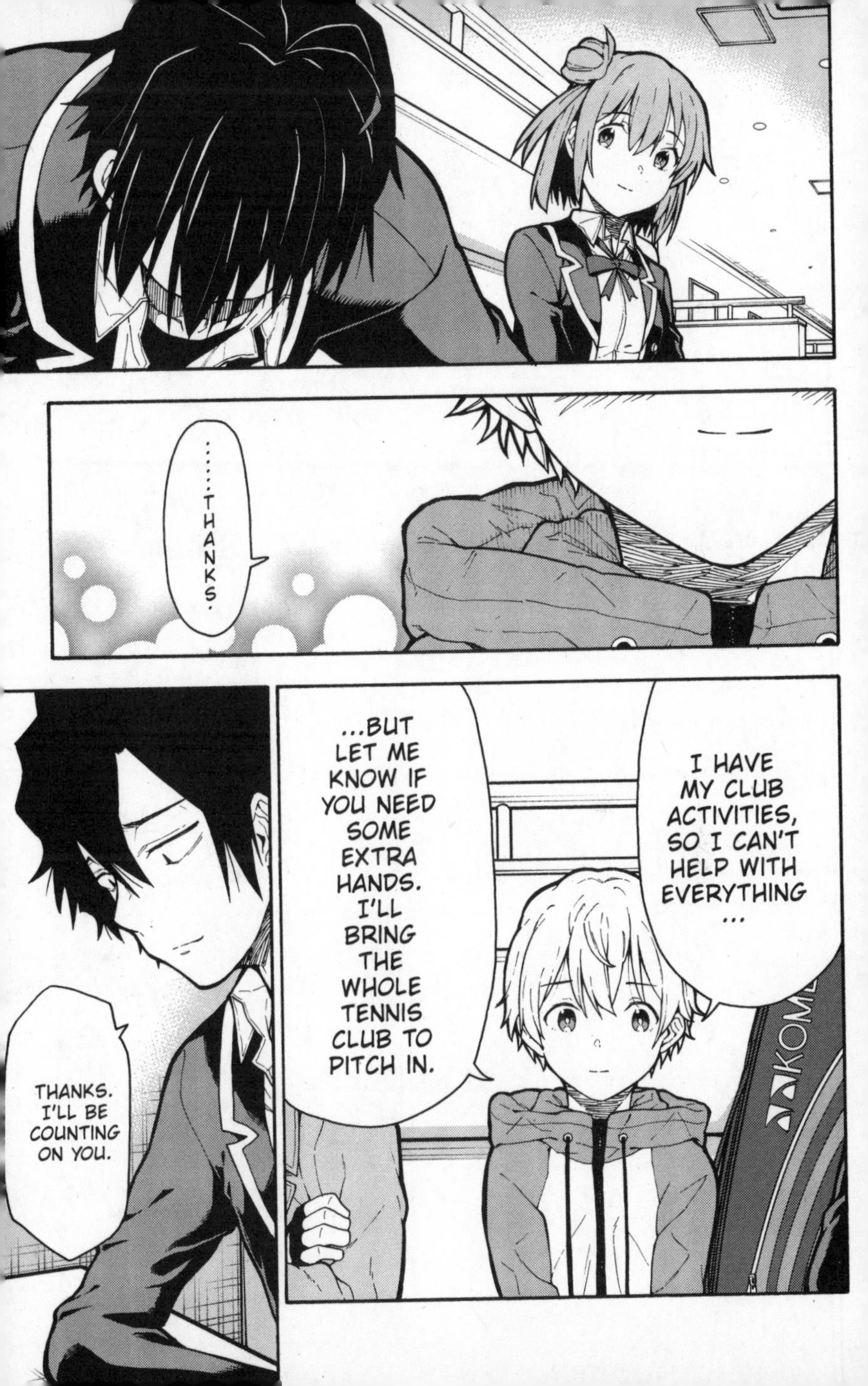
......THANKS.
I HAVE MY CLUB ACTIVITIES, SO I CAN'T HELP WITH EVERYTHING...
...BUT LET ME KNOW IF YOU NEED SOME EXTRA HANDS. I'LL BRING THE WHOLE TENNIS CLUB TO PITCH IN.
THANKS. I'LL BE COUNTING ON YOU.

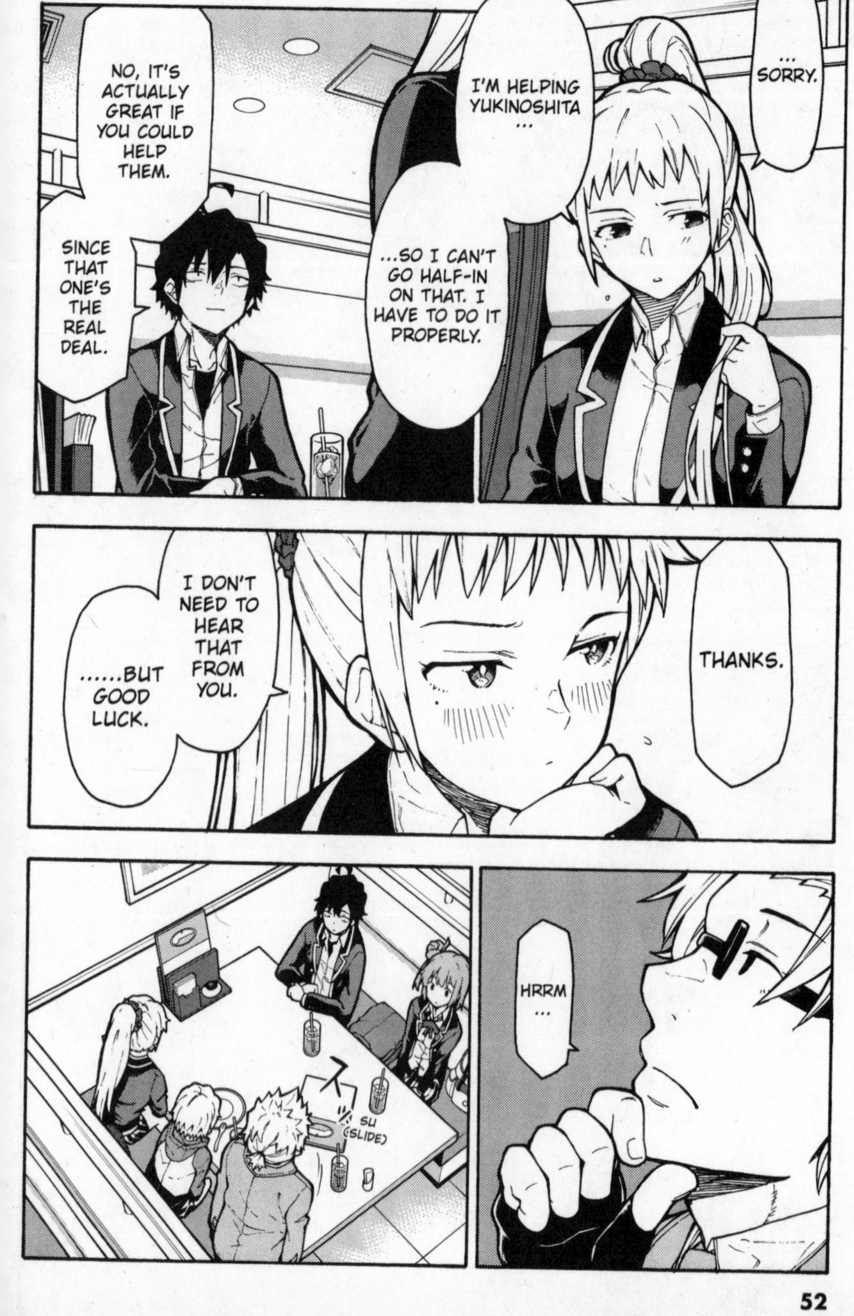
... SORRY.
I'M HELPING YUKINOSHITA ...
...SO I CAN'T GO HALF-IN ON THAT. I HAVE TO DO IT PROPERLY.
NO, IT'S ACTUALLY GREAT IF YOU COULD HELP THEM.
SINCE THAT ONE'S THE REAL DEAL.
THANKS.
I DON'T NEED TO HEAR THAT FROM YOU.
......BUT GOOD LUCK.
HRRM ...
SU (SLIDE)

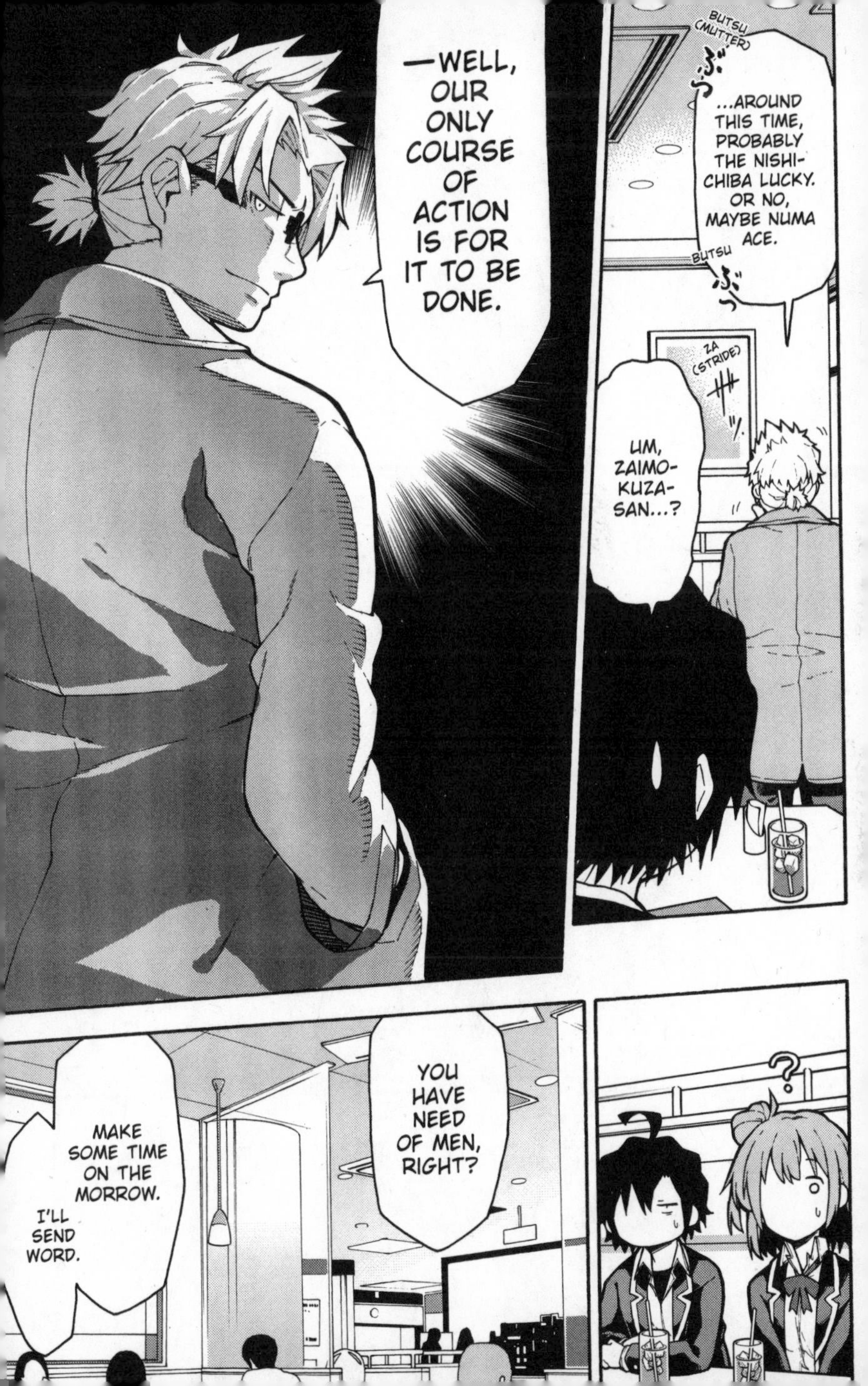
BUTSU (MUTTER)
...AROUND THIS TIME, PROBABLY THE NISHI-CHIBA LUCKY. OR NO, MAYBE NUMA ACE.
BUTSU
ZA (STRIDE)
UM, ZAIMOKUZA-SAN...?
—WELL, OUR ONLY COURSE OF ACTION IS FOR IT TO BE DONE.
?
YOU HAVE NEED OF MEN, RIGHT?
MAKE SOME TIME ON THE MORROW.
I'LL SEND WORD.

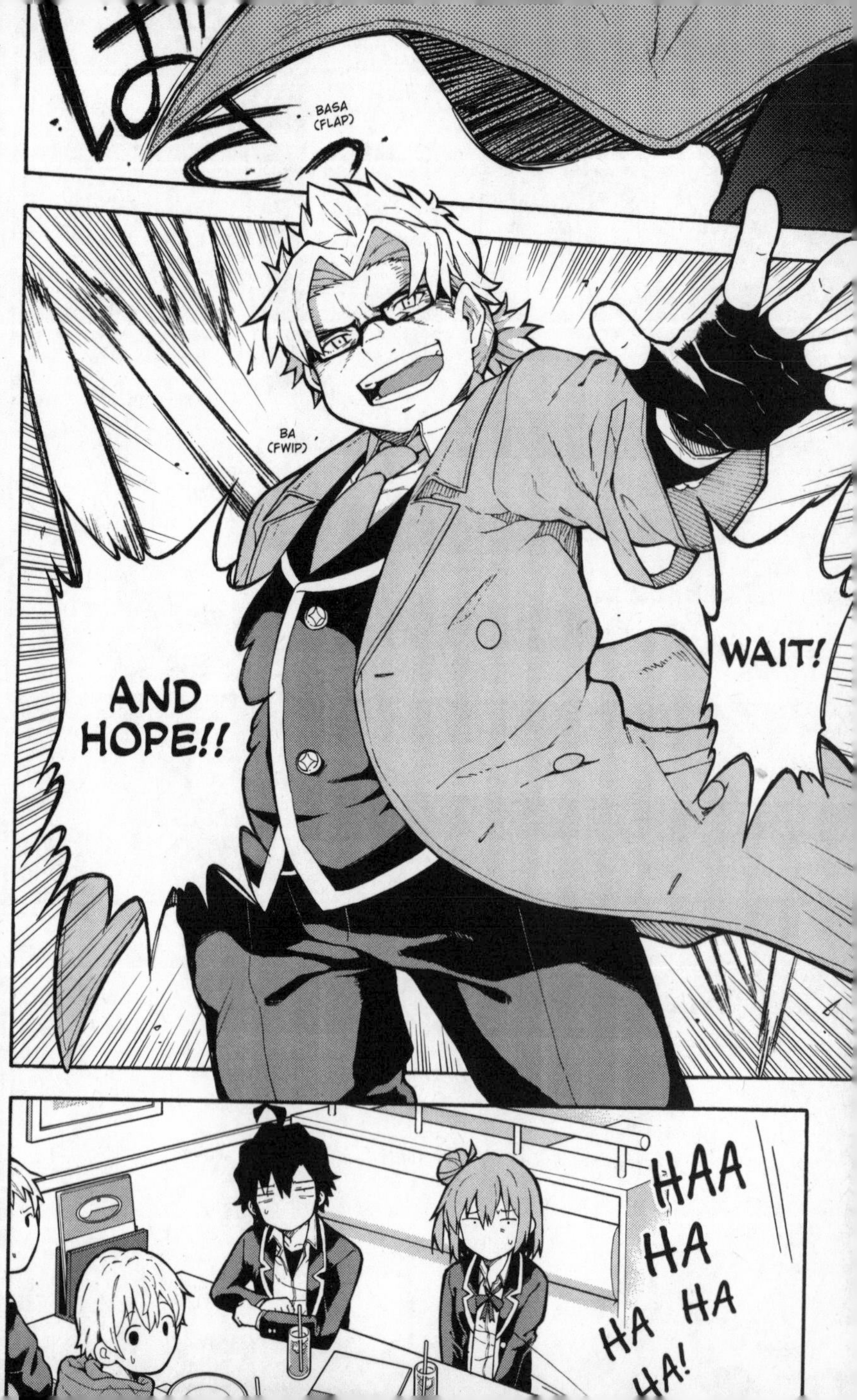
BASA
(FLAP)
BA
(FWIP)
WAIT!
AND HOPE!!
HAA HA HA HA HA!

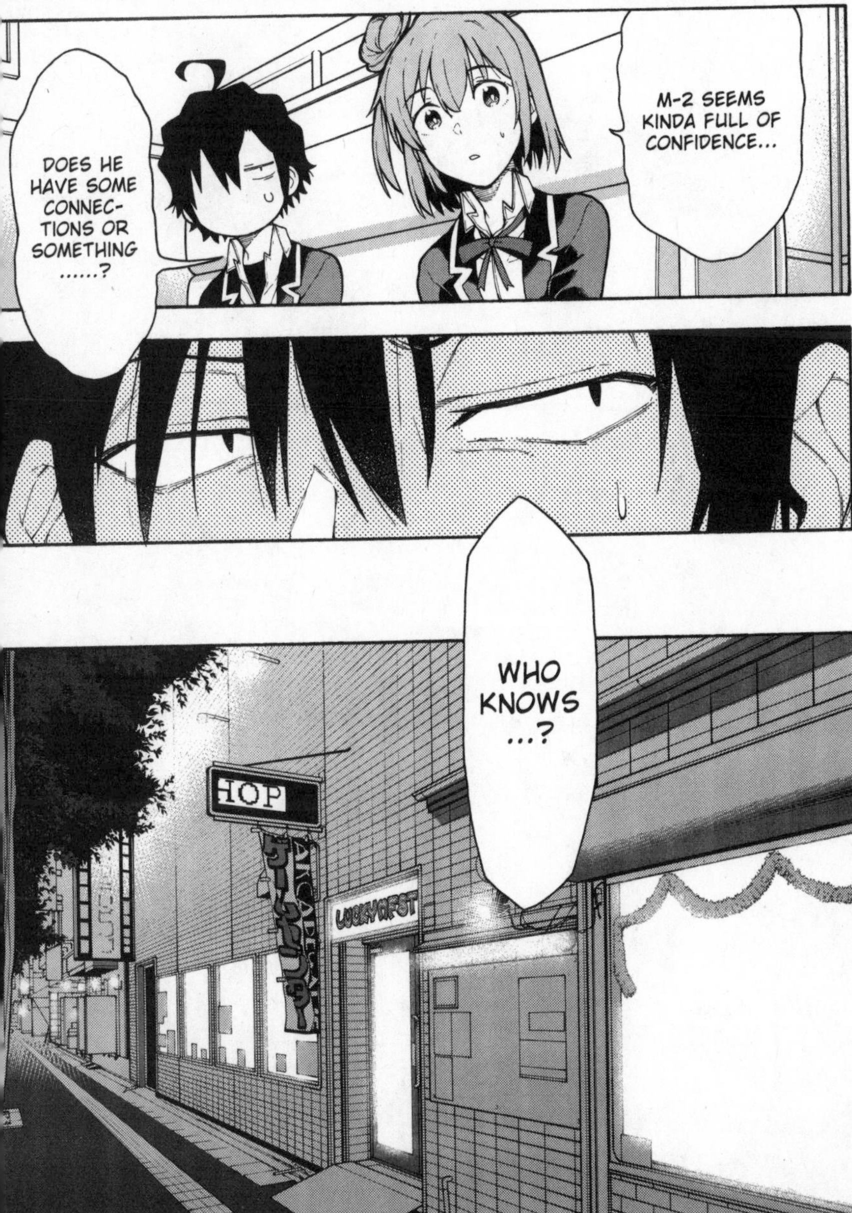
M-2 SEEMS KINDA FULL OF CONFIDENCE...
DOES HE HAVE SOME CONNECTIONS OR SOMETHING ......?
WHO KNOWS ...?
HOP

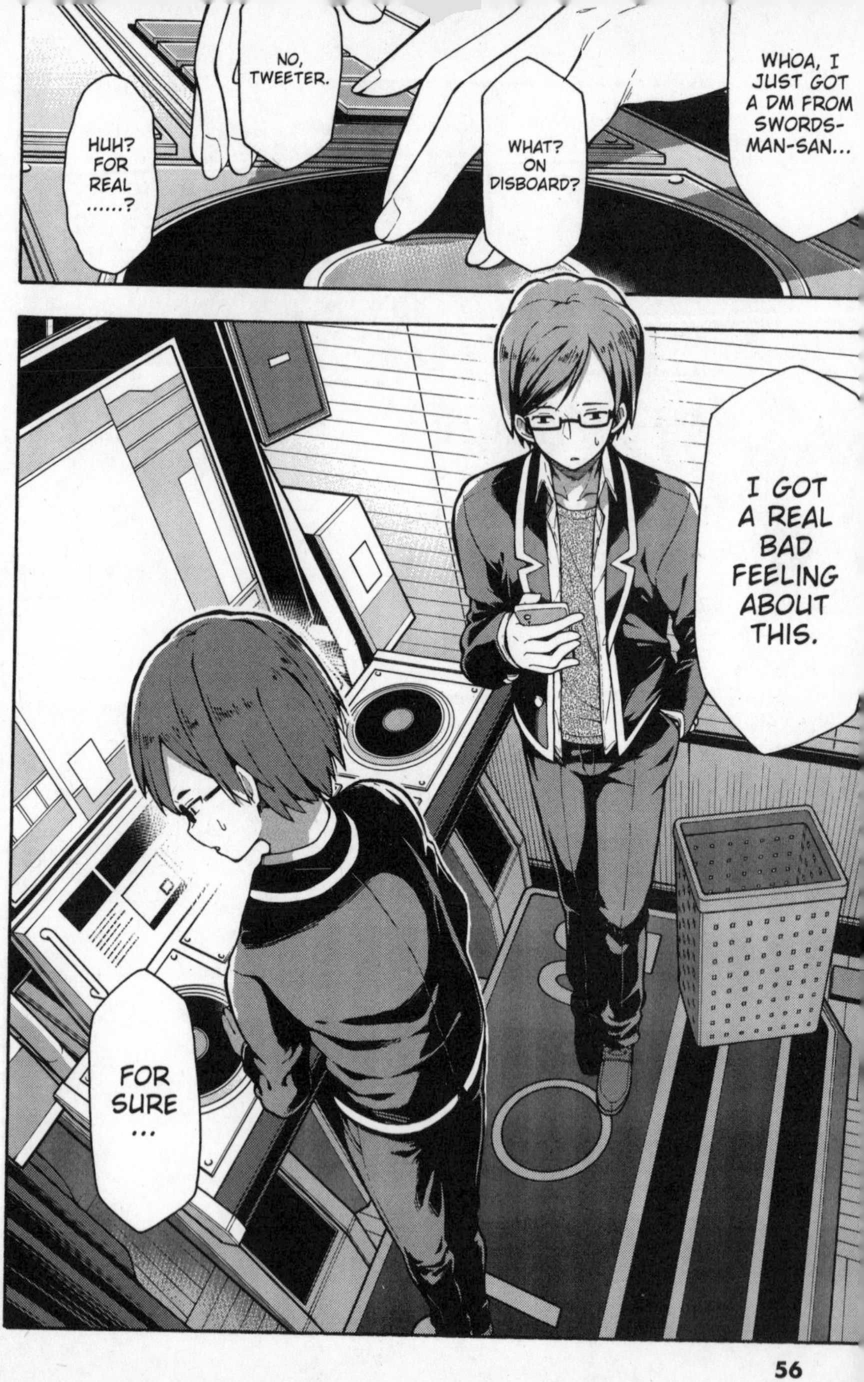
WHOA, I JUST GOT A DM FROM SWORDS-MAN-SAN...
WHAT? ON DISBOARD?
NO, TWEETER.
HUH? FOR REAL ......?
I GOT A REAL BAD FEELING ABOUT THIS.
FOR SURE ...

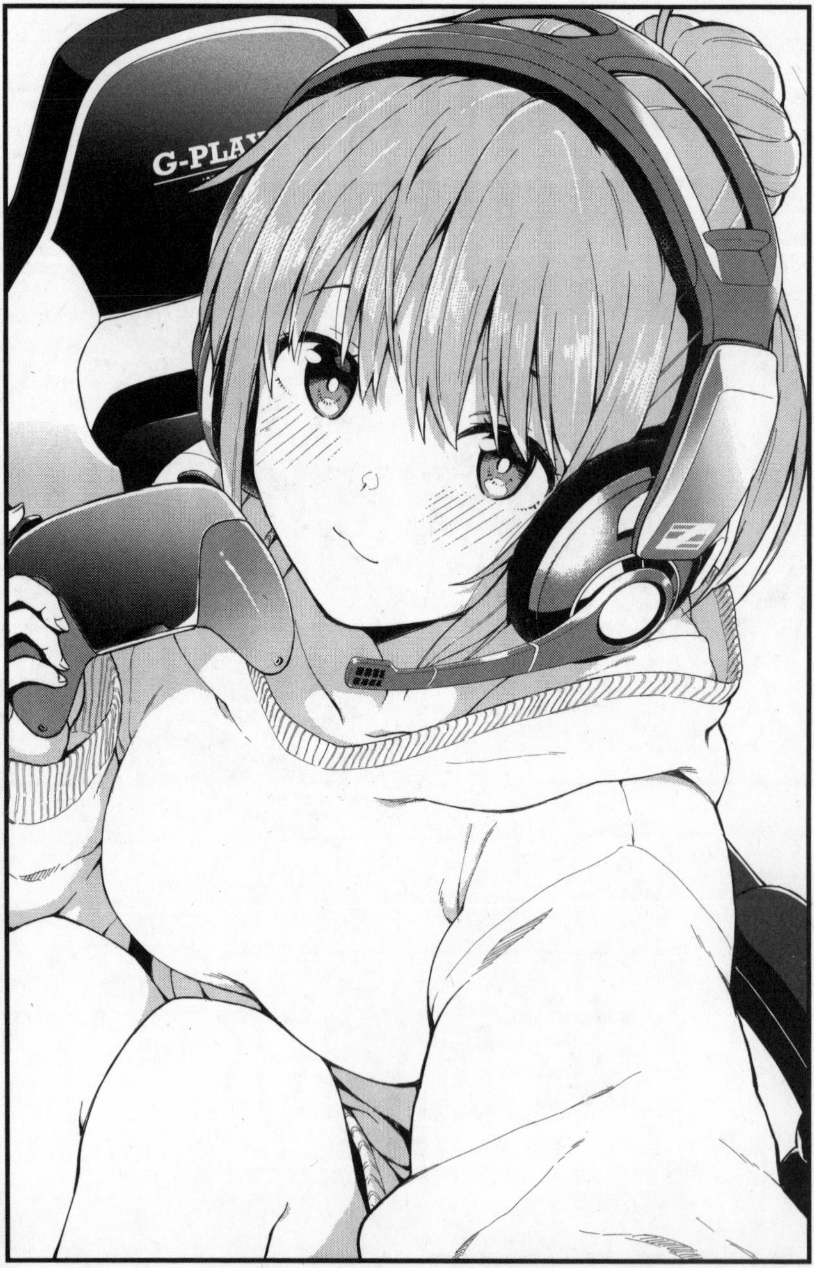
G-PLAY

CHAPTER 99 … AT SOME UNKNOWN POINT, THE ENDING CREDITS BEGIN TO ROLL.

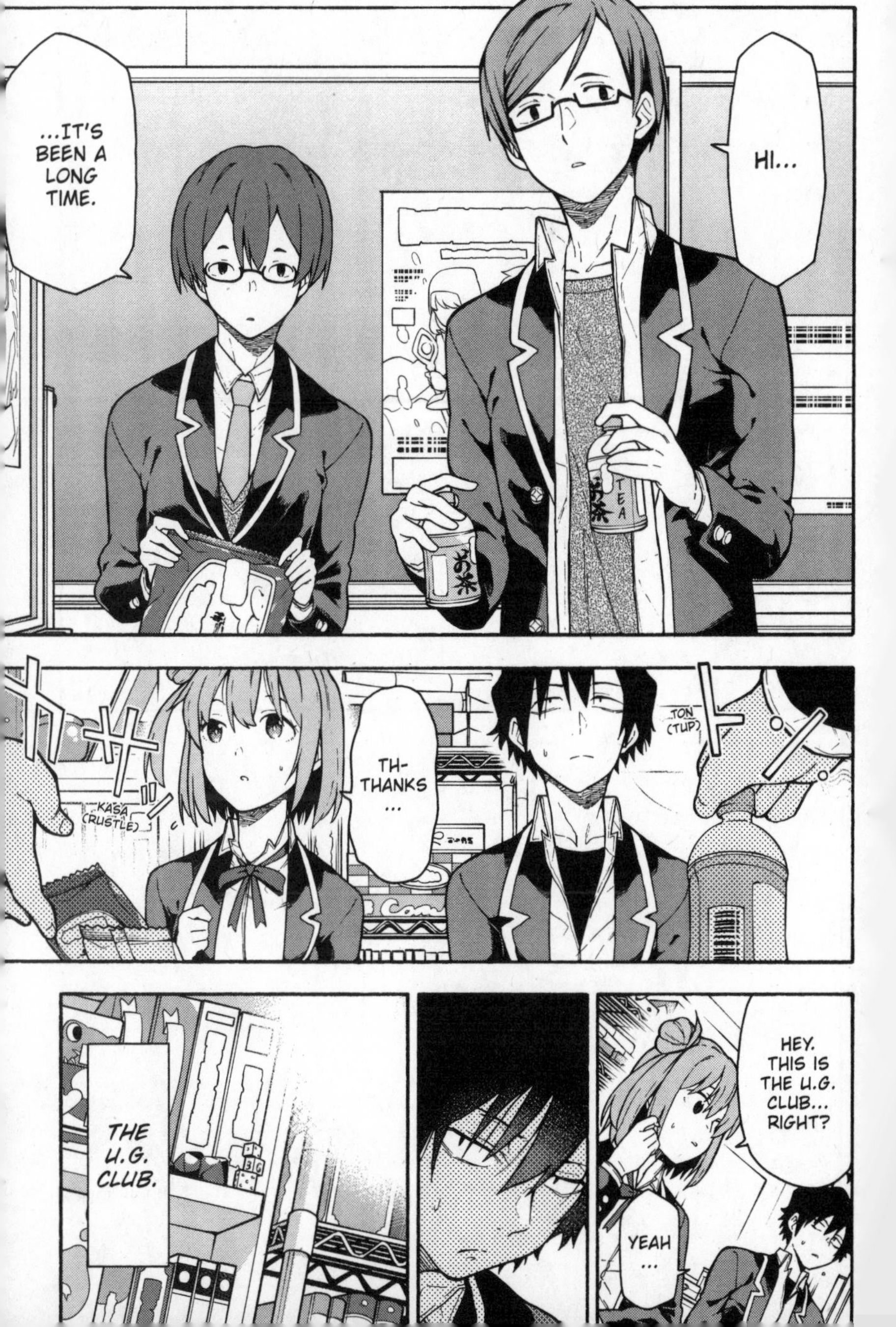
HI...
...IT'S BEEN A LONG TIME.
TON (TUP)
TH-THANKS ...
KASA (RUSTLE)
HEY. THIS IS THE U.G. CLUB... RIGHT?
YEAH ...
THE U.G. CLUB.

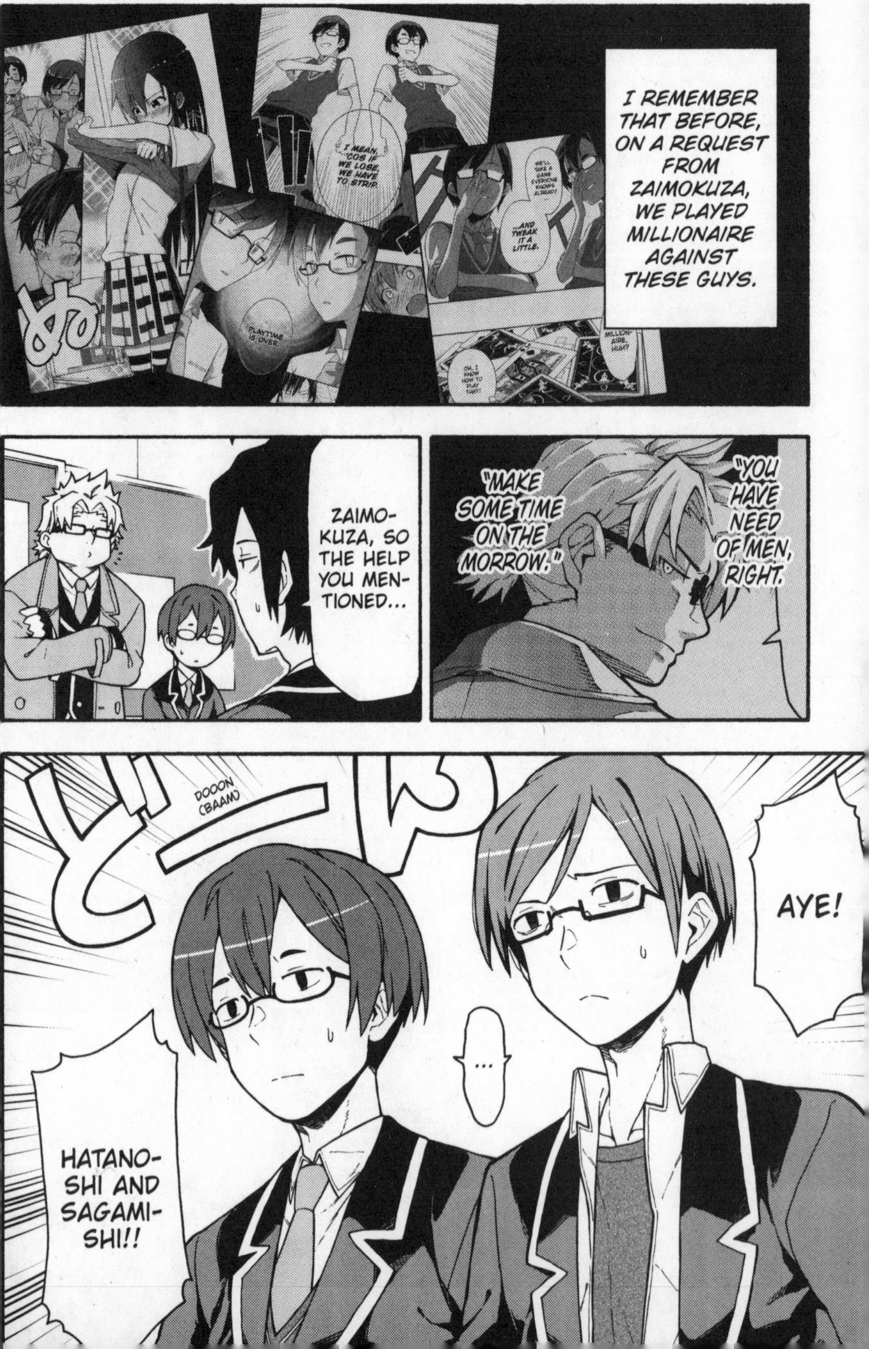
I REMEMBER THAT BEFORE, ON A REQUEST FROM ZAIMOKUZA, WE PLAYED MILLIONAIRE AGAINST THESE GUYS.
I MEAN, 'COS IF WE LOSE, WE HAVE TO STRIP.
WE'LL TAKE A GAME EVERYONE KNOWS ALREADY
...AND TWEAK IT A LITTLE.
MILLIONAIRE, HUH?
OH, I KNOW HOW TO PLAY THAT!
PLAYTIME IS OVER.
"YOU HAVE NEED OF MEN, RIGHT.
"MAKE SOME TIME ON THE MORROW."
ZAIMOKUZA, SO THE HELP YOU MENTIONED...
DOOON (BAAM)
AYE!
...
HATANO-SHI AND SAGAMI-SHI!!

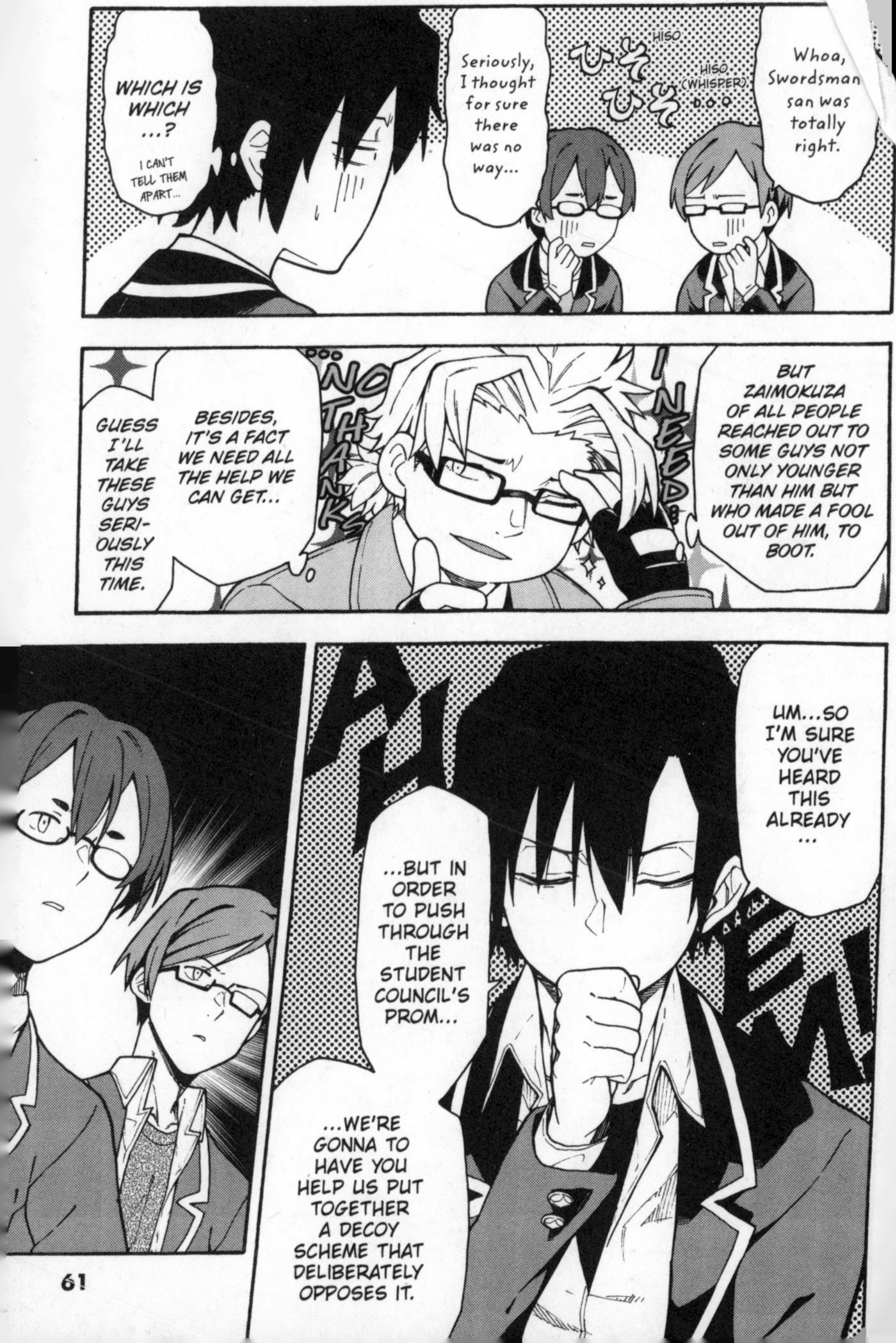
Whoa, Swordsman-san was totally right.
HISO
HISO (WHISPER)
Seriously, I thought for sure there was no way...
WHICH IS WHICH ...?
I CAN'T TELL THEM APART...
BUT ZAIMOKUZA OF ALL PEOPLE REACHED OUT TO SOME GUYS NOT ONLY YOUNGER THAN HIM BUT WHO MADE A FOOL OUT OF HIM, TO BOOT.
I NEED...
NO THANKS...
BESIDES, IT'S A FACT WE NEED ALL THE HELP WE CAN GET...
GUESS I'LL TAKE THESE GUYS SERIOUSLY THIS TIME.
UM...SO I'M SURE YOU'VE HEARD THIS ALREADY...
...BUT IN ORDER TO PUSH THROUGH THE STUDENT COUNCIL'S PROM...
...WE'RE GONNA TO HAVE YOU HELP US PUT TOGETHER A DECOY SCHEME THAT DELIBERATELY OPPOSES IT.

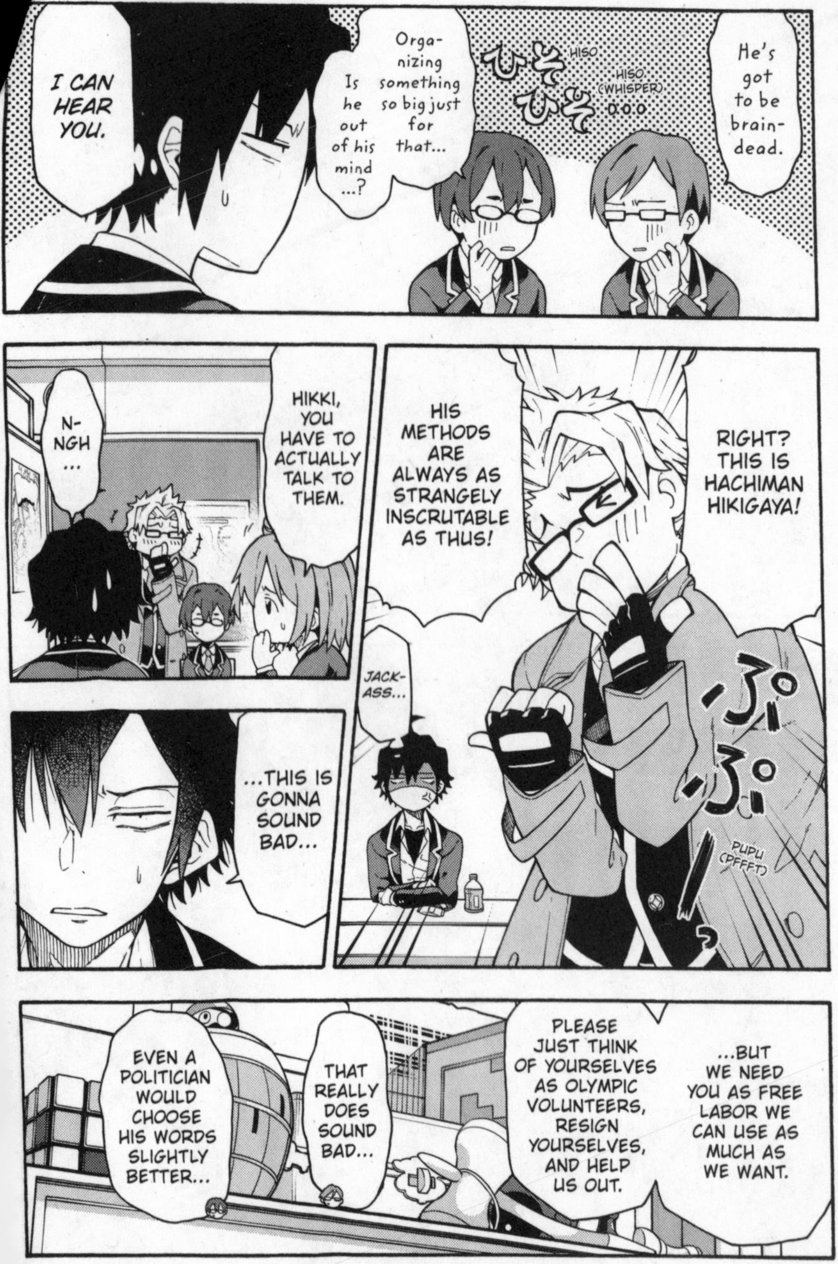
He's got to be brain-dead.
HISO HISO (WHISPER)
Organizing something so big just for that...
Is he out of his mind...?
I CAN HEAR YOU.
RIGHT? THIS IS HACHIMAN HIKIGAYA!
HIS METHODS ARE ALWAYS AS STRANGELY INSCRUTABLE AS THUS!
PUPU (PFFFT)
JACK-ASS...
HIKKI, YOU HAVE TO ACTUALLY TALK TO THEM.
N-NGH...
...THIS IS GONNA SOUND BAD...
...BUT WE NEED YOU AS FREE LABOR WE CAN USE AS MUCH AS WE WANT.
PLEASE JUST THINK OF YOURSELVES AS OLYMPIC VOLUNTEERS, RESIGN YOURSELVES, AND HELP US OUT.
THAT REALLY DOES SOUND BAD...
EVEN A POLITICIAN WOULD CHOOSE HIS WORDS SLIGHTLY BETTER...

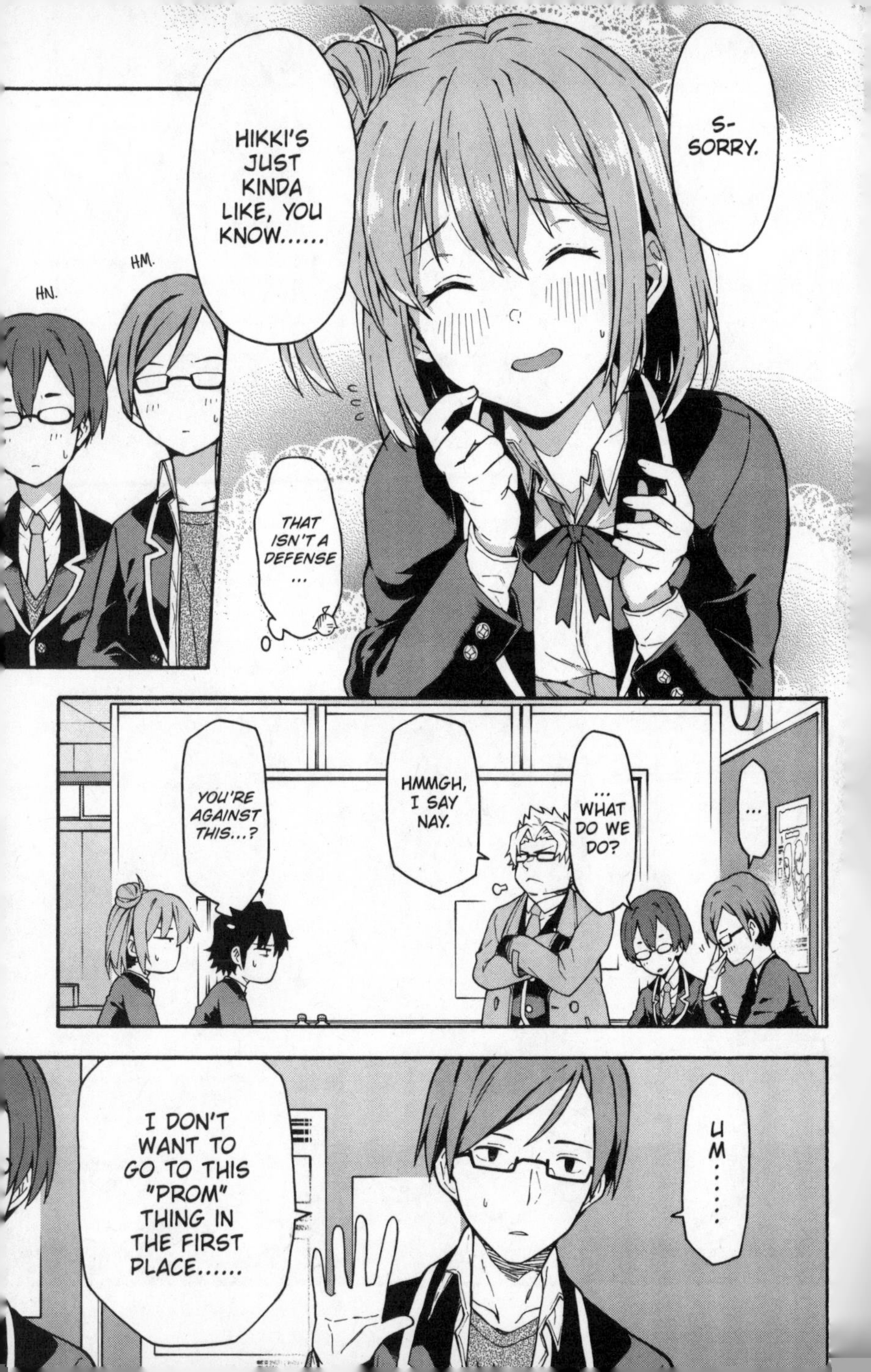
S-SORRY.
HIKKI'S JUST KINDA LIKE, YOU KNOW......
HM.
HN.
THAT ISN'T A DEFENSE ...
...
... WHAT DO WE DO?
HMMGH, I SAY NAY.
YOU'RE AGAINST THIS...?
UM......
I DON'T WANT TO GO TO THIS "PROM" THING IN THE FIRST PLACE......

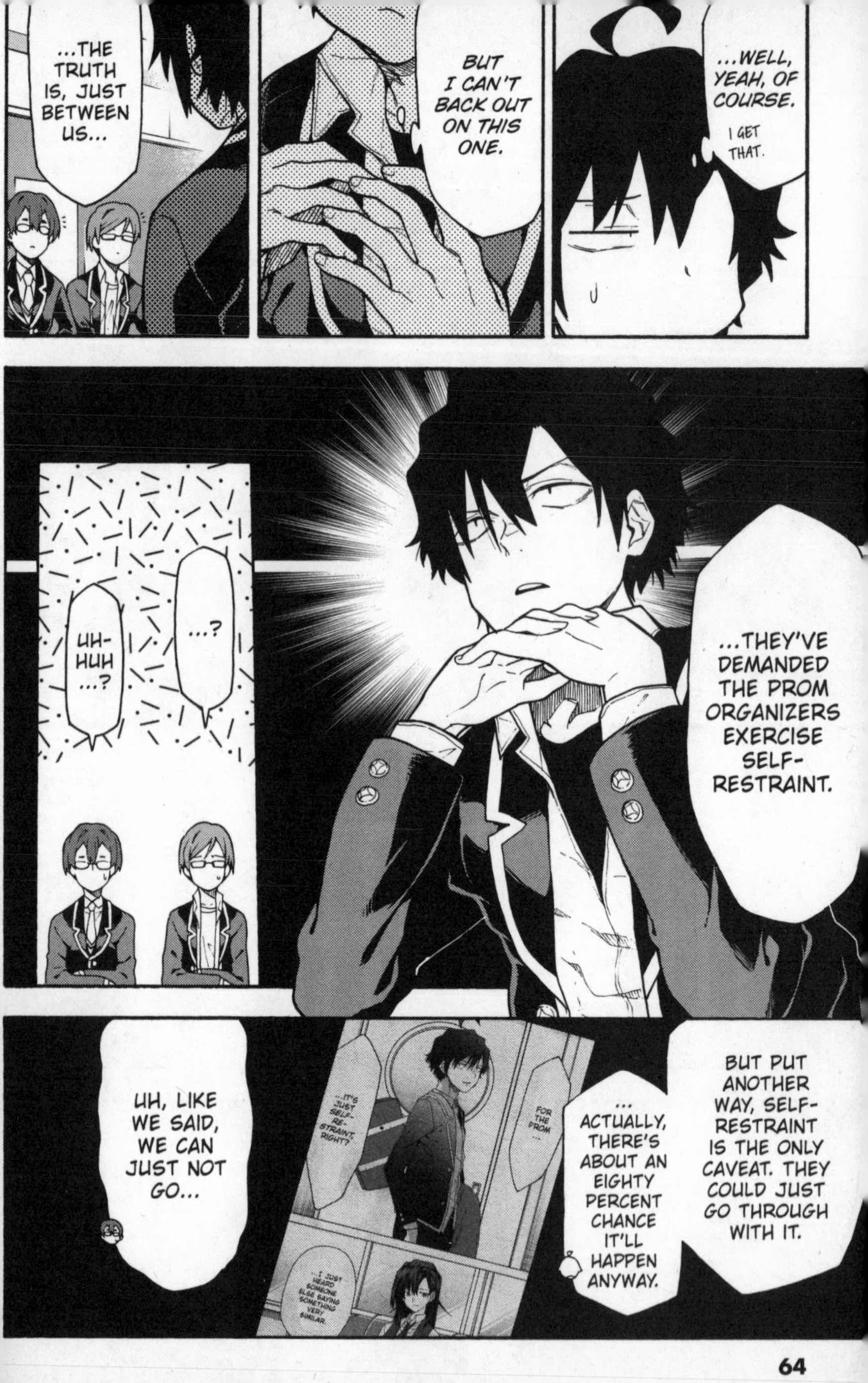
...WELL, YEAH, OF COURSE.
I GET THAT.
BUT I CAN'T BACK OUT ON THIS ONE.
...THE TRUTH IS, JUST BETWEEN US...
...THEY'VE DEMANDED THE PROM ORGANIZERS EXERCISE SELF-RESTRAINT.
...?
UH-HUH...?
BUT PUT ANOTHER WAY, SELF-RESTRAINT IS THE ONLY CAVEAT. THEY COULD JUST GO THROUGH WITH IT.
...ACTUALLY, THERE'S ABOUT AN EIGHTY PERCENT CHANCE IT'LL HAPPEN ANYWAY.
FOR THE PROM...
...IT'S JUST SELF-RESTRAINT, RIGHT?
...I JUST HEARD SOMEONE ELSE SAYING SOMETHING VERY SIMILAR.
UH, LIKE WE SAID, WE CAN JUST NOT GO...

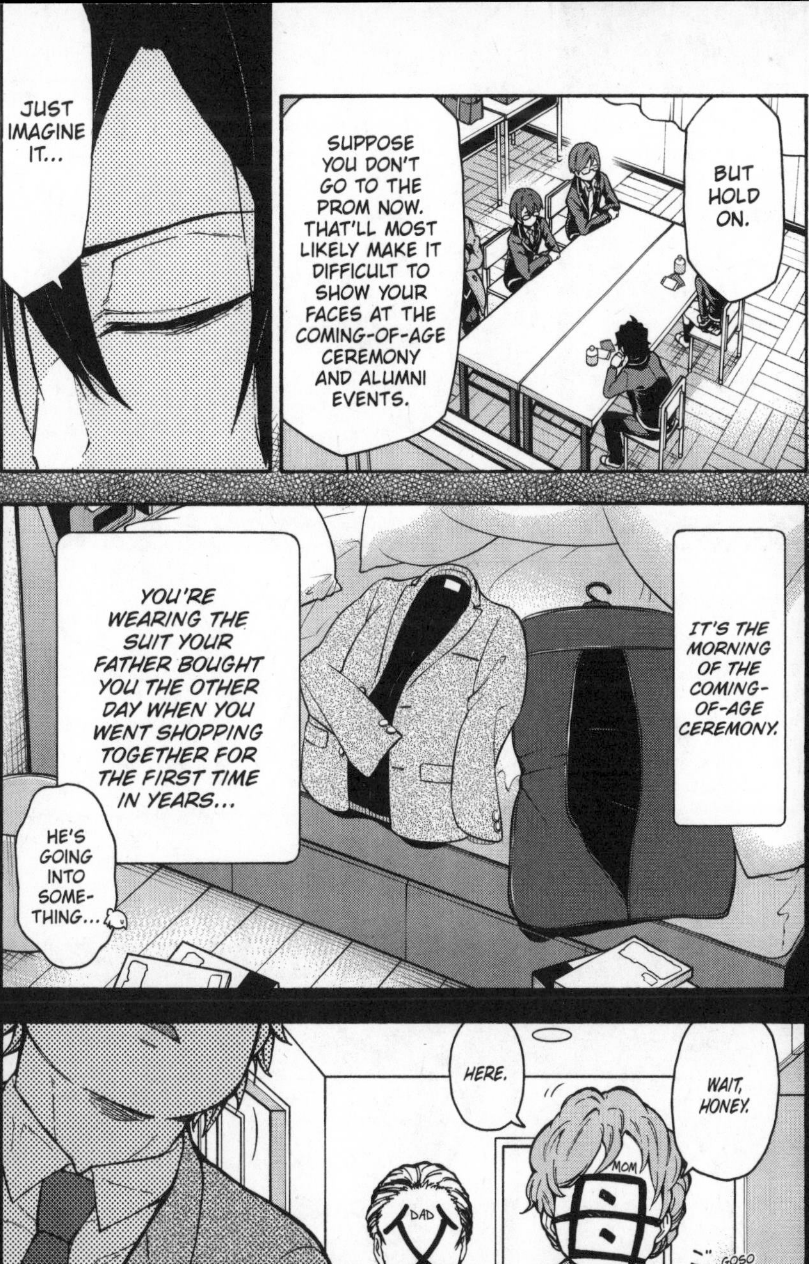
BUT HOLD ON.
SUPPOSE YOU DON'T GO TO THE PROM NOW. THAT'LL MOST LIKELY MAKE IT DIFFICULT TO SHOW YOUR FACES AT THE COMING-OF-AGE CEREMONY AND ALUMNI EVENTS.
JUST IMAGINE IT...
IT'S THE MORNING OF THE COMING-OF-AGE CEREMONY.
YOU'RE WEARING THE SUIT YOUR FATHER BOUGHT YOU THE OTHER DAY WHEN YOU WENT SHOPPING TOGETHER FOR THE FIRST TIME IN YEARS...
HE'S GOING INTO SOME-THING...
WAIT, HONEY.
HERE.
MOM
DAD
GOSO (RUSTLE)

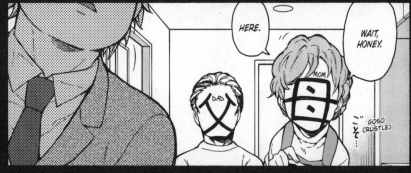

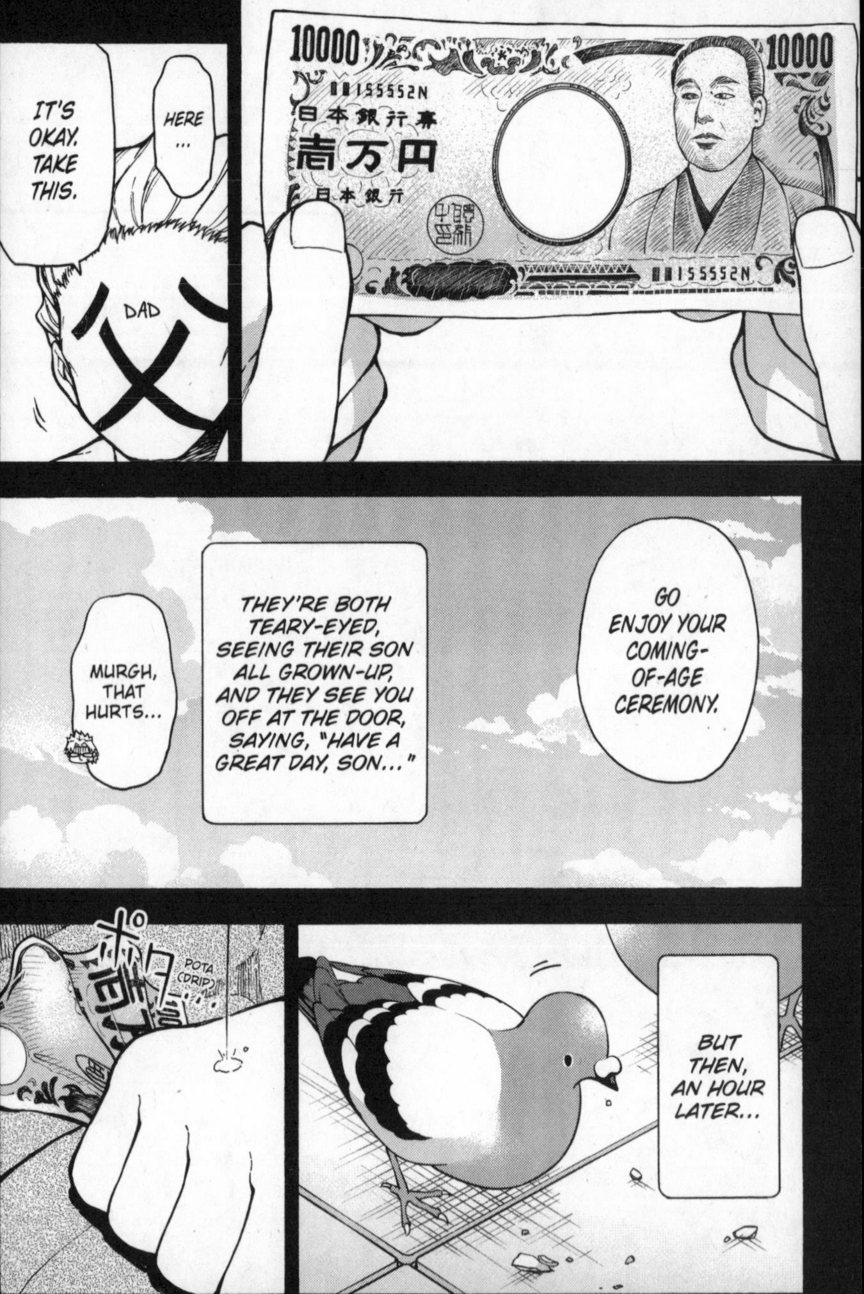
10000
日本銀行券
壱万円
日本銀行
HERE ...
IT'S OKAY. TAKE THIS.
DAD
GO ENJOY YOUR COMING-OF-AGE CEREMONY.
THEY'RE BOTH TEARY-EYED, SEEING THEIR SON ALL GROWN-UP, AND THEY SEE YOU OFF AT THE DOOR, SAYING, "HAVE A GREAT DAY, SON..."
MURGH, THAT HURTS...
BUT THEN, AN HOUR LATER...
POTA (DRIP)

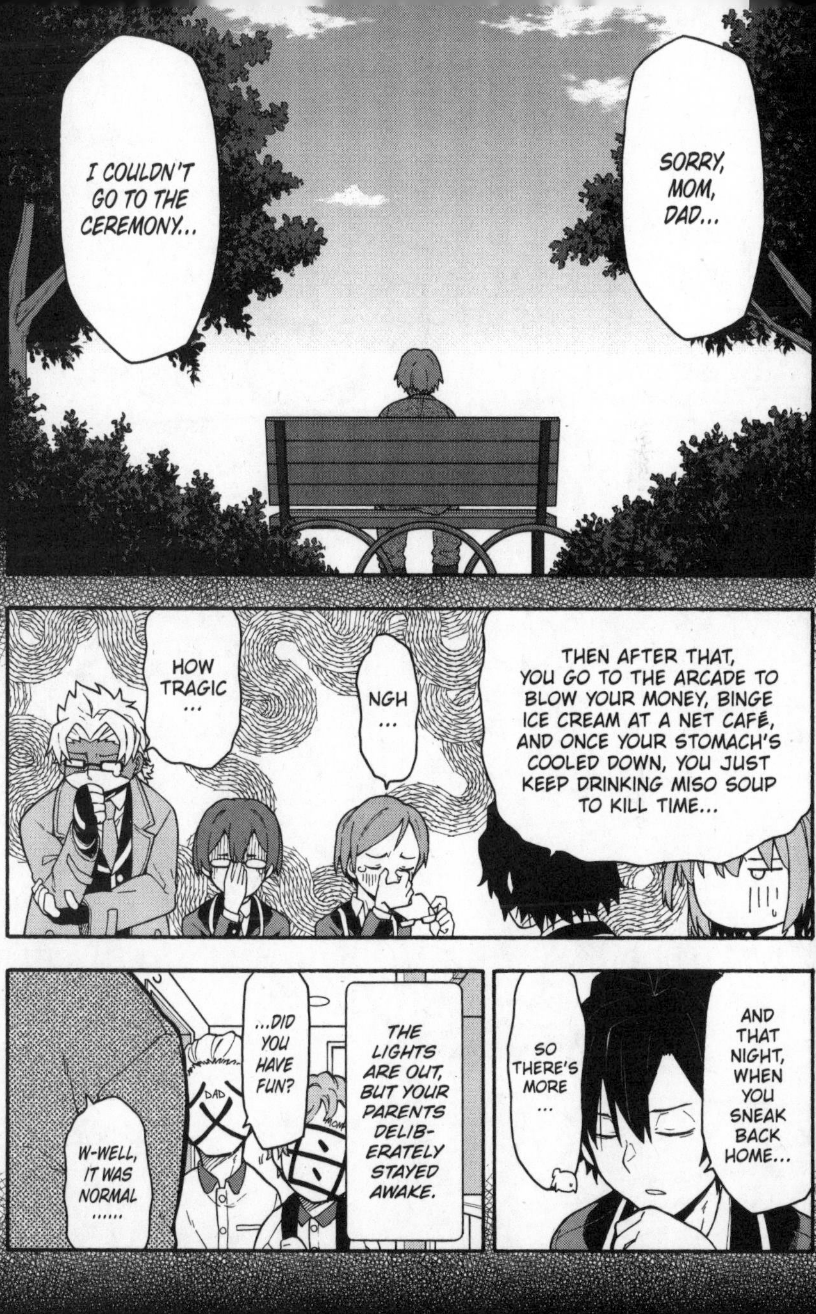
SORRY, MOM, DAD...
I COULDN'T GO TO THE CEREMONY...
THEN AFTER THAT, YOU GO TO THE ARCADE TO BLOW YOUR MONEY, BINGE ICE CREAM AT A NET CAFÉ, AND ONCE YOUR STOMACH'S COOLED DOWN, YOU JUST KEEP DRINKING MISO SOUP TO KILL TIME...
NGH ...
HOW TRAGIC ...
AND THAT NIGHT, WHEN YOU SNEAK BACK HOME...
SO THERE'S MORE ...
THE LIGHTS ARE OUT, BUT YOUR PARENTS DELIBERATELY STAYED AWAKE.
...DID YOU HAVE FUN?
DAD
MOM
W-WELL, IT WAS NORMAL ......

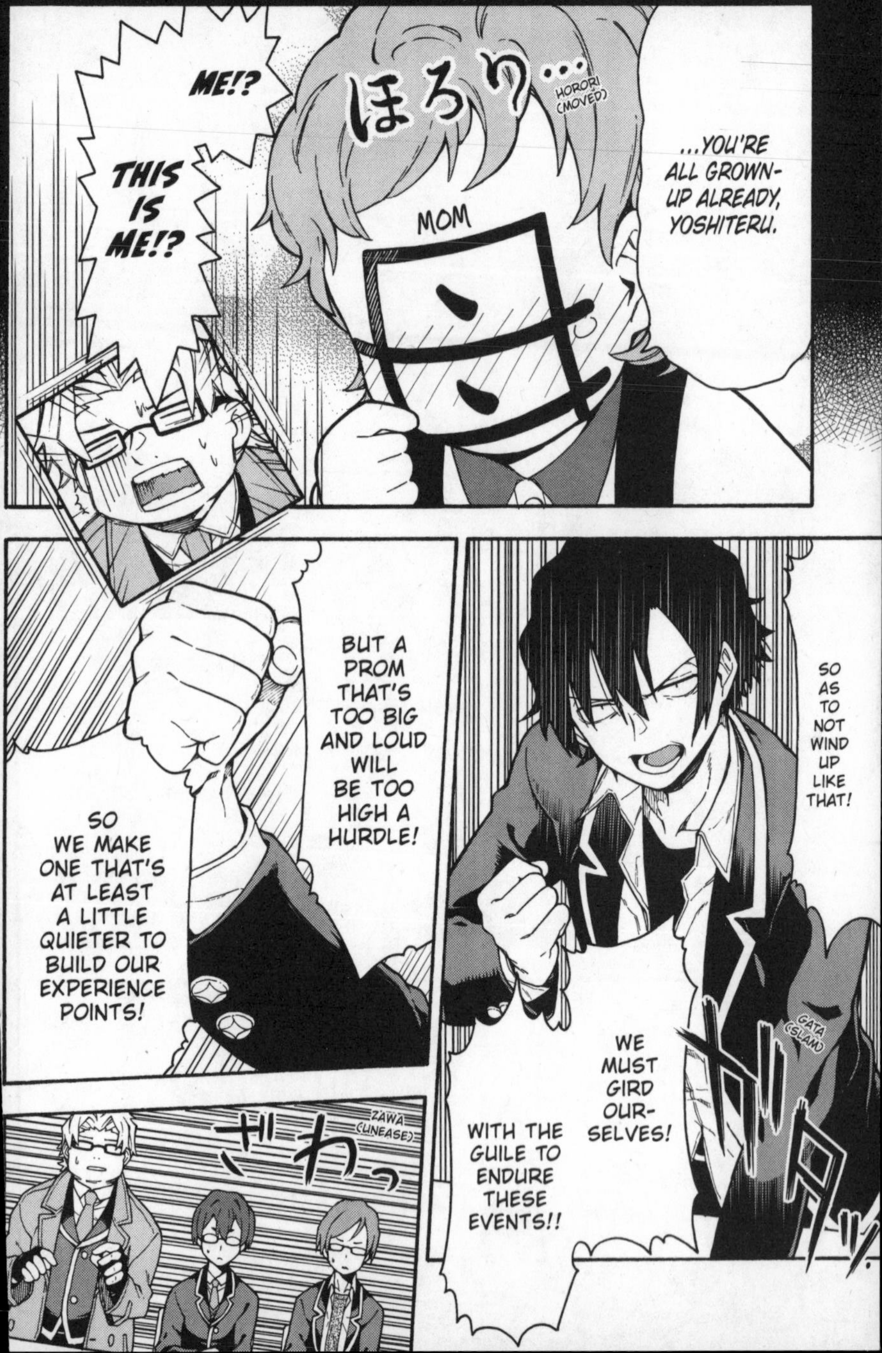

...YOU'RE ALL GROWN-UP ALREADY, YOSHITERU.
ほろり…
HORORI (MOVED)
MOM
ME!?
THIS IS ME!?
SO AS TO NOT WIND UP LIKE THAT!
WE MUST GIRD OURSELVES!
WITH THE GUILE TO ENDURE THESE EVENTS!!
GATA (SLAM)
BUT A PROM THAT'S TOO BIG AND LOUD WILL BE TOO HIGH A HURDLE!
SO WE MAKE ONE THAT'S AT LEAST A LITTLE QUIETER TO BUILD OUR EXPERIENCE POINTS!
ざわっ
ZAWA (UNEASE)

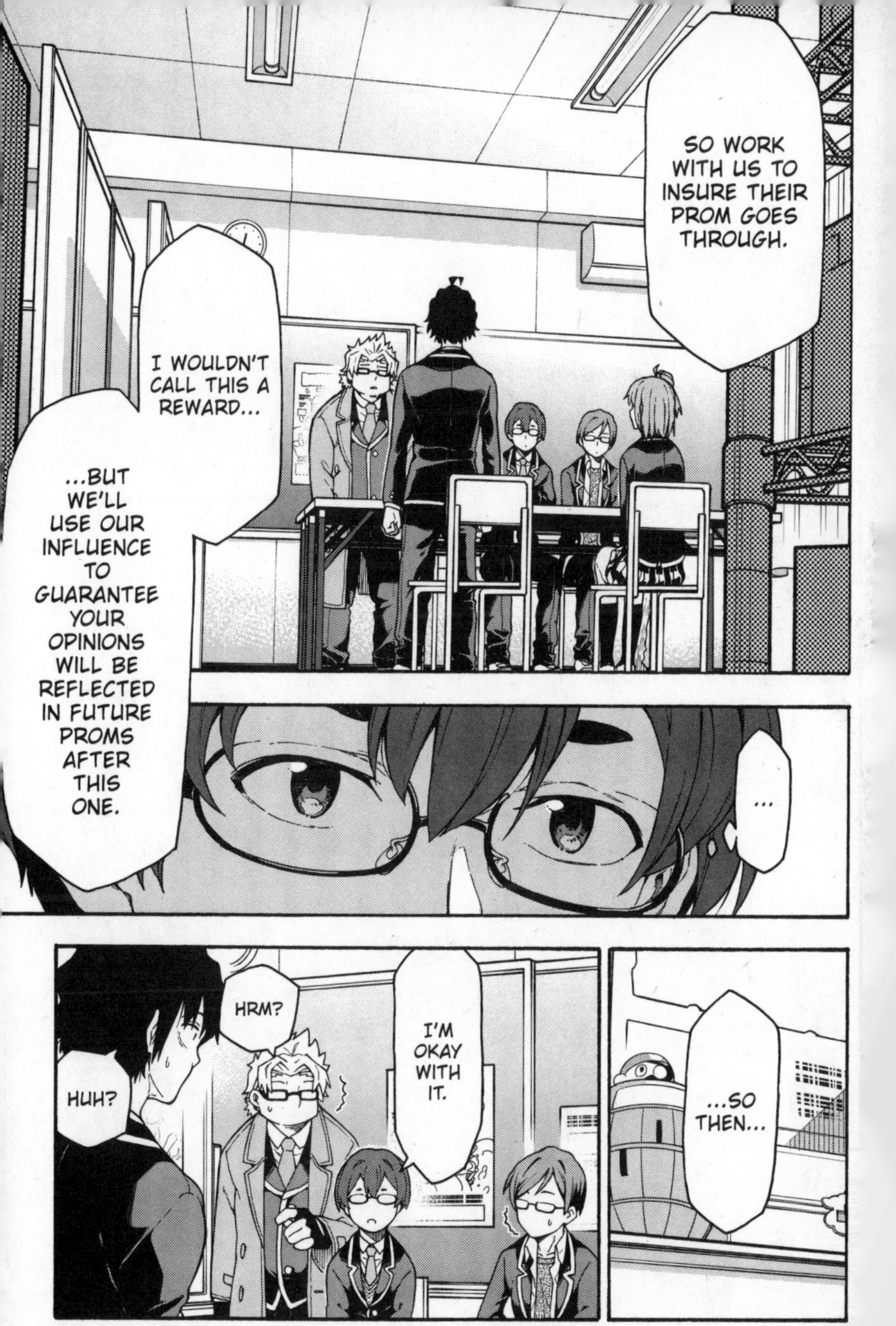
SO WORK WITH US TO INSURE THEIR PROM GOES THROUGH.
I WOULDN'T CALL THIS A REWARD...
...BUT WE'LL USE OUR INFLUENCE TO GUARANTEE YOUR OPINIONS WILL BE REFLECTED IN FUTURE PROMS AFTER THIS ONE.
...
...SO THEN...
I'M OKAY WITH IT.
HRM?
HUH?

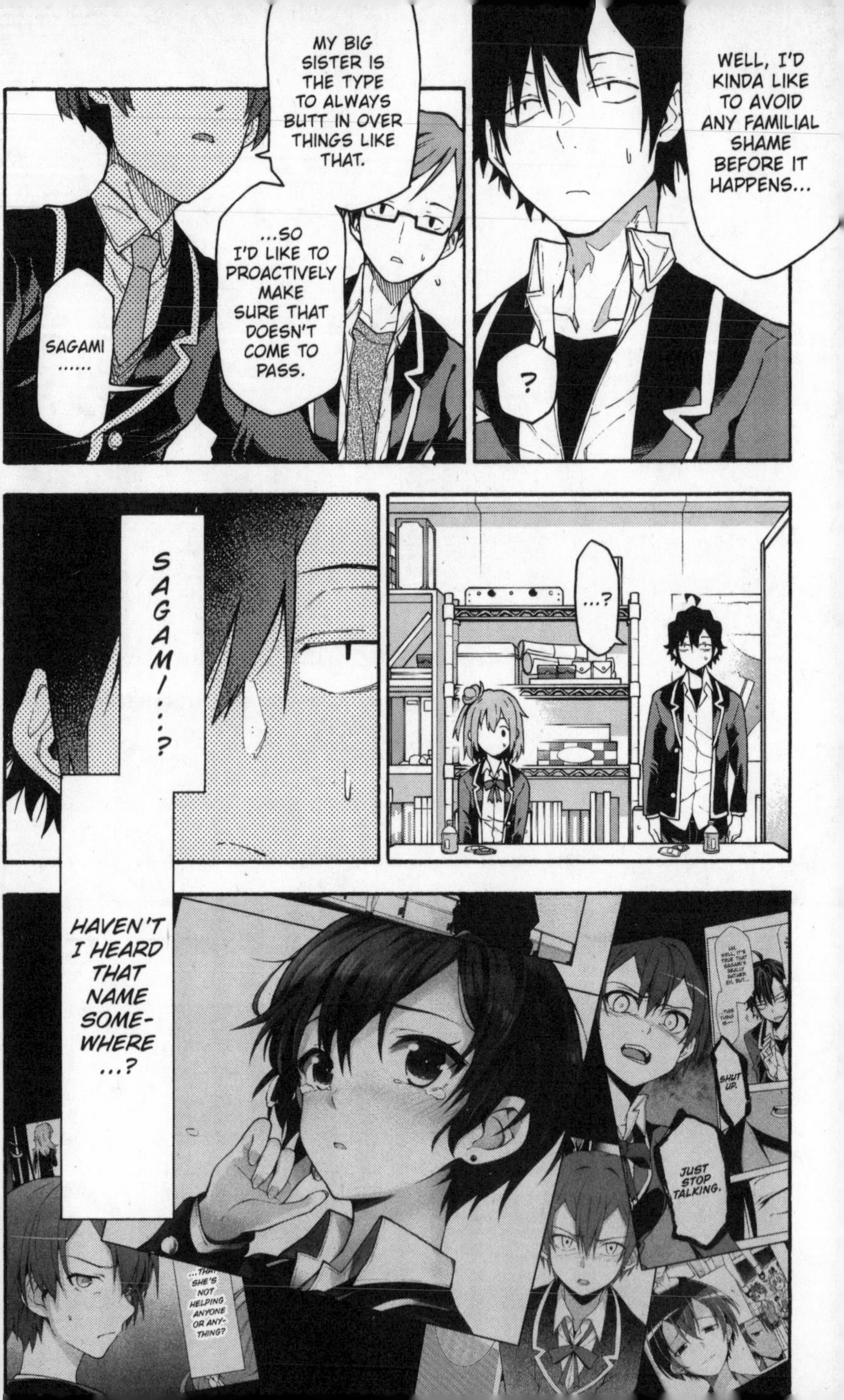
WELL, I'D KINDA LIKE TO AVOID ANY FAMILIAL SHAME BEFORE IT HAPPENS...
?
MY BIG SISTER IS THE TYPE TO ALWAYS BUTT IN OVER THINGS LIKE THAT.
...SO I'D LIKE TO PROACTIVELY MAKE SURE THAT DOESN'T COME TO PASS.
SAGAMI......
...?
SAGAMI...?
HAVEN'T I HEARD THAT NAME SOME-WHERE...?
UH, WELL, IT'S TRUE THAT SAGAMI'S REALLY RATHER EVIL, BUT...
THIS THING IS—
SHUT UP.
JUST STOP TALKING.
...THAT SHE'S NOT HELPING ANYONE OR ANYTHING?

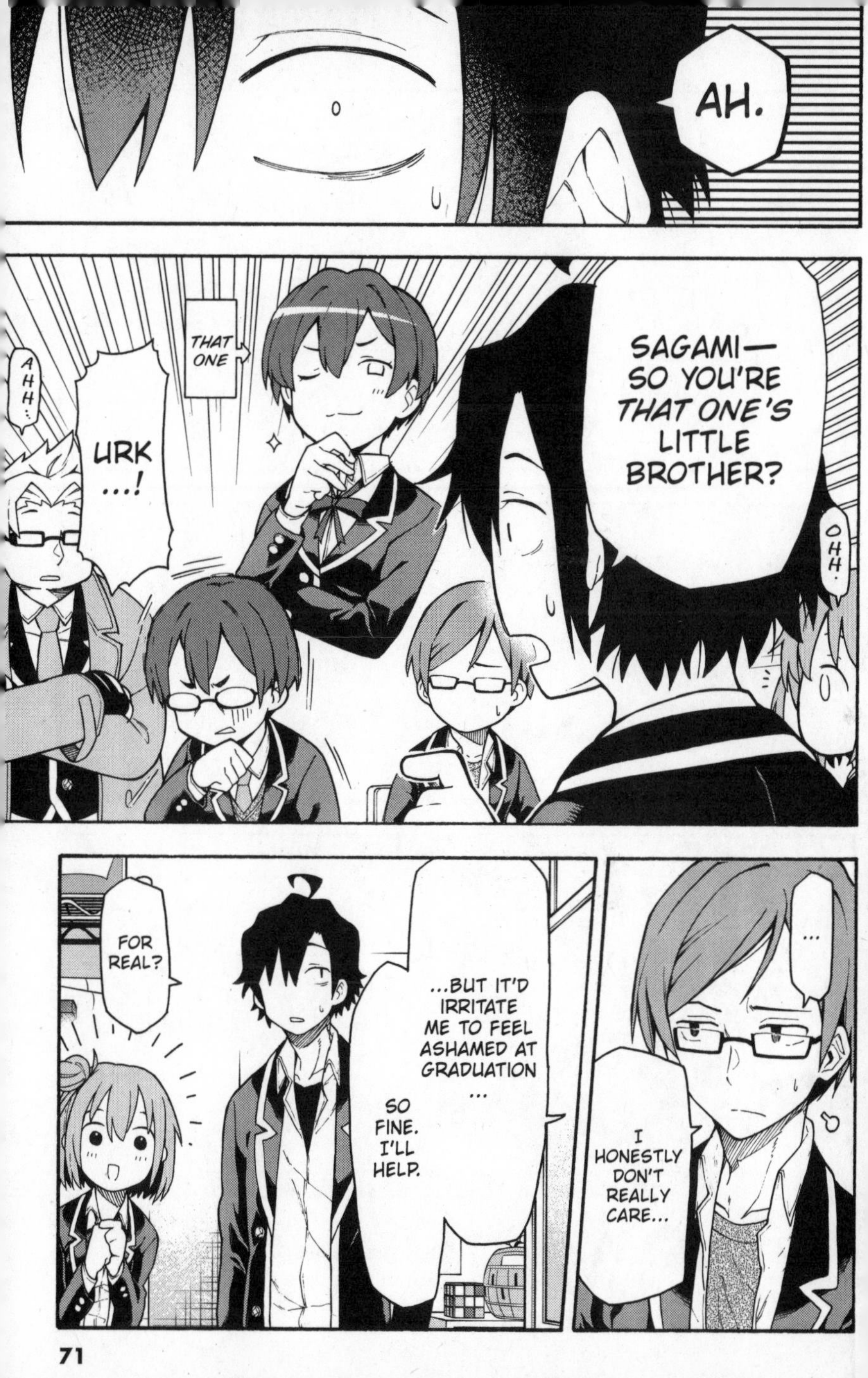
AH.
SAGAMI— SO YOU'RE *THAT ONE'S* LITTLE BROTHER?
OHH.
THAT ONE
URK ...!
AHH...
...
I HONESTLY DON'T REALLY CARE...
...BUT IT'D IRRITATE ME TO FEEL ASHAMED AT GRADUATION ...
SO FINE. I'LL HELP.
FOR REAL?

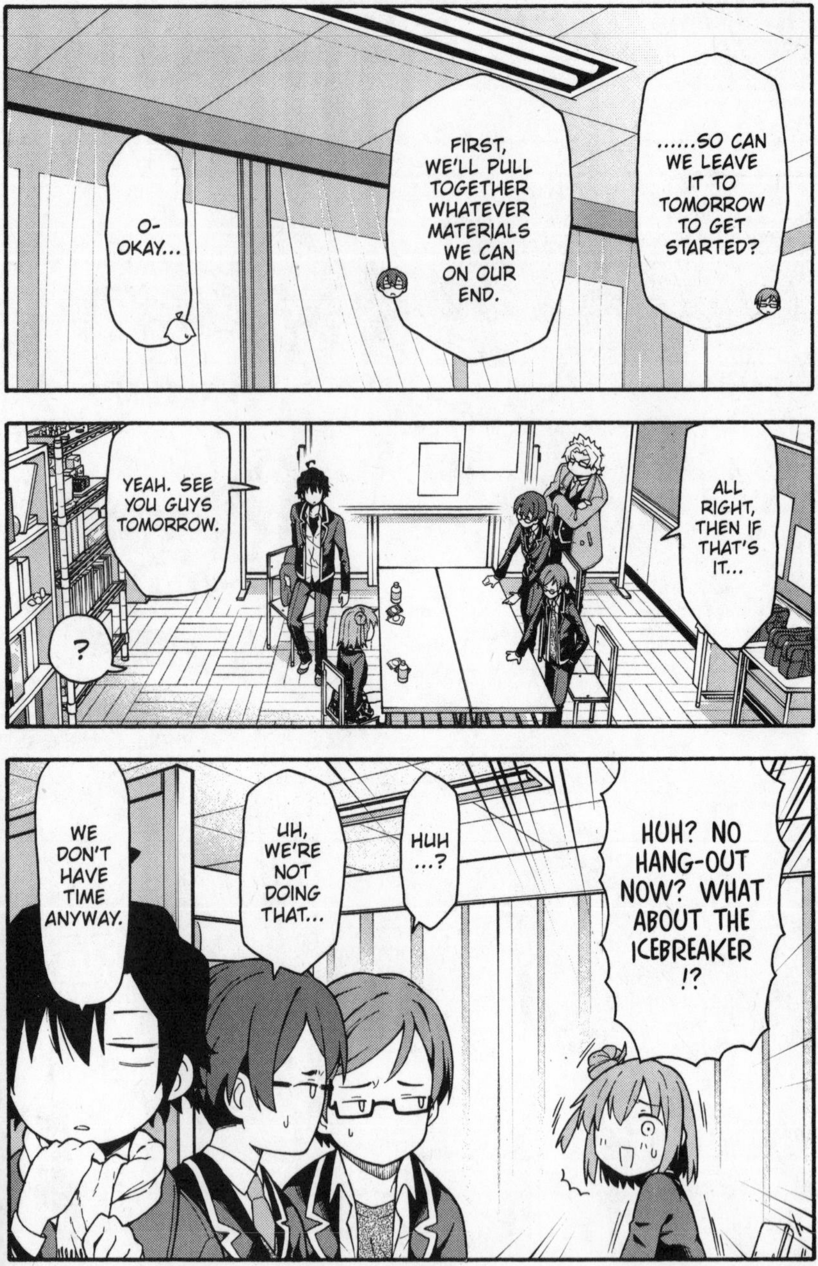
......SO CAN WE LEAVE IT TO TOMORROW TO GET STARTED?
FIRST, WE'LL PULL TOGETHER WHATEVER MATERIALS WE CAN ON OUR END.
O-OKAY...
ALL RIGHT, THEN IF THAT'S IT...
YEAH. SEE YOU GUYS TOMORROW.
?
HUH? NO HANG-OUT NOW? WHAT ABOUT THE ICEBREAKER!?
HUH...?
UH, WE'RE NOT DOING THAT...
WE DON'T HAVE TIME ANYWAY.

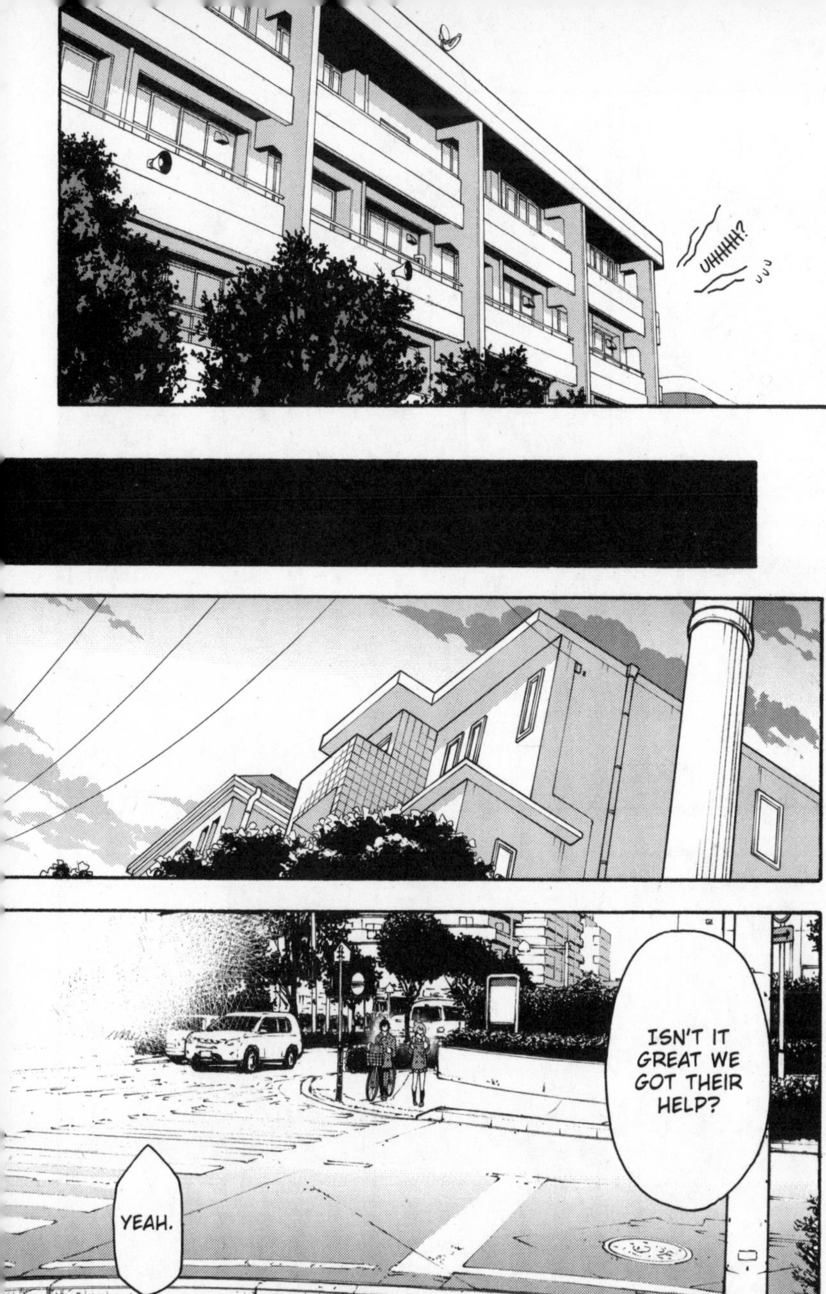
UHHHHH?
ISN'T IT GREAT WE GOT THEIR HELP?
YEAH.

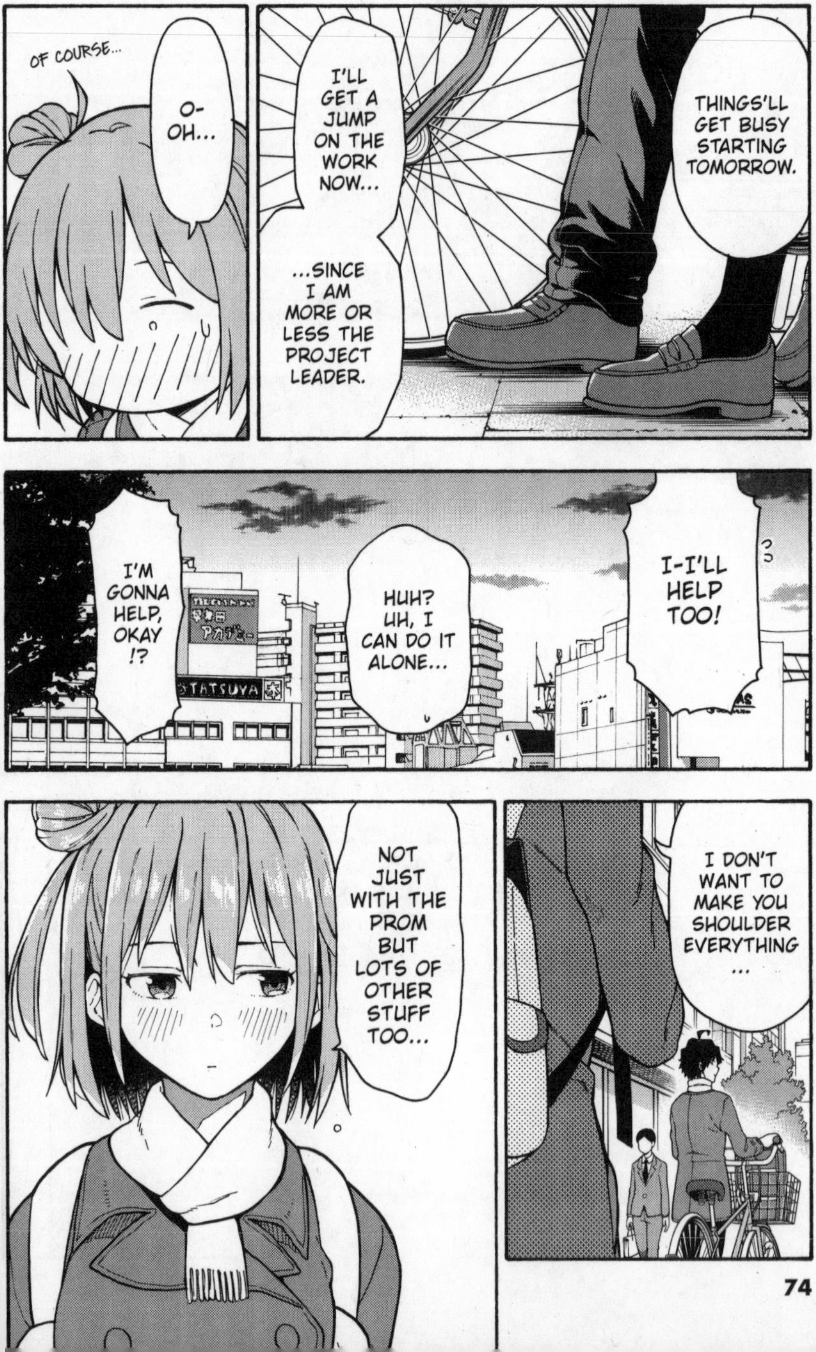
THINGS'LL GET BUSY STARTING TOMORROW.
I'LL GET A JUMP ON THE WORK NOW...
...SINCE I AM MORE OR LESS THE PROJECT LEADER.
O-OH...
OF COURSE...
I-I'LL HELP TOO!
HUH? UH, I CAN DO IT ALONE...
I'M GONNA HELP, OKAY!?
I DON'T WANT TO MAKE YOU SHOULDER EVERYTHING...
NOT JUST WITH THE PROM BUT LOTS OF OTHER STUFF TOO...

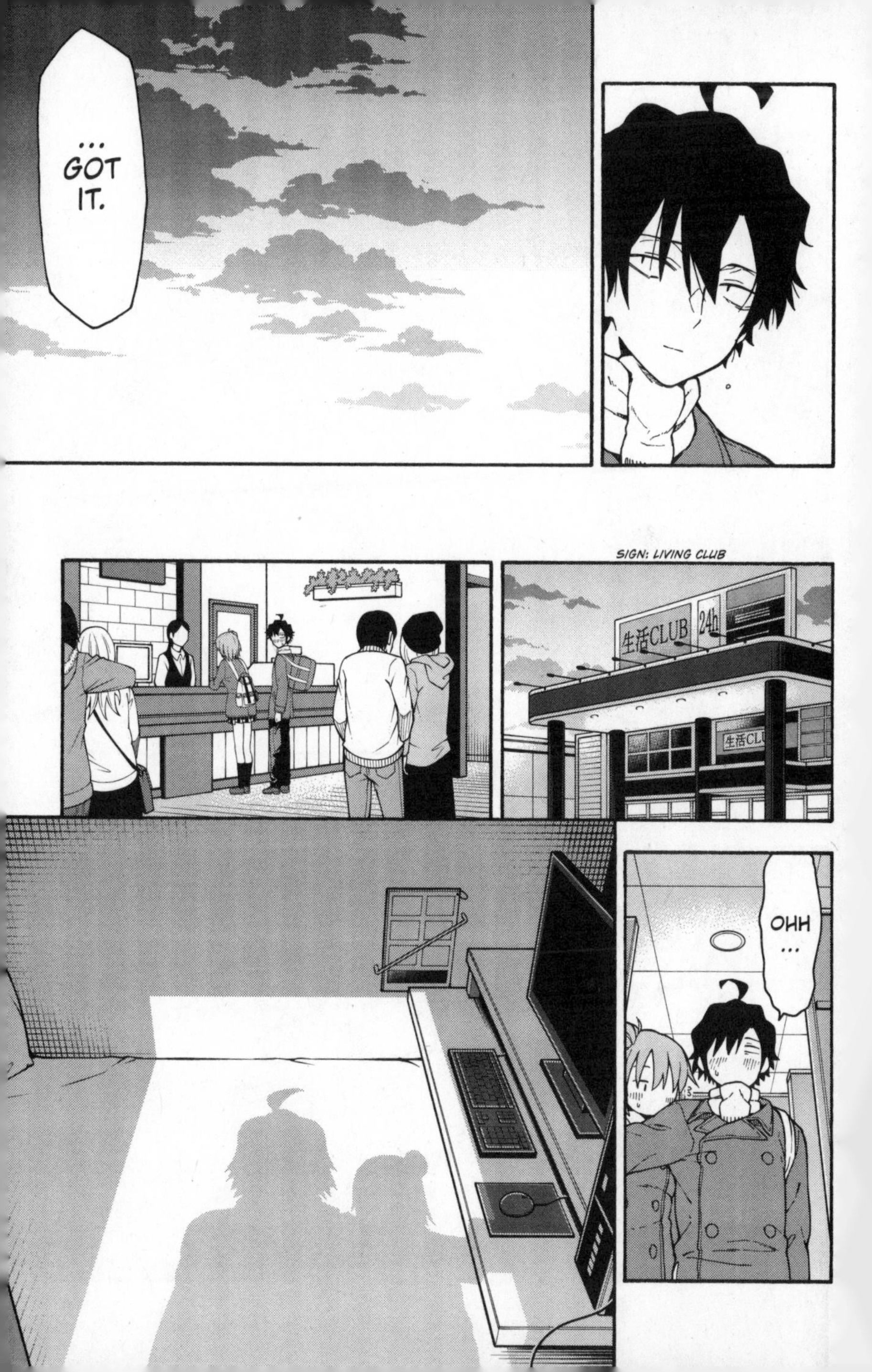
... GOT IT.
SIGN: LIVING CLUB
生活CLUB
24h
OHH ...

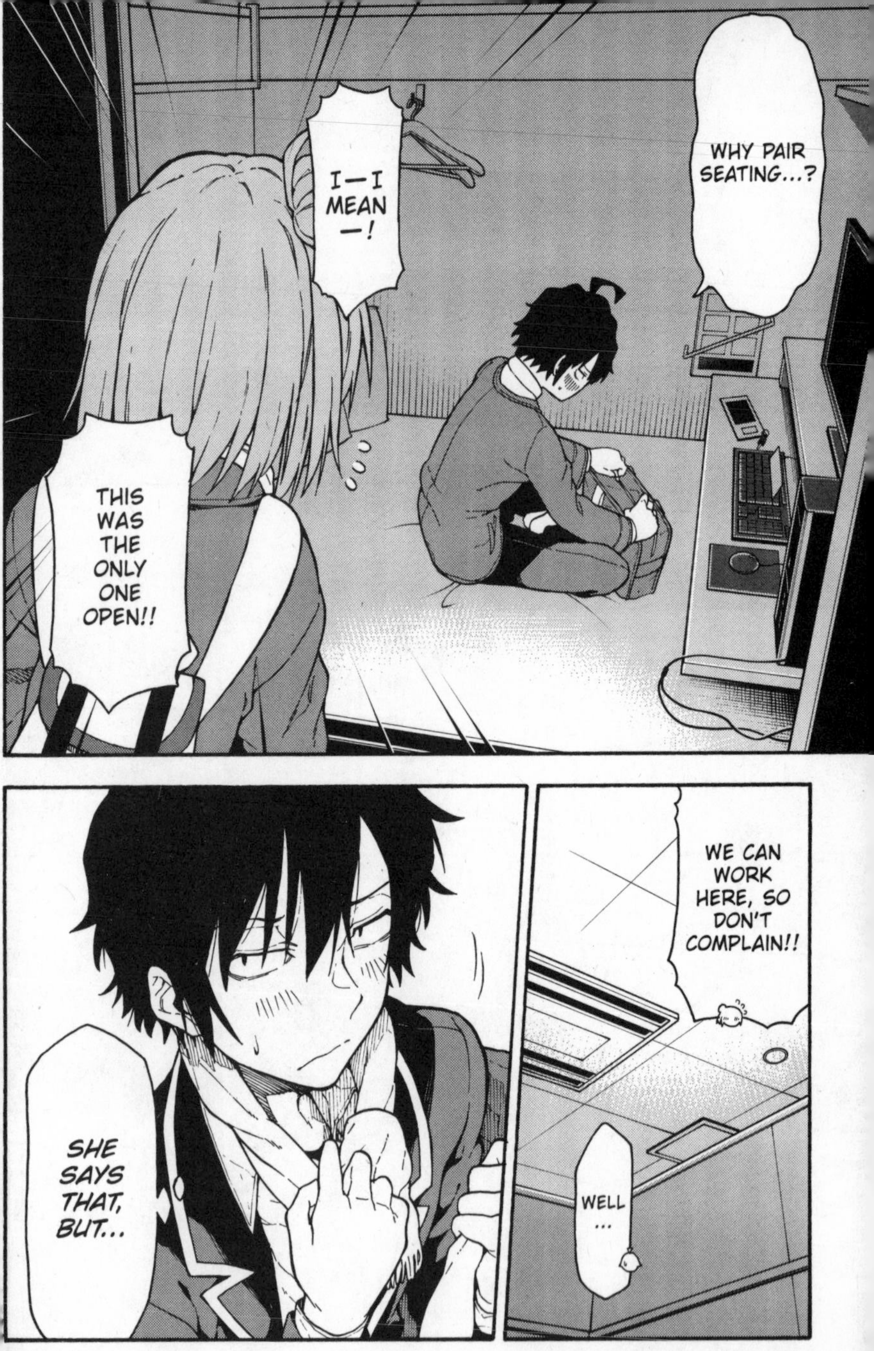

WHY PAIR SEATING...?
I—I MEAN—!
THIS WAS THE ONLY ONE OPEN!!
WE CAN WORK HERE, SO DON'T COMPLAIN!!
WELL...
SHE SAYS THAT, BUT...

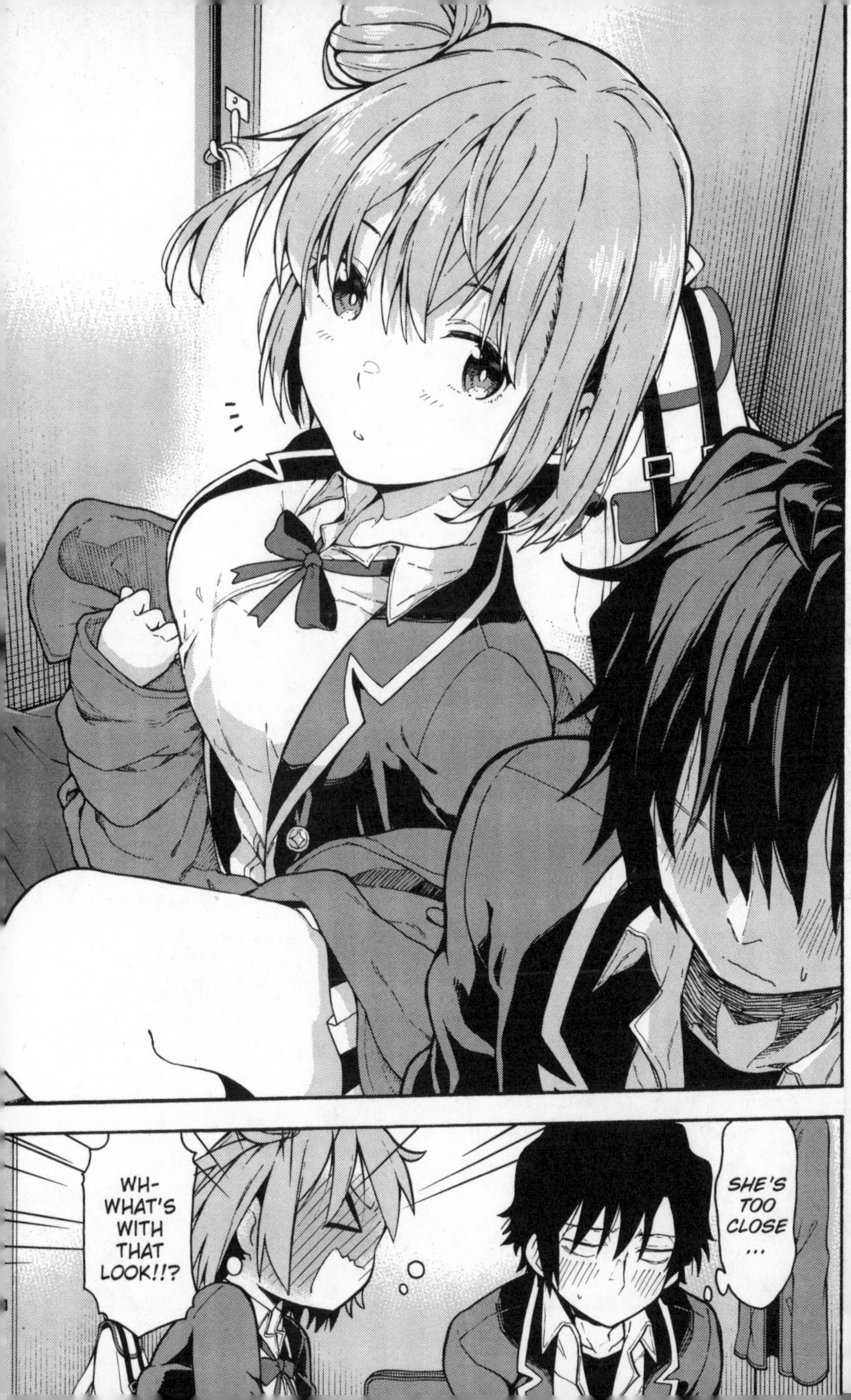
SHE'S TOO CLOSE ...
WH-WHAT'S WITH THAT LOOK!!?

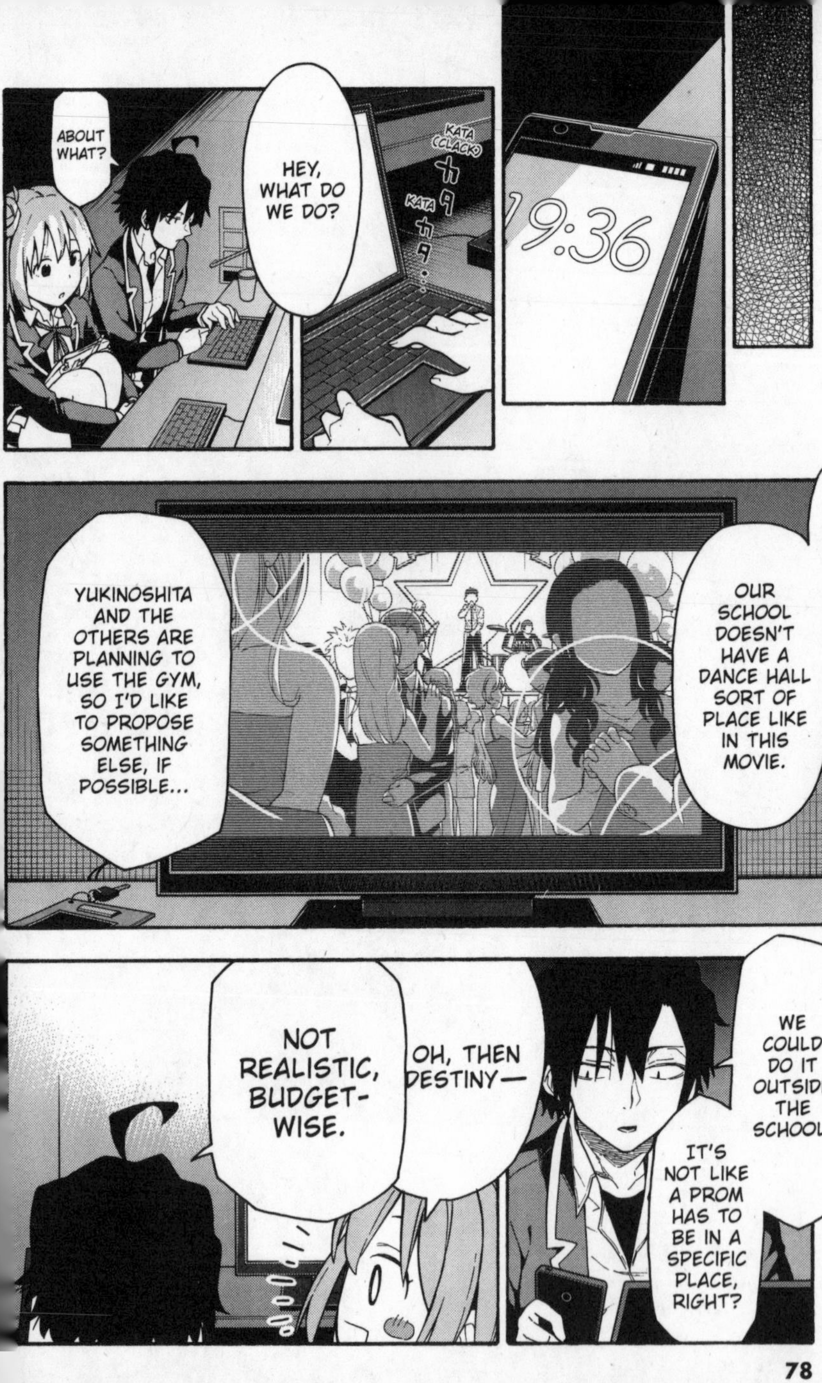
19:36
KATA (CLACK)
カタ
KATA
カタ…
HEY, WHAT DO WE DO?
ABOUT WHAT?
VENUE.
OUR SCHOOL DOESN'T HAVE A DANCE HALL SORT OF PLACE LIKE IN THIS MOVIE.
YUKINOSHITA AND THE OTHERS ARE PLANNING TO USE THE GYM, SO I'D LIKE TO PROPOSE SOMETHING ELSE, IF POSSIBLE...
WE COULD DO IT OUTSIDE THE SCHOOL.
IT'S NOT LIKE A PROM HAS TO BE IN A SPECIFIC PLACE, RIGHT?
OH, THEN DESTINY—
NOT REALISTIC, BUDGET-WISE.

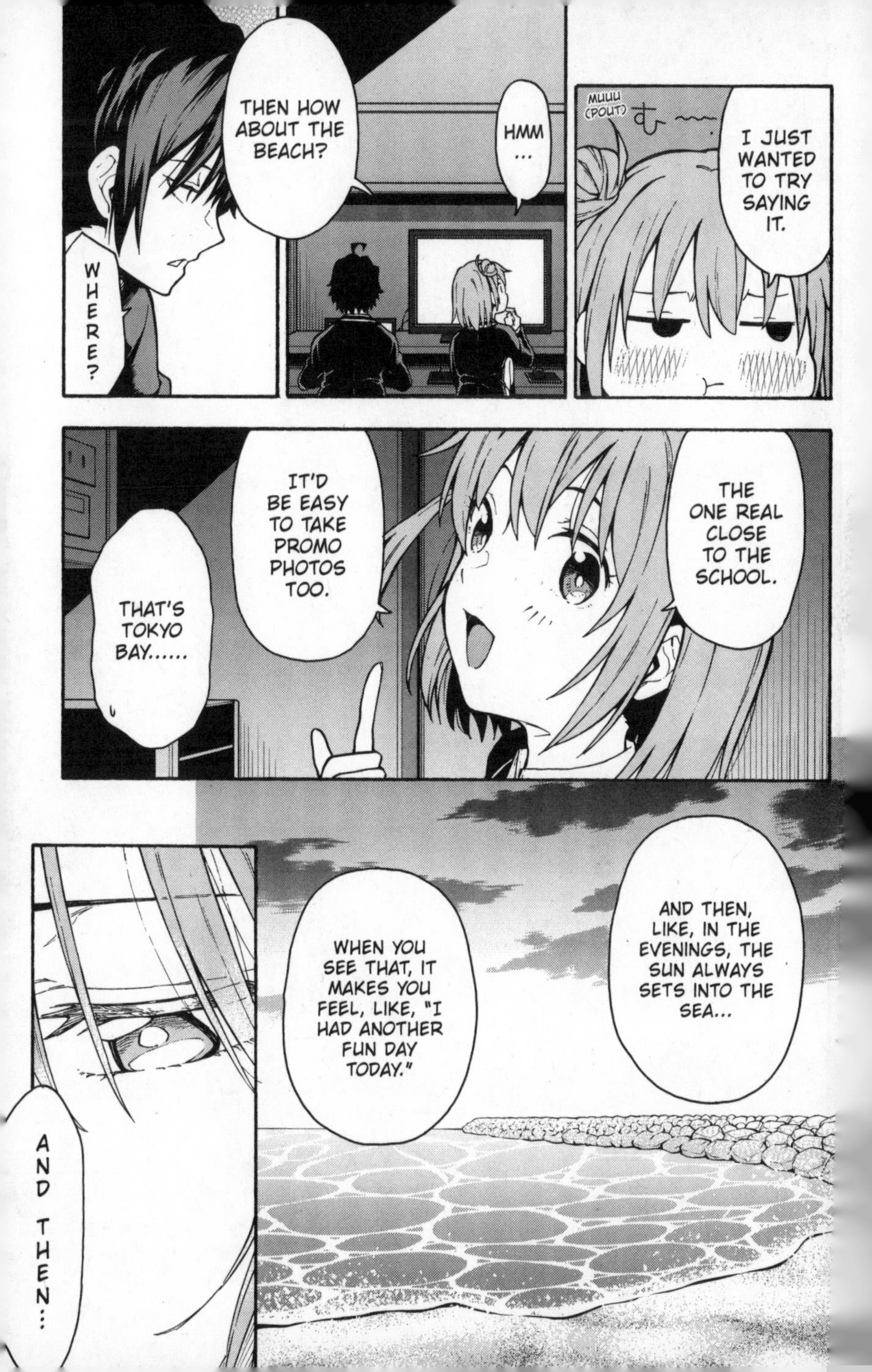
MUUU (POUT)
I JUST WANTED TO TRY SAYING IT.
HMM ...
THEN HOW ABOUT THE BEACH?
WHERE?
THE ONE REAL CLOSE TO THE SCHOOL.
IT'D BE EASY TO TAKE PROMO PHOTOS TOO.
THAT'S TOKYO BAY......
AND THEN, LIKE, IN THE EVENINGS, THE SUN ALWAYS SETS INTO THE SEA...
WHEN YOU SEE THAT, IT MAKES YOU FEEL, LIKE, "I HAD ANOTHER FUN DAY TODAY."
AND THEN...

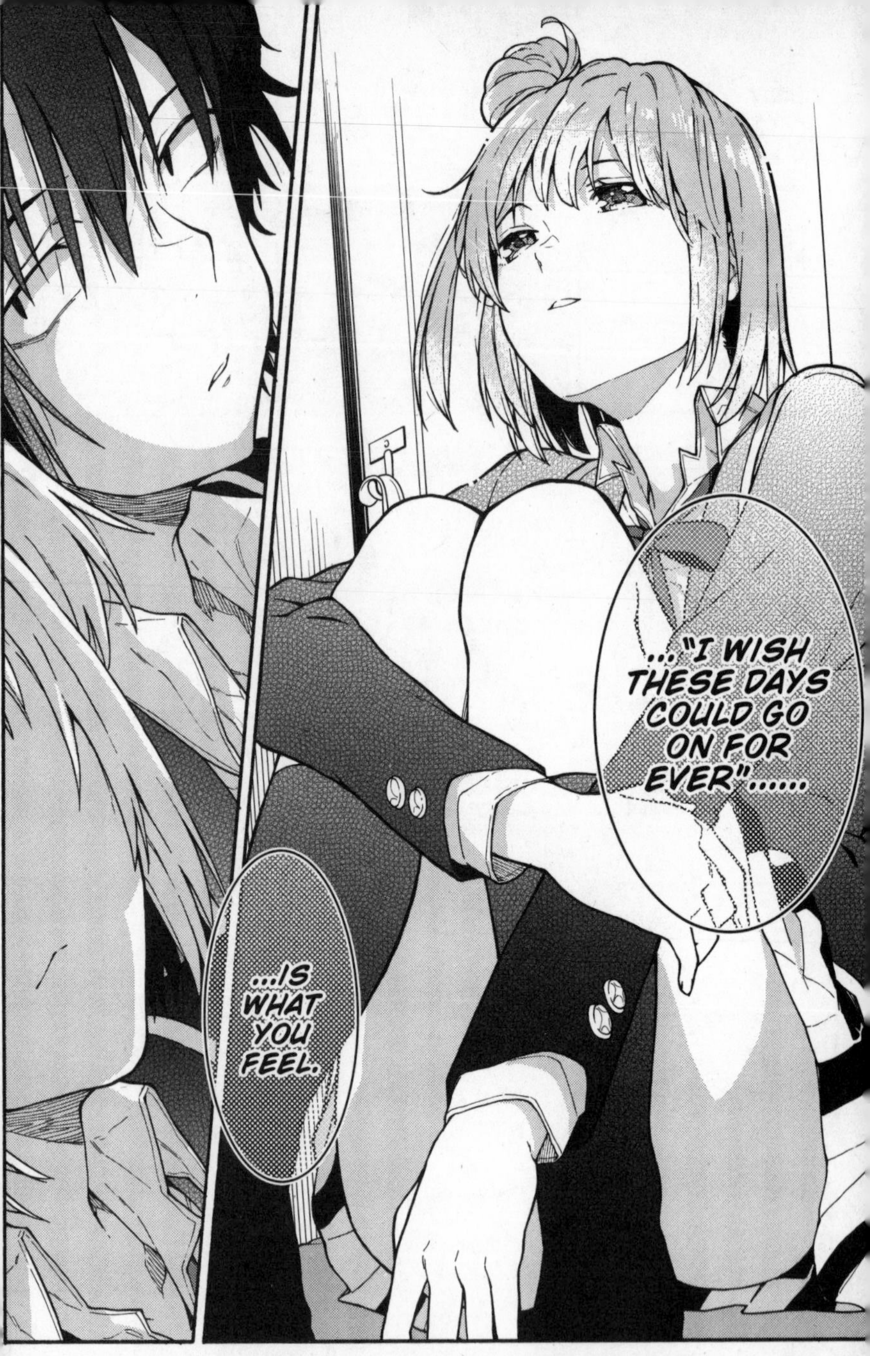
..."I WISH THESE DAYS COULD GO ON FOR EVER"......
...IS WHAT YOU FEEL.

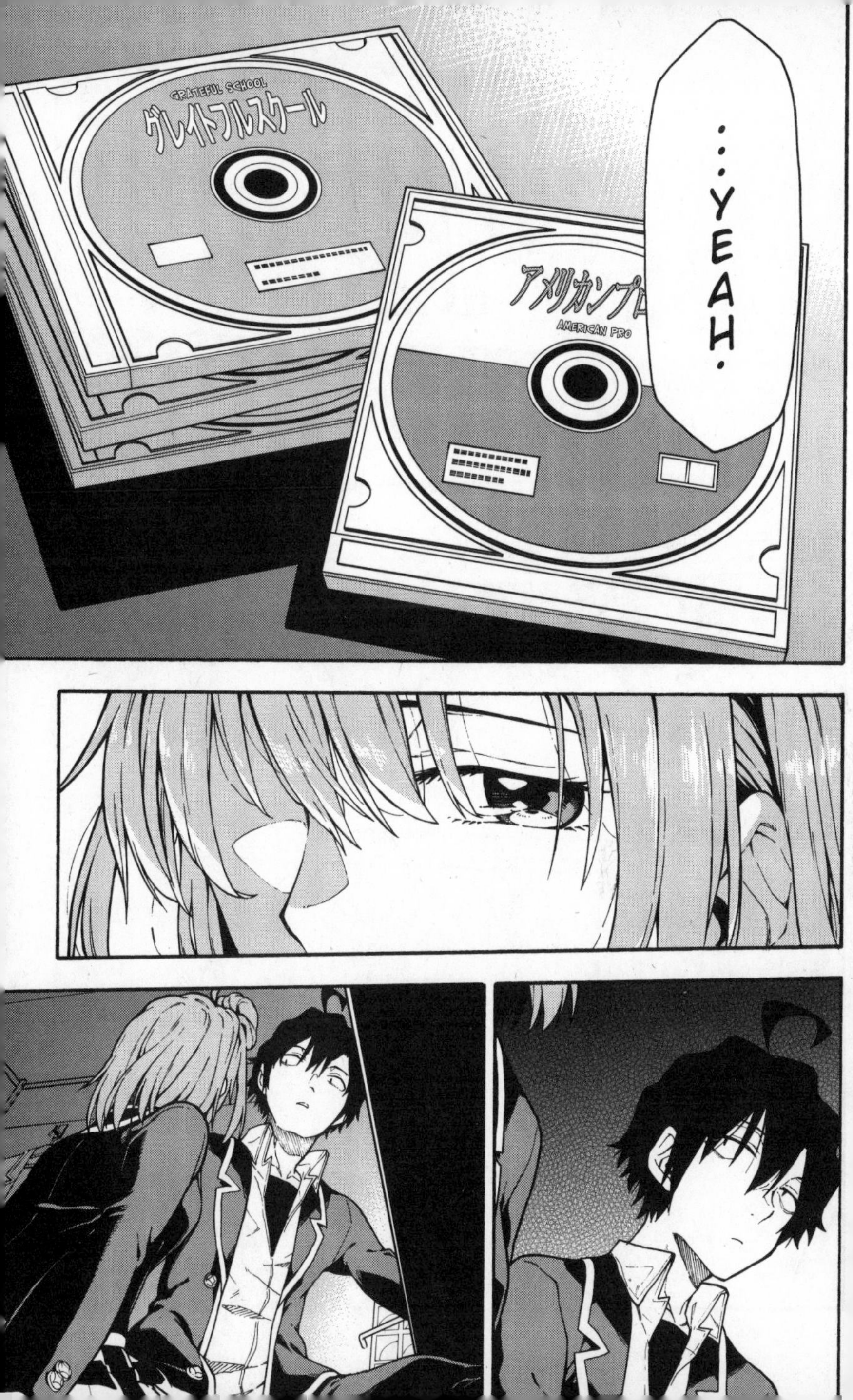
...YEAH.
GRATEFUL SCHOOL
グレイトフルスクール
アメリカンプロ
AMERICAN PRO

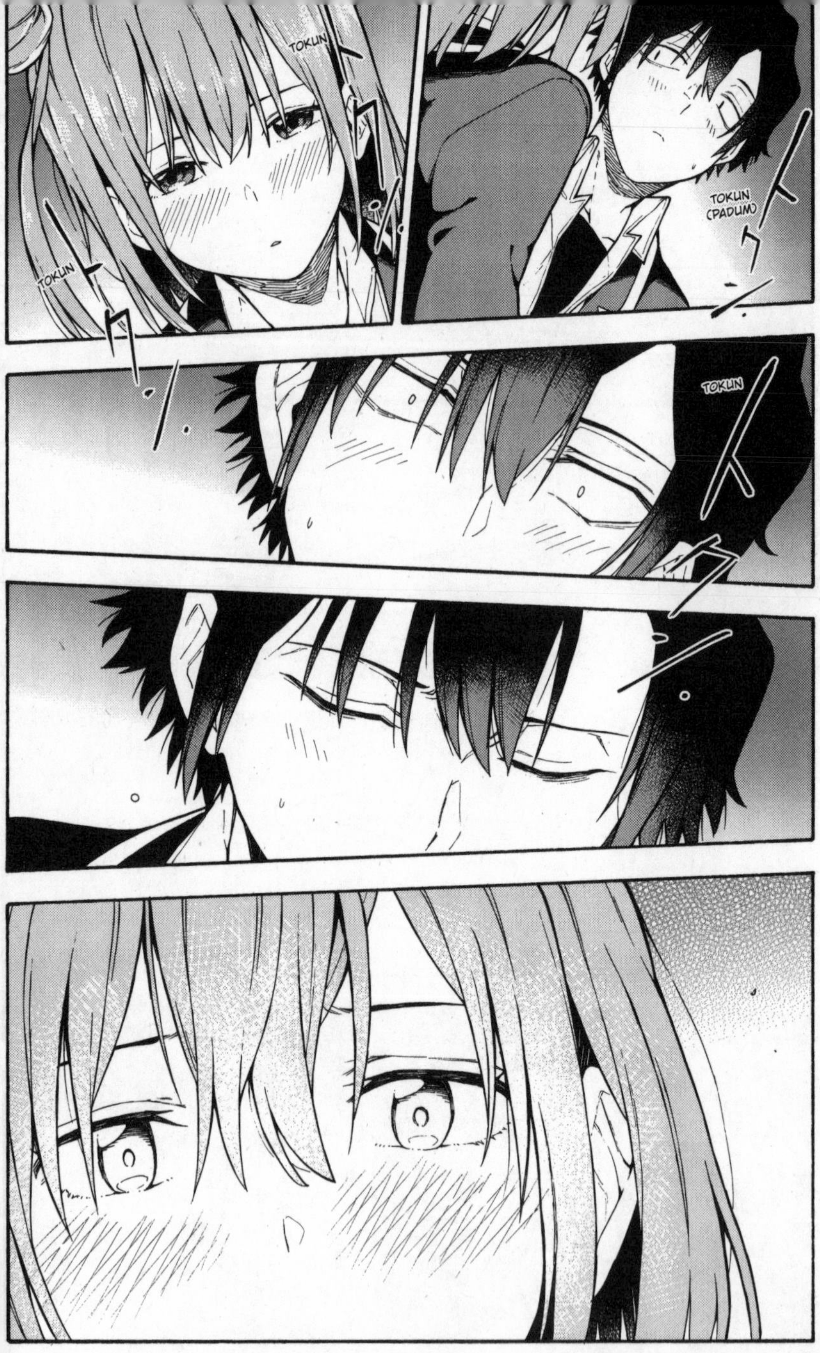
TOKUN
(PADUM)
TOKUN
TOKUN
TOKUN

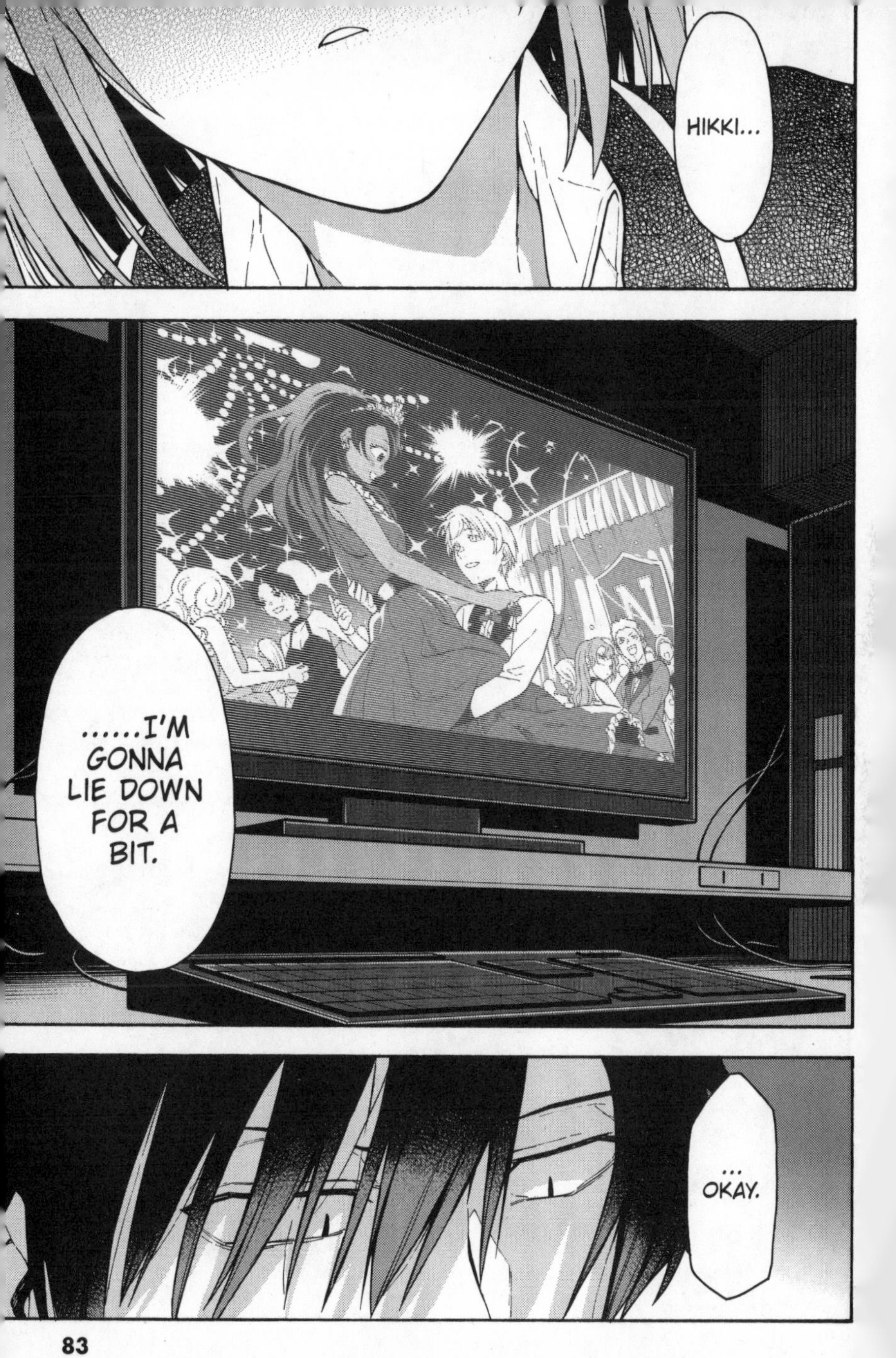
HIKKI...
......I'M GONNA LIE DOWN FOR A BIT.
...OKAY.

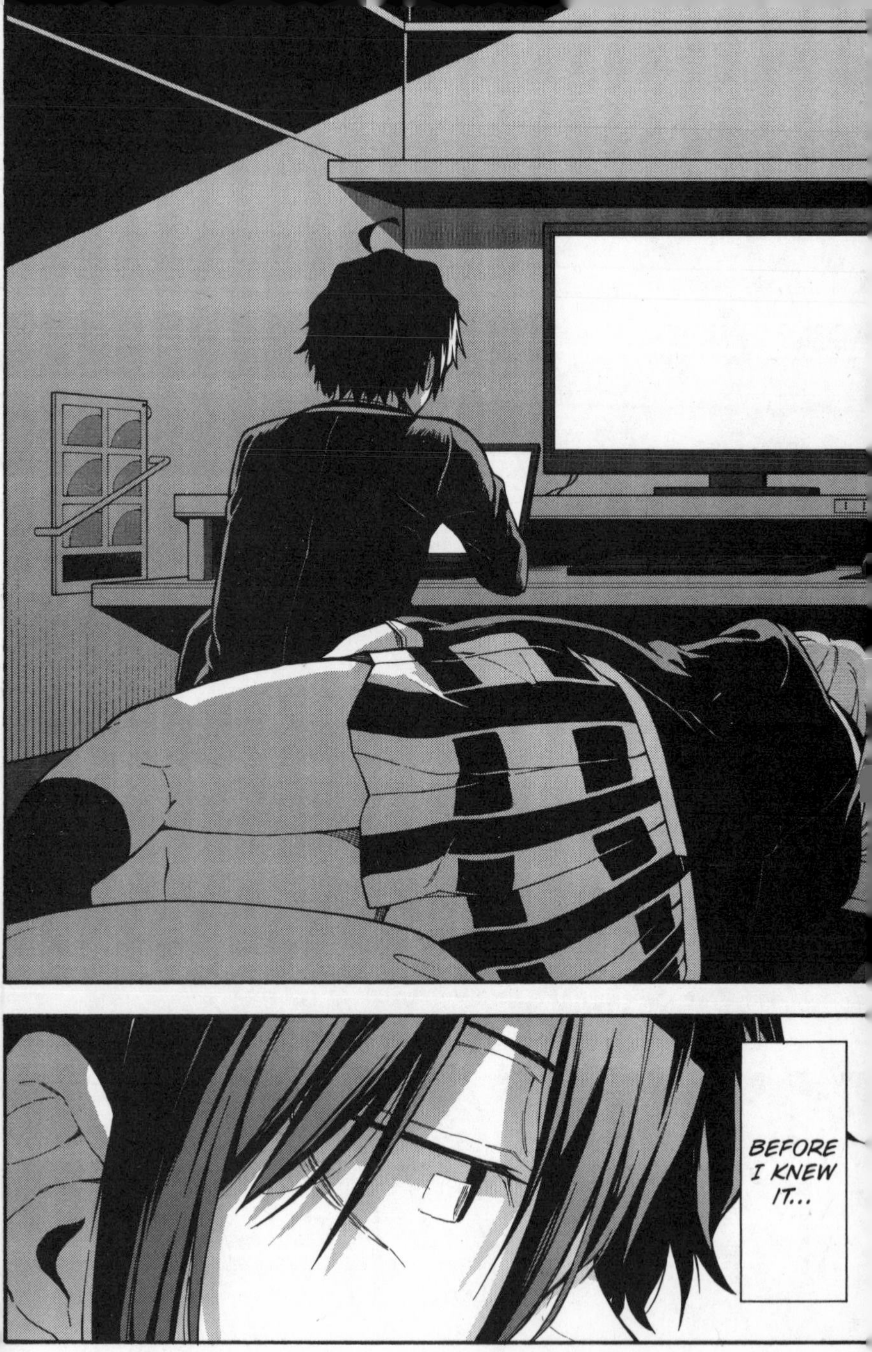
BEFORE I KNEW IT...

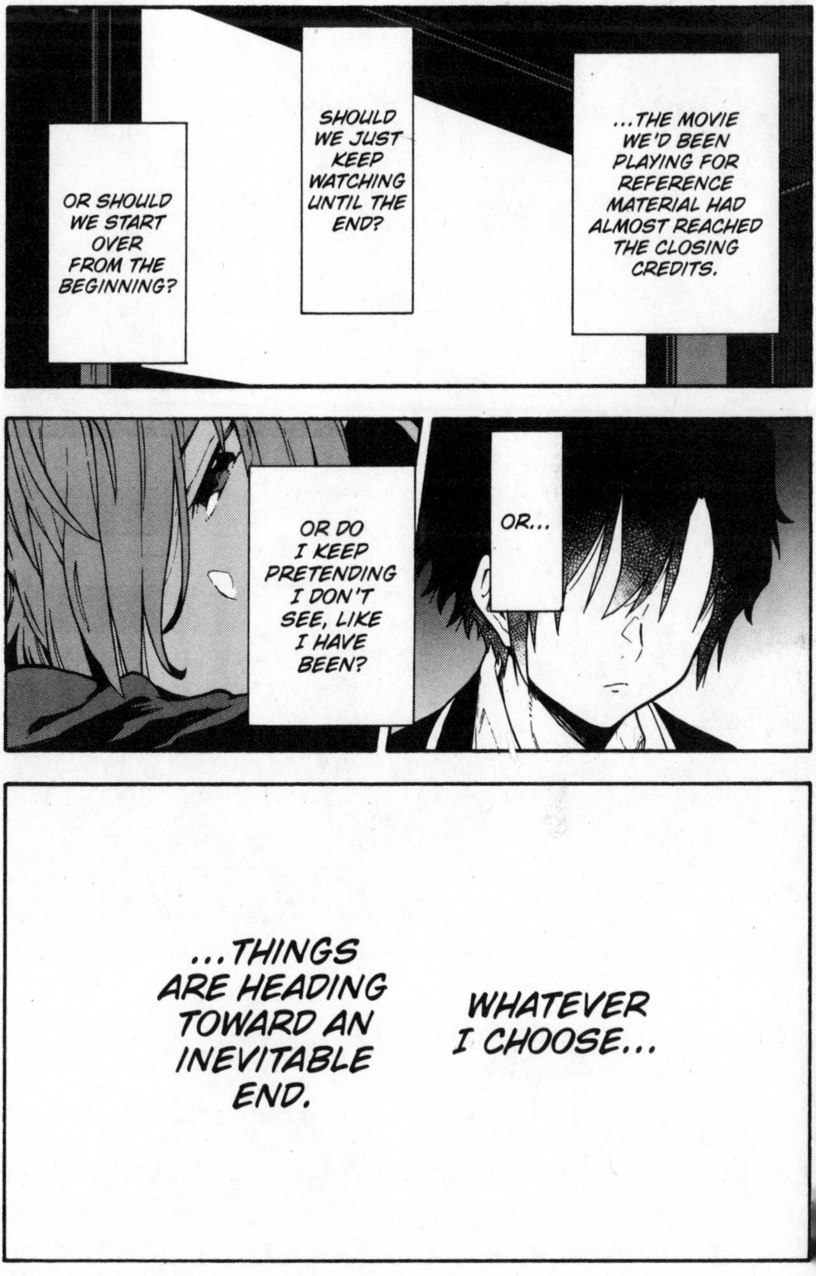
...THE MOVIE WE'D BEEN PLAYING FOR REFERENCE MATERIAL HAD ALMOST REACHED THE CLOSING CREDITS.
SHOULD WE JUST KEEP WATCHING UNTIL THE END?
OR SHOULD WE START OVER FROM THE BEGINNING?
OR...
OR DO I KEEP PRETENDING I DON'T SEE, LIKE I HAVE BEEN?
WHATEVER I CHOOSE...
...THINGS ARE HEADING TOWARD AN INEVITABLE END.

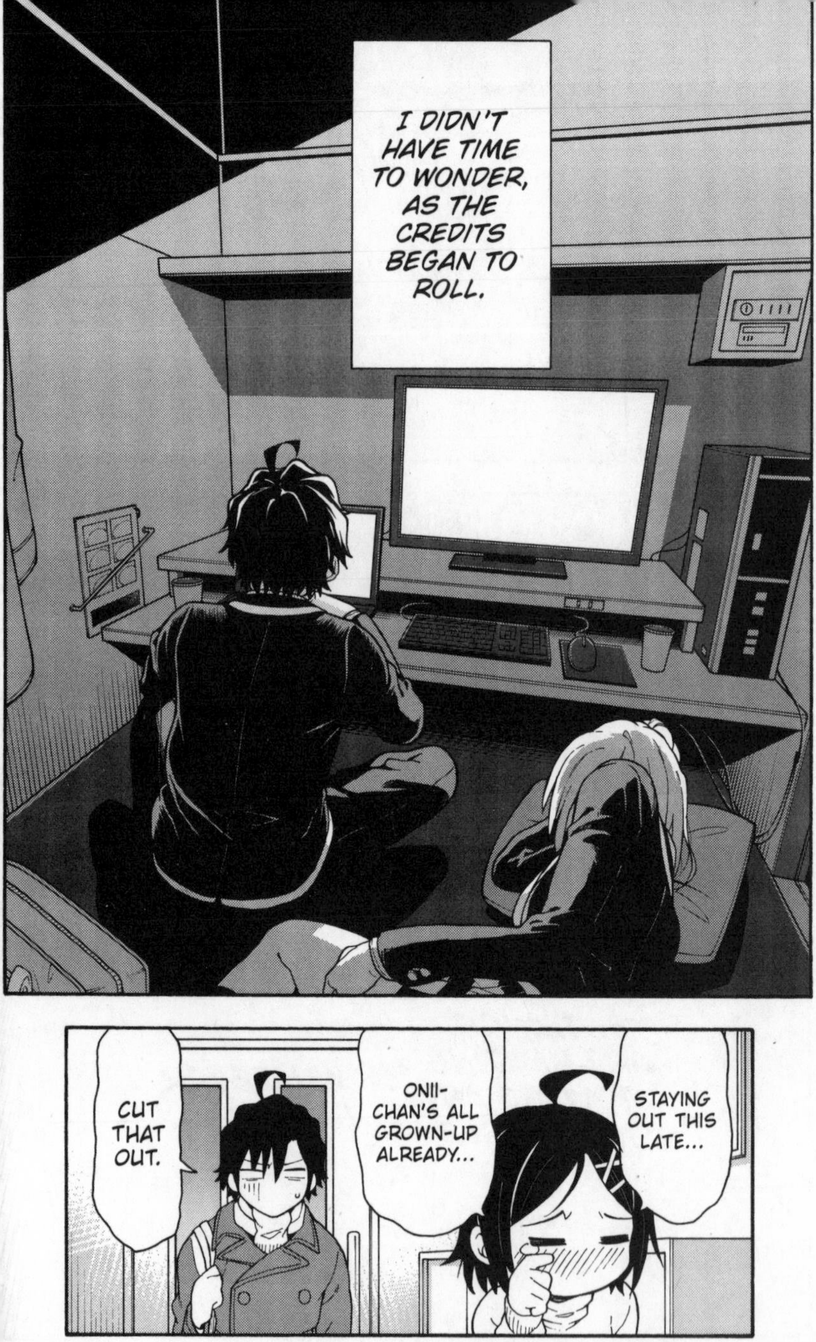
I DIDN'T HAVE TIME TO WONDER, AS THE CREDITS BEGAN TO ROLL.
STAYING OUT THIS LATE...
ONII-CHAN'S ALL GROWN-UP ALREADY...
CUT THAT OUT.

CHAPTER 100 ··· PRIVATELY, HAYATO HAYAMA FEELS REGRET.

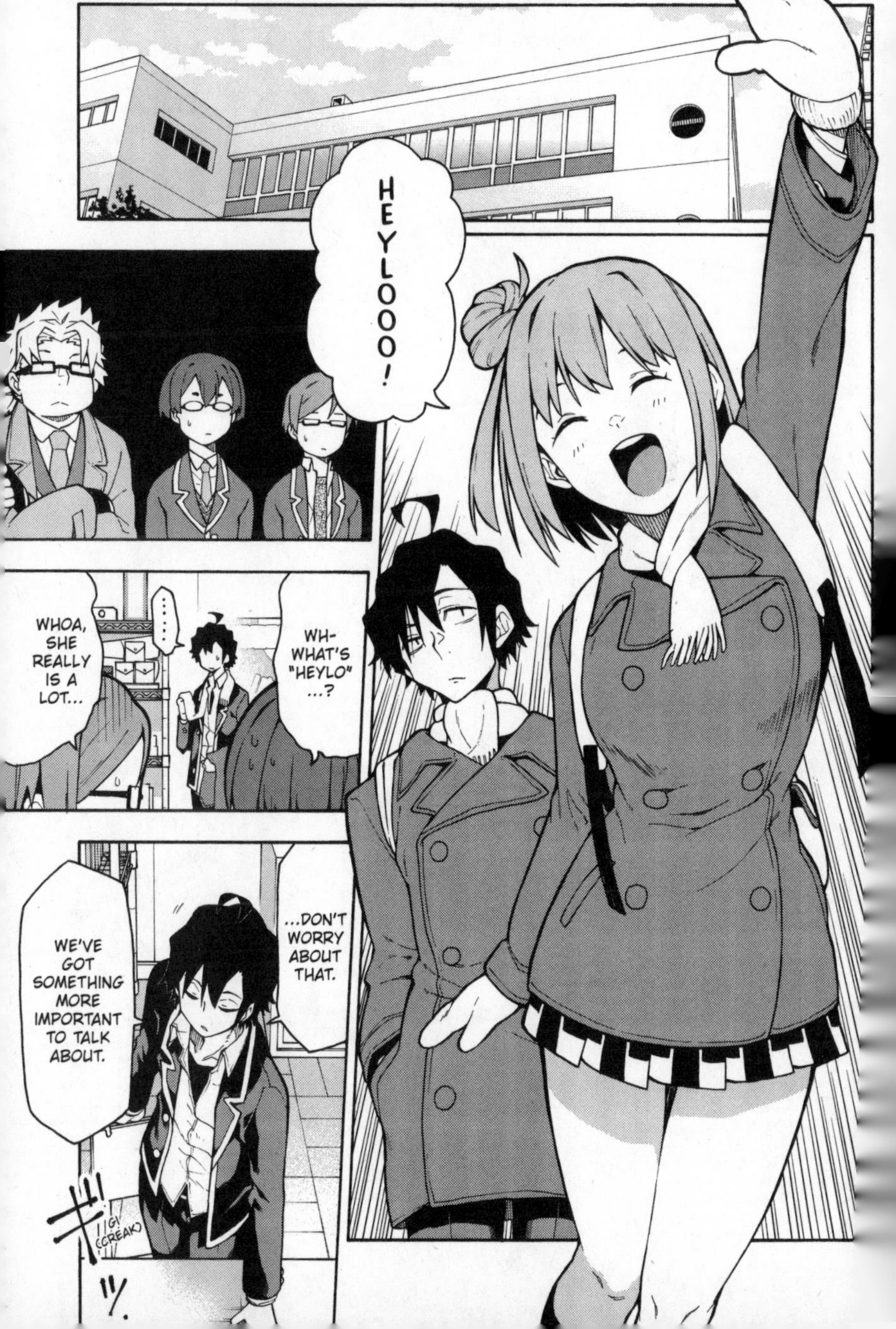
HEYLOOO!
WH-WHAT'S "HEYLO" ...?
......
WHOA, SHE REALLY IS A LOT...
...DON'T WORRY ABOUT THAT.
WE'VE GOT SOMETHING MORE IMPORTANT TO TALK ABOUT.
GI (CREAK)

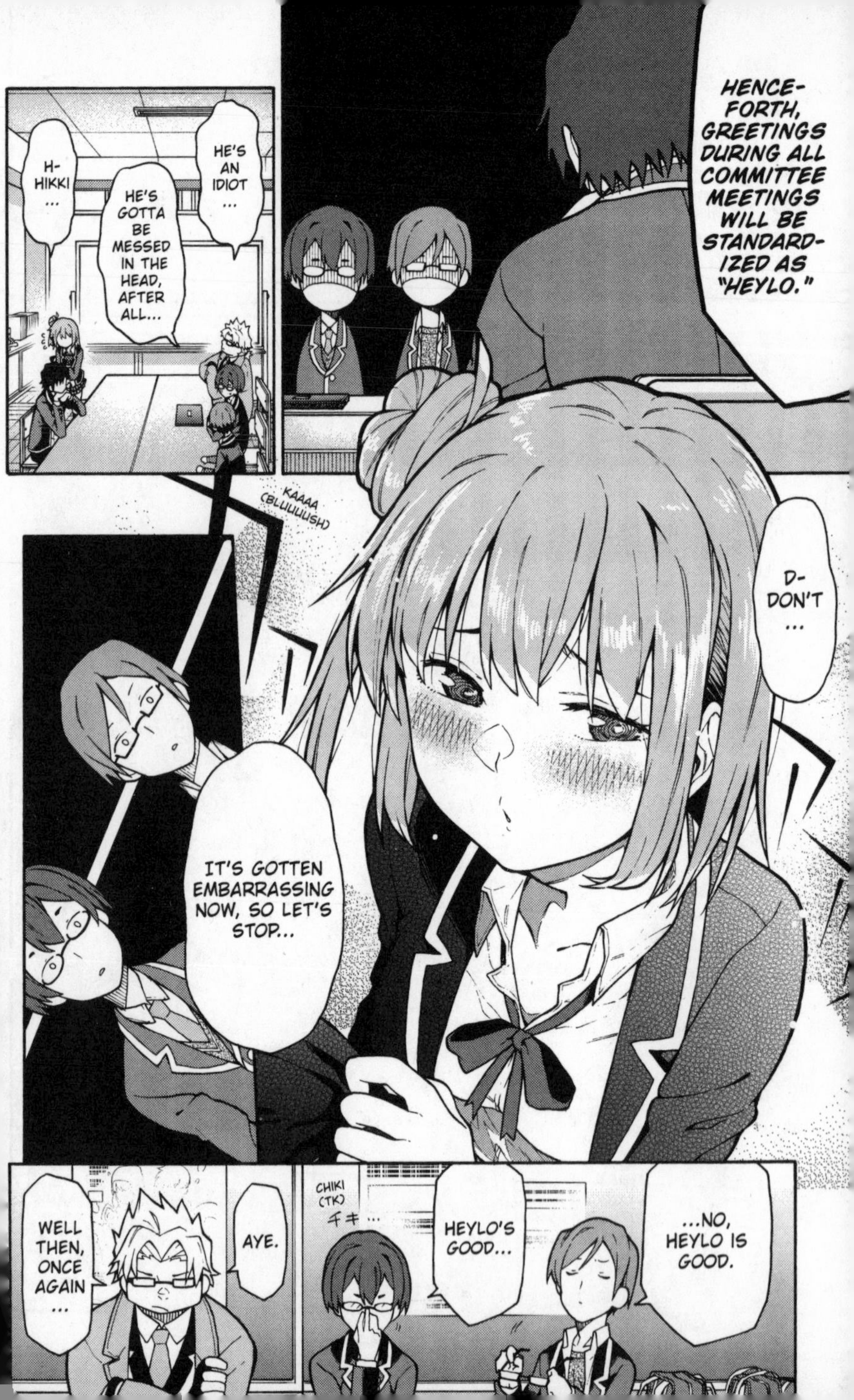
HENCE-FORTH, GREETINGS DURING ALL COMMITTEE MEETINGS WILL BE STANDARDIZED AS "HEYLO."
HE'S AN IDIOT...
HE'S GOTTA BE MESSED IN THE HEAD, AFTER ALL...
H-HIKKI...
KAAAA (BLUUUUSH)
D-DON'T...
IT'S GOTTEN EMBARRASSING NOW, SO LET'S STOP...
...NO, HEYLO IS GOOD.
HEYLO'S GOOD...
CHIKI (TK)
チキ...
AYE.
WELL THEN, ONCE AGAIN...

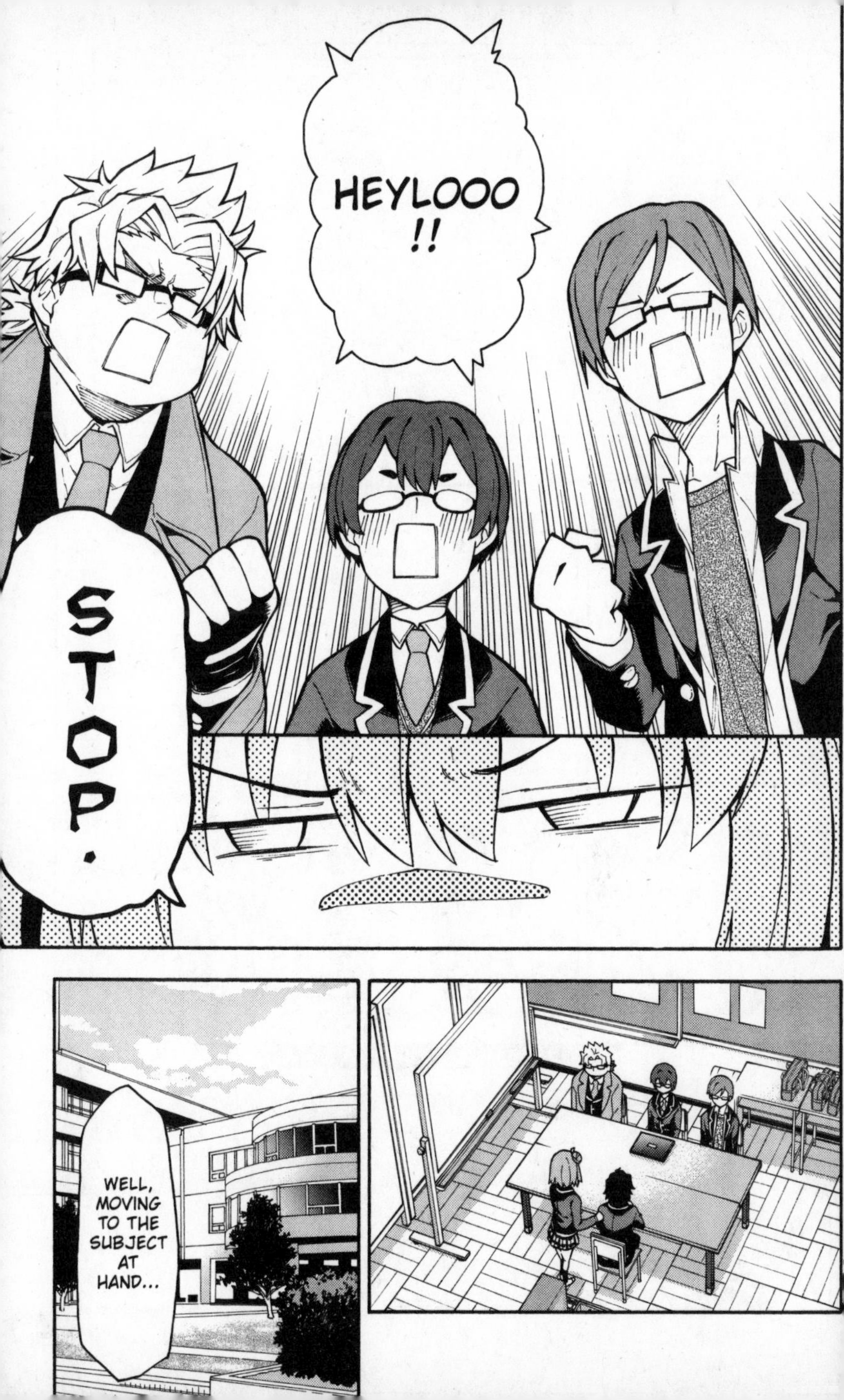
HEYLOOO !!
STOP.
WELL, MOVING TO THE SUBJECT AT HAND...

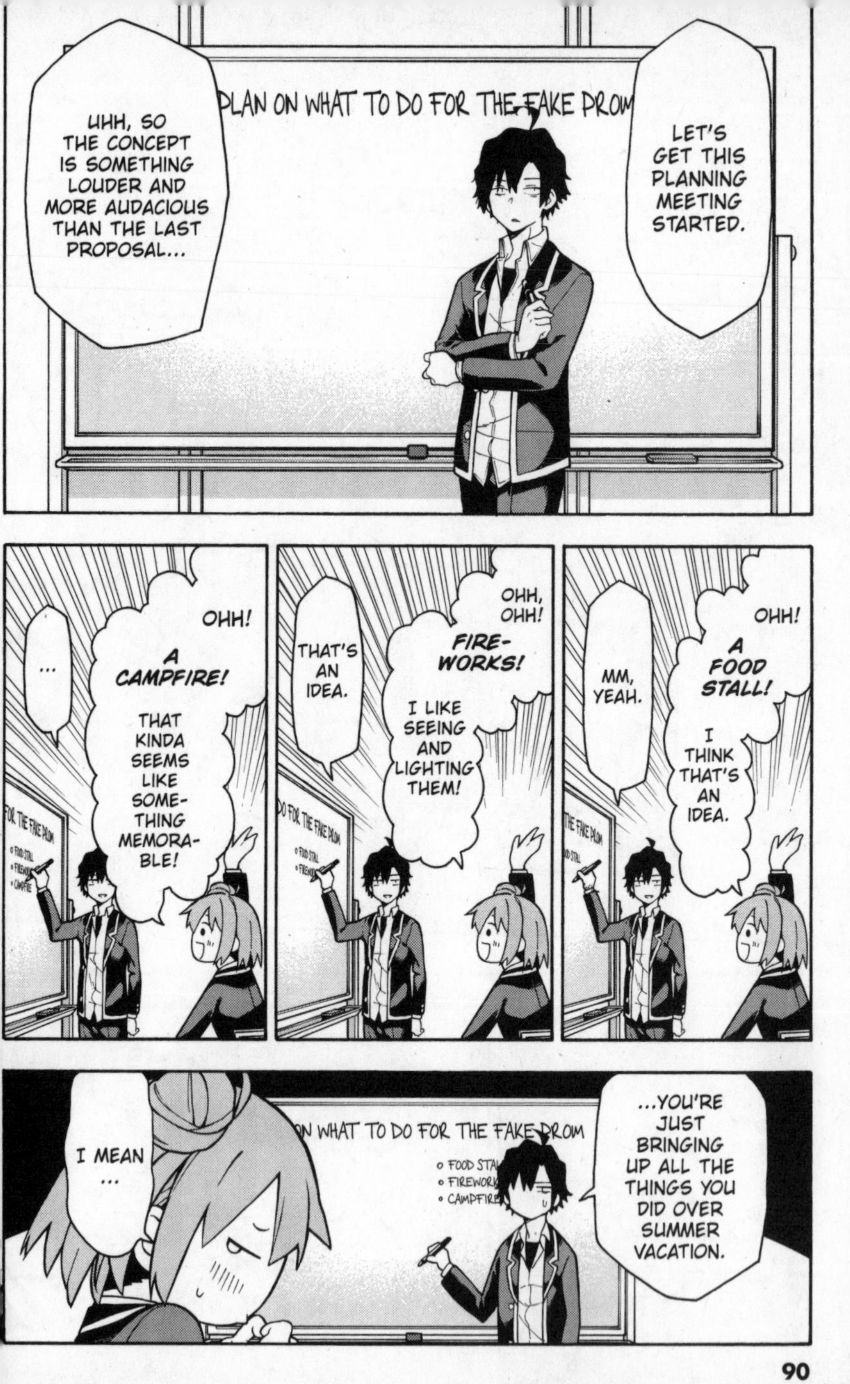
PLAN ON WHAT TO DO FOR THE FAKE PROM
LET'S GET THIS PLANNING MEETING STARTED.
UHH, SO THE CONCEPT IS SOMETHING LOUDER AND MORE AUDACIOUS THAN THE LAST PROPOSAL...
OHH! A FOOD STALL! I THINK THAT'S AN IDEA.
MM, YEAH.
OHH, OHH! FIRE-WORKS! I LIKE SEEING AND LIGHTING THEM!
THAT'S AN IDEA.
OHH! A CAMPFIRE! THAT KINDA SEEMS LIKE SOME-THING MEMORA-BLE!
...
ON WHAT TO DO FOR THE FAKE PROM
...YOU'RE JUST BRINGING UP ALL THE THINGS YOU DID OVER SUMMER VACATION.
I MEAN ...

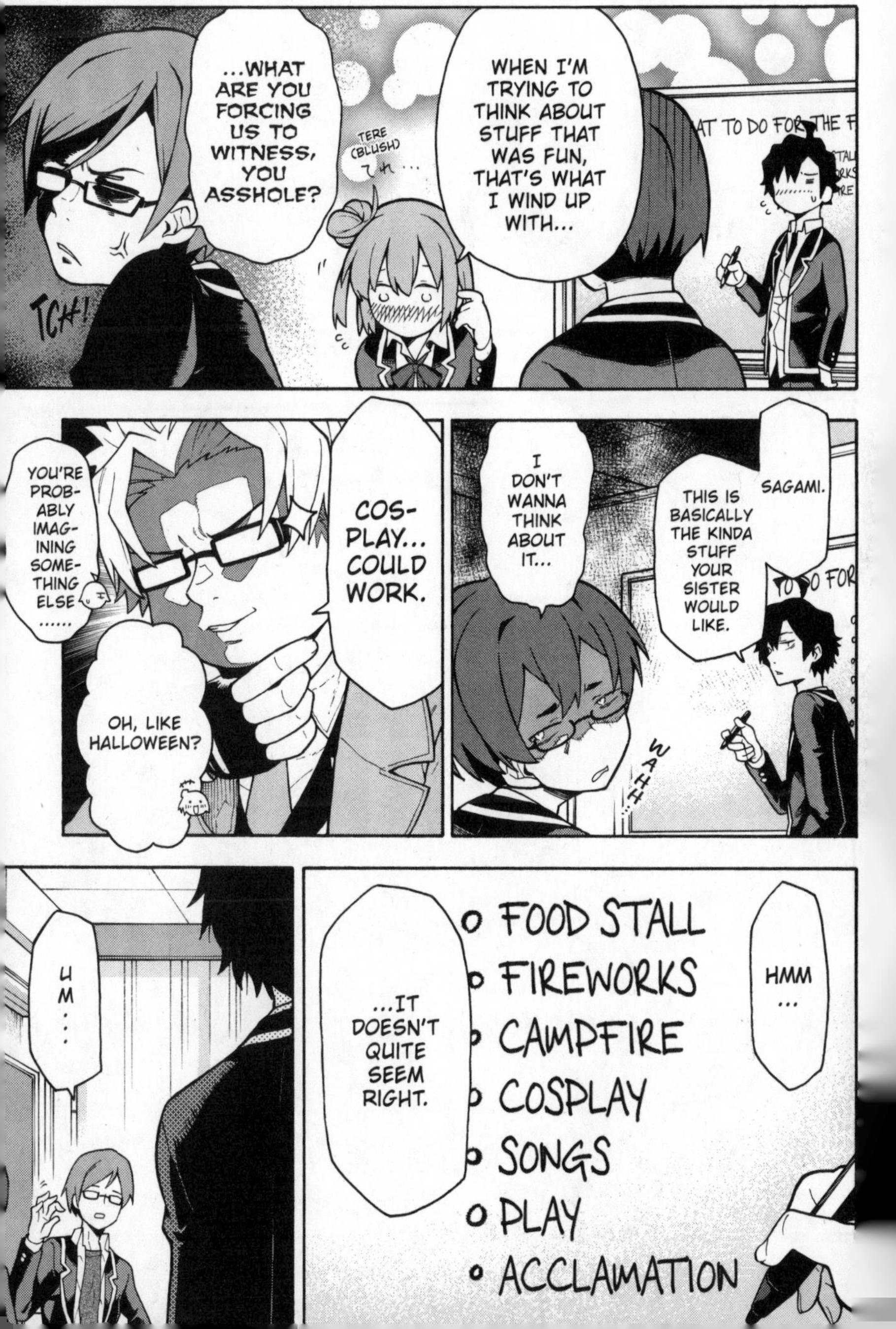
WHEN I'M TRYING TO THINK ABOUT STUFF THAT WAS FUN, THAT'S WHAT I WIND UP WITH...
TERE (BLUSH) てれ…
...WHAT ARE YOU FORCING US TO WITNESS, YOU ASSHOLE?
TCH!
SAGAMI.
THIS IS BASICALLY THE KINDA STUFF YOUR SISTER WOULD LIKE.
I DON'T WANNA THINK ABOUT IT...
WAHH...
COS-PLAY... COULD WORK.
YOU'RE PROB-ABLY IMAG-INING SOME-THING ELSE......
OH, LIKE HALLOWEEN?
HMM...
FOOD STALL
FIREWORKS
CAMPFIRE
COSPLAY
SONGS
PLAY
ACCLAMATION
...IT DOESN'T QUITE SEEM RIGHT.
UM...

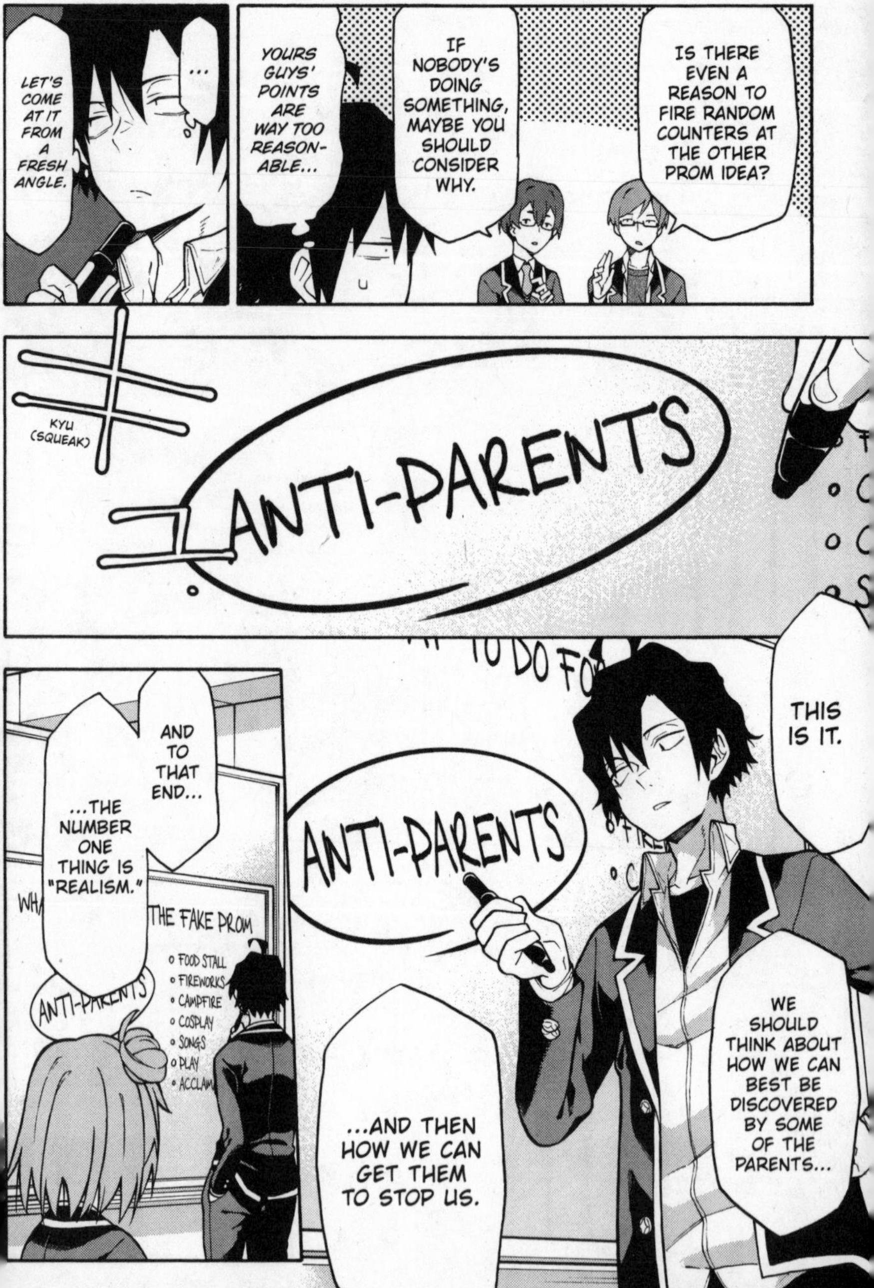
IS THERE EVEN A REASON TO FIRE RANDOM COUNTERS AT THE OTHER PROM IDEA?
IF NOBODY'S DOING SOMETHING, MAYBE YOU SHOULD CONSIDER WHY.
YOURS GUYS' POINTS ARE WAY TOO REASON-ABLE...
...
LET'S COME AT IT FROM A FRESH ANGLE.
ANTI-PARENTS
KYU (SQUEAK)
THIS IS IT.
WE SHOULD THINK ABOUT HOW WE CAN BEST BE DISCOVERED BY SOME OF THE PARENTS...
...AND THEN HOW WE CAN GET THEM TO STOP US.
ANTI-PARENTS
AND TO THAT END...
...THE NUMBER ONE THING IS "REALISM."
THE FAKE PROM
FOOD STALL
FIREWORKS
CAMPFIRE
COSPLAY
SONGS
PLAY
ANTI-PARENTS

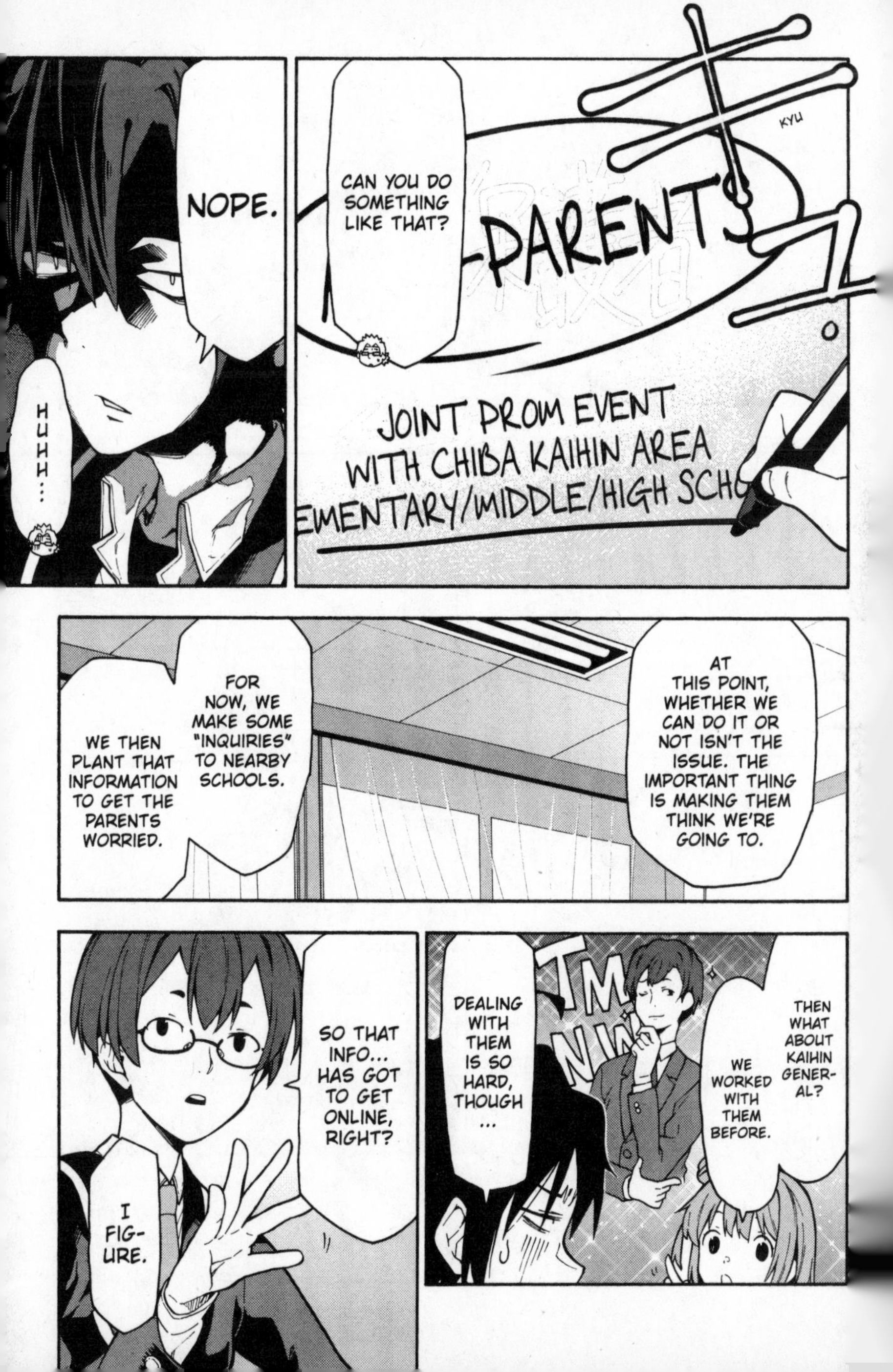
KYU
CAN YOU DO SOMETHING LIKE THAT?
PARENTS
JOINT PROM EVENT
WITH CHIBA KAIHIN AREA
EMENTARY/MIDDLE/HIGH SCH
NOPE.
HUHH...
AT THIS POINT, WHETHER WE CAN DO IT OR NOT ISN'T THE ISSUE. THE IMPORTANT THING IS MAKING THEM THINK WE'RE GOING TO.
FOR NOW, WE MAKE SOME "INQUIRIES" TO NEARBY SCHOOLS.
WE THEN PLANT THAT INFORMATION TO GET THE PARENTS WORRIED.
THEN WHAT ABOUT KAIHIN GENERAL?
WE WORKED WITH THEM BEFORE.
DEALING WITH THEM IS SO HARD, THOUGH...
SO THAT INFO... HAS GOT TO GET ONLINE, RIGHT?
I FIGURE.

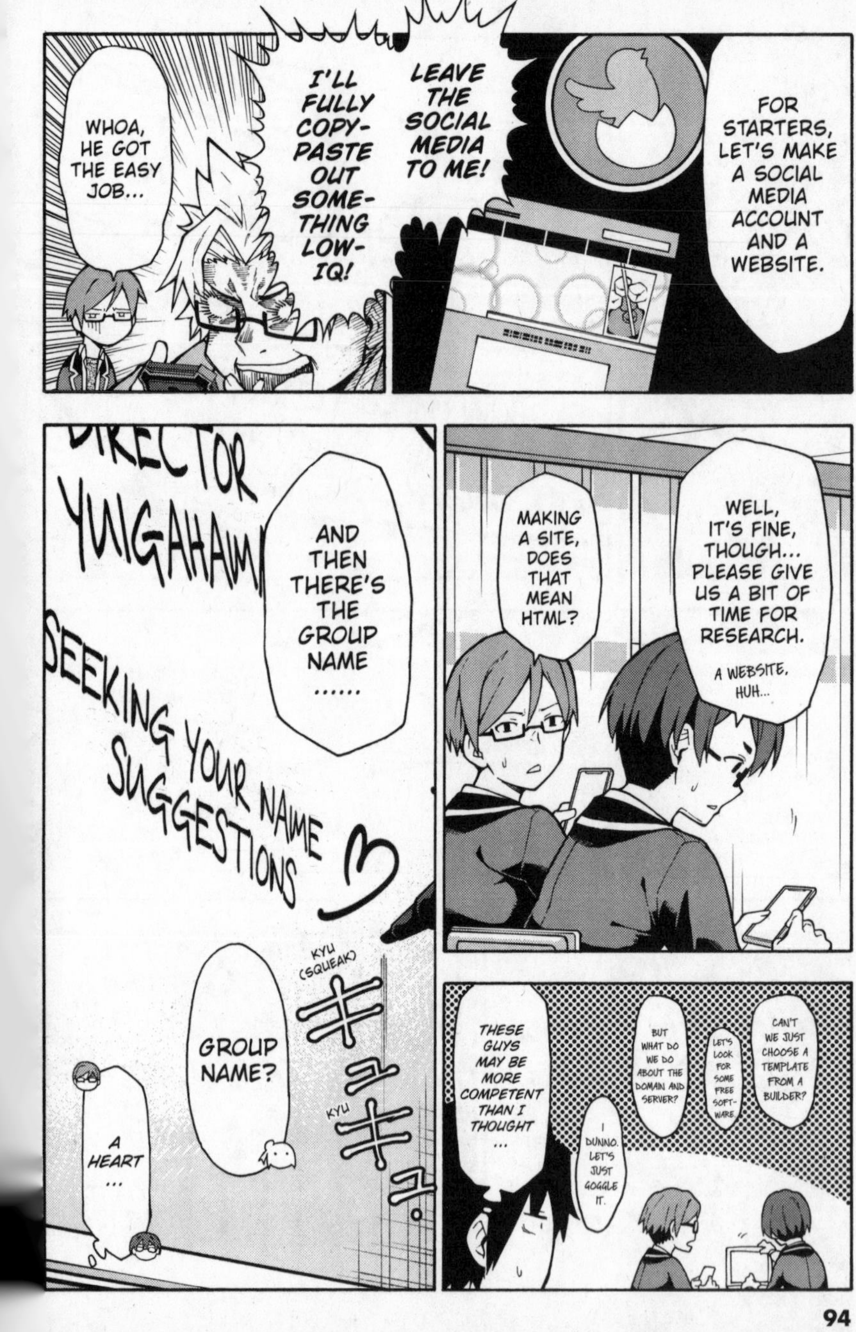
FOR STARTERS, LET'S MAKE A SOCIAL MEDIA ACCOUNT AND A WEBSITE.
LEAVE THE SOCIAL MEDIA TO ME!
I'LL FULLY COPY-PASTE OUT SOMETHING LOW-IQ!
WHOA, HE GOT THE EASY JOB...
WELL, IT'S FINE, THOUGH... PLEASE GIVE US A BIT OF TIME FOR RESEARCH.
MAKING A SITE, DOES THAT MEAN HTML?
A WEBSITE, HUH...
CAN'T WE JUST CHOOSE A TEMPLATE FROM A BUILDER?
LET'S LOOK FOR SOME FREE SOFT-WARE.
BUT WHAT DO WE DO ABOUT THE DOMAIN AND SERVER?
I DUNNO. LET'S JUST GOGGLE IT.
THESE GUYS MAY BE MORE COMPETENT THAN I THOUGHT ...
AND THEN THERE'S THE GROUP NAME ......
DIRECTOR YUIGAHAM
SEEKING YOUR NAME SUGGESTIONS
KYU (SQUEAK)
KYU
GROUP NAME?
A HEART ...

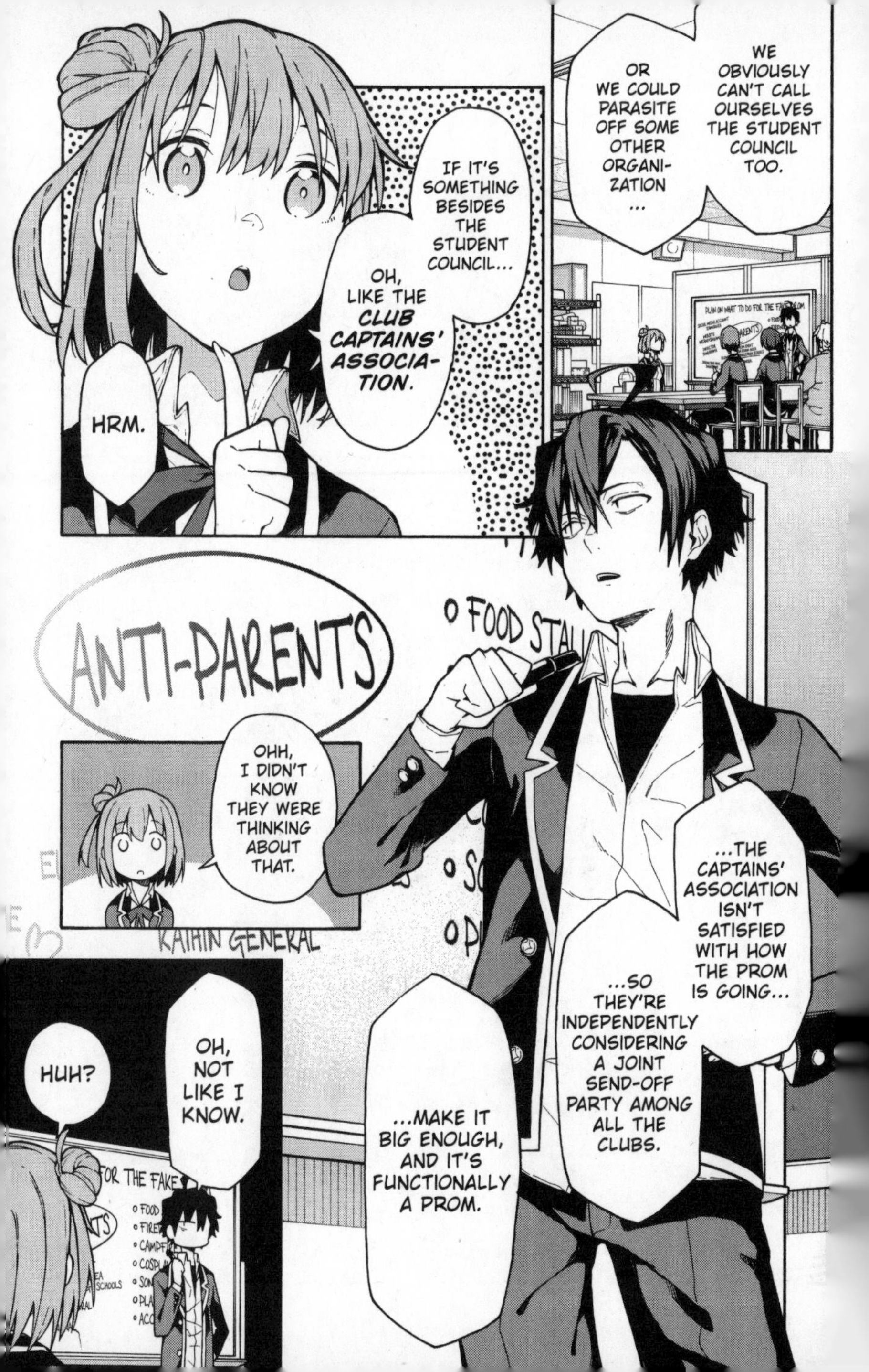
WE OBVIOUSLY CAN'T CALL OURSELVES THE STUDENT COUNCIL TOO.
OR WE COULD PARASITE OFF SOME OTHER ORGANIZATION...
IF IT'S SOMETHING BESIDES THE STUDENT COUNCIL...
OH, LIKE THE *CLUB CAPTAINS' ASSOCIATION.*
HRM.
ANTI-PARENTS
...THE CAPTAINS' ASSOCIATION ISN'T SATISFIED WITH HOW THE PROM IS GOING...
...SO THEY'RE INDEPENDENTLY CONSIDERING A JOINT SEND-OFF PARTY AMONG ALL THE CLUBS.
OHH, I DIDN'T KNOW THEY WERE THINKING ABOUT THAT.
KAIHIN GENERAL
...MAKE IT BIG ENOUGH, AND IT'S FUNCTIONALLY A PROM.
OH, NOT LIKE I KNOW.
HUH?

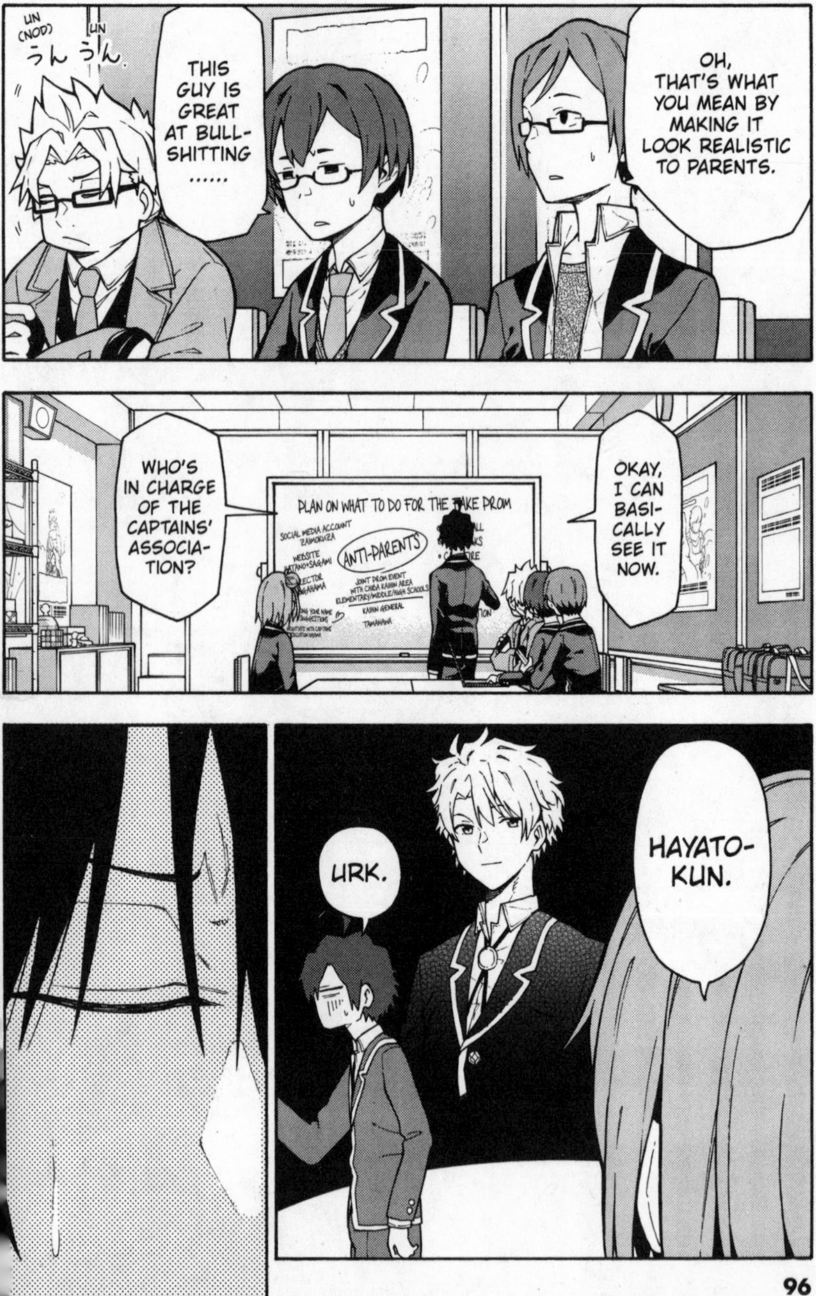
OH, THAT'S WHAT YOU MEAN BY MAKING IT LOOK REALISTIC TO PARENTS.
THIS GUY IS GREAT AT BULL-SHITTING ......
UN (NOD) UN
うん うん。
OKAY, I CAN BASI-CALLY SEE IT NOW.
PLAN ON WHAT TO DO FOR THE FAKE PROM
SOCIAL MEDIA ACCOUNT ZAIMOKUZA
WEBSITE HATANO+SAGAMI
ANTI-PARENTS
JOINT PROM EVENT WITH CHIBA KAIHIN AREA ELEMENTARY/MIDDLE/HIGH SCHOOLS
KAIHIN GENERAL
TAMANAWA
WHO'S IN CHARGE OF THE CAPTAINS' ASSOCIATION?
HAYATO-KUN.
URK.

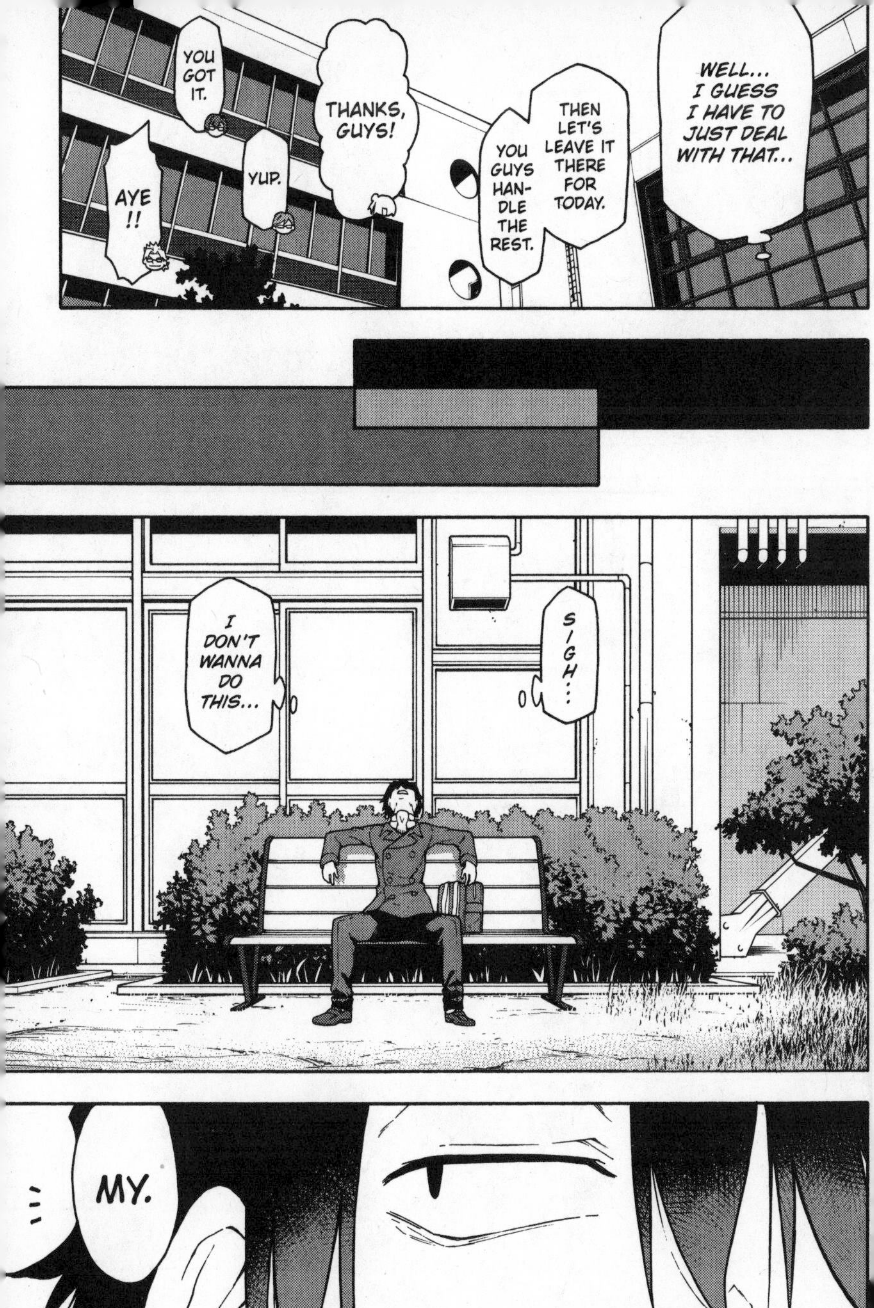
WELL... I GUESS I HAVE TO JUST DEAL WITH THAT...
THEN LET'S LEAVE IT THERE FOR TODAY.
YOU GUYS HAN-DLE THE REST.
THANKS, GUYS!
YUP.
YOU GOT IT.
AYE!!
SIGH...
I DON'T WANNA DO THIS...
MY.

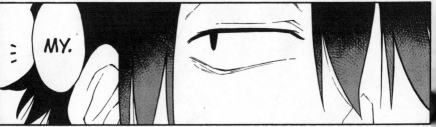

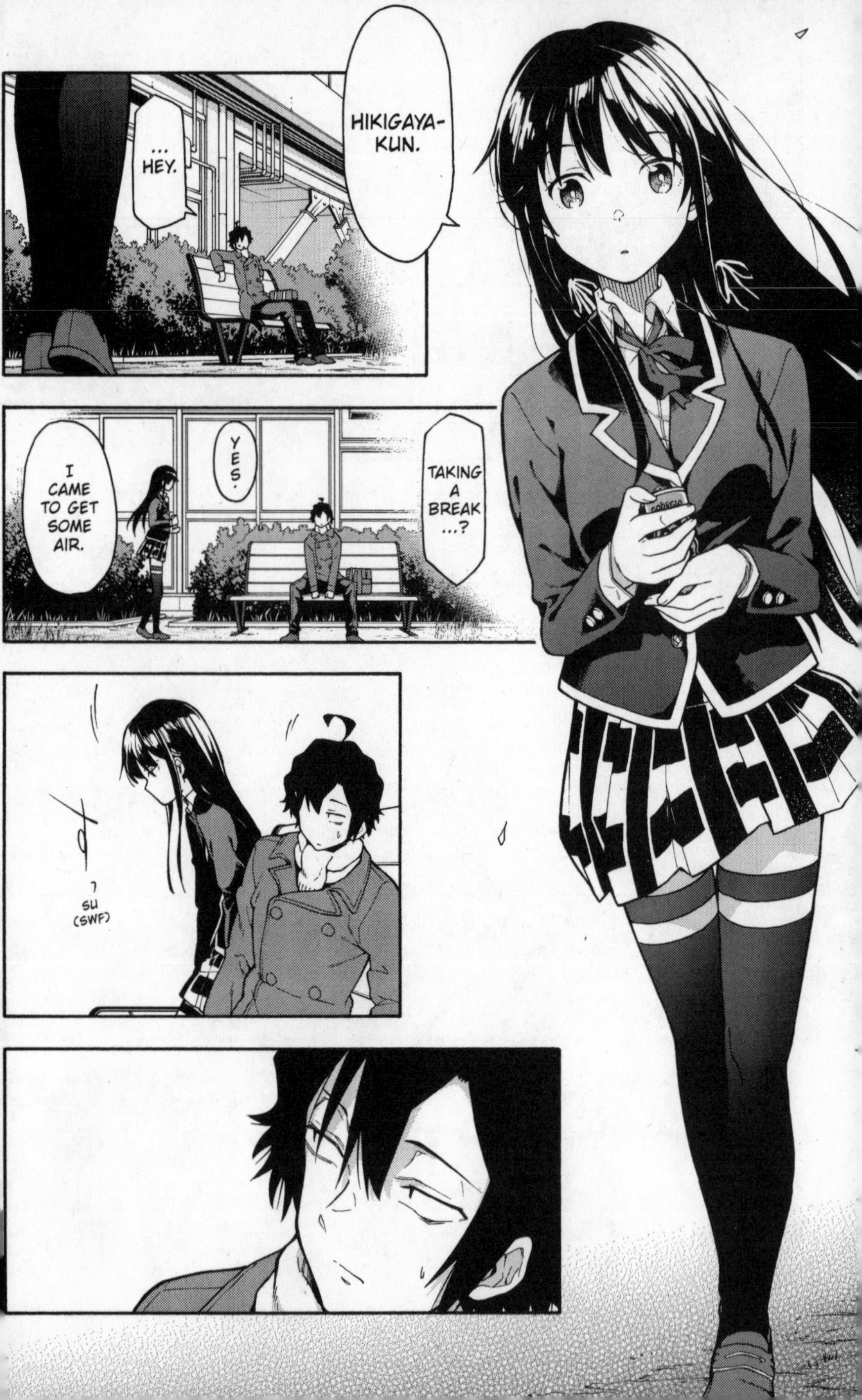
HIKIGAYA-KUN.
...HEY.
TAKING A BREAK...?
YES.
I CAME TO GET SOME AIR.
SU (SWF)

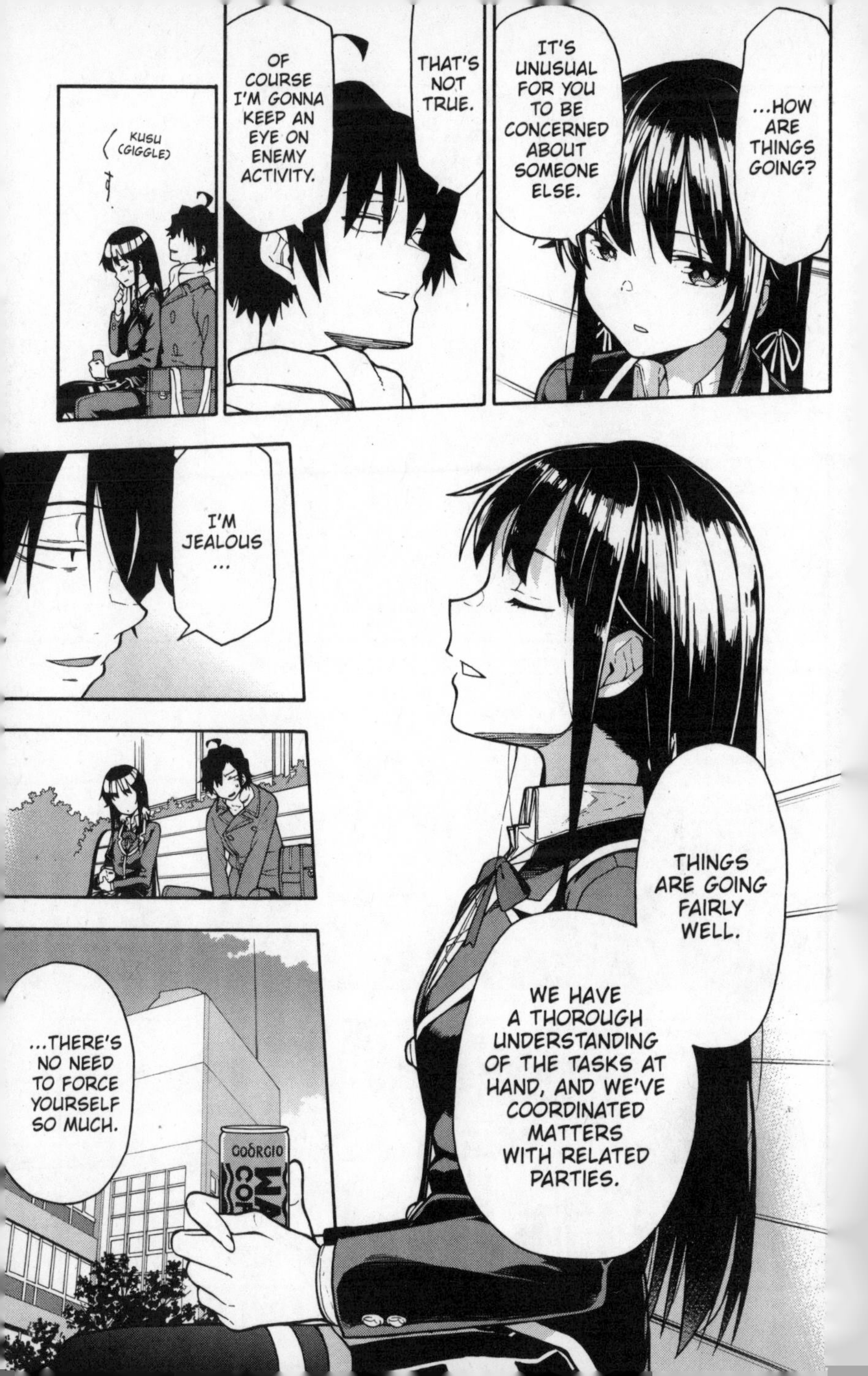
...HOW ARE THINGS GOING?
IT'S UNUSUAL FOR YOU TO BE CONCERNED ABOUT SOMEONE ELSE.
THAT'S NOT TRUE.
OF COURSE I'M GONNA KEEP AN EYE ON ENEMY ACTIVITY.
KUSU (GIGGLE)
す
THINGS ARE GOING FAIRLY WELL.
WE HAVE A THOROUGH UNDERSTANDING OF THE TASKS AT HAND, AND WE'VE COORDINATED MATTERS WITH RELATED PARTIES.
I'M JEALOUS ...
...THERE'S NO NEED TO FORCE YOURSELF SO MUCH.

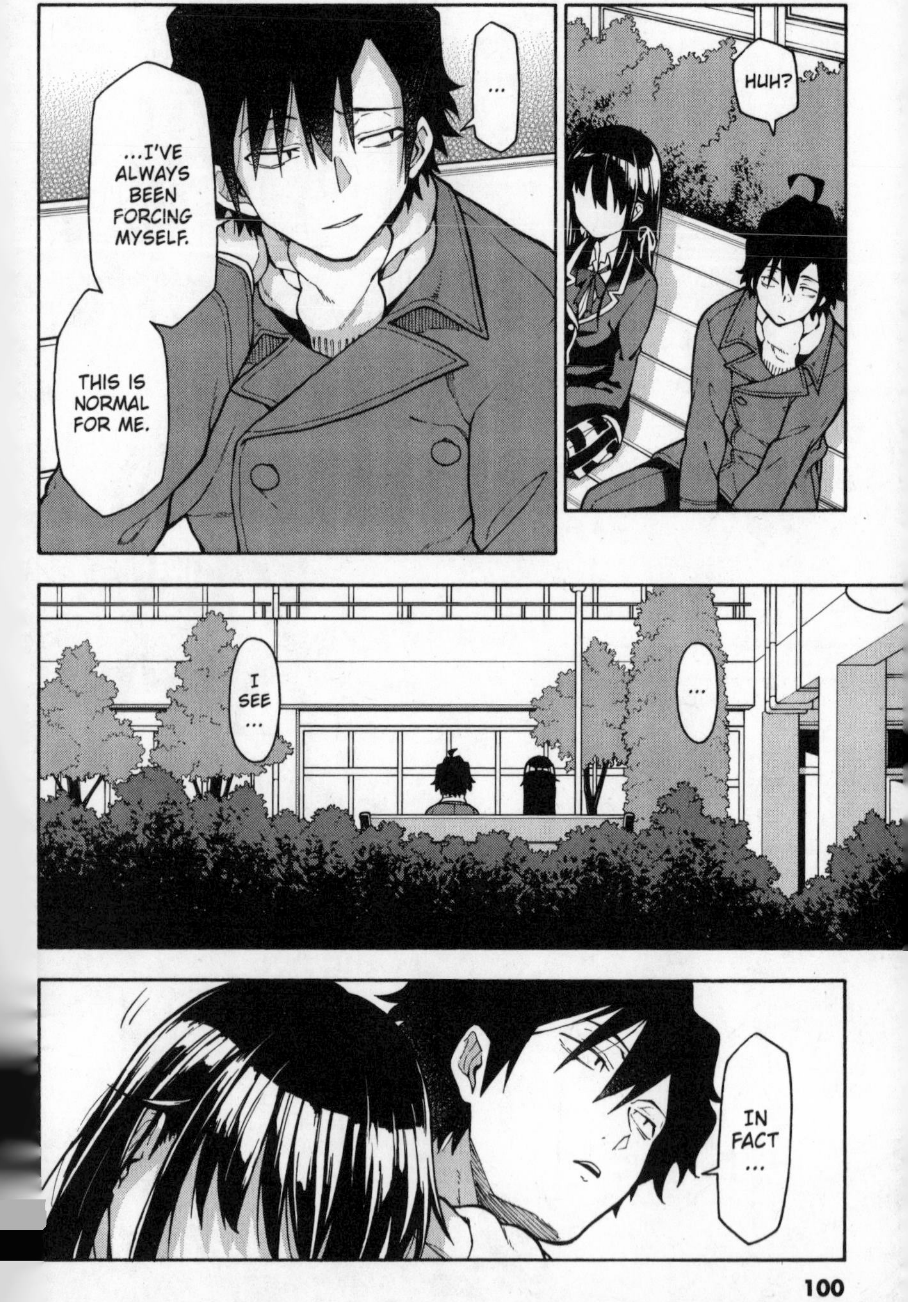
HUH?
...
...I'VE ALWAYS BEEN FORCING MYSELF.
THIS IS NORMAL FOR ME.
...
I SEE ...
IN FACT ...

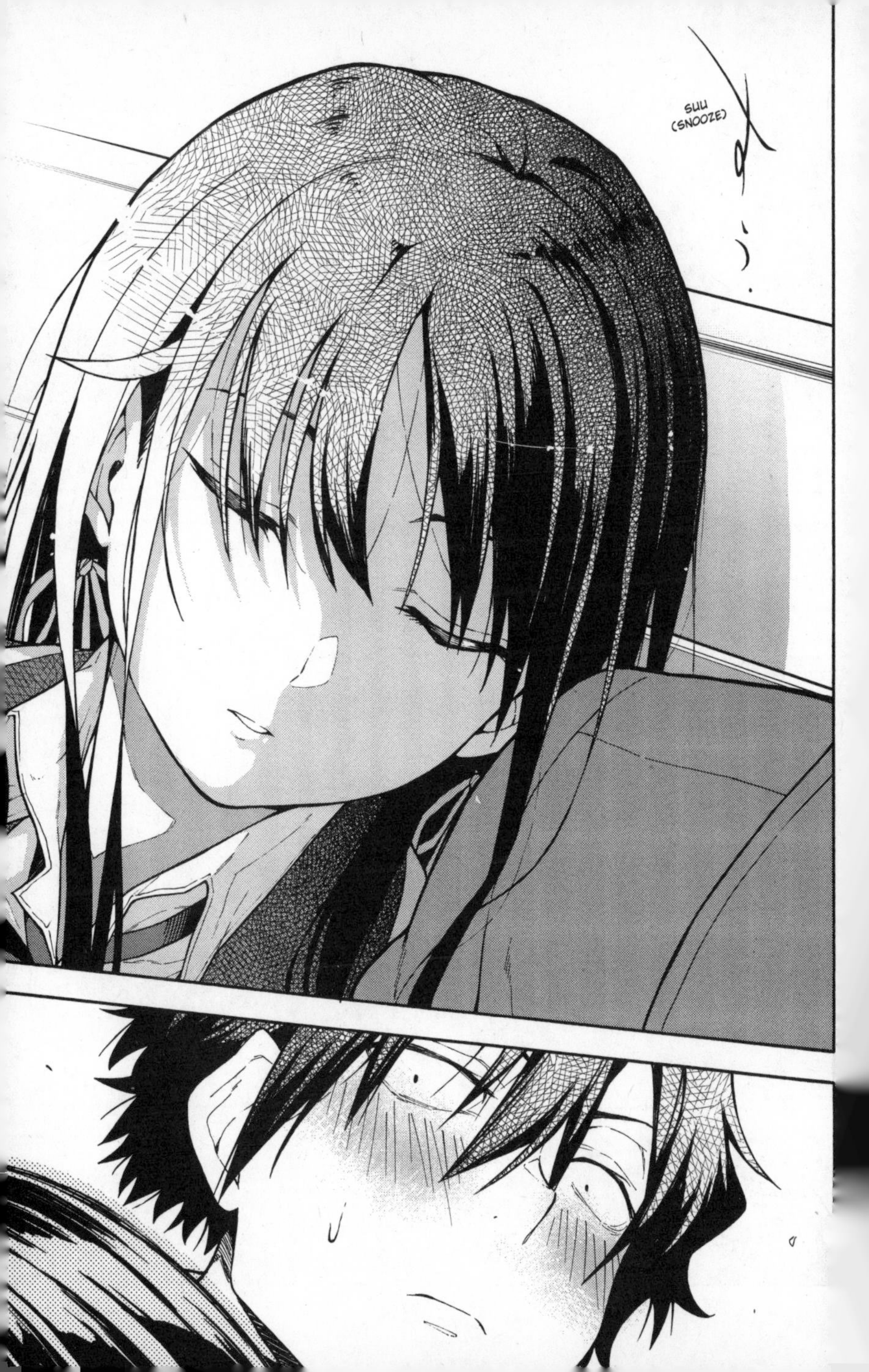
SUU (SNOOZE)

WHICH ONE OF US IS FORCING THEMSELVES ...?

GOOD GRIEF...

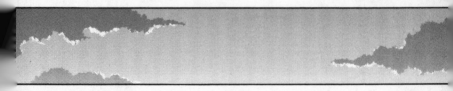

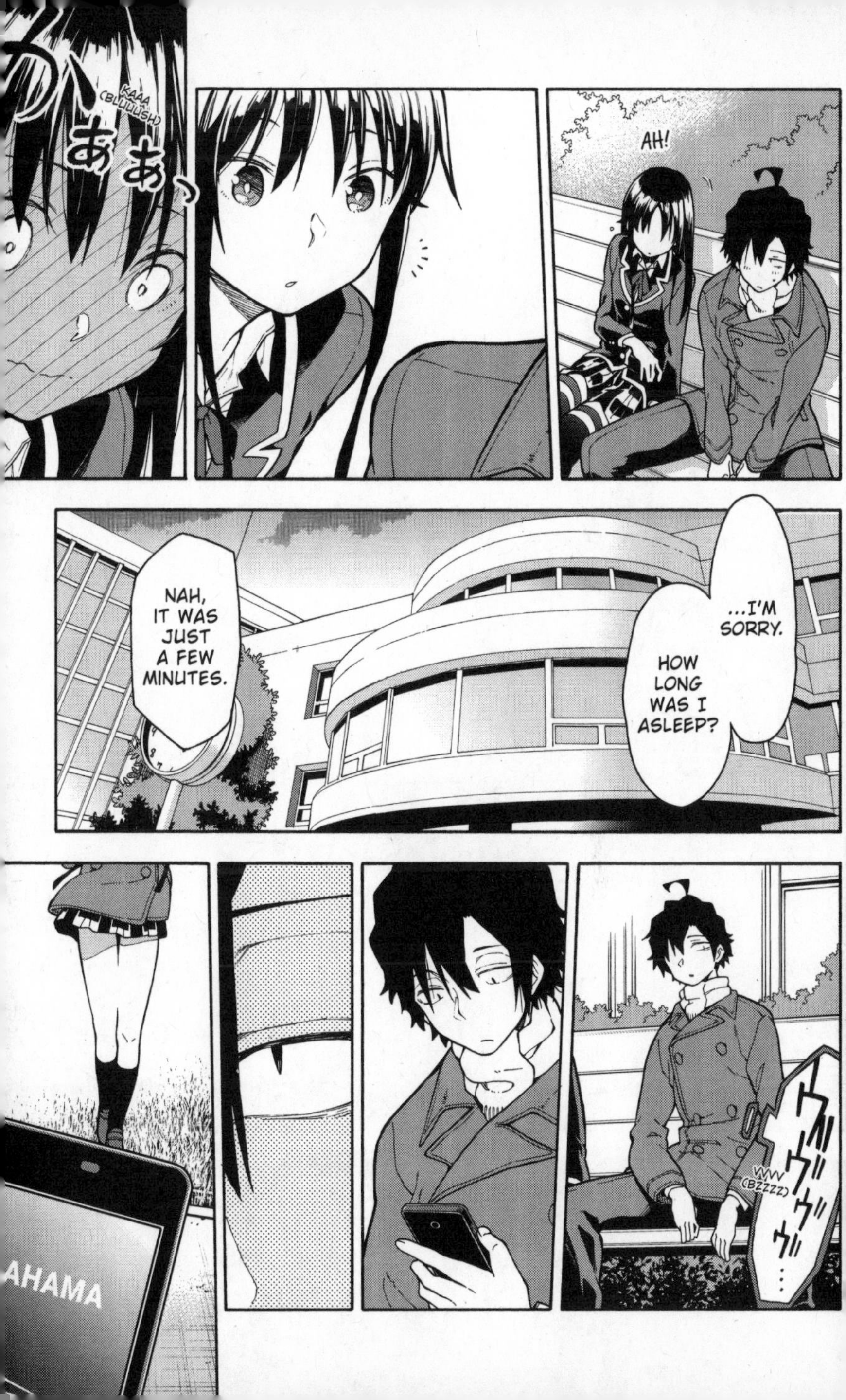
AH!
KAAA (BLUUUSH)
...I'M SORRY.
HOW LONG WAS I ASLEEP?
NAH, IT WAS JUST A FEW MINUTES.
VVVV (BZZZZ)
AHAMA

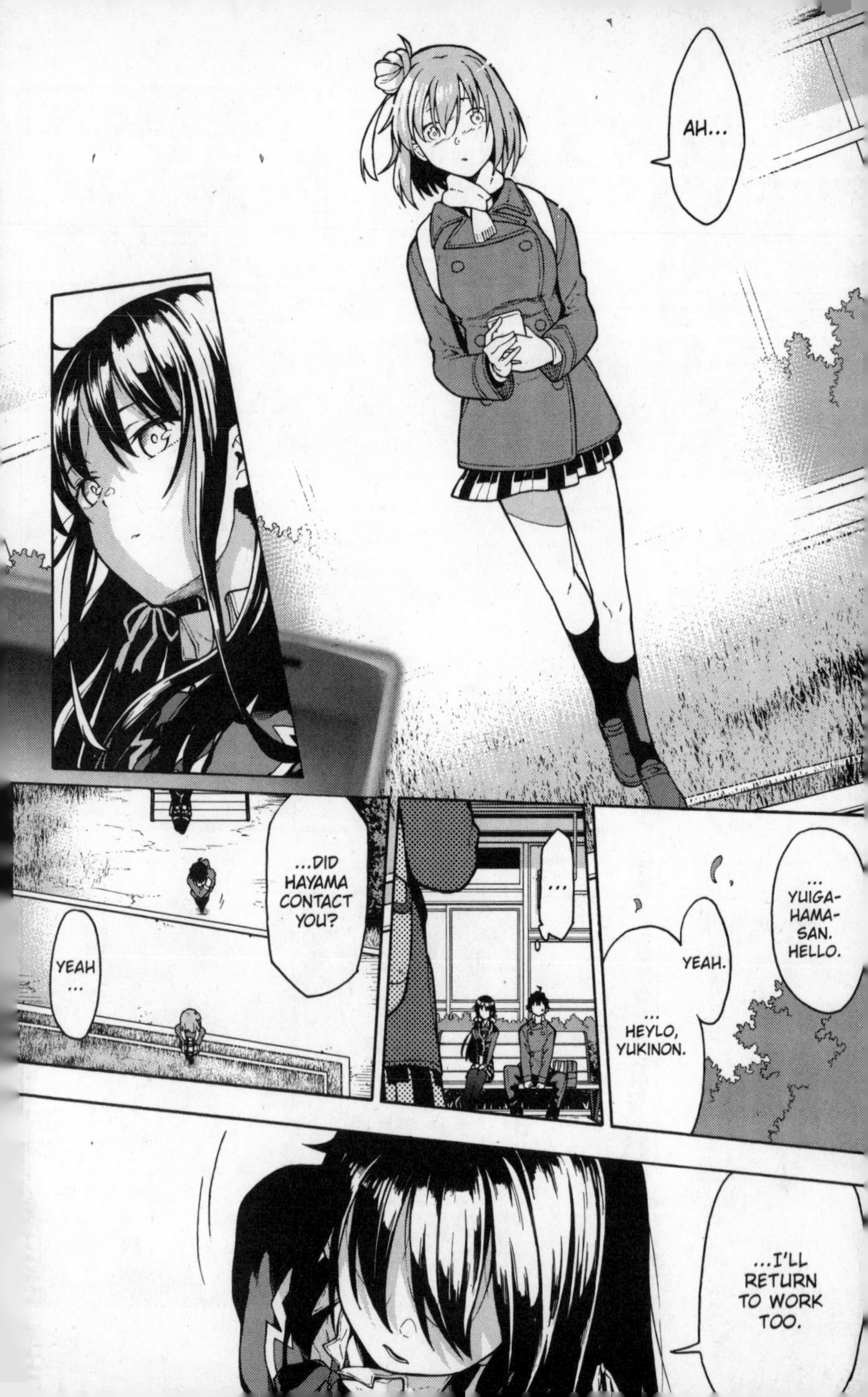
AH...
... YUIGA-HAMA-SAN. HELLO.
YEAH.
... HEYLO, YUKINON.
...
...DID HAYAMA CONTACT YOU?
YEAH ...
...I'LL RETURN TO WORK TOO.

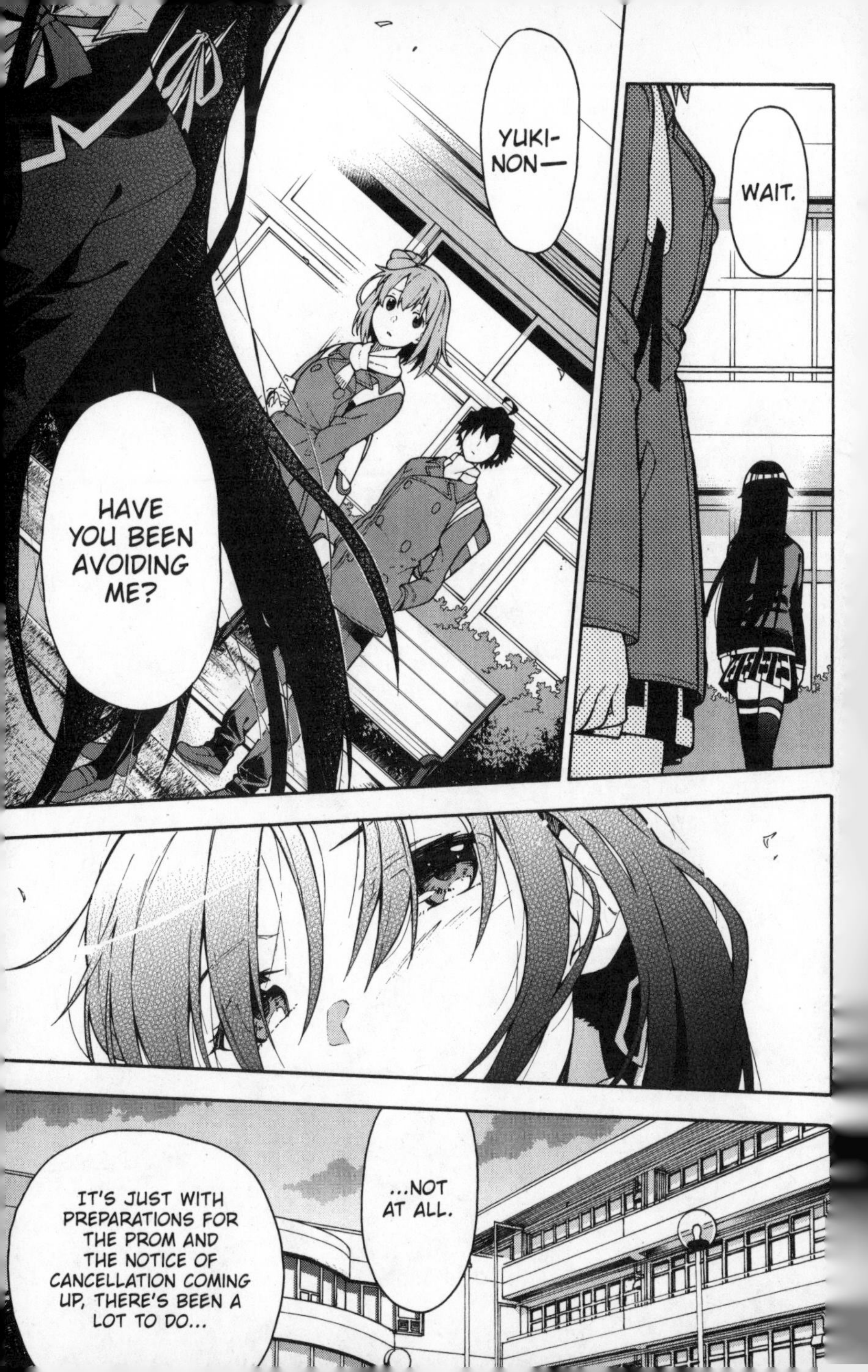
WAIT.
YUKI-NON—
HAVE YOU BEEN AVOIDING ME?
...NOT AT ALL.
IT'S JUST WITH PREPARATIONS FOR THE PROM AND THE NOTICE OF CANCELLATION COMING UP, THERE'S BEEN A LOT TO DO...

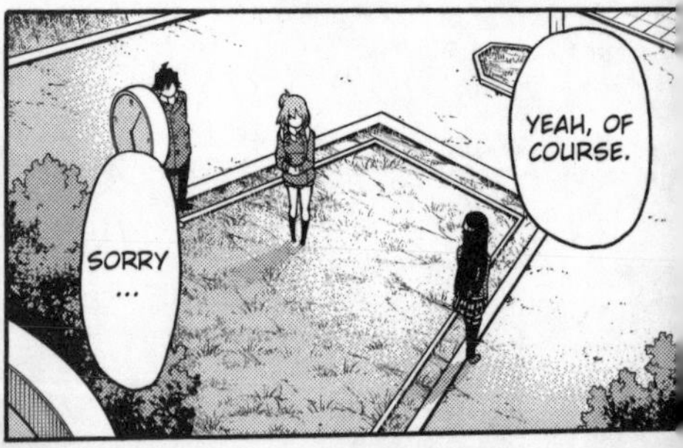
YEAH, OF COURSE.
SORRY ...

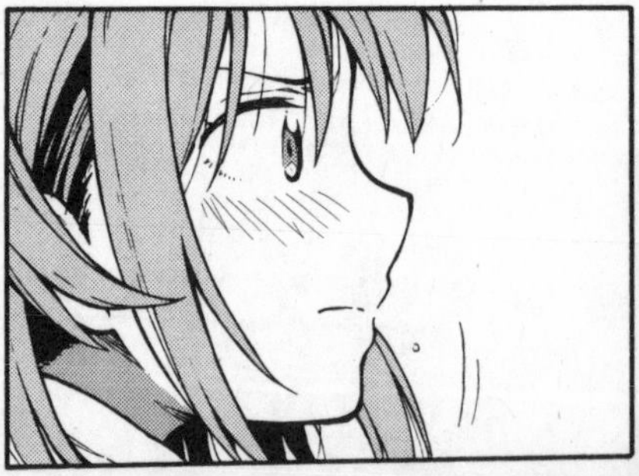

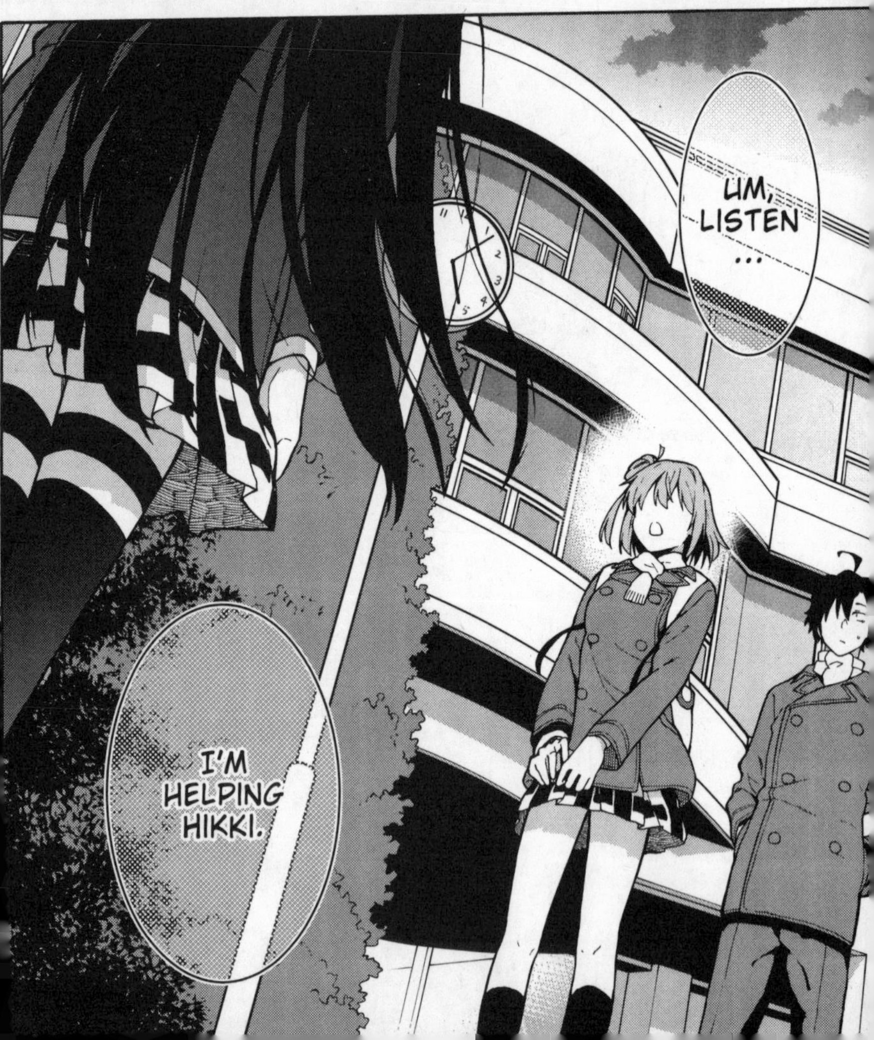
UM, LISTEN ...
I'M HELPING HIKKI.

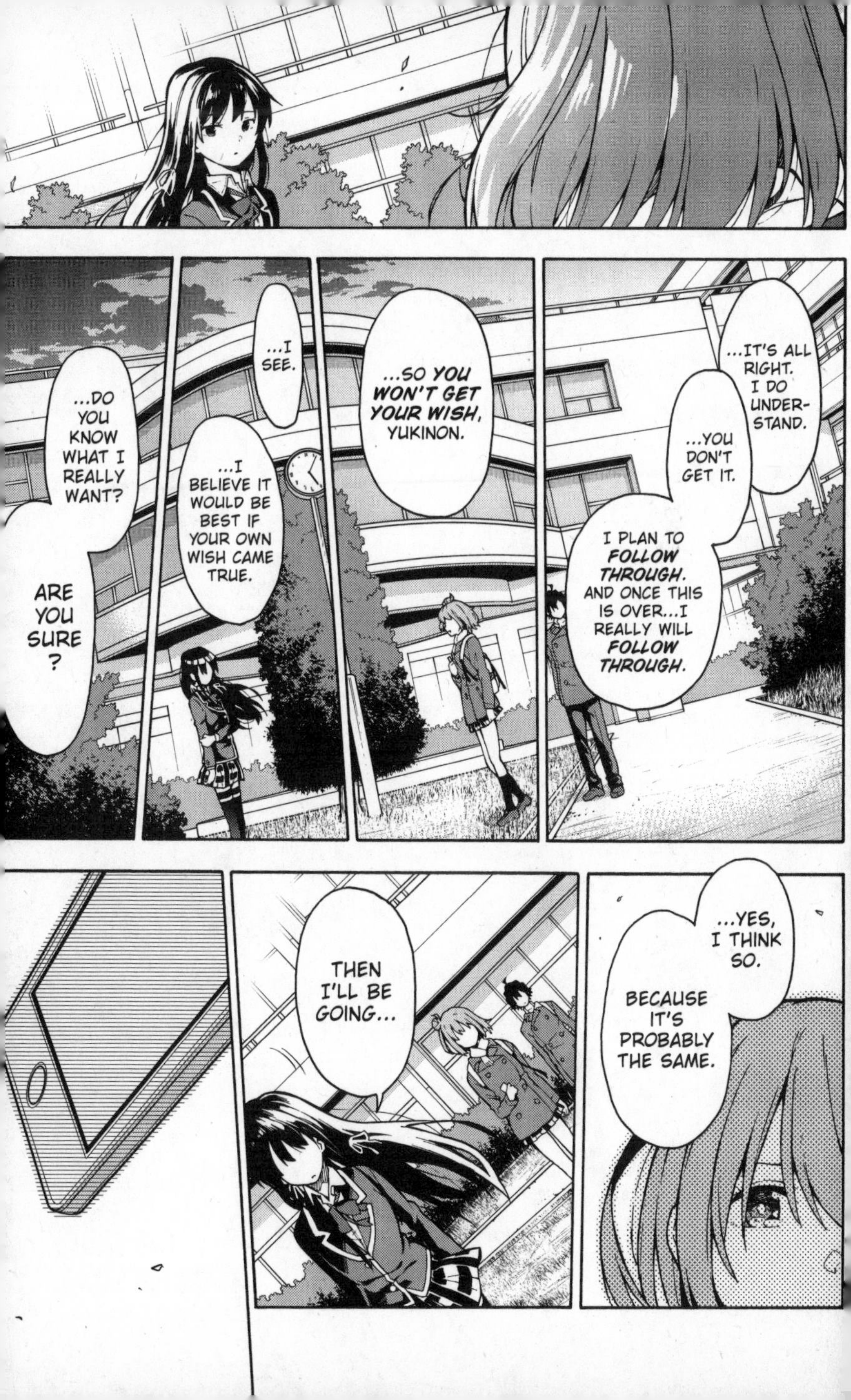
...IT'S ALL RIGHT. I DO UNDERSTAND.
...YOU DON'T GET IT.
I PLAN TO FOLLOW THROUGH. AND ONCE THIS IS OVER...I REALLY WILL FOLLOW THROUGH.
...SO YOU WON'T GET YOUR WISH, YUKINON.
...I SEE.
...I BELIEVE IT WOULD BE BEST IF YOUR OWN WISH CAME TRUE.
...DO YOU KNOW WHAT I REALLY WANT?
ARE YOU SURE?
...YES, I THINK SO.
BECAUSE IT'S PROBABLY THE SAME.
THEN I'LL BE GOING...

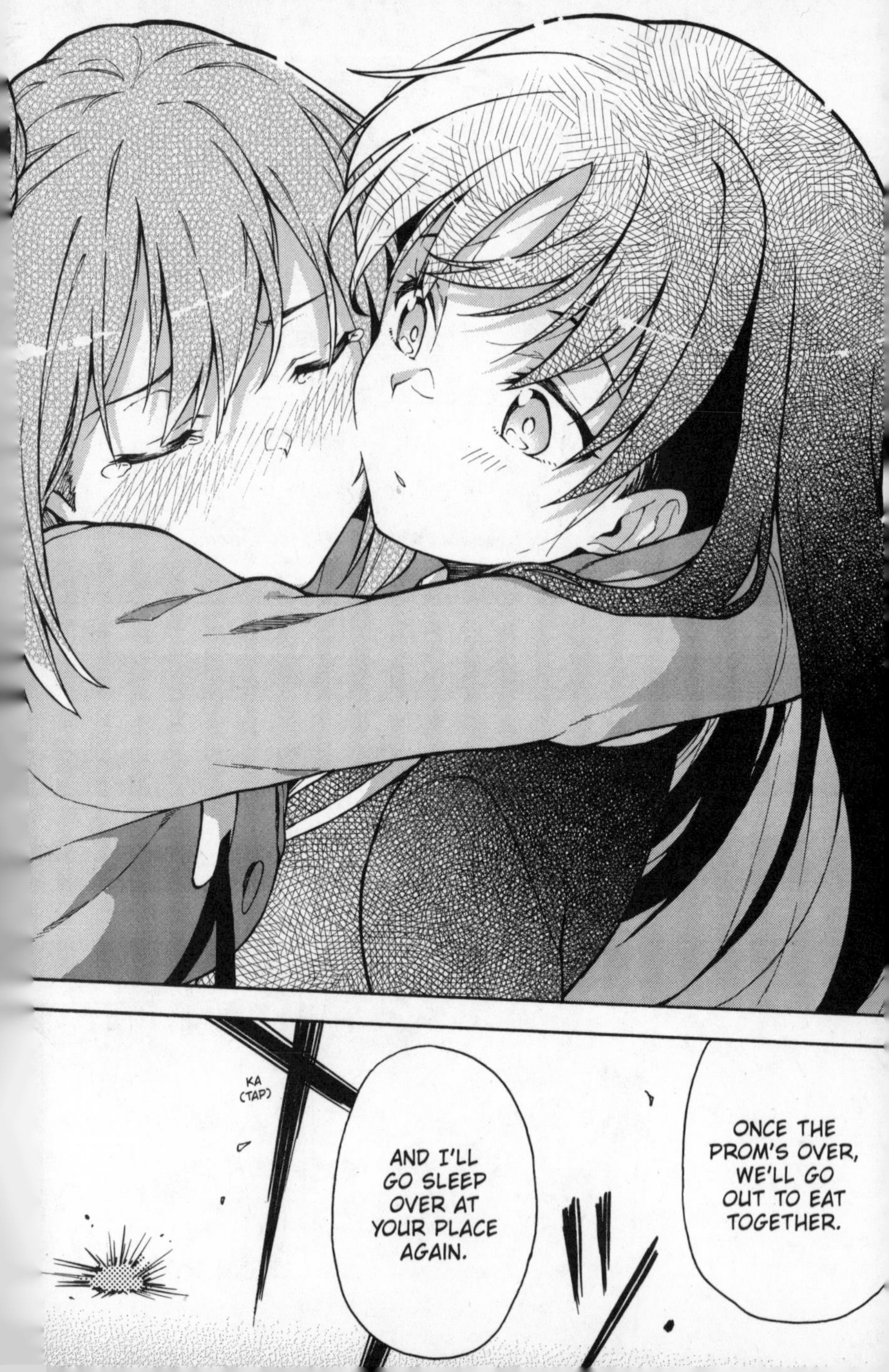
ONCE THE PROM'S OVER, WE'LL GO OUT TO EAT TOGETHER.
AND I'LL GO SLEEP OVER AT YOUR PLACE AGAIN.
KA (TAP)

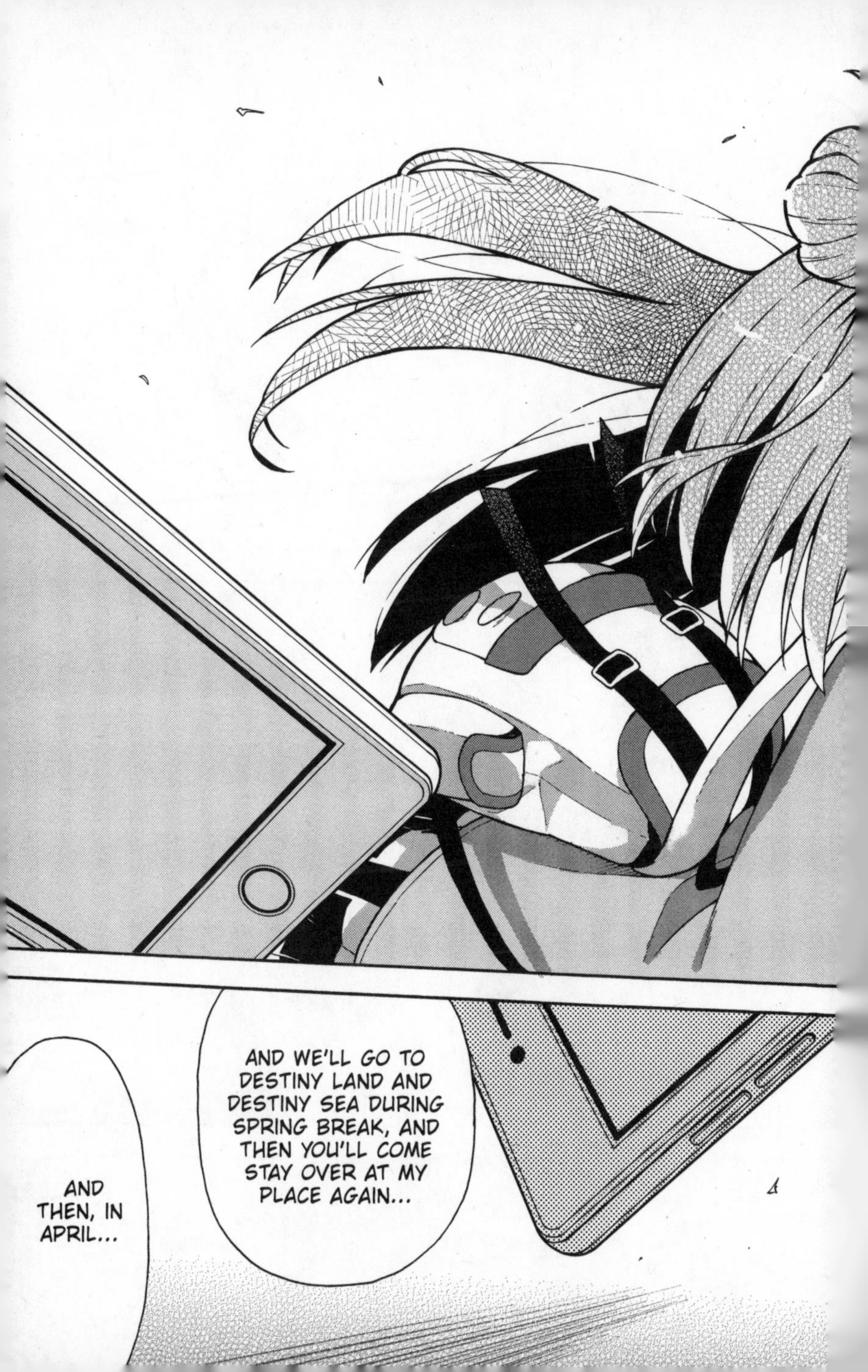
AND WE'LL GO TO DESTINY LAND AND DESTINY SEA DURING SPRING BREAK, AND THEN YOU'LL COME STAY OVER AT MY PLACE AGAIN...
AND THEN, IN APRIL...

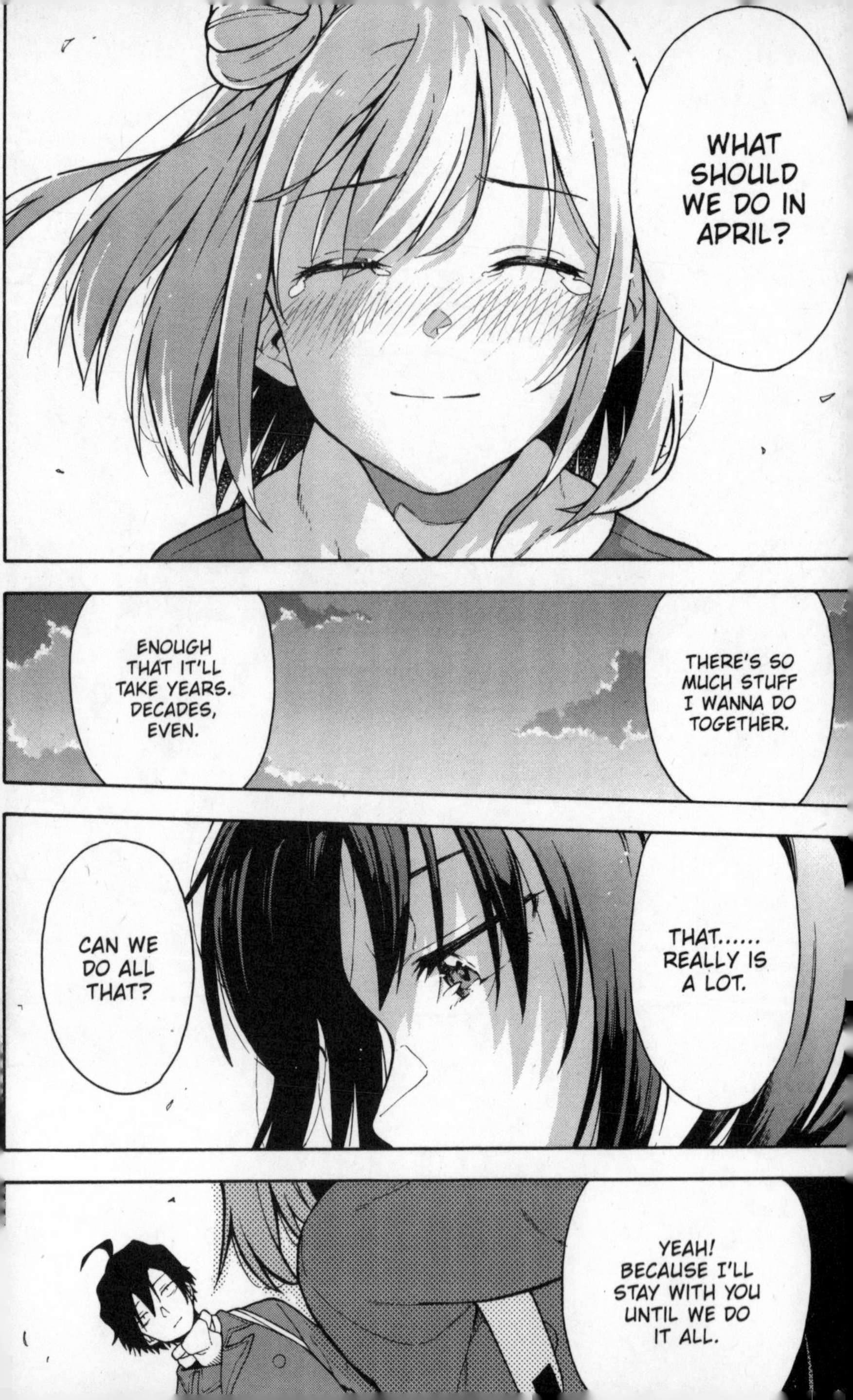
WHAT SHOULD WE DO IN APRIL?
THERE'S SO MUCH STUFF I WANNA DO TOGETHER.
ENOUGH THAT IT'LL TAKE YEARS. DECADES, EVEN.
THAT...... REALLY IS A LOT.
CAN WE DO ALL THAT?
YEAH! BECAUSE I'LL STAY WITH YOU UNTIL WE DO IT ALL.

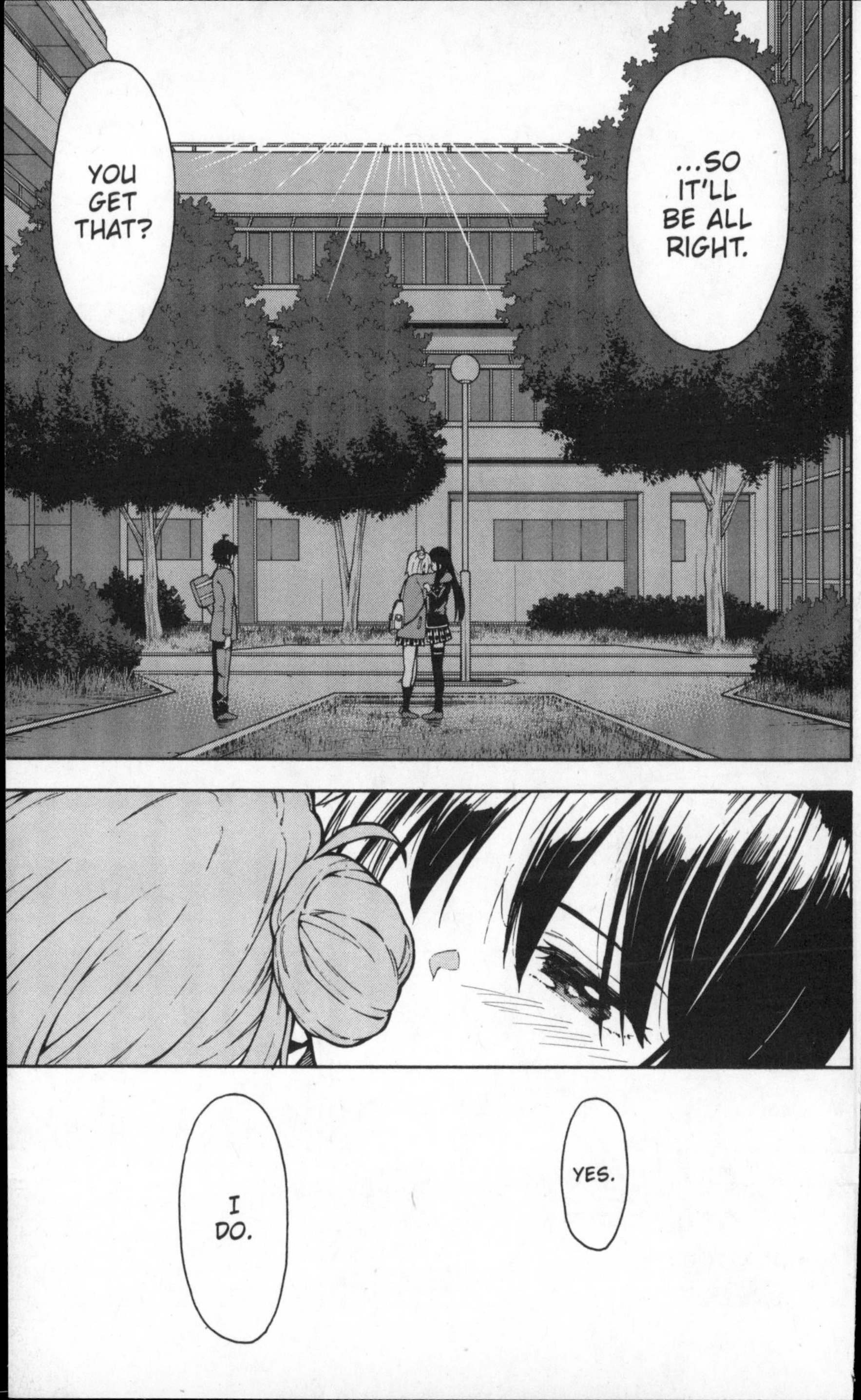
...SO IT'LL BE ALL RIGHT.
YOU GET THAT?
YES.
I DO.

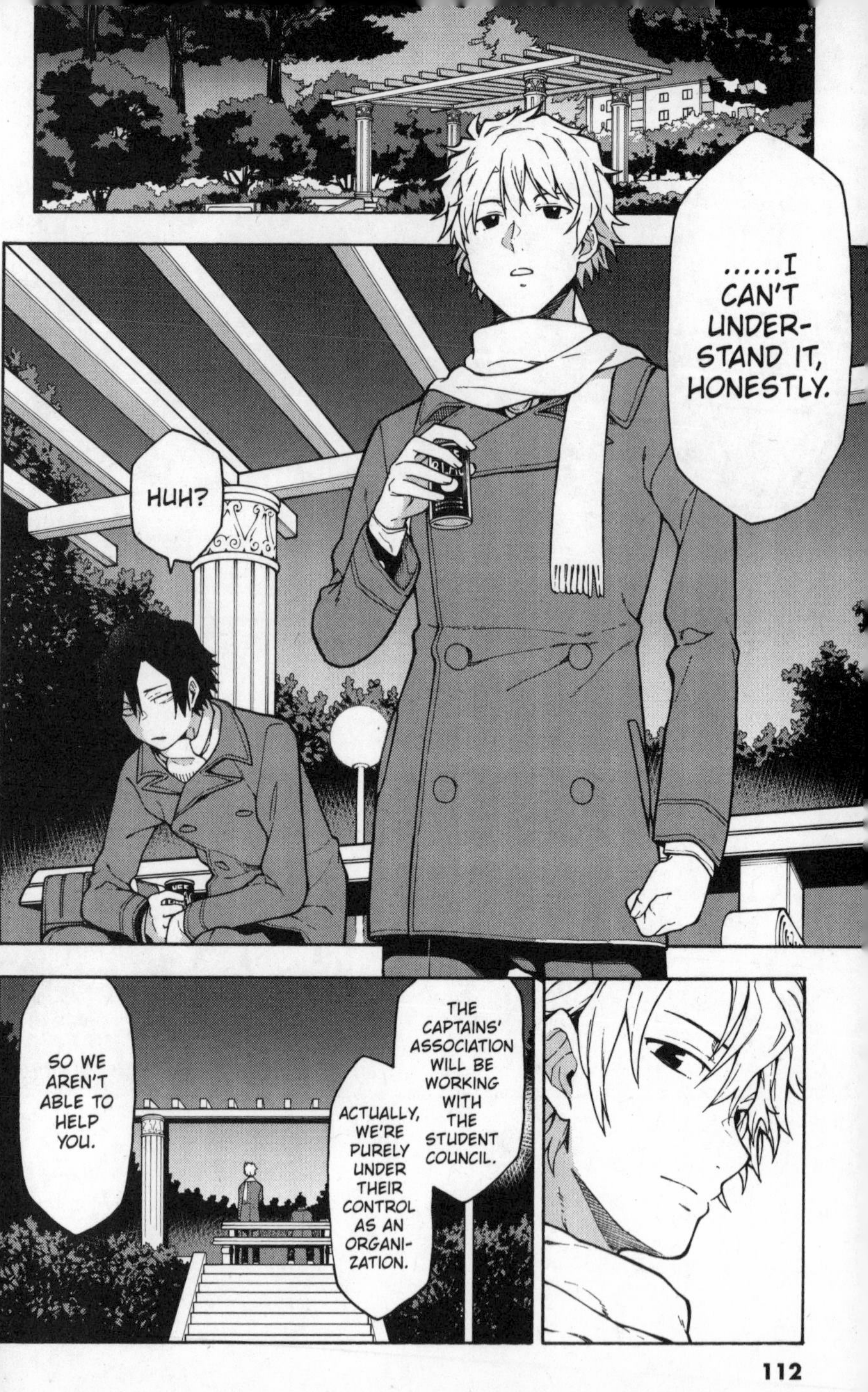
......I CAN'T UNDER-STAND IT, HONESTLY.
HUH?
THE CAPTAINS' ASSOCIATION WILL BE WORKING WITH THE STUDENT COUNCIL.
ACTUALLY, WE'RE PURELY UNDER THEIR CONTROL AS AN ORGANI-ZATION.
SO WE AREN'T ABLE TO HELP YOU.

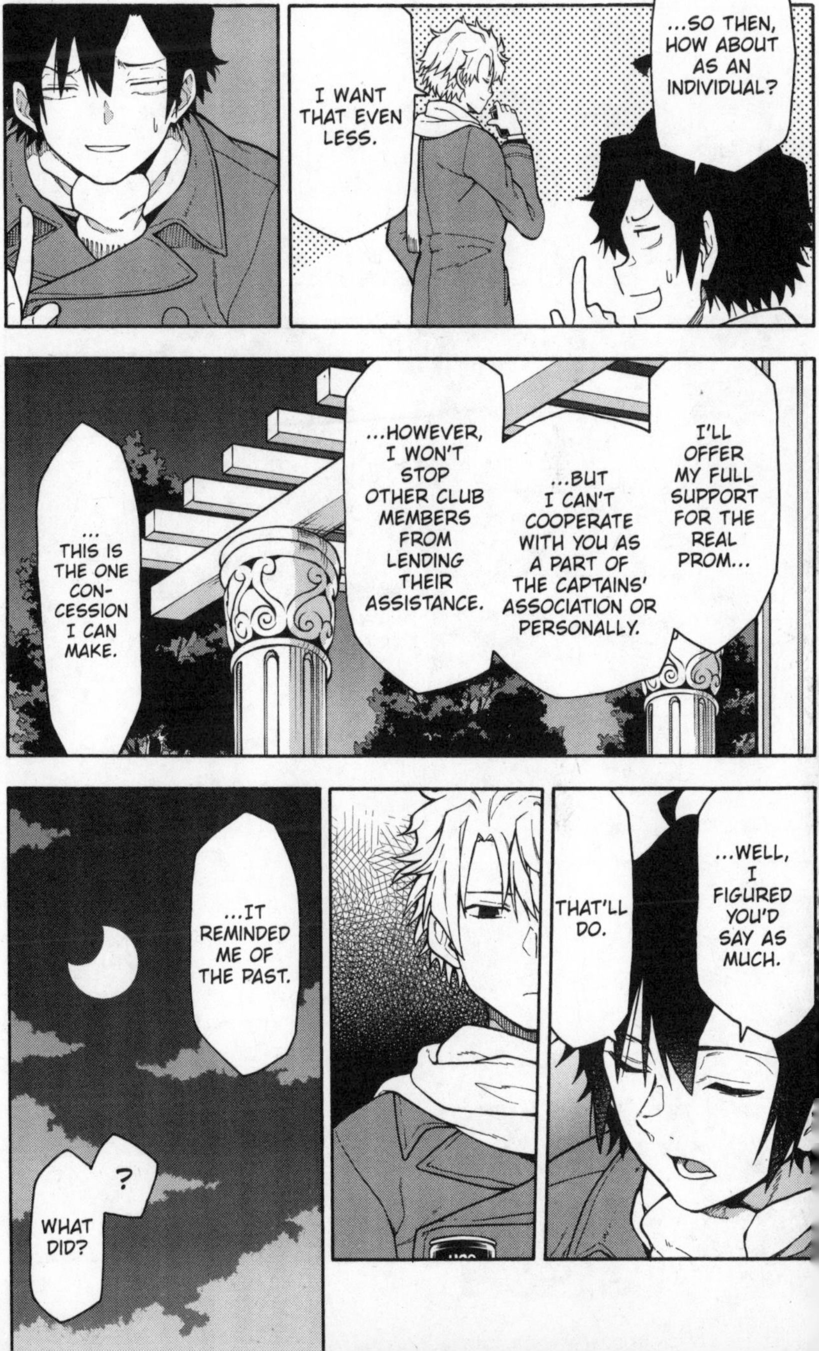
...SO THEN, HOW ABOUT AS AN INDIVIDUAL?
I WANT THAT EVEN LESS.
I'LL OFFER MY FULL SUPPORT FOR THE REAL PROM...
...BUT I CAN'T COOPERATE WITH YOU AS A PART OF THE CAPTAINS' ASSOCIATION OR PERSONALLY.
...HOWEVER, I WON'T STOP OTHER CLUB MEMBERS FROM LENDING THEIR ASSISTANCE.
... THIS IS THE ONE CON-CESSION I CAN MAKE.
...WELL, I FIGURED YOU'D SAY AS MUCH.
THAT'LL DO.
...IT REMINDED ME OF THE PAST.
?
WHAT DID?

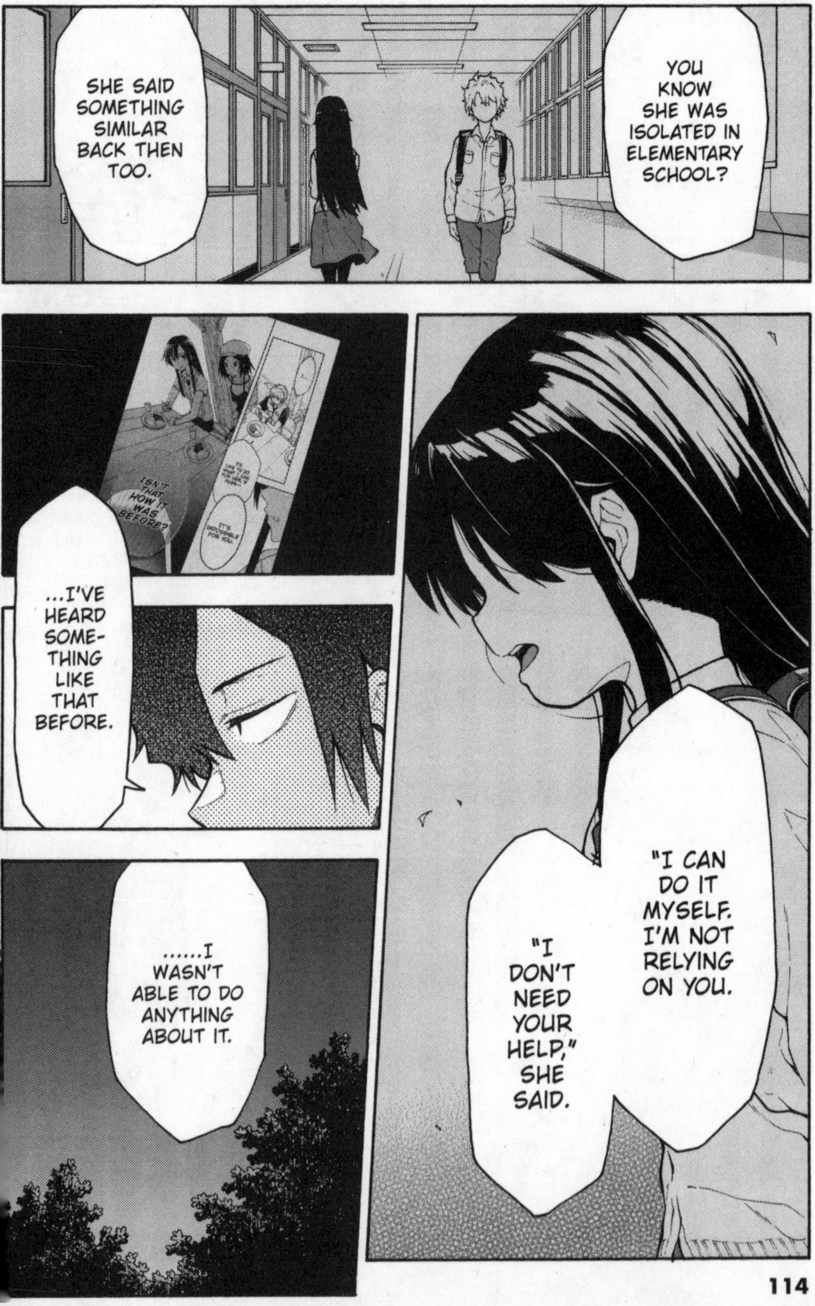
YOU KNOW SHE WAS ISOLATED IN ELEMENTARY SCHOOL?
SHE SAID SOMETHING SIMILAR BACK THEN TOO.
"I CAN DO IT MYSELF. I'M NOT RELYING ON YOU.
"I DON'T NEED YOUR HELP," SHE SAID.
ISN'T THAT HOW IT WAS BEFORE?
...I'VE HEARD SOMETHING LIKE THAT BEFORE.
......I WASN'T ABLE TO DO ANYTHING ABOUT IT.

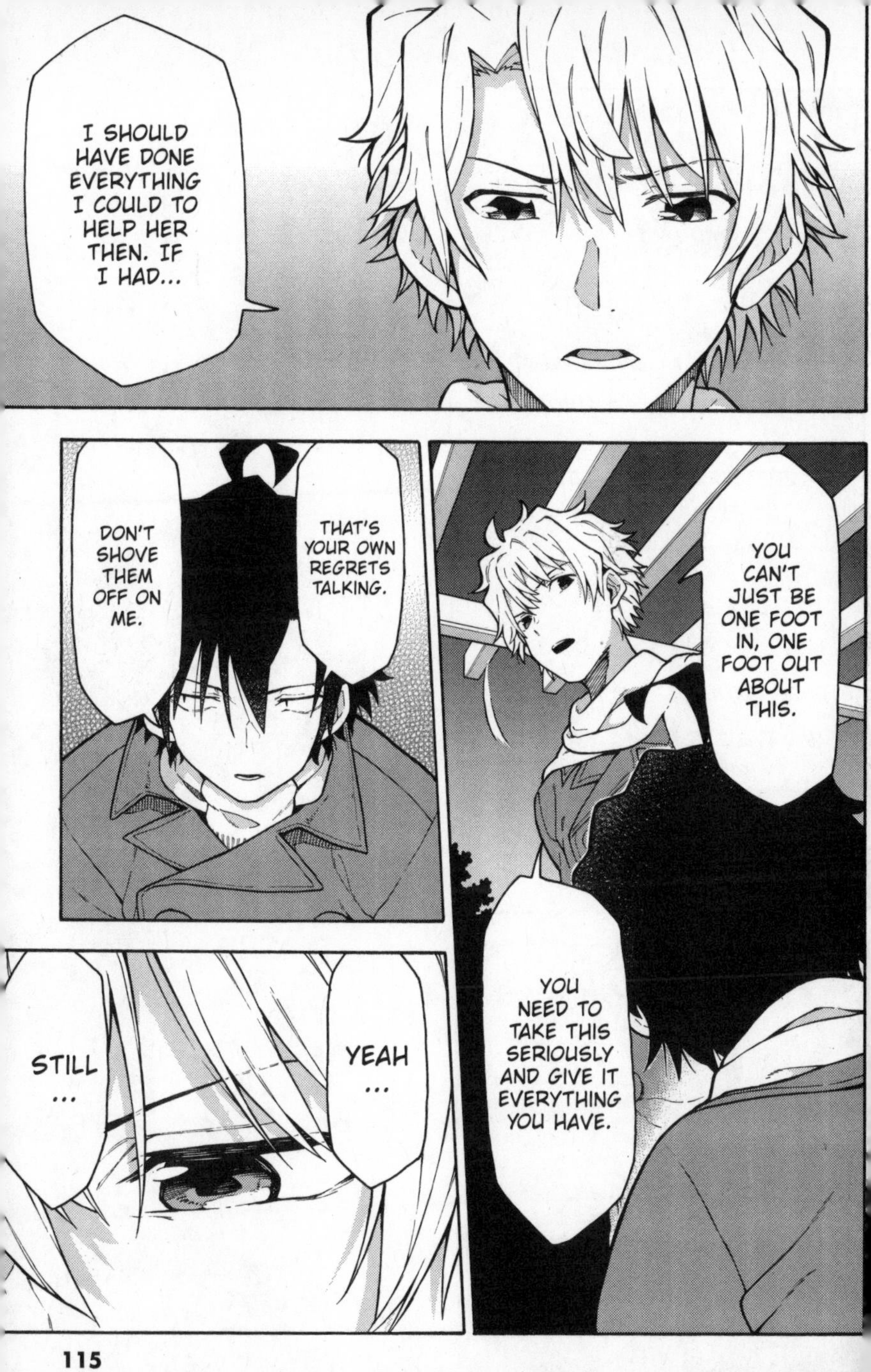
I SHOULD HAVE DONE EVERYTHING I COULD TO HELP HER THEN. IF I HAD...
YOU CAN'T JUST BE ONE FOOT IN, ONE FOOT OUT ABOUT THIS.
YOU NEED TO TAKE THIS SERIOUSLY AND GIVE IT EVERYTHING YOU HAVE.
THAT'S YOUR OWN REGRETS TALKING.
DON'T SHOVE THEM OFF ON ME.
YEAH ...
STILL ...

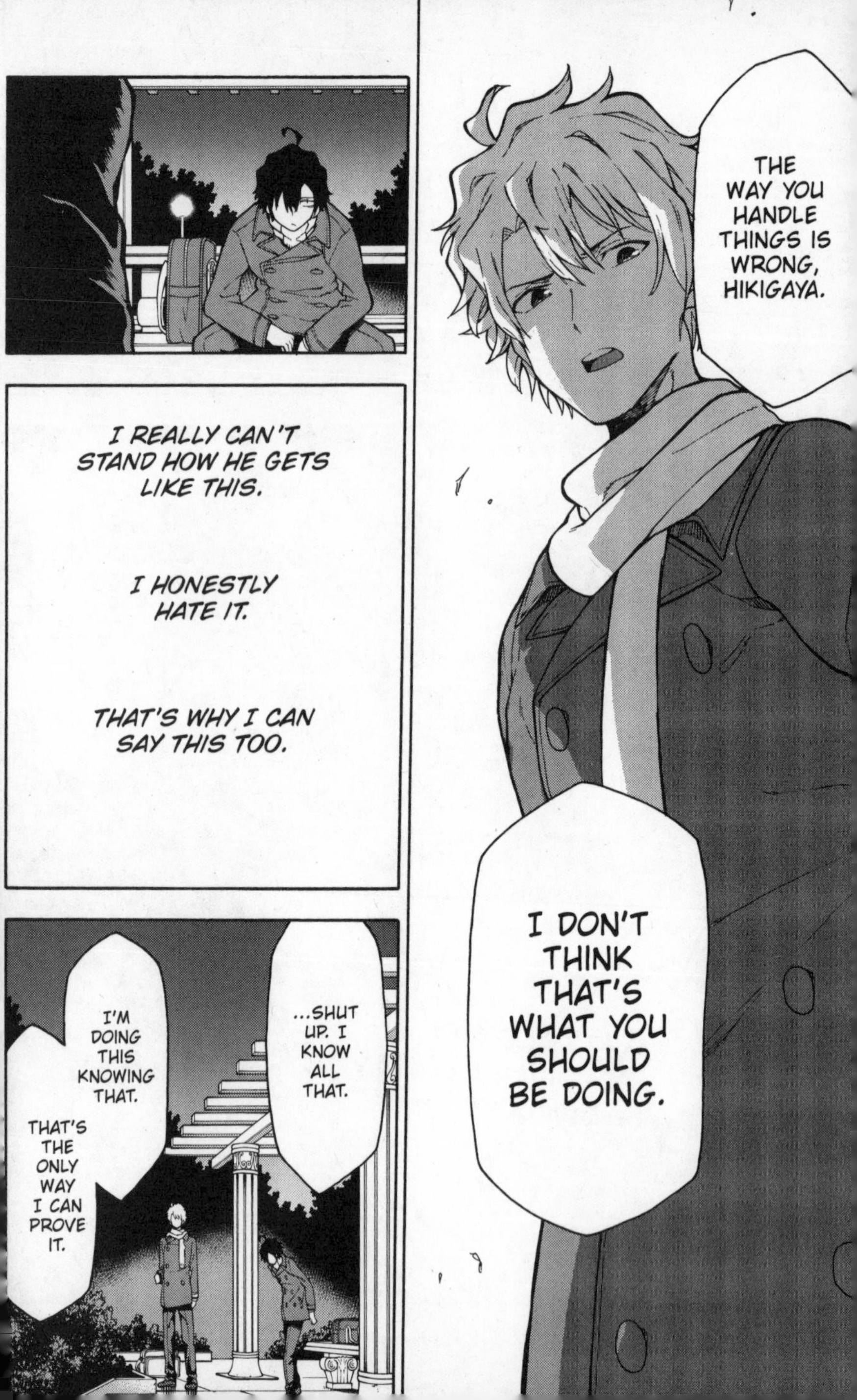
THE WAY YOU HANDLE THINGS IS WRONG, HIKIGAYA.
I DON'T THINK THAT'S WHAT YOU SHOULD BE DOING.
I REALLY CAN'T STAND HOW HE GETS LIKE THIS.
I HONESTLY HATE IT.
THAT'S WHY I CAN SAY THIS TOO.
...SHUT UP. I KNOW ALL THAT.
I'M DOING THIS KNOWING THAT.
THAT'S THE ONLY WAY I CAN PROVE IT.

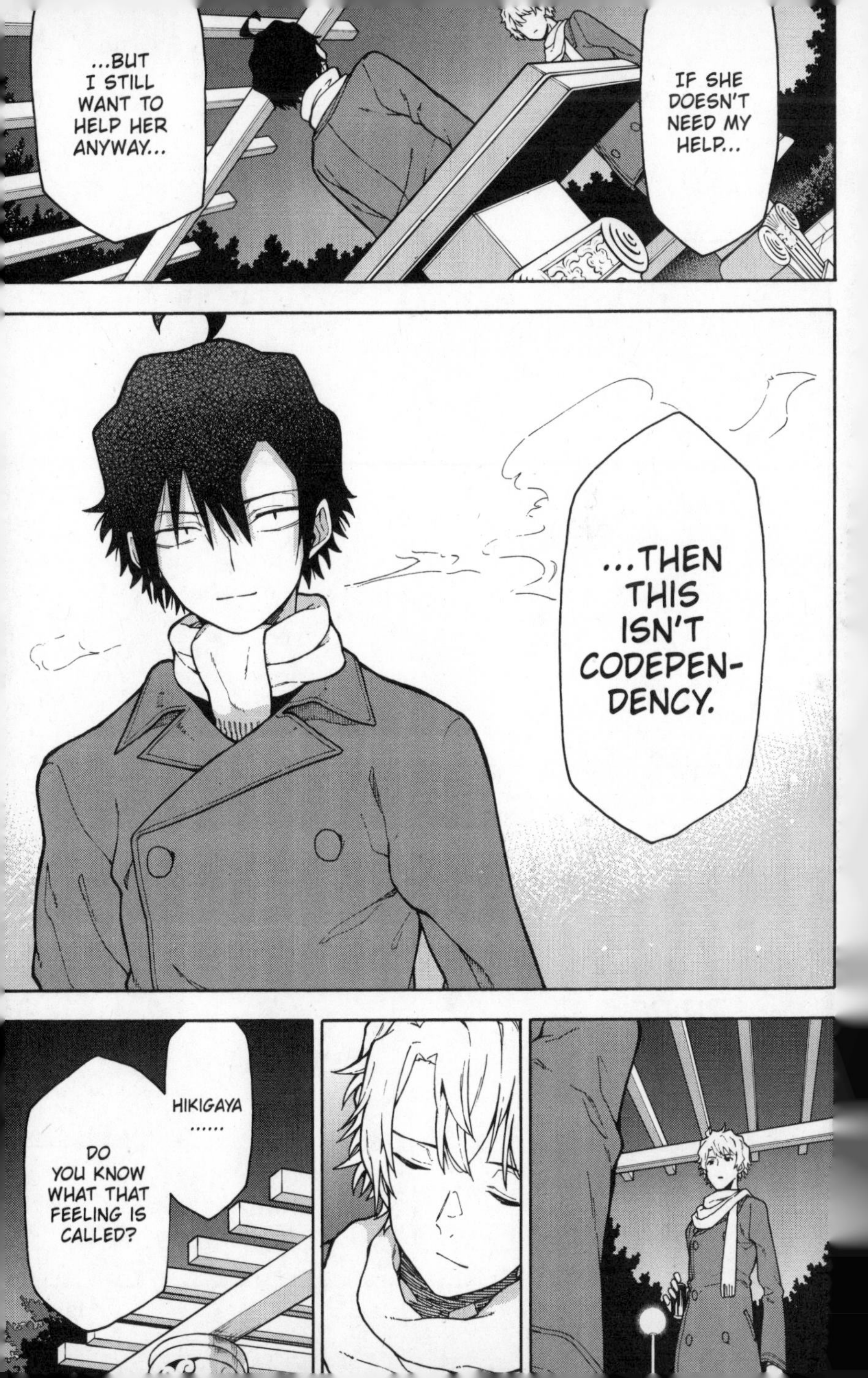
IF SHE DOESN'T NEED MY HELP...
...BUT I STILL WANT TO HELP HER ANYWAY...
...THEN THIS ISN'T CODEPEN-DENCY.
HIKIGAYA ......
DO YOU KNOW WHAT THAT FEELING IS CALLED?

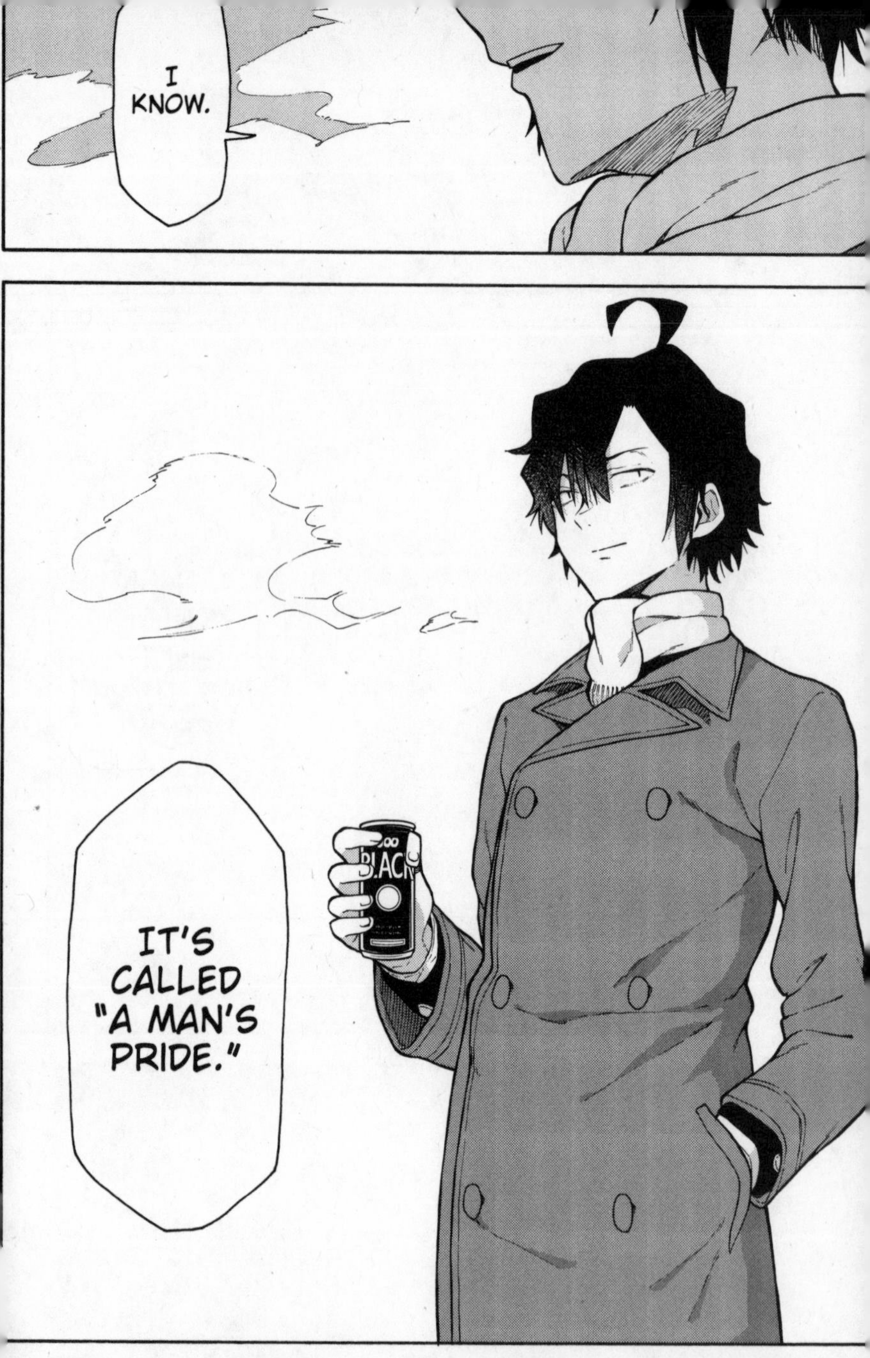
I KNOW.
IT'S CALLED "A MAN'S PRIDE."

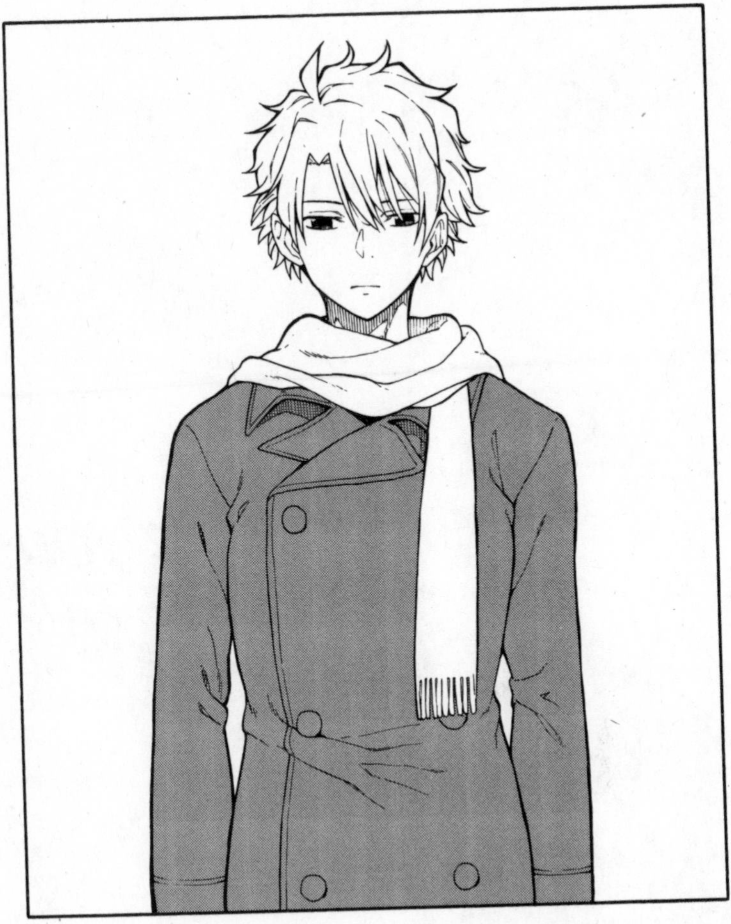

CHAPTER 100.5 ··· INTERLUDE HAYATO HAYAMA.

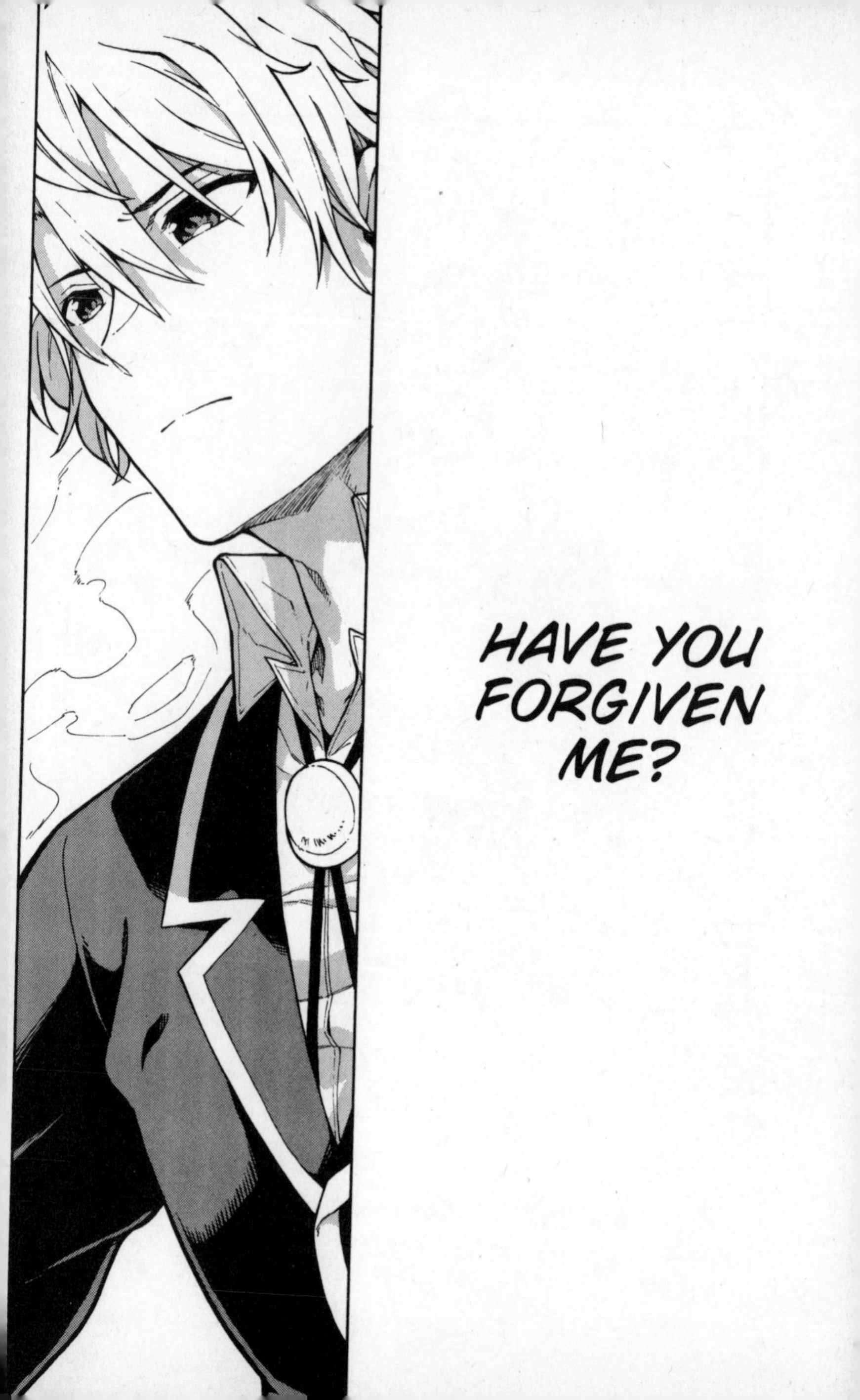
HAVE YOU FORGIVEN ME?

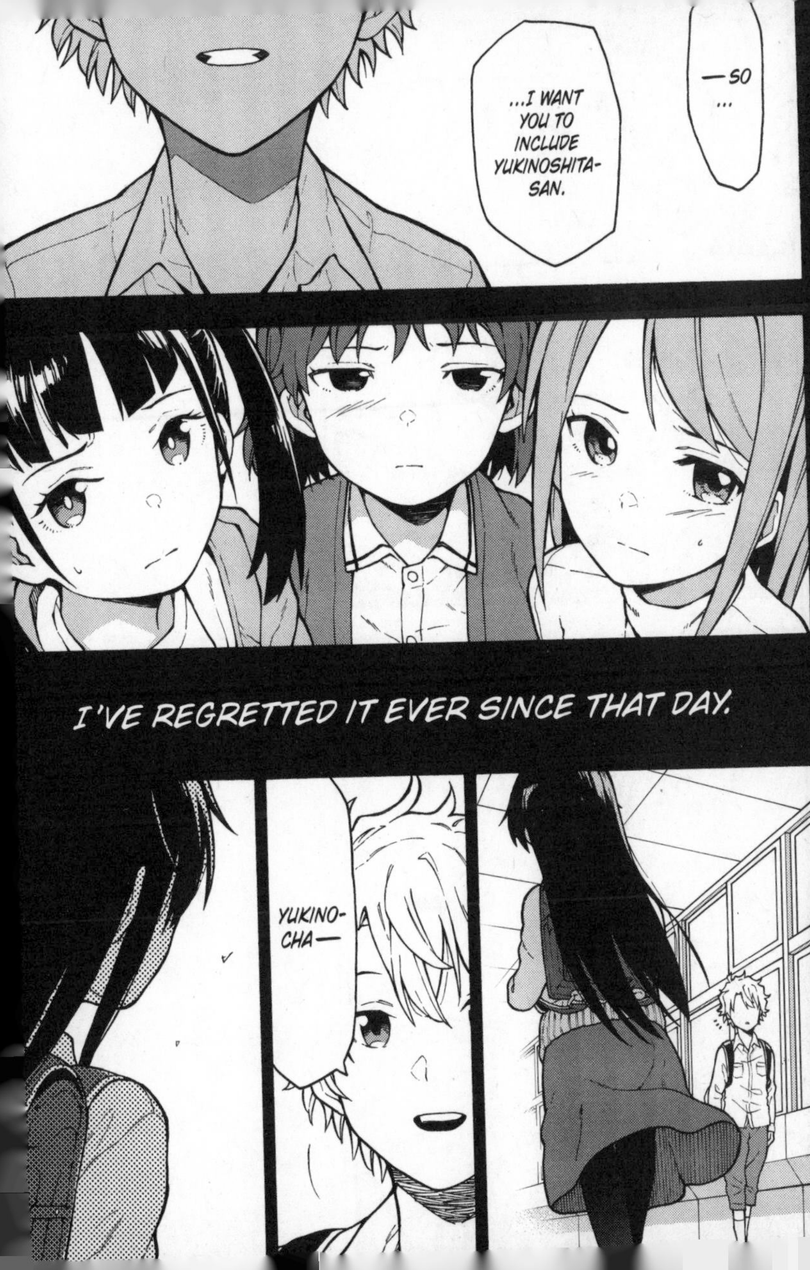
—SO ...
...I WANT YOU TO INCLUDE YUKINOSHITA-SAN.
I'VE REGRETTED IT EVER SINCE THAT DAY.
YUKINO-CHA—

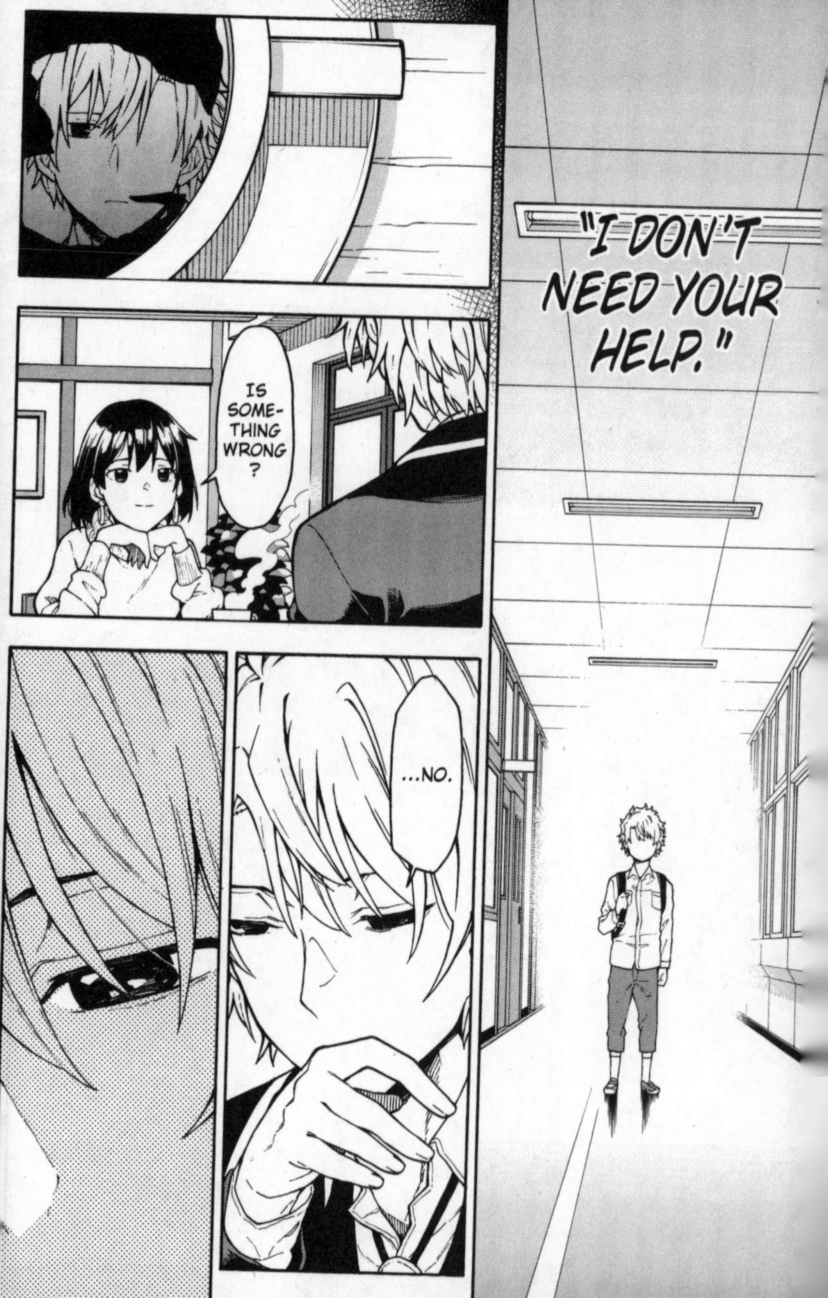
"I DON'T NEED YOUR HELP."
IS SOMETHING WRONG?
...NO.

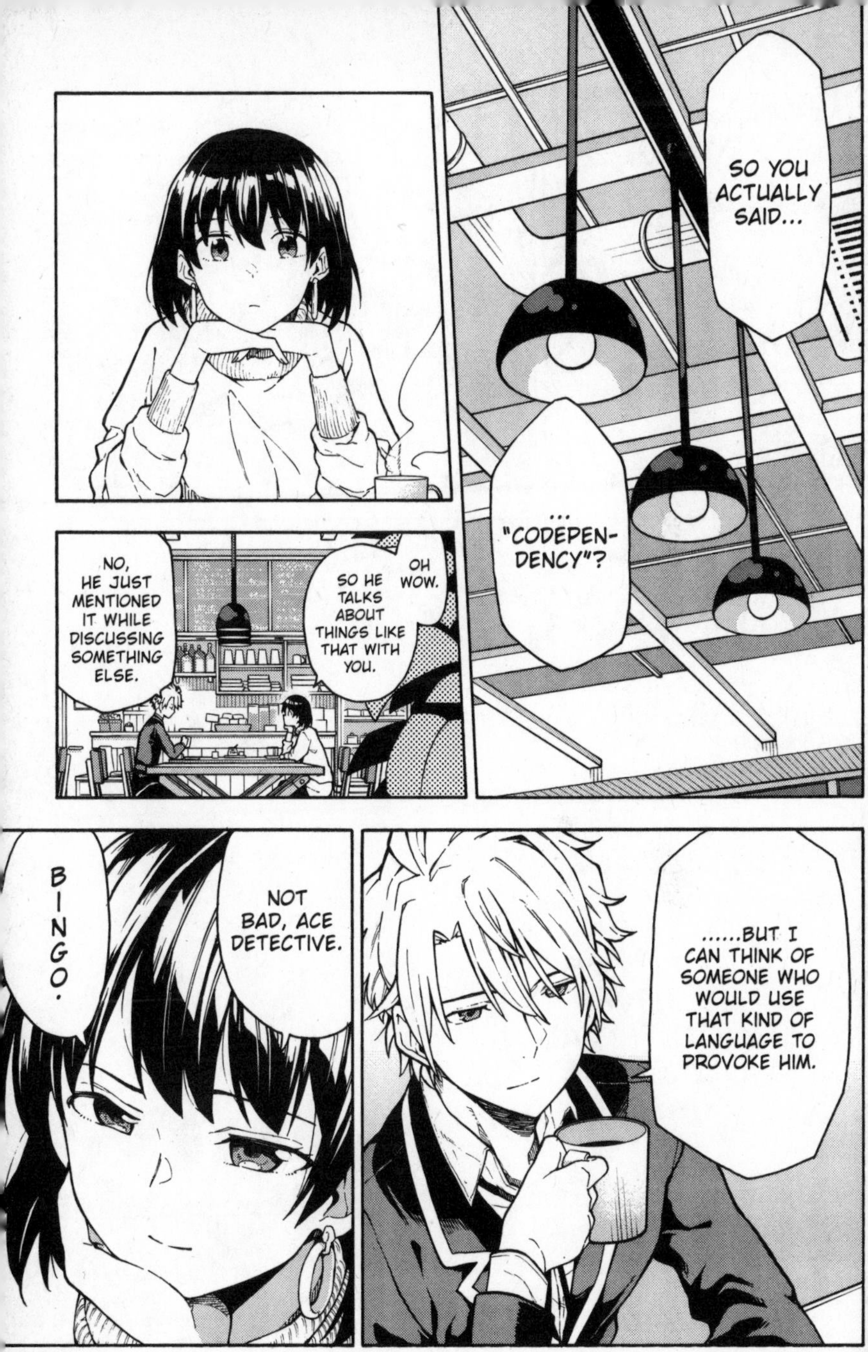
SO YOU ACTUALLY SAID...
... "CODEPENDENCY"?
OH WOW.
SO HE TALKS ABOUT THINGS LIKE THAT WITH YOU.
NO, HE JUST MENTIONED IT WHILE DISCUSSING SOMETHING ELSE.
......BUT I CAN THINK OF SOMEONE WHO WOULD USE THAT KIND OF LANGUAGE TO PROVOKE HIM.
NOT BAD, ACE DETECTIVE.
BINGO.

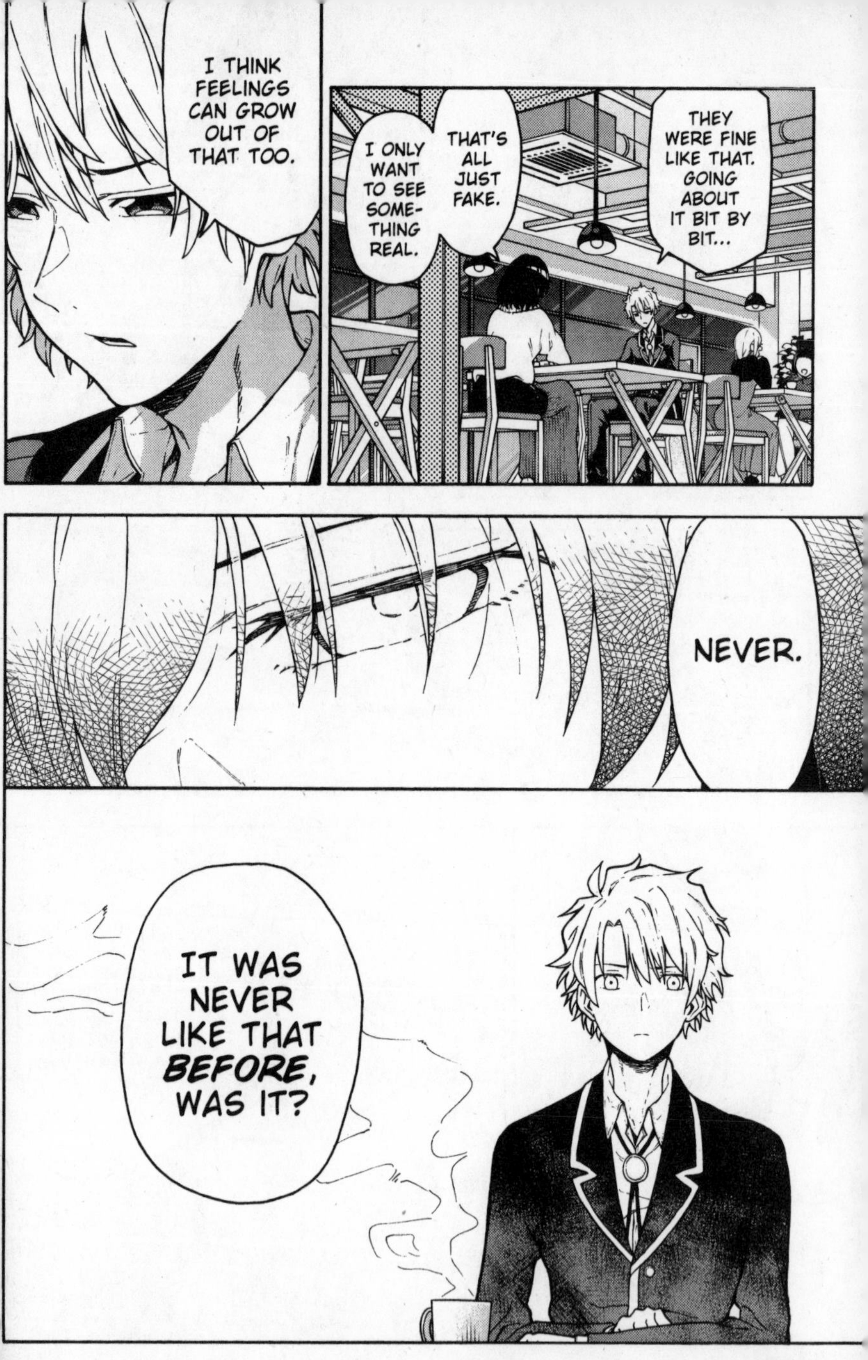
THEY WERE FINE LIKE THAT. GOING ABOUT IT BIT BY BIT...
THAT'S ALL JUST FAKE.
I ONLY WANT TO SEE SOME-THING REAL.
I THINK FEELINGS CAN GROW OUT OF THAT TOO.
NEVER.
IT WAS NEVER LIKE THAT *BEFORE*, WAS IT?

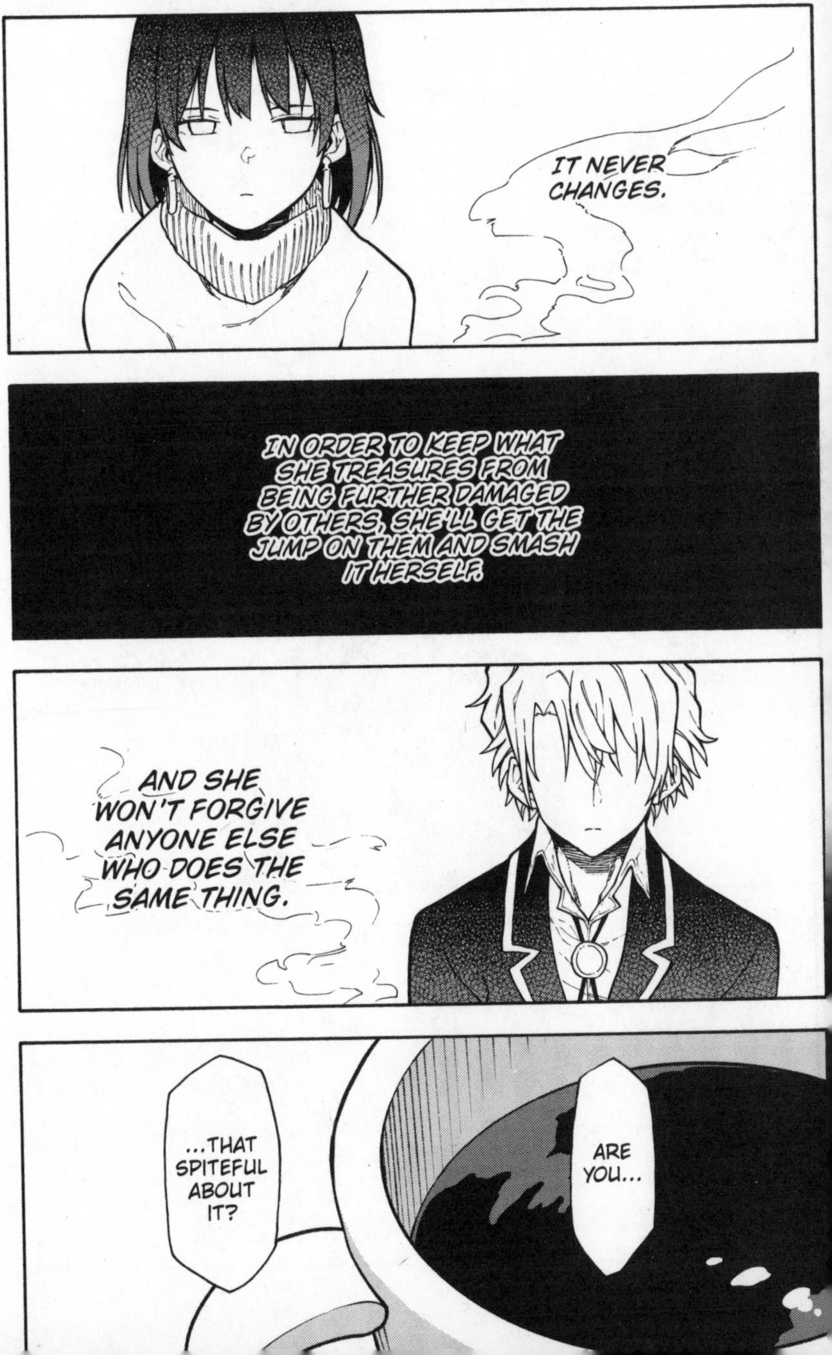
IT NEVER CHANGES.
IN ORDER TO KEEP WHAT SHE TREASURES FROM BEING FURTHER DAMAGED BY OTHERS, SHE'LL GET THE JUMP ON THEM AND SMASH IT HERSELF.
AND SHE WON'T FORGIVE ANYONE ELSE WHO DOES THE SAME THING.
ARE YOU...
...THAT SPITEFUL ABOUT IT?

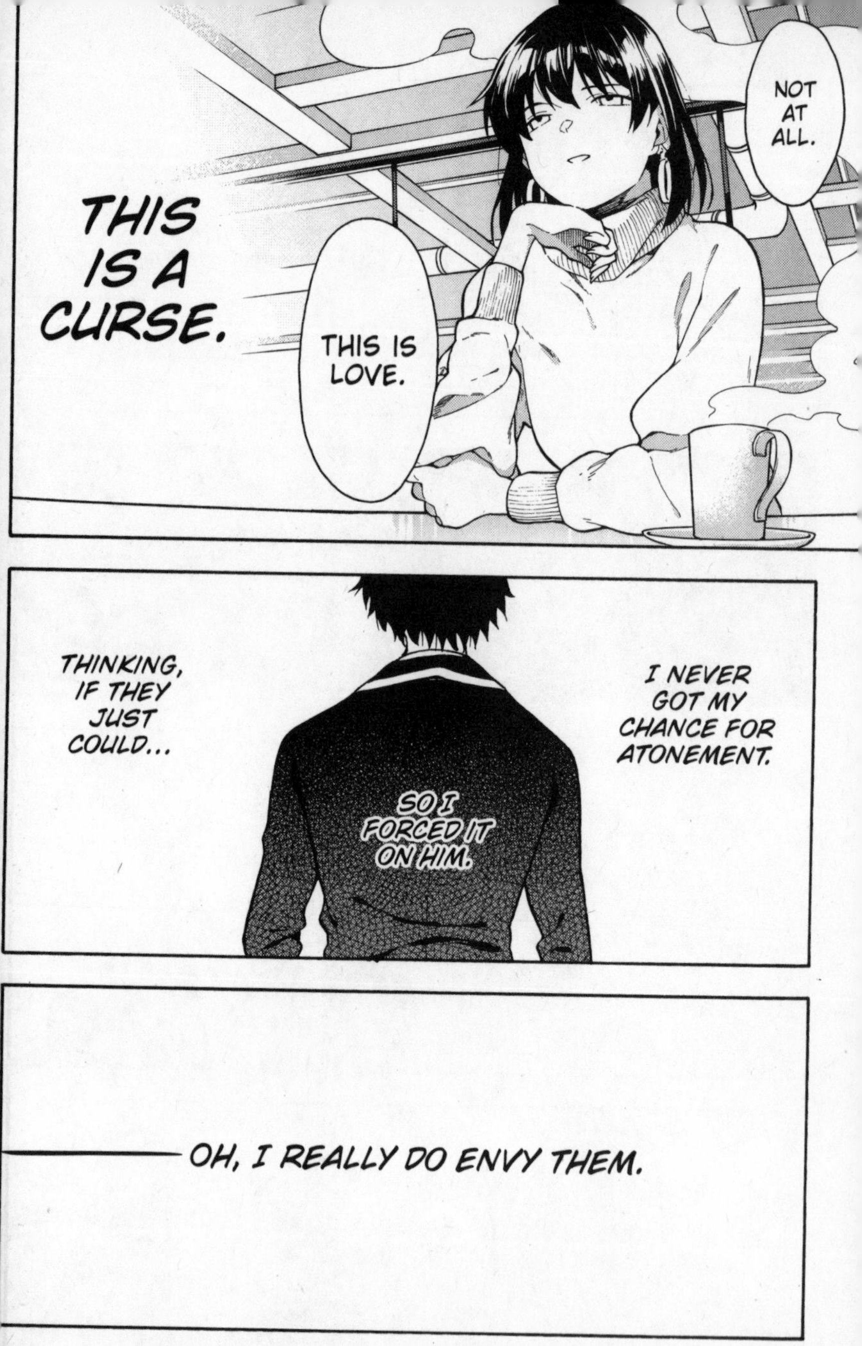
NOT AT ALL.
THIS IS LOVE.
THIS IS A CURSE.
I NEVER GOT MY CHANCE FOR ATONEMENT.
SO I FORCED IT ON HIM.
THINKING, IF THEY JUST COULD...
—OH, I REALLY DO ENVY THEM.

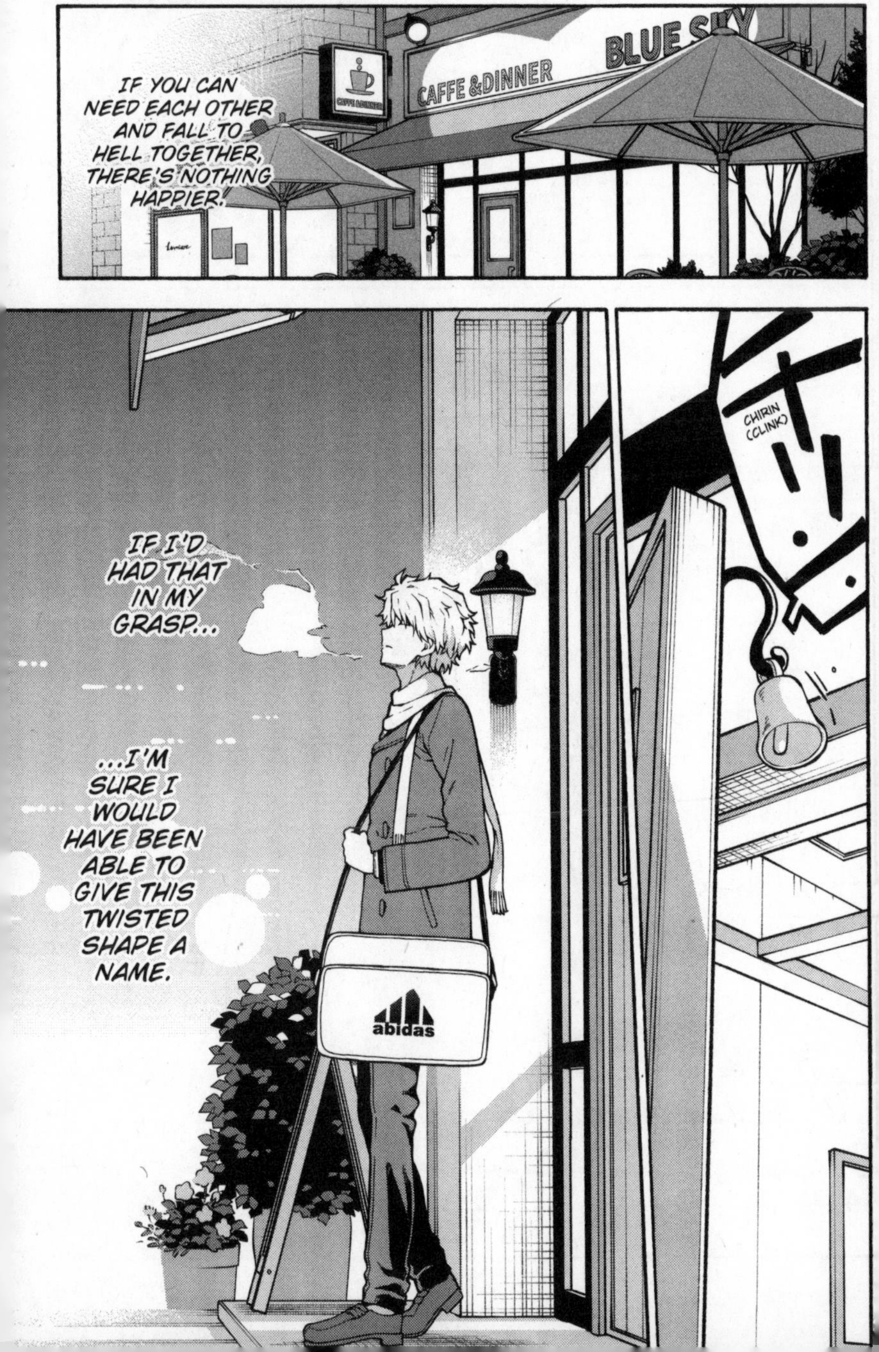
BLUE SKY
CAFFE &DINNER
IF YOU CAN NEED EACH OTHER AND FALL TO HELL TOGETHER, THERE'S NOTHING HAPPIER.
CHIRIN (CLINK)
IF I'D HAD THAT IN MY GRASP...
...I'M SURE I WOULD HAVE BEEN ABLE TO GIVE THIS TWISTED SHAPE A NAME.
abidas

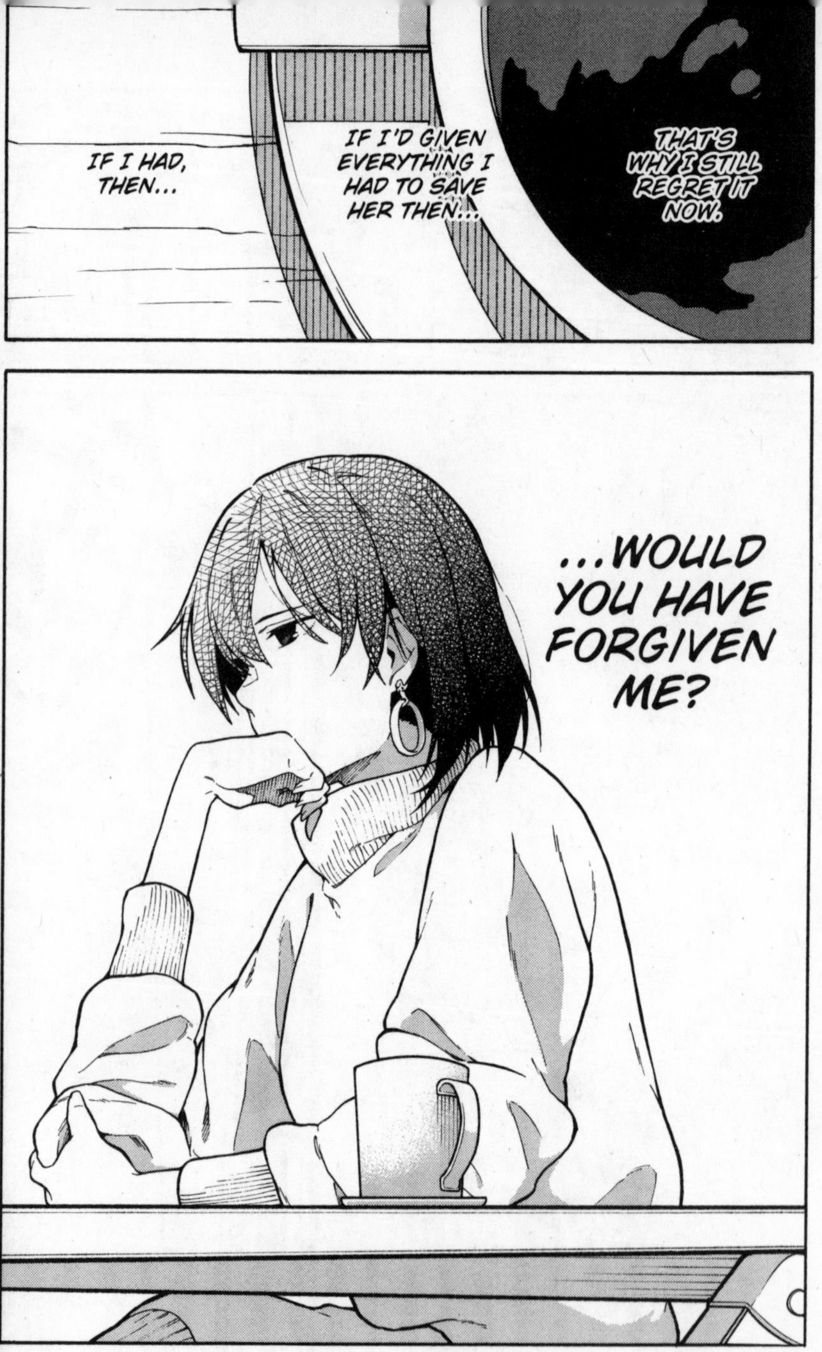
THAT'S WHY I STILL REGRET IT NOW.
IF I'D GIVEN EVERYTHING I HAD TO SAVE HER THEN...
IF I HAD, THEN...
...WOULD YOU HAVE FORGIVEN ME?

CHAPTER 101 … WHAT HIBA EBINA SEES THROUGH THE LENS IS.

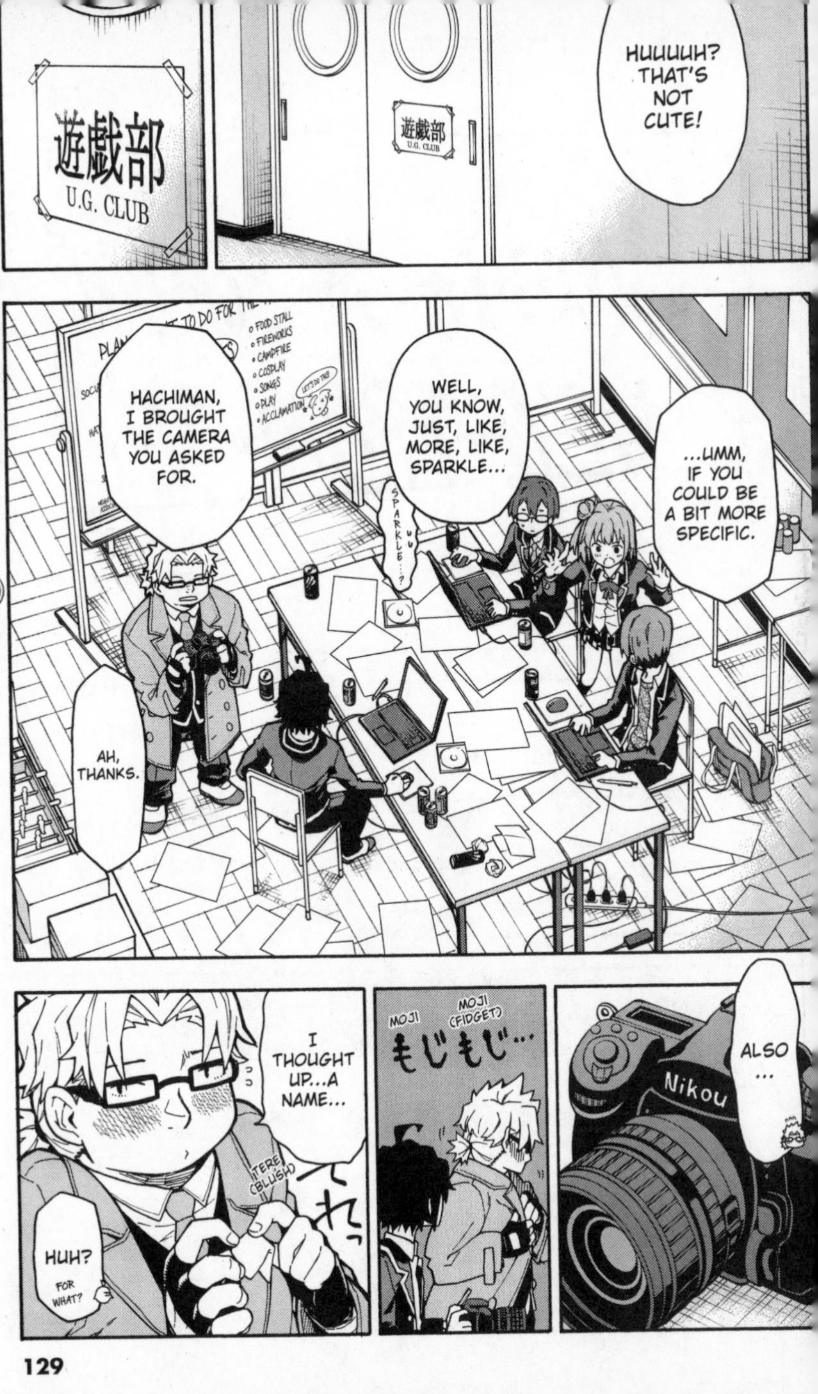
HUUUUH? THAT'S NOT CUTE!
遊戯部 U.G. CLUB
遊戯部 U.G. CLUB
...UMM, IF YOU COULD BE A BIT MORE SPECIFIC.
WELL, YOU KNOW, JUST, LIKE, MORE, LIKE, SPARKLE...
SPARKLE...?
FOOD STALL
FIREWORKS
CAMPFIRE
COSPLAY
SONGS
PLAY
ACCLAMATION
LET'S DO THIS!
HACHIMAN, I BROUGHT THE CAMERA YOU ASKED FOR.
AH, THANKS.
ALSO...
Nikou
MOJI MOJI (FIDGET)
もじもじ…
I THOUGHT UP...A NAME...
TERE (BLUSH)
てれっ
HUH?
FOR WHAT?

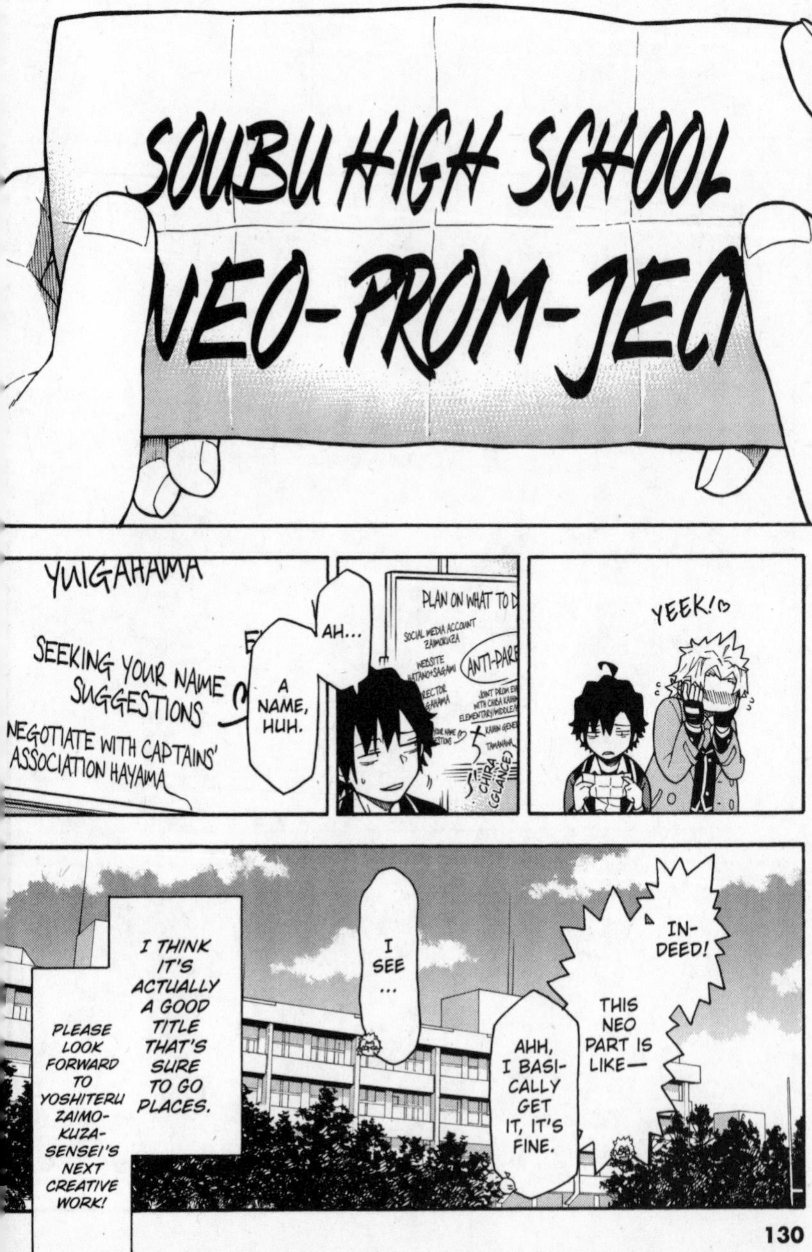
SOUBU HIGH SCHOOL
NEO-PROM-JEC
YEEK!♡
AH...
A NAME, HUH.
PLAN ON WHAT TO D
SOCIAL MEDIA ACCOUNT ZAIMOKUZA
CHIRA (GLANCE)
YUIGAHAMA
SEEKING YOUR NAME SUGGESTIONS
NEGOTIATE WITH CAPTAINS' ASSOCIATION HAYAMA
IN-DEED!
THIS NEO PART IS LIKE—
AHH, I BASICALLY GET IT, IT'S FINE.
I SEE...
I THINK IT'S ACTUALLY A GOOD TITLE THAT'S SURE TO GO PLACES.
PLEASE LOOK FORWARD TO YOSHITERU ZAIMOKUZA-SENSEI'S NEXT CREATIVE WORK!

CHAPTER 101 ··· WHAT HINA EBINA SEES THROUGH THE LENS IS...

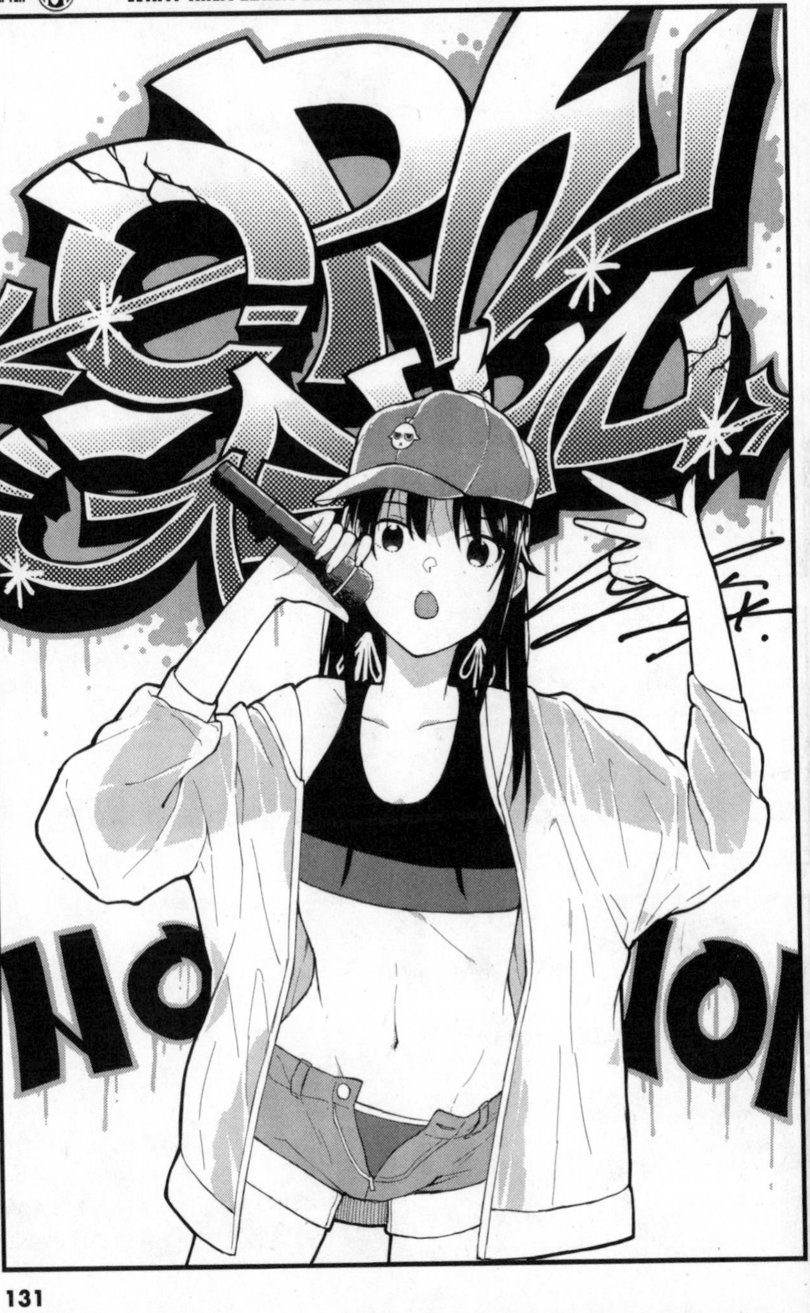

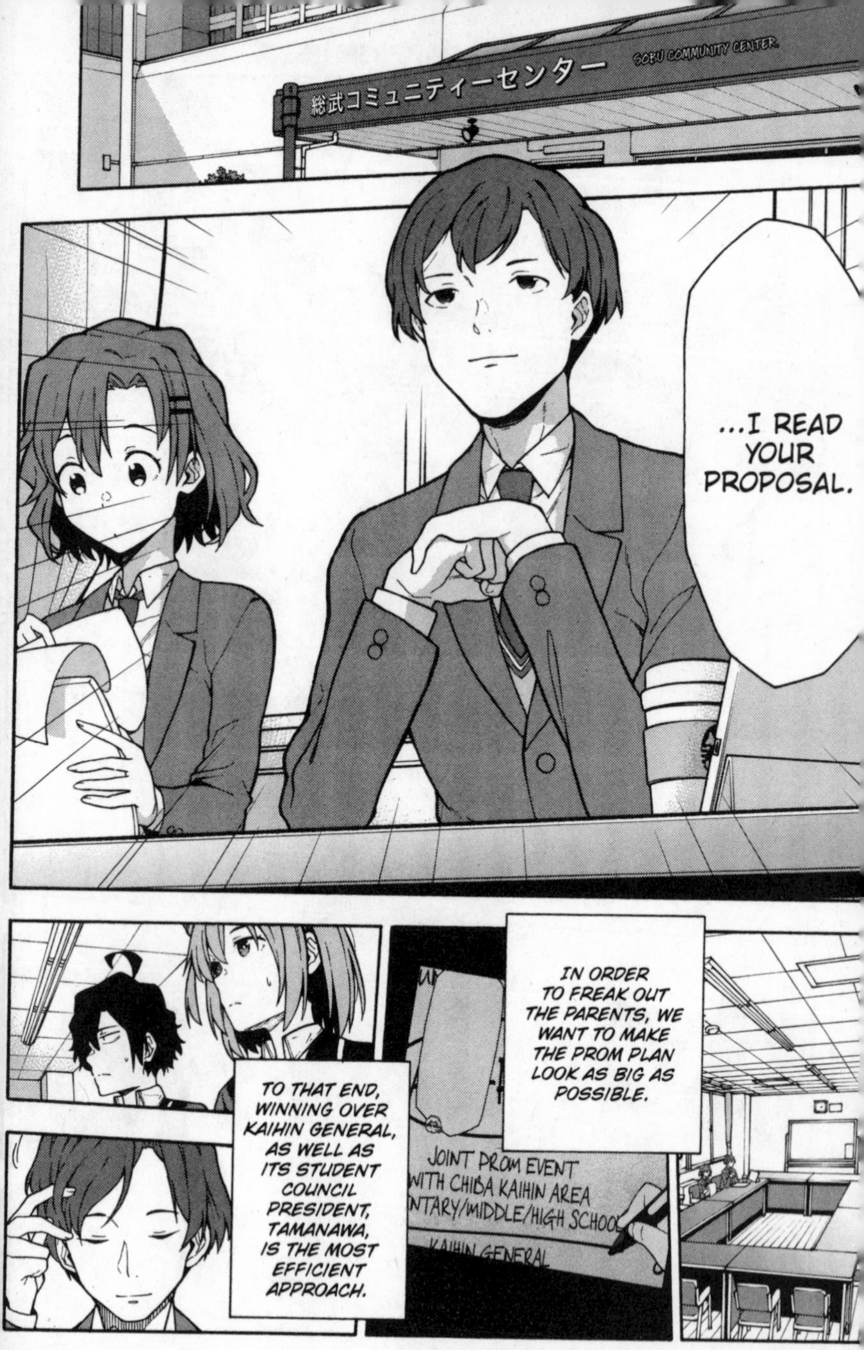
総武コミュニティーセンター
SOBU COMMUNITY CENTER.
...I READ YOUR PROPOSAL.
IN ORDER TO FREAK OUT THE PARENTS, WE WANT TO MAKE THE PROM PLAN LOOK AS BIG AS POSSIBLE.
JOINT PROM EVENT WITH CHIBA KAIHIN AREA
NTARY/MIDDLE/HIGH SCHOOL
KAIHIN GENERAL
TO THAT END, WINNING OVER KAIHIN GENERAL, AS WELL AS ITS STUDENT COUNCIL PRESIDENT, TAMANAWA, IS THE MOST EFFICIENT APPROACH.

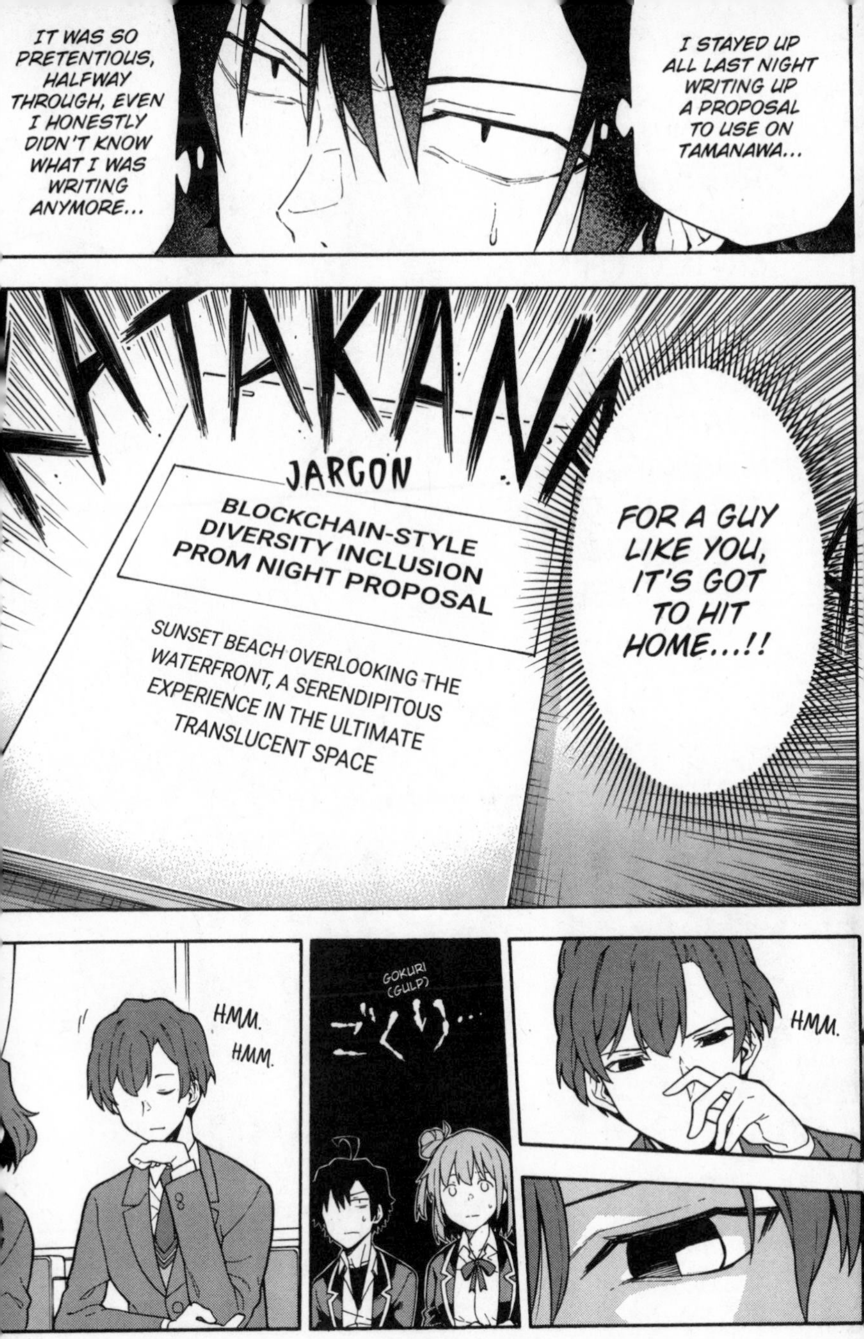
I STAYED UP ALL LAST NIGHT WRITING UP A PROPOSAL TO USE ON TAMANAWA...
IT WAS SO PRETENTIOUS, HALFWAY THROUGH, EVEN I HONESTLY DIDN'T KNOW WHAT I WAS WRITING ANYMORE...
KATAKANA
JARGON
FOR A GUY LIKE YOU, IT'S GOT TO HIT HOME...!!
BLOCKCHAIN-STYLE DIVERSITY INCLUSION PROM NIGHT PROPOSAL
SUNSET BEACH OVERLOOKING THE WATERFRONT, A SERENDIPITOUS EXPERIENCE IN THE ULTIMATE TRANSLUCENT SPACE
HMM.
GOKURI (GULP)
ごくり…
HMM.
HMM.

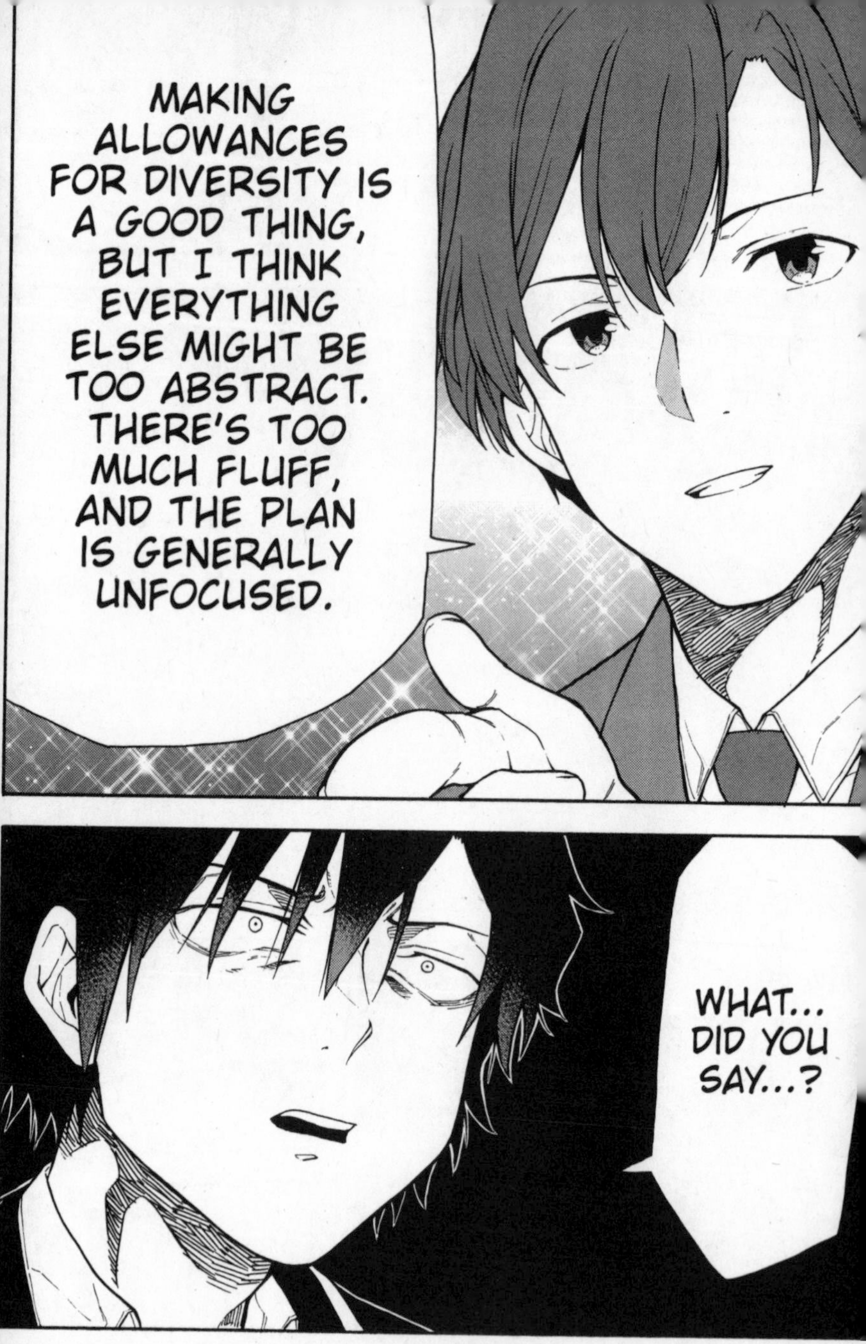
MAKING ALLOWANCES FOR DIVERSITY IS A GOOD THING, BUT I THINK EVERYTHING ELSE MIGHT BE TOO ABSTRACT. THERE'S TOO MUCH FLUFF, AND THE PLAN IS GENERALLY UNFOCUSED.
WHAT... DID YOU SAY...?

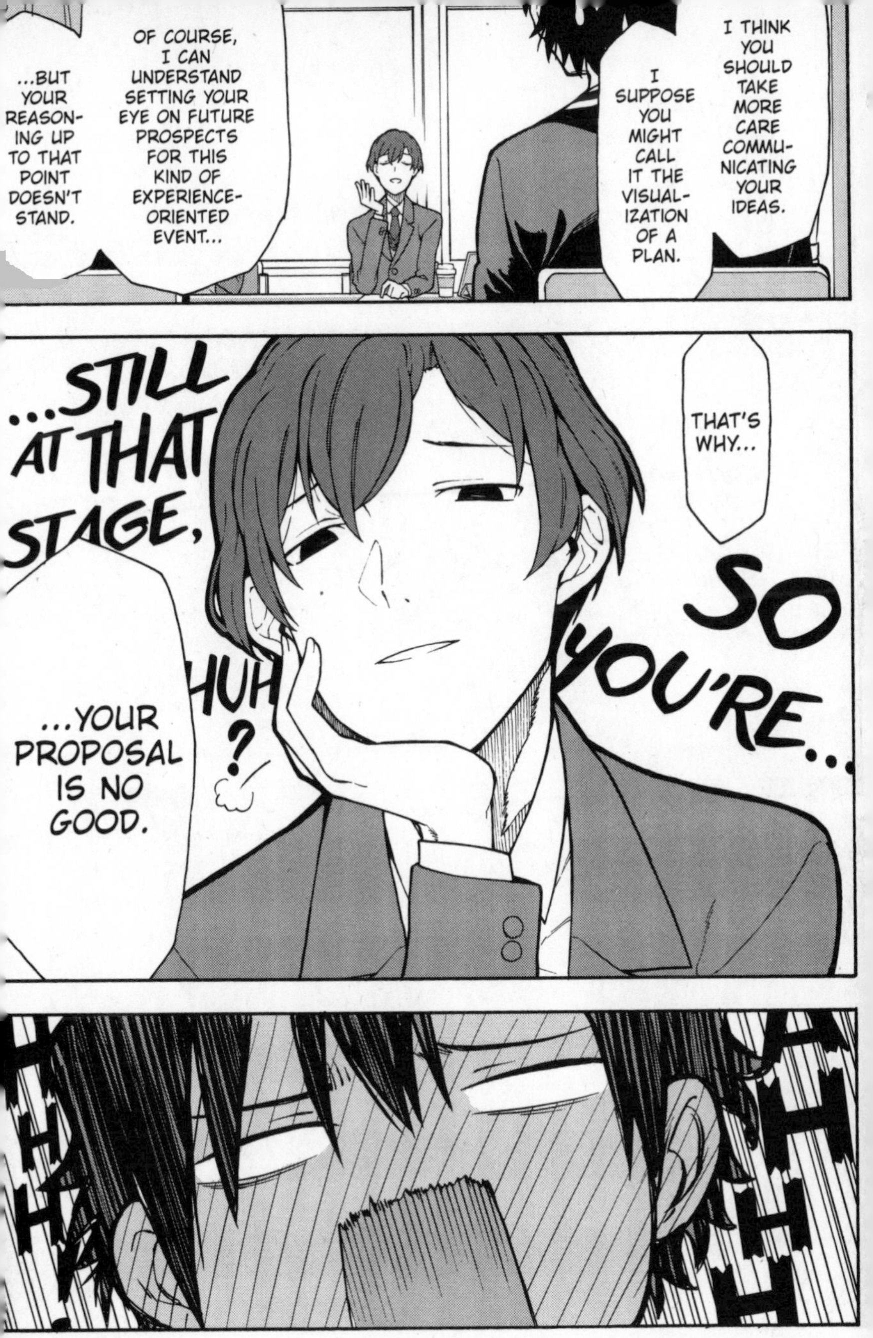
I THINK YOU SHOULD TAKE MORE CARE COMMUNICATING YOUR IDEAS.
I SUPPOSE YOU MIGHT CALL IT THE VISUALIZATION OF A PLAN.
OF COURSE, I CAN UNDERSTAND SETTING YOUR EYE ON FUTURE PROSPECTS FOR THIS KIND OF EXPERIENCE-ORIENTED EVENT...
...BUT YOUR REASONING UP TO THAT POINT DOESN'T STAND.
THAT'S WHY...
SO YOU'RE...
...STILL AT THAT STAGE,
HUH?
...YOUR PROPOSAL IS NO GOOD.

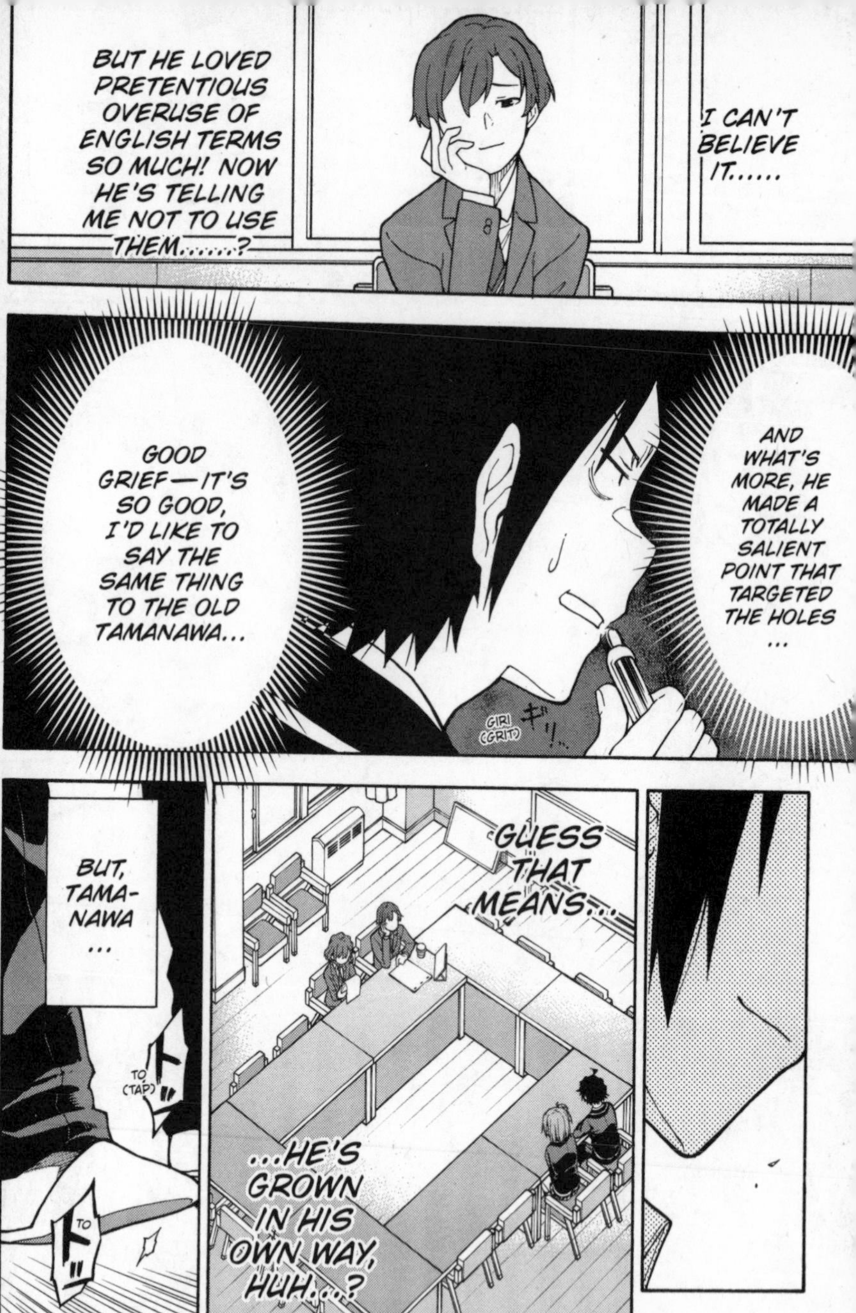

I CAN'T BELIEVE IT......
BUT HE LOVED PRETENTIOUS OVERUSE OF ENGLISH TERMS SO MUCH! NOW HE'S TELLING ME NOT TO USE THEM......?
AND WHAT'S MORE, HE MADE A TOTALLY SALIENT POINT THAT TARGETED THE HOLES ...
GOOD GRIEF—IT'S SO GOOD, I'D LIKE TO SAY THE SAME THING TO THE OLD TAMANAWA...
ギリ…
GIRI (GRIT)
GUESS THAT MEANS...
...HE'S GROWN IN HIS OWN WAY, HUH...?
BUT, TAMA-NAWA ...
ト
TO (TAP)
ト
TO

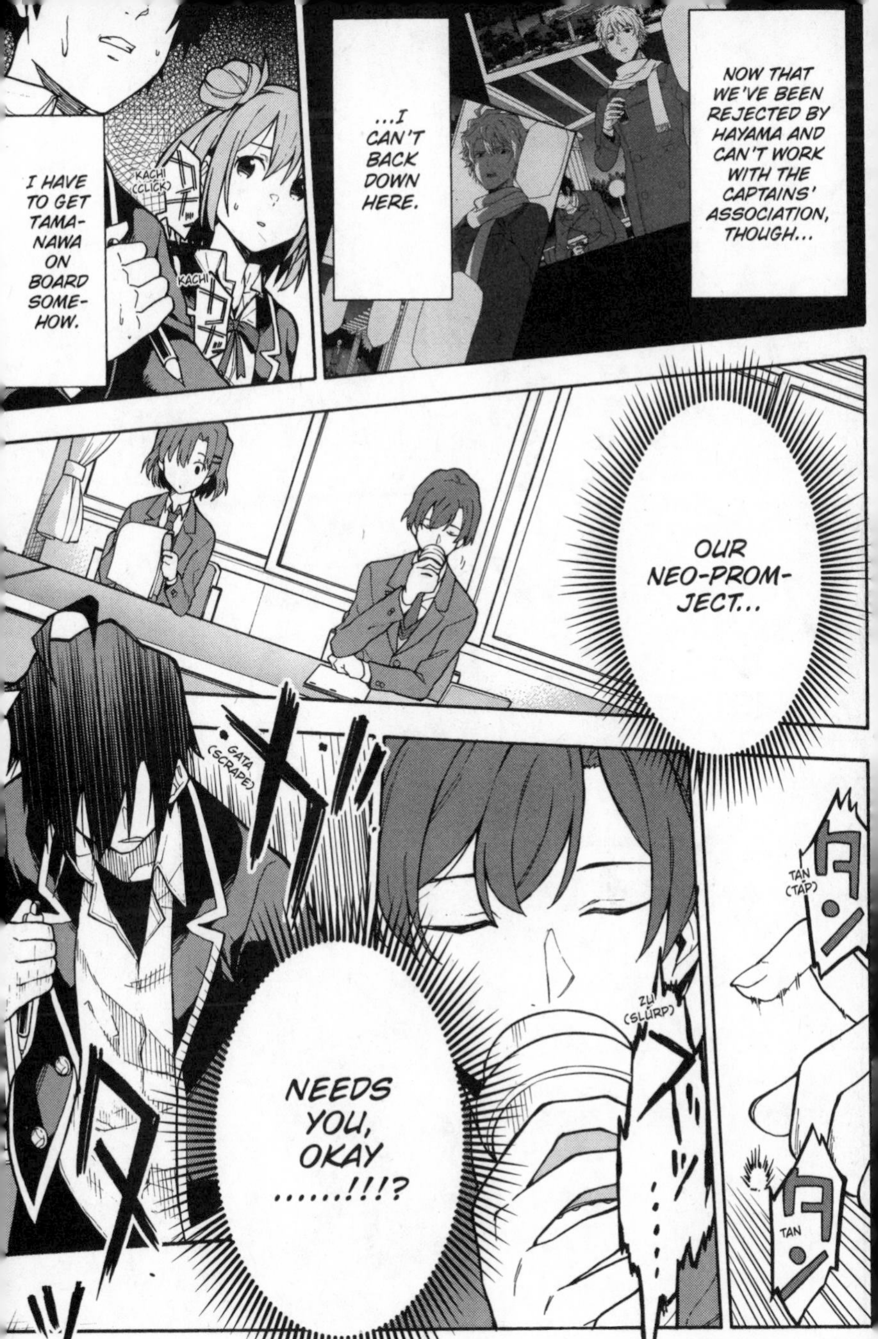
NOW THAT WE'VE BEEN REJECTED BY HAYAMA AND CAN'T WORK WITH THE CAPTAINS' ASSOCIATION, THOUGH...
...I CAN'T BACK DOWN HERE.
KACHI (CLICK)
KACHI
I HAVE TO GET TAMA-NAWA ON BOARD SOME-HOW.
OUR NEO-PROM-JECT...
TAN (TAP)
TAN
ZU (SLURP)
NEEDS YOU, OKAY ......!!!?
GATA (SCRAPE)

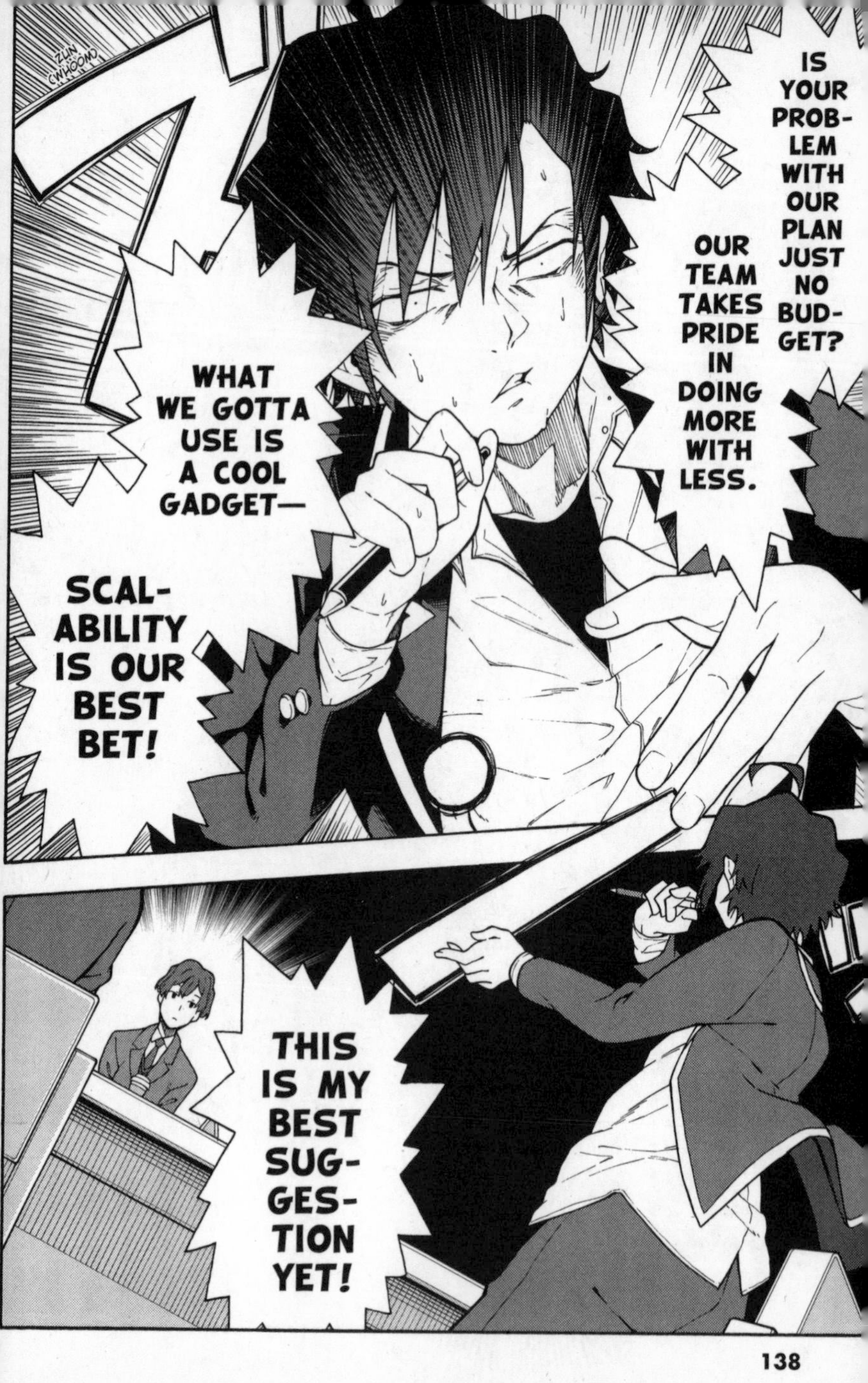
IS YOUR PROBLEM WITH OUR PLAN JUST NO BUDGET?
OUR TEAM TAKES PRIDE IN DOING MORE WITH LESS.
ZUN (WHOOOM)
WHAT WE GOTTA USE IS A COOL GADGET—
SCALABILITY IS OUR BEST BET!
THIS IS MY BEST SUGGESTION YET!

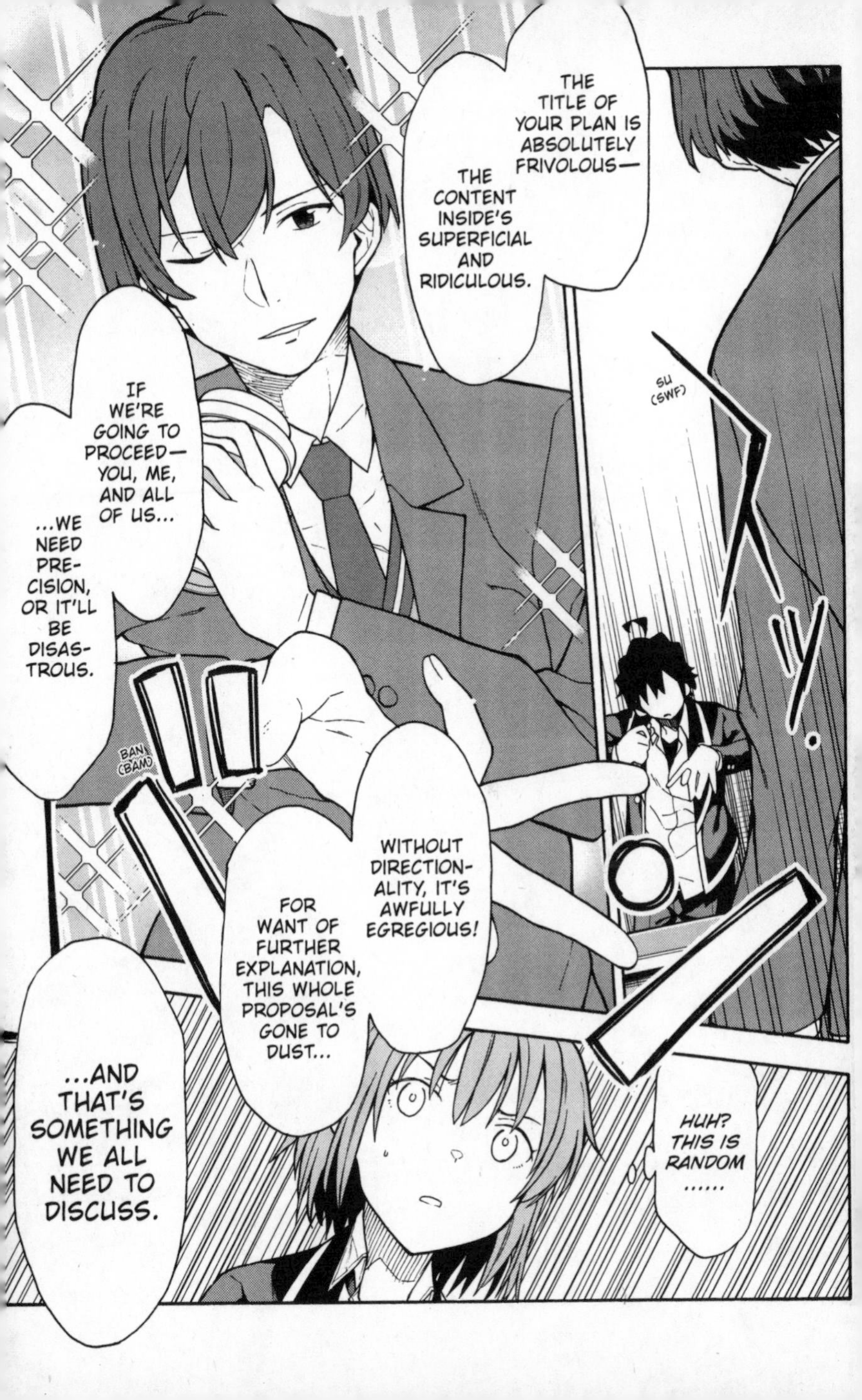
THE TITLE OF YOUR PLAN IS ABSOLUTELY FRIVOLOUS—
THE CONTENT INSIDE'S SUPERFICIAL AND RIDICULOUS.
SU (SWF)
IF WE'RE GOING TO PROCEED—YOU, ME, AND ALL OF US...
...WE NEED PRE-CISION, OR IT'LL BE DISAS-TROUS.
BAN (BAM)
WITHOUT DIRECTION-ALITY, IT'S AWFULLY EGREGIOUS!
FOR WANT OF FURTHER EXPLANATION, THIS WHOLE PROPOSAL'S GONE TO DUST...
HUH? THIS IS RANDOM......
...AND THAT'S SOMETHING WE ALL NEED TO DISCUSS.

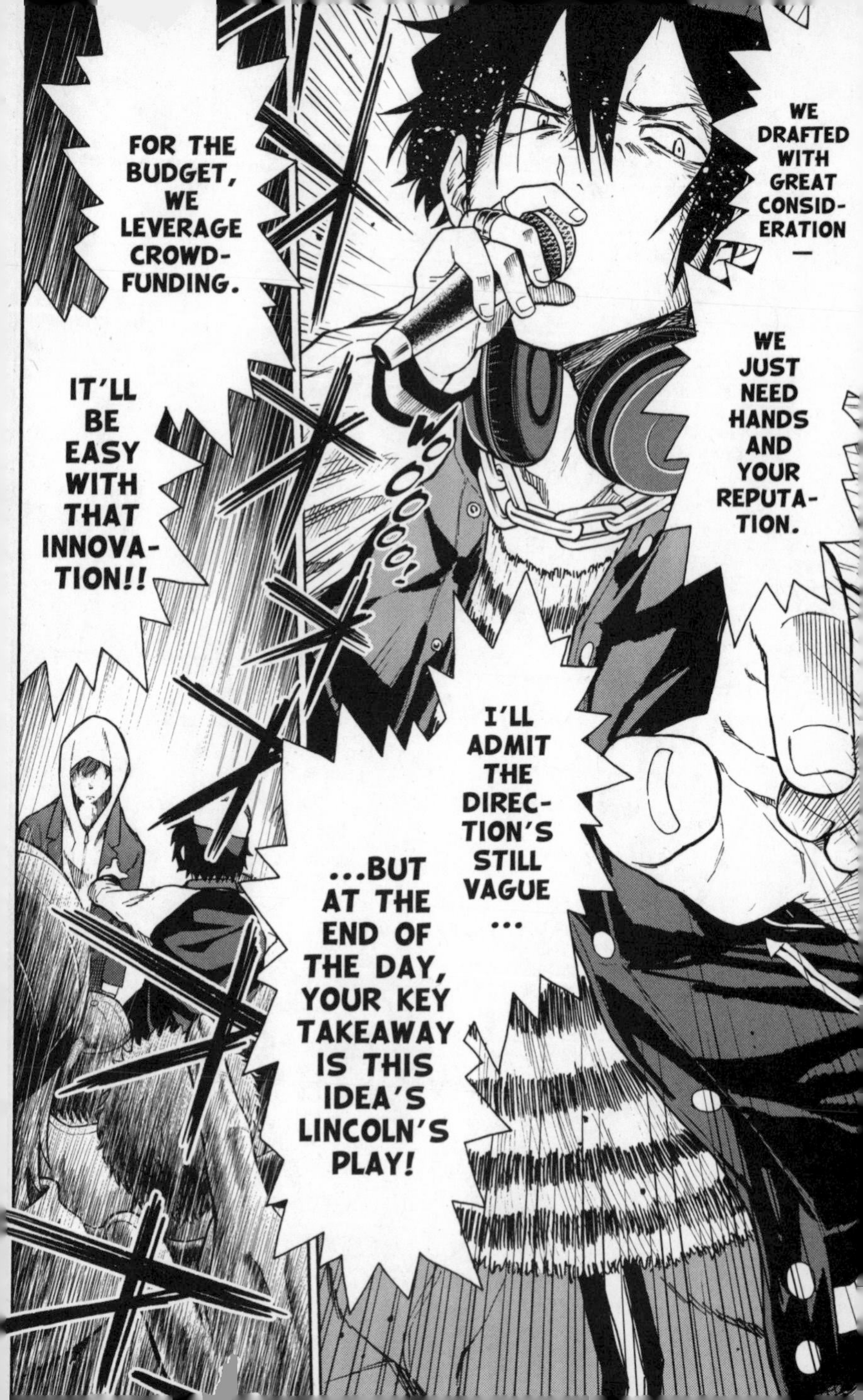
WE DRAFTED WITH GREAT CONSID-ERATION—
FOR THE BUDGET, WE LEVERAGE CROWD-FUNDING.
WE JUST NEED HANDS AND YOUR REPUTA-TION.
IT'LL BE EASY WITH THAT INNOVA-TION!!
WOOOOOOO!
I'LL ADMIT THE DIREC-TION'S STILL VAGUE...
...BUT AT THE END OF THE DAY, YOUR KEY TAKEAWAY IS THIS IDEA'S LINCOLN'S PLAY!

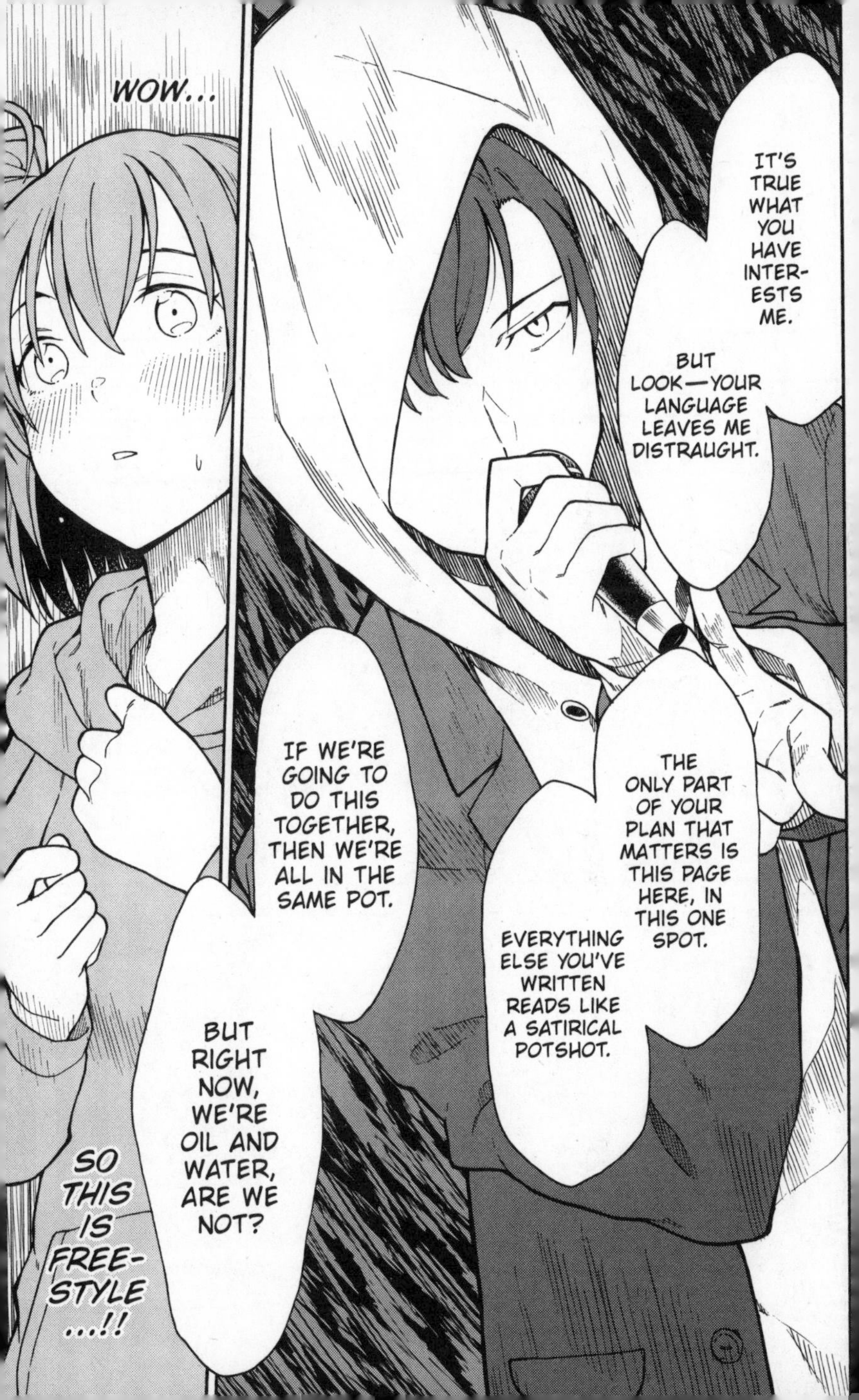
IT'S TRUE WHAT YOU HAVE INTERESTS ME.
BUT LOOK—YOUR LANGUAGE LEAVES ME DISTRAUGHT.
THE ONLY PART OF YOUR PLAN THAT MATTERS IS THIS PAGE HERE, IN THIS ONE SPOT.
EVERYTHING ELSE YOU'VE WRITTEN READS LIKE A SATIRICAL POTSHOT.
IF WE'RE GOING TO DO THIS TOGETHER, THEN WE'RE ALL IN THE SAME POT.
BUT RIGHT NOW, WE'RE OIL AND WATER, ARE WE NOT?
WOW...
SO THIS IS FREE-STYLE ...!!

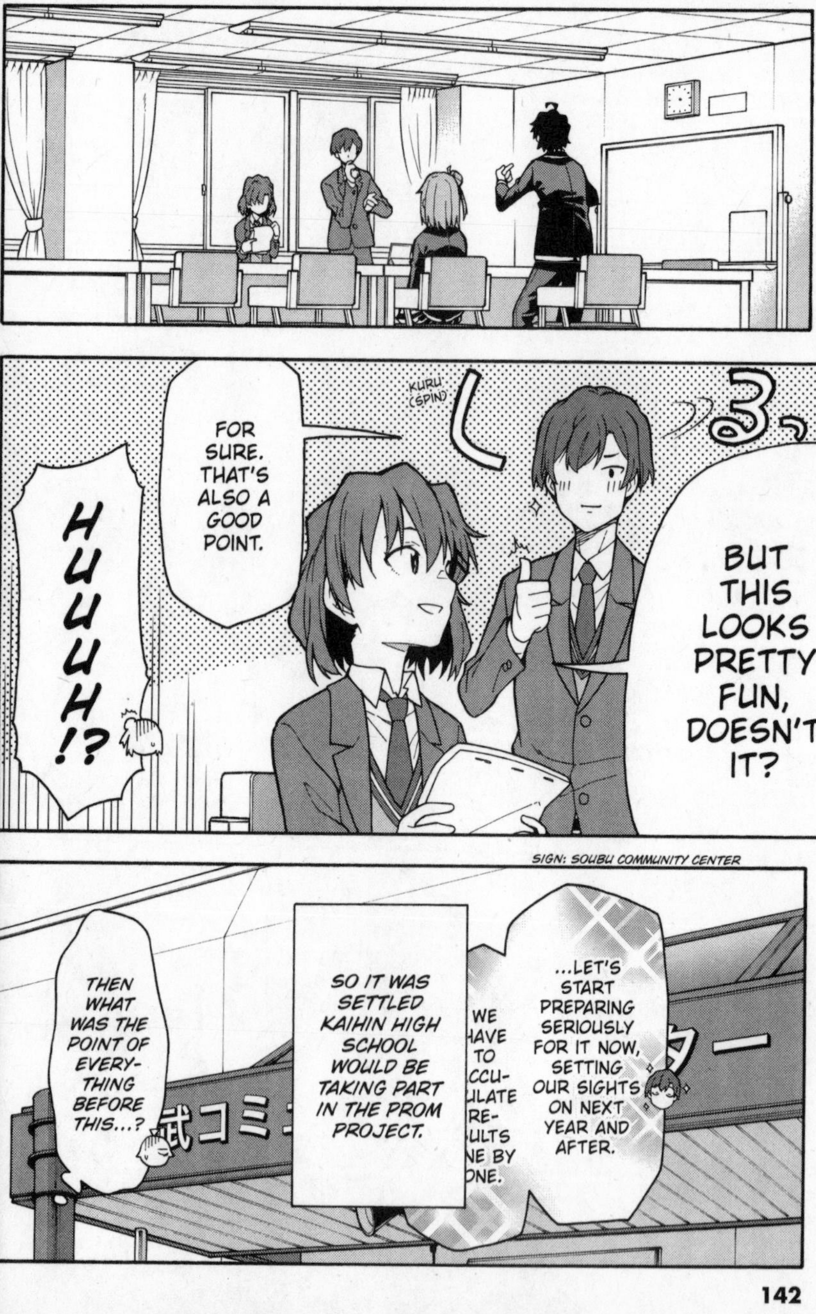
BUT THIS LOOKS PRETTY FUN, DOESN'T IT?
KURU (SPIN)
FOR SURE. THAT'S ALSO A GOOD POINT.
HUUUH!?
SIGN: SOUBU COMMUNITY CENTER
...LET'S START PREPARING SERIOUSLY FOR IT NOW, SETTING OUR SIGHTS ON NEXT YEAR AND AFTER.
WE HAVE TO CCU- ULATE RE- ULTS NE BY ONE.
SO IT WAS SETTLED KAIHIN HIGH SCHOOL WOULD BE TAKING PART IN THE PROM PROJECT.
THEN WHAT WAS THE POINT OF EVERY- THING BEFORE THIS...?

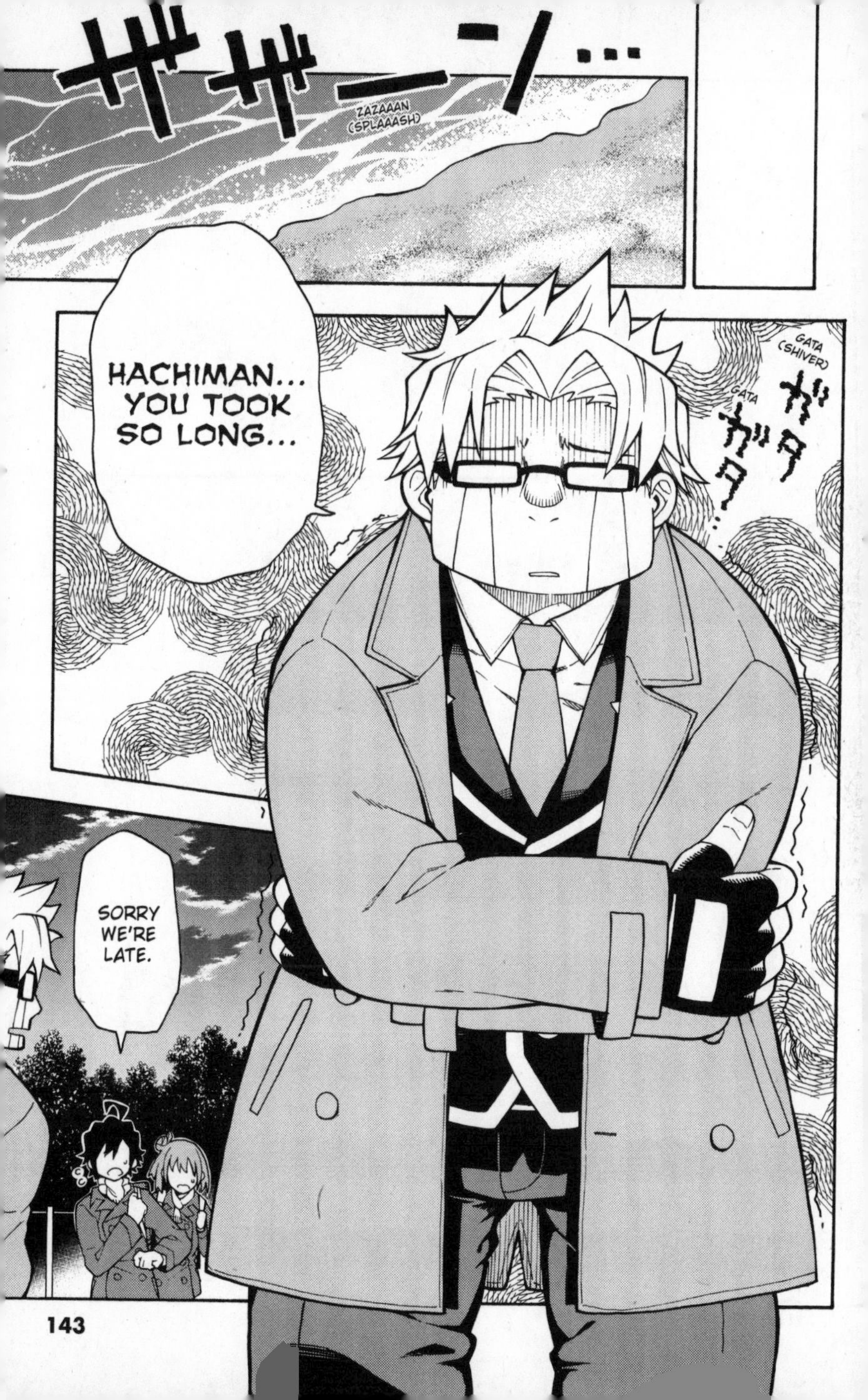
ザザーン…
ZAZAAAN
(SPLAAASH)
HACHIMAN... YOU TOOK SO LONG...
GATA (SHIVER)
ガタ
GATA
ガタ…
SORRY WE'RE LATE.

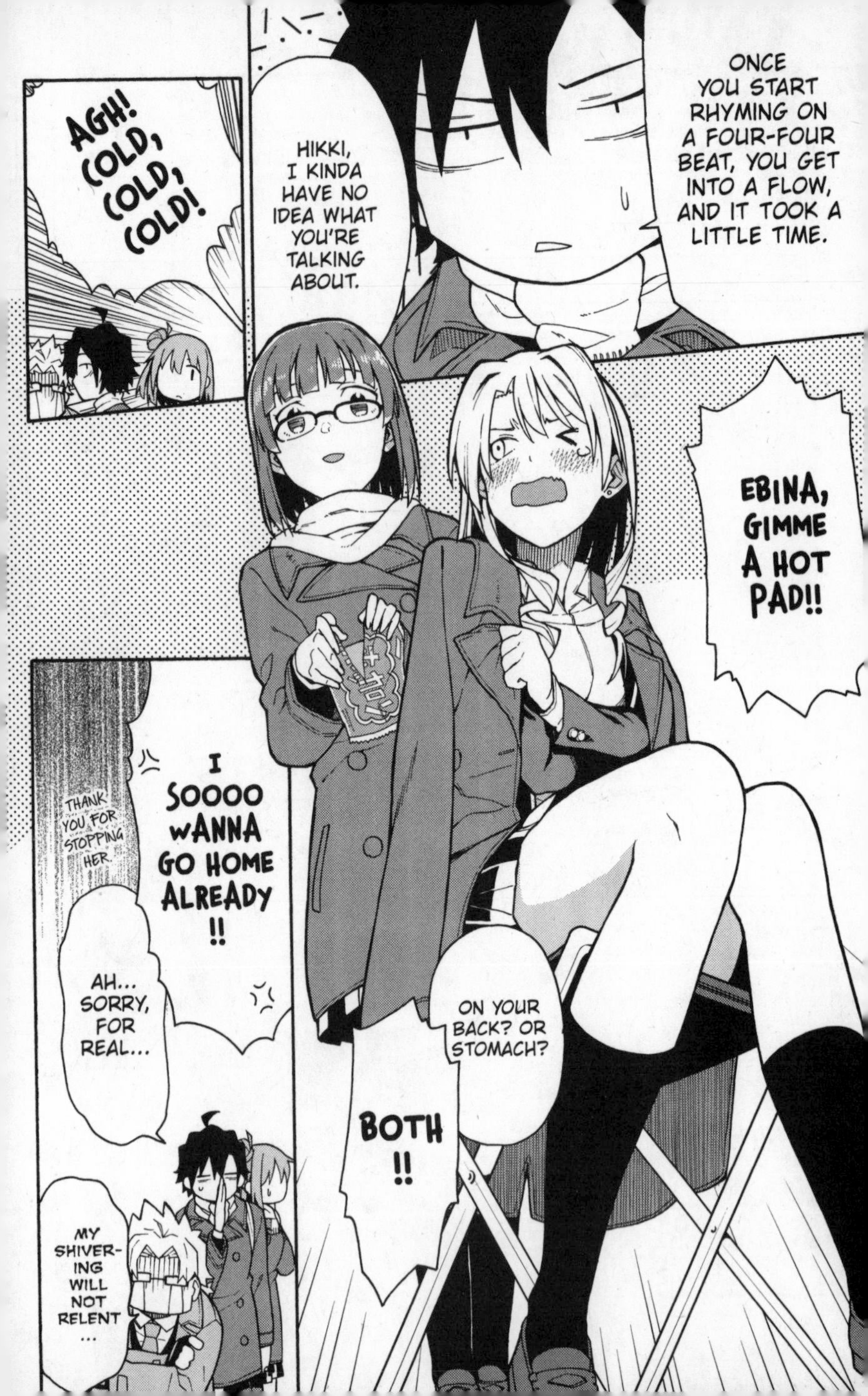

ONCE YOU START RHYMING ON A FOUR-FOUR BEAT, YOU GET INTO A FLOW, AND IT TOOK A LITTLE TIME.
HIKKI, I KINDA HAVE NO IDEA WHAT YOU'RE TALKING ABOUT.
AGH! COLD, COLD, COLD!
EBINA, GIMME A HOT PAD!!
ON YOUR BACK? OR STOMACH?
BOTH !!
I SOOOO wANNA GO HOME ALREADY !!
THANK YOU FOR STOPPING HER.
AH... SORRY, FOR REAL...
MY SHIVER-ING WILL NOT RELENT ...

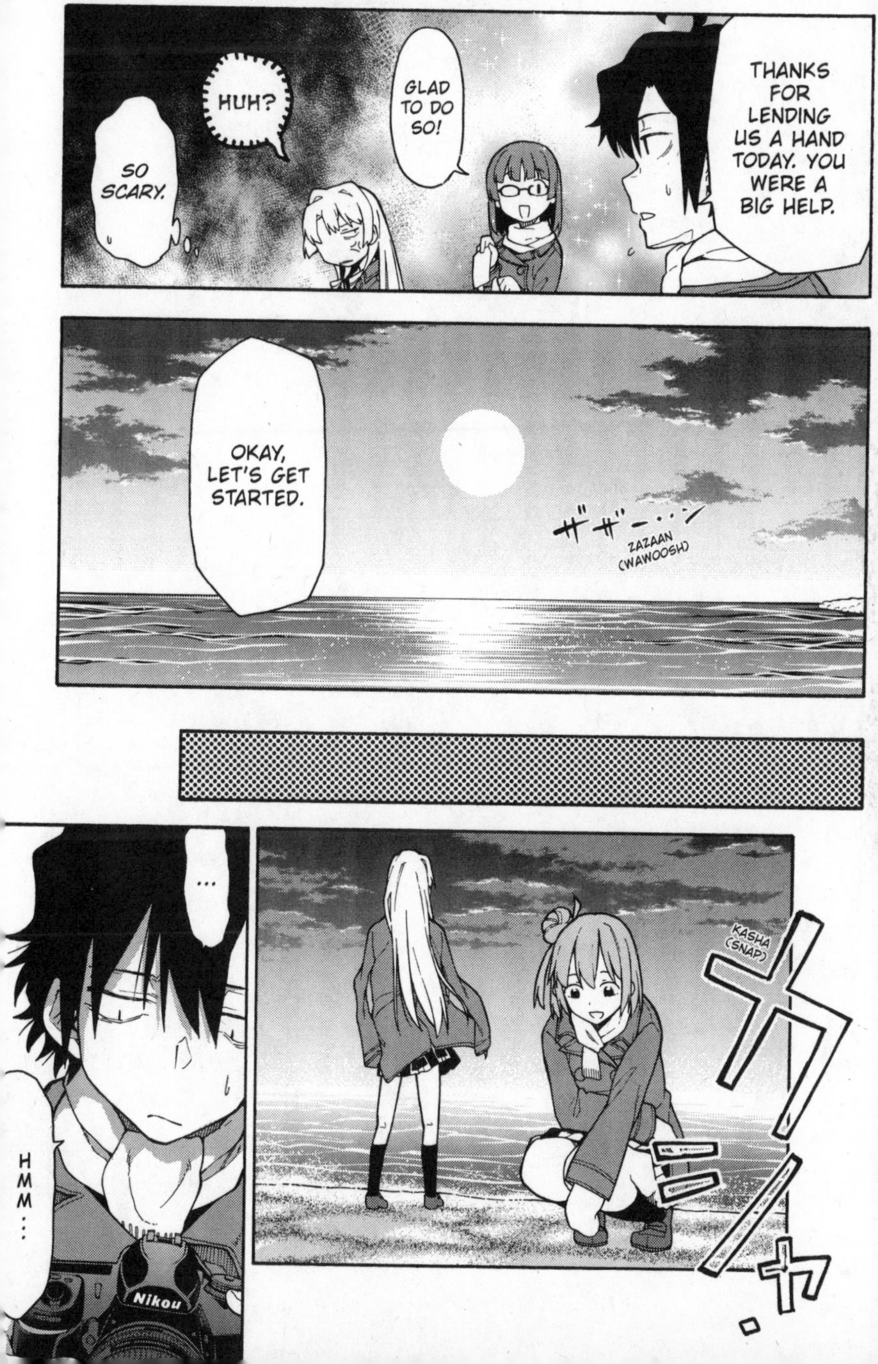
THANKS FOR LENDING US A HAND TODAY. YOU WERE A BIG HELP.
GLAD TO DO SO!
HUH?
SO SCARY.
OKAY, LET'S GET STARTED.
ZAZAAN (WAWOOSH)
KASHA (SNAP)
...
HMM...
Nikou

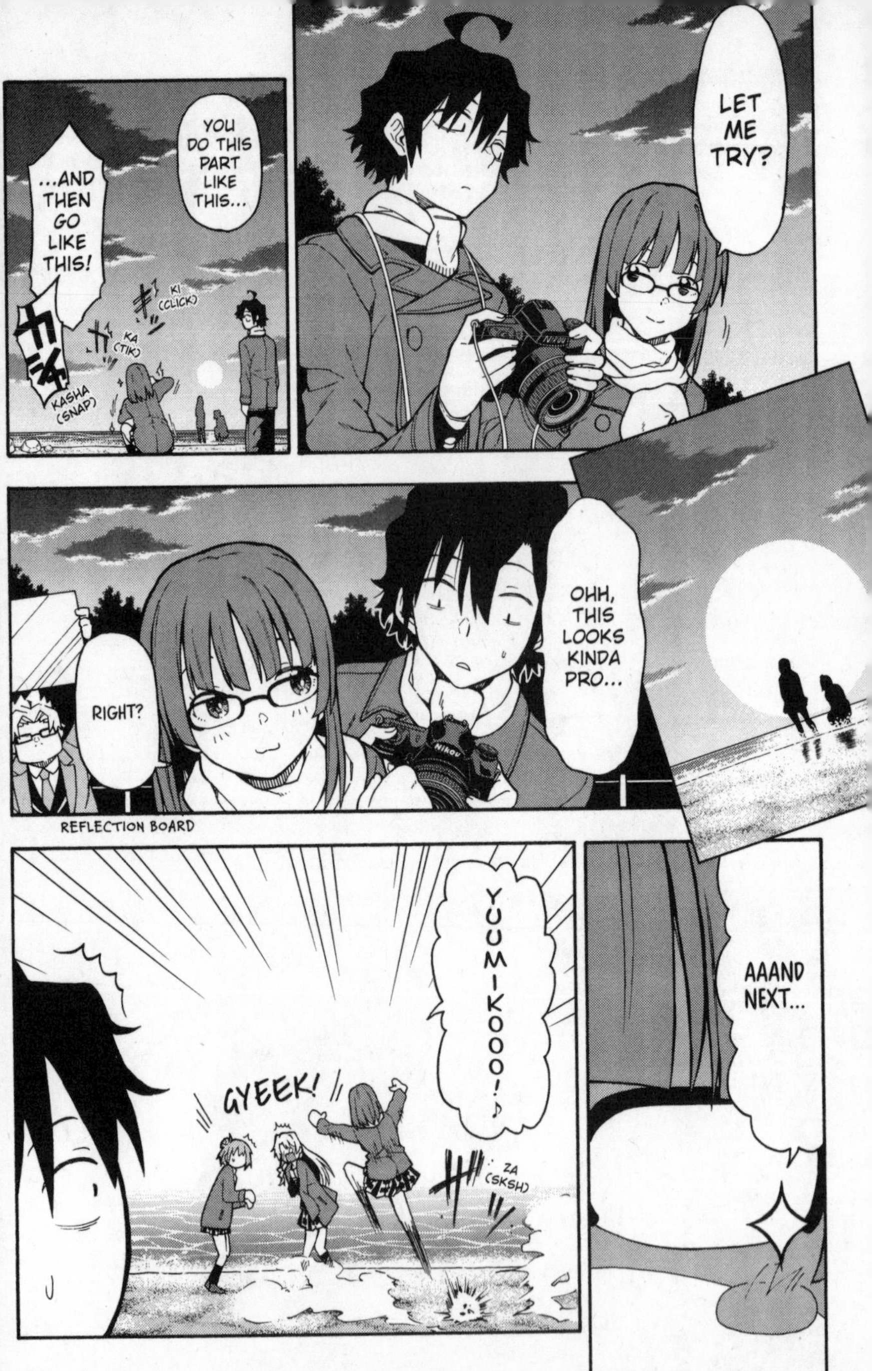
LET ME TRY?
YOU DO THIS PART LIKE THIS...
...AND THEN GO LIKE THIS!
KI (CLICK)
KA (TIK)
KASHA (SNAP)
OHH, THIS LOOKS KINDA PRO...
RIGHT?
REFLECTION BOARD
AAAND NEXT...
YUUMIKOOOO!♪
GYEEK!
ZA (SKSH)

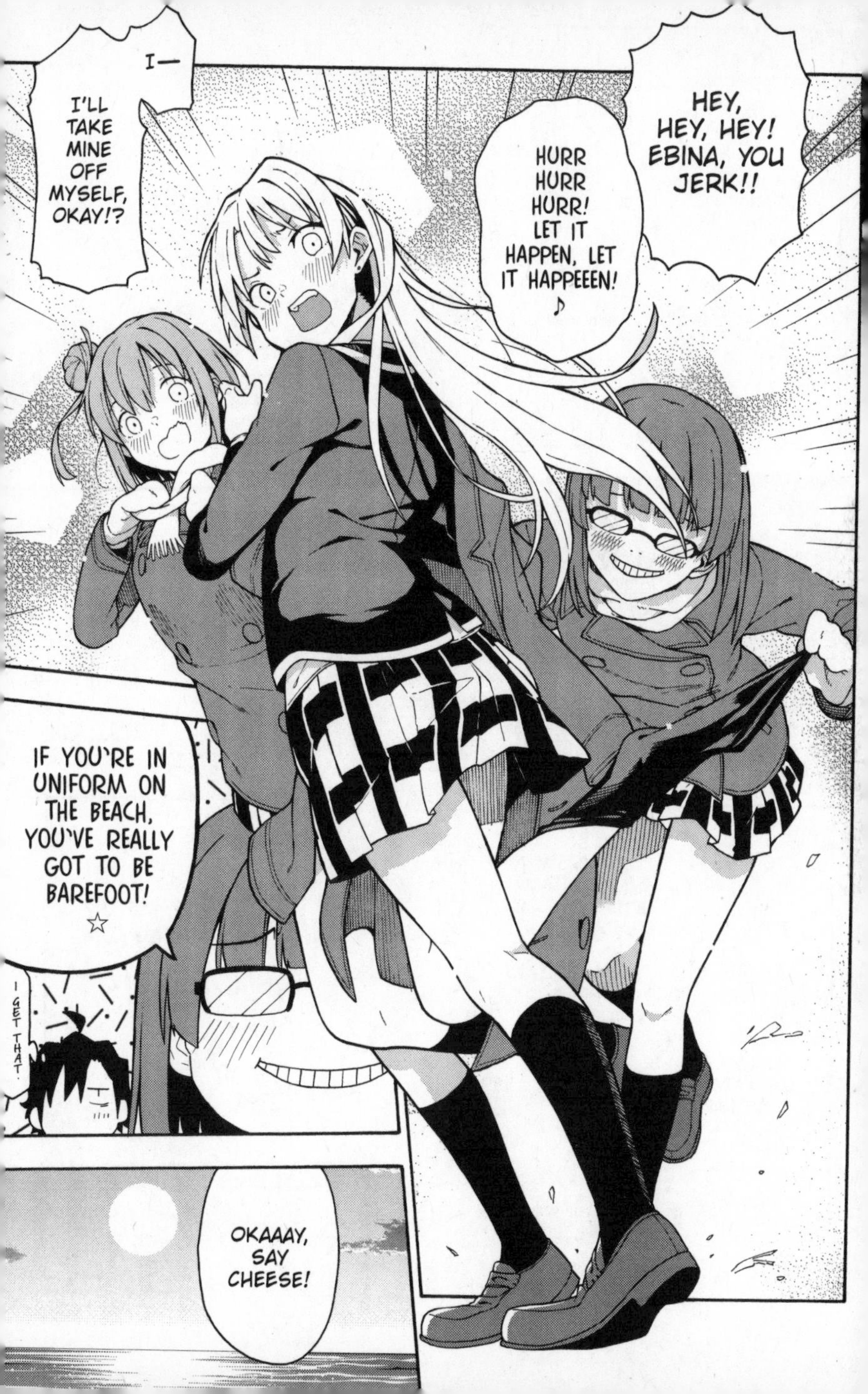
HEY, HEY, HEY! EBINA, YOU JERK!!
HURR HURR HURR! LET IT HAPPEN, LET IT HAPPEEEN! ♪
I— I'LL TAKE MINE OFF MYSELF, OKAY!?
IF YOU'RE IN UNIFORM ON THE BEACH, YOU'VE REALLY GOT TO BE BAREFOOT! ☆
I GET THAT.
OKAAAY, SAY CHEESE!

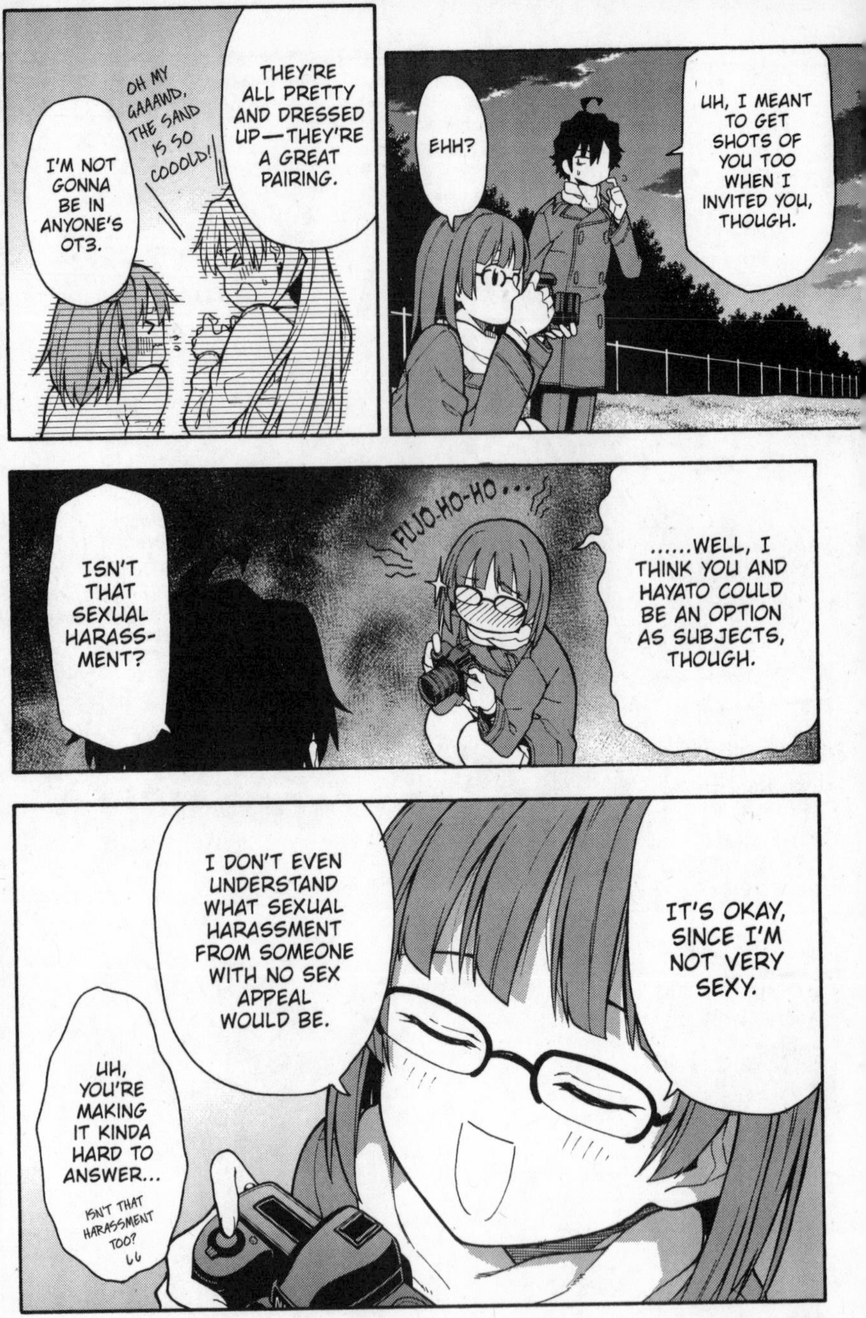
UH, I MEANT TO GET SHOTS OF YOU TOO WHEN I INVITED YOU, THOUGH.
EHH?
THEY'RE ALL PRETTY AND DRESSED UP—THEY'RE A GREAT PAIRING.
OH MY GAAAWD, THE SAND IS SO COOOLD!
I'M NOT GONNA BE IN ANYONE'S OT3.
......WELL, I THINK YOU AND HAYATO COULD BE AN OPTION AS SUBJECTS, THOUGH.
FUJO-HO-HO...
ISN'T THAT SEXUAL HARASS-MENT?
IT'S OKAY, SINCE I'M NOT VERY SEXY.
I DON'T EVEN UNDERSTAND WHAT SEXUAL HARASSMENT FROM SOMEONE WITH NO SEX APPEAL WOULD BE.
UH, YOU'RE MAKING IT KINDA HARD TO ANSWER...
ISN'T THAT HARASSMENT TOO?

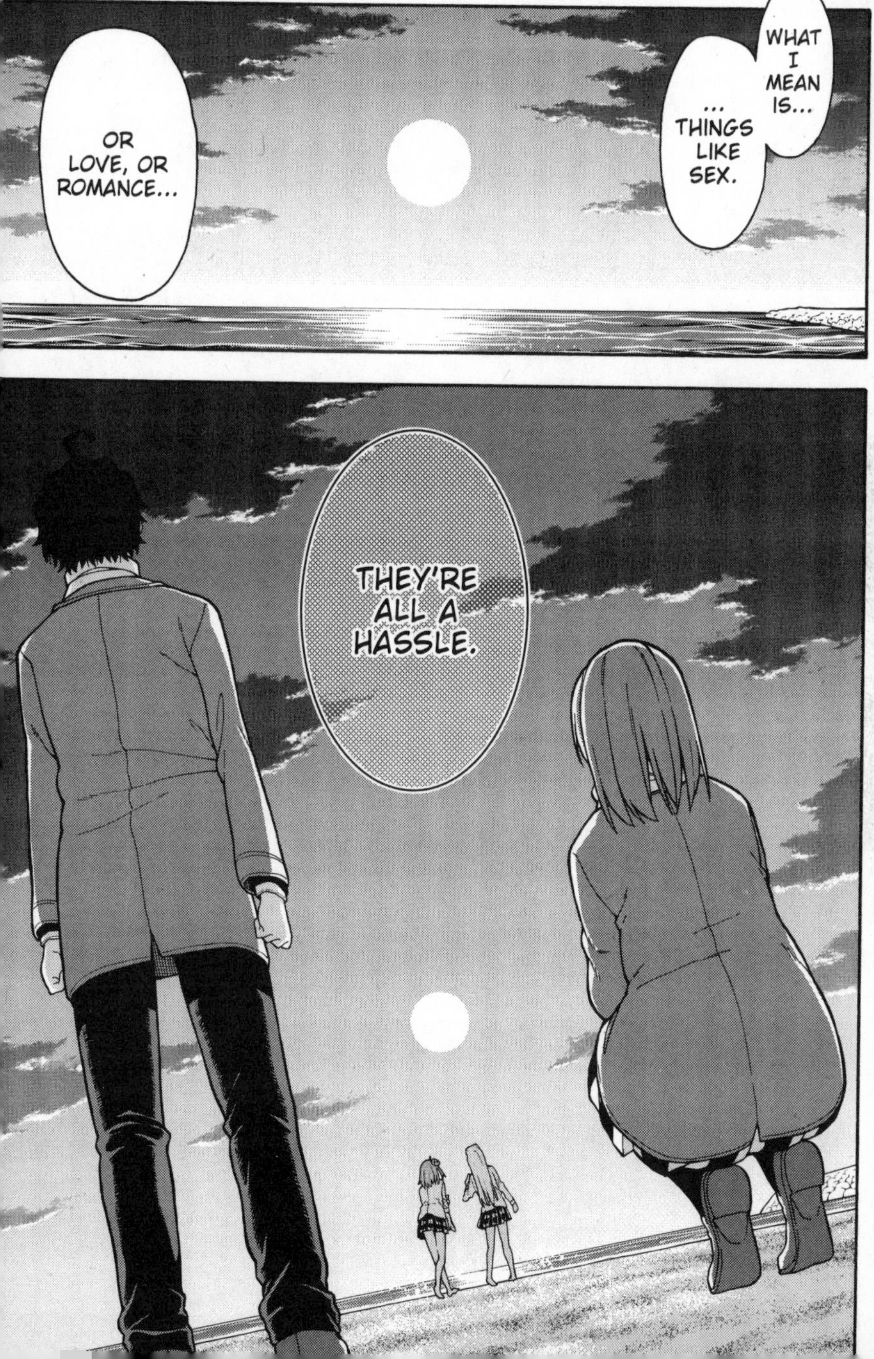
WHAT I MEAN IS...
...THINGS LIKE SEX.
OR LOVE, OR ROMANCE...
THEY'RE ALL A HASSLE.

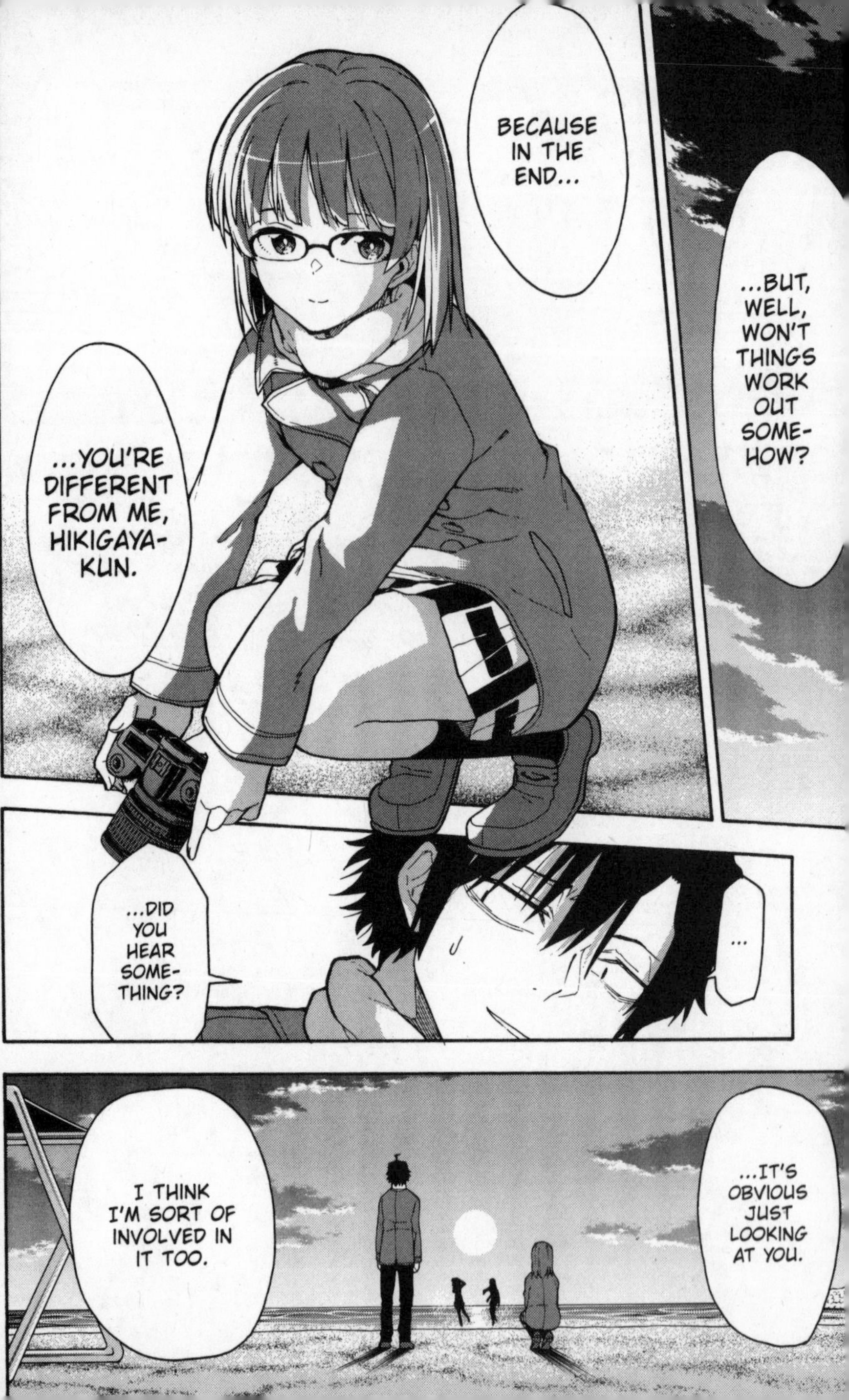
...BUT, WELL, WON'T THINGS WORK OUT SOME-HOW?
BECAUSE IN THE END...
...YOU'RE DIFFERENT FROM ME, HIKIGAYA-KUN.
...
...DID YOU HEAR SOME-THING?
...IT'S OBVIOUS JUST LOOKING AT YOU.
I THINK I'M SORT OF INVOLVED IN IT TOO.

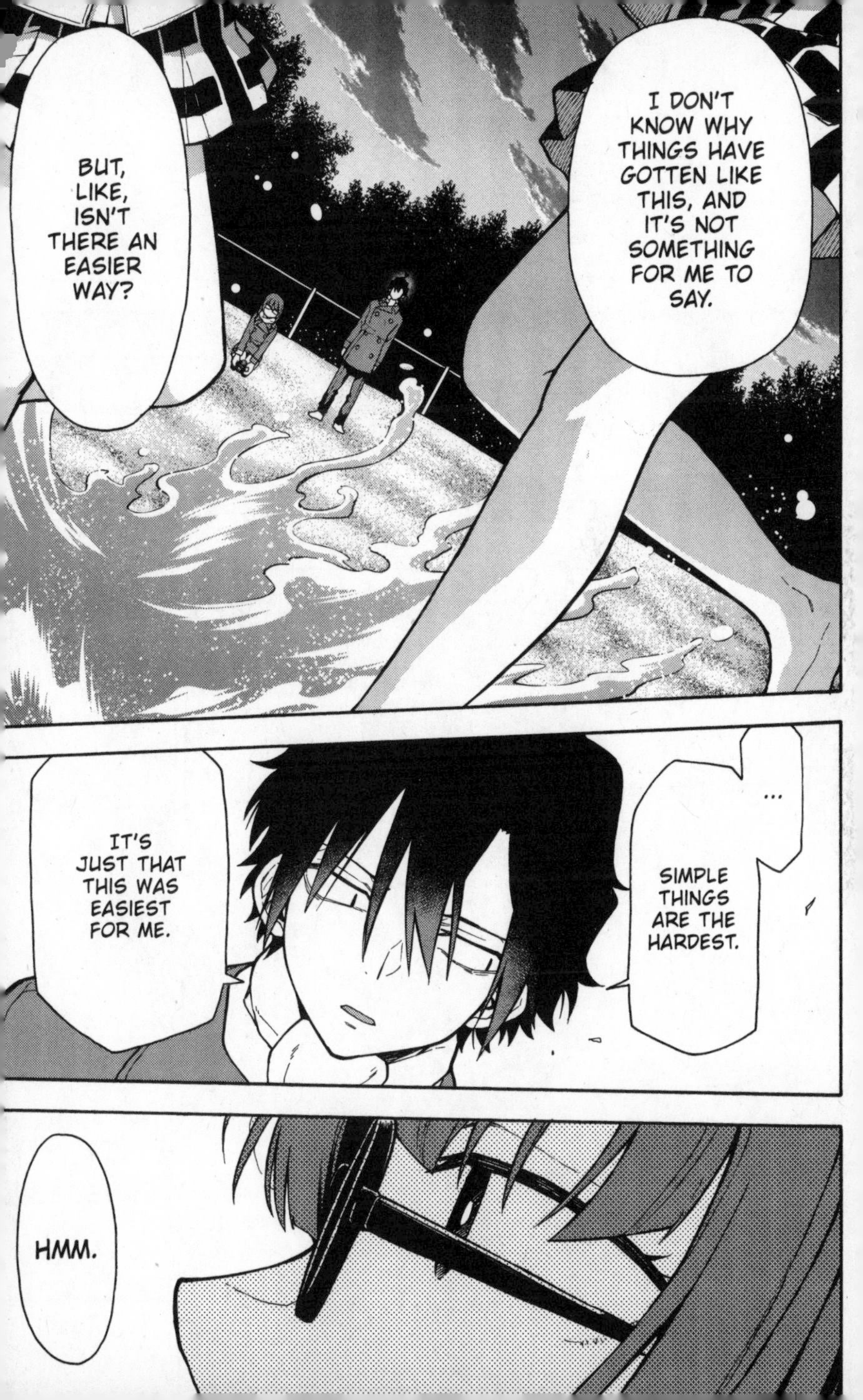
I DON'T KNOW WHY THINGS HAVE GOTTEN LIKE THIS, AND IT'S NOT SOMETHING FOR ME TO SAY.
BUT, LIKE, ISN'T THERE AN EASIER WAY?
...
SIMPLE THINGS ARE THE HARDEST.
IT'S JUST THAT THIS WAS EASIEST FOR ME.
HMM.

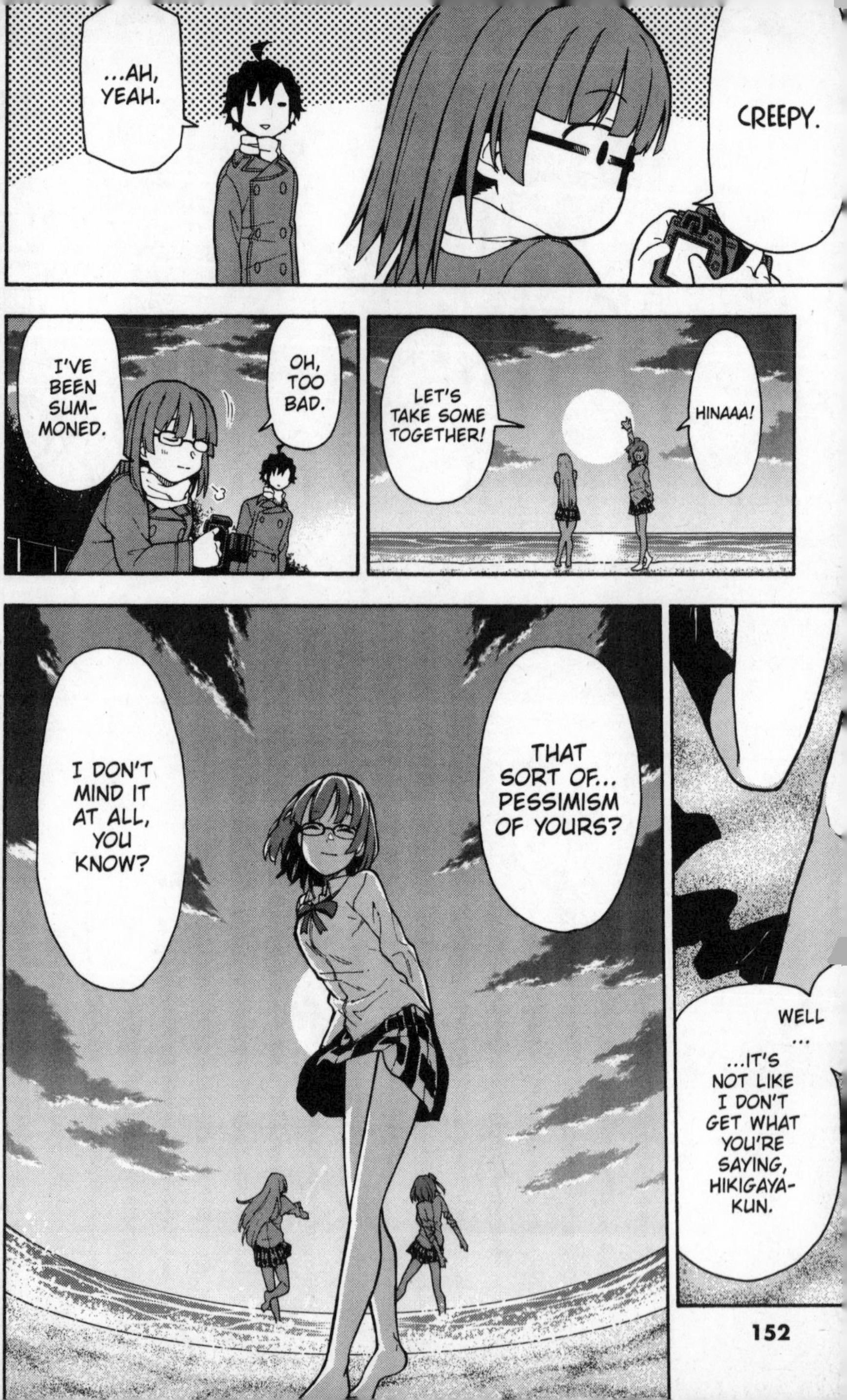
CREEPY.
...AH, YEAH.
HINAAA!
LET'S TAKE SOME TOGETHER!
OH, TOO BAD.
I'VE BEEN SUM-MONED.
WELL... ...IT'S NOT LIKE I DON'T GET WHAT YOU'RE SAYING, HIKIGAYA-KUN.
THAT SORT OF... PESSIMISM OF YOURS?
I DON'T MIND IT AT ALL, YOU KNOW?

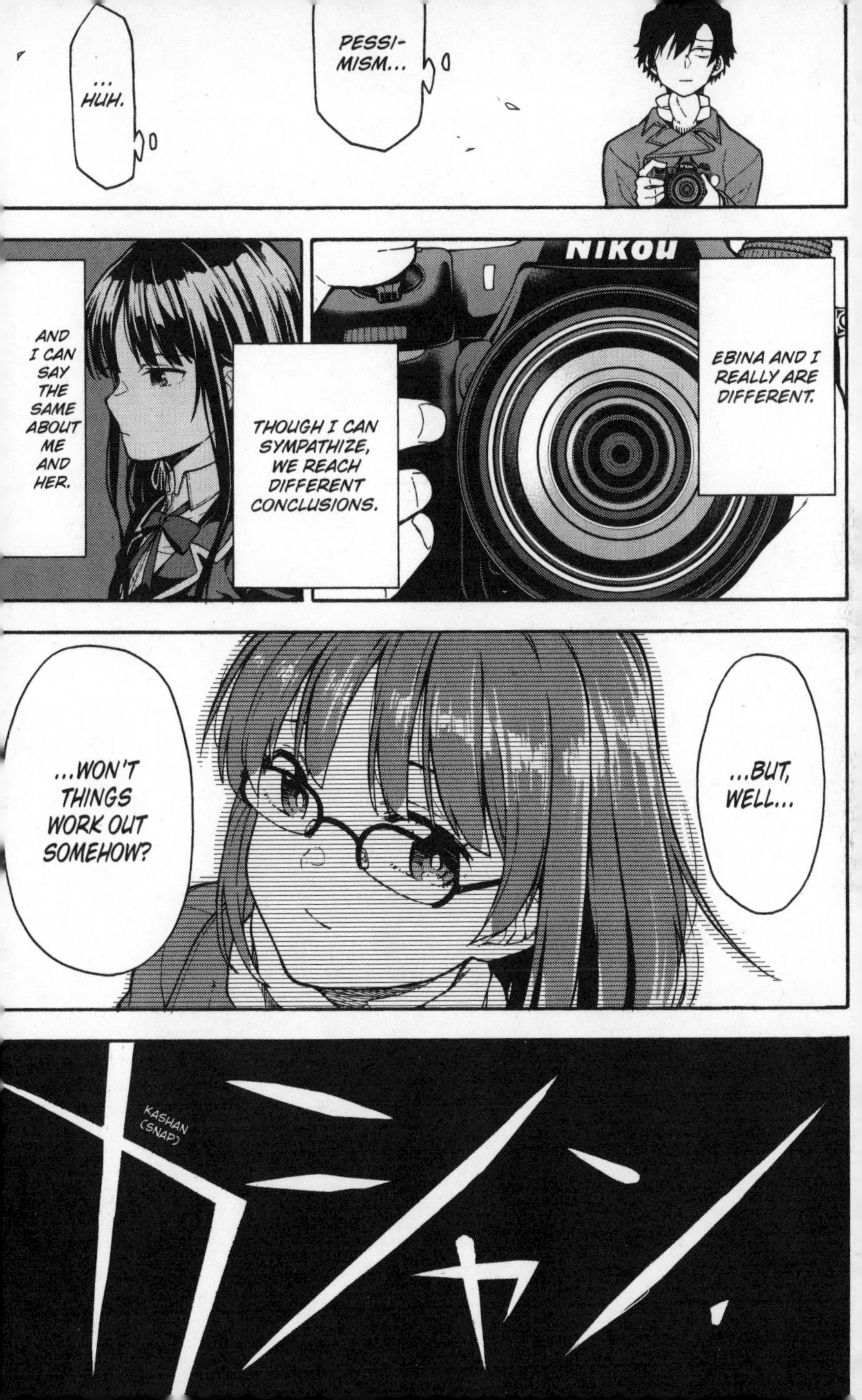
PESSI-MISM...
...HUH.
EBINA AND I REALLY ARE DIFFERENT.
THOUGH I CAN SYMPATHIZE, WE REACH DIFFERENT CONCLUSIONS.
AND I CAN SAY THE SAME ABOUT ME AND HER.
...BUT, WELL...
...WON'T THINGS WORK OUT SOMEHOW?
KASHAN (SNAP)

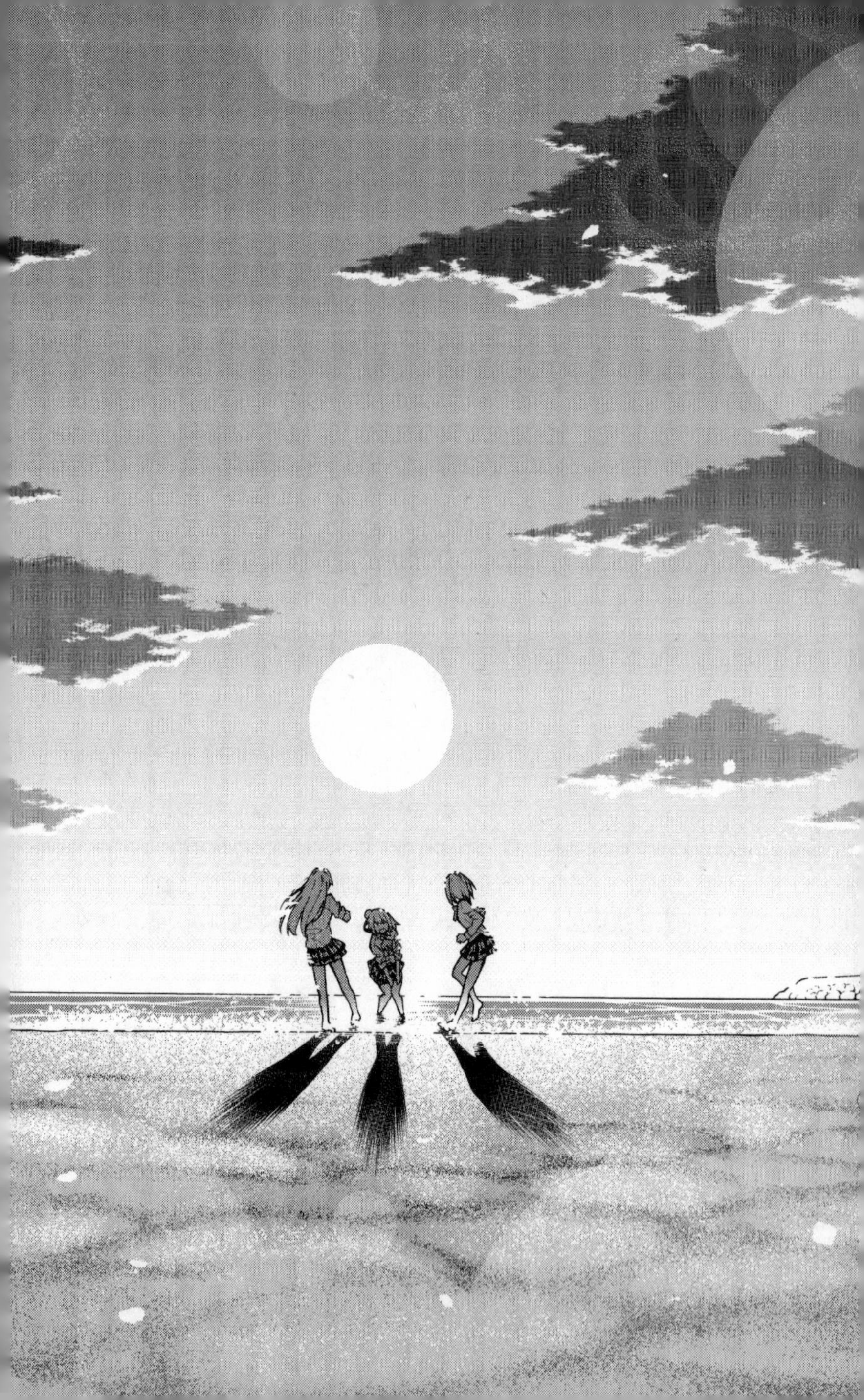

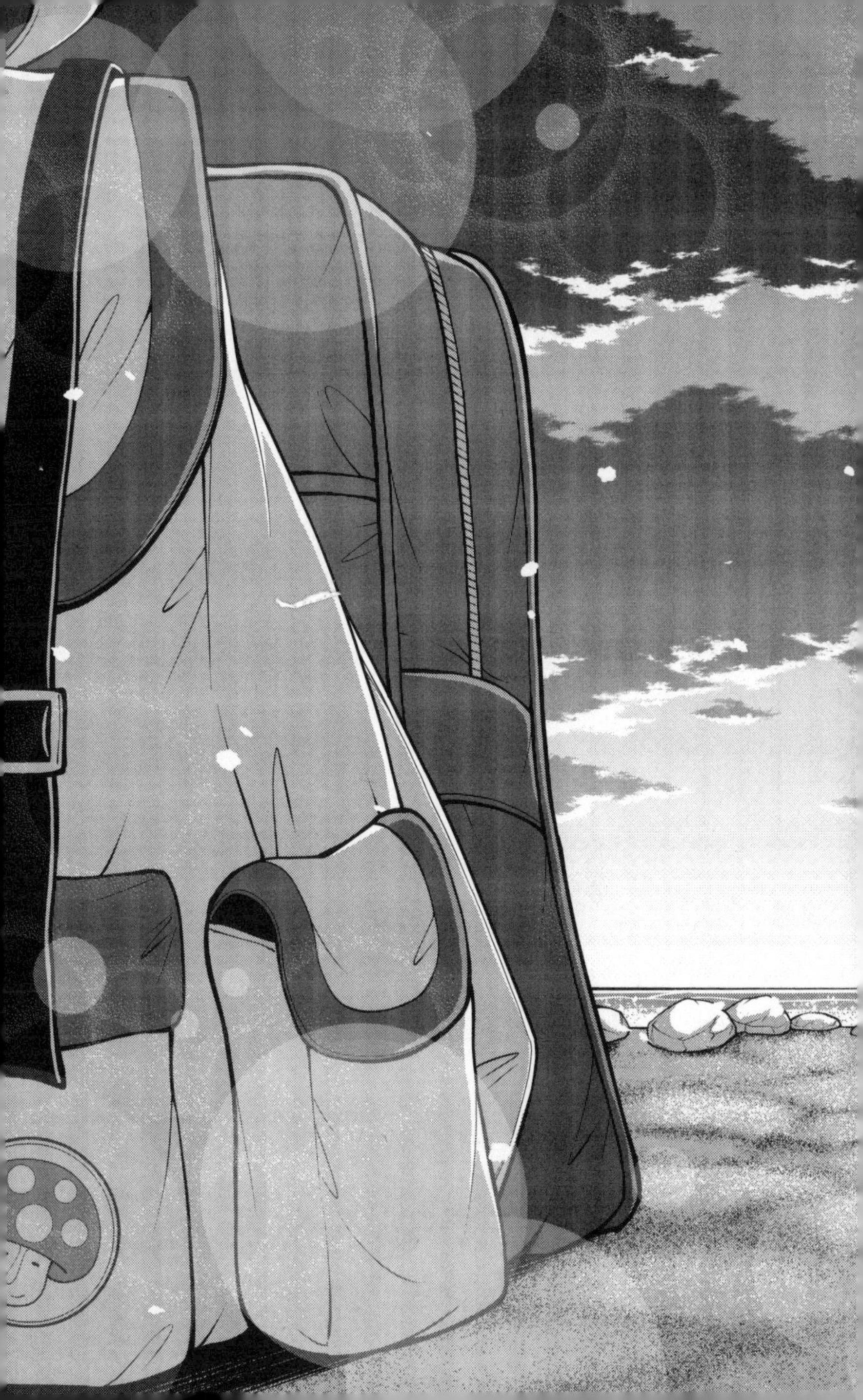

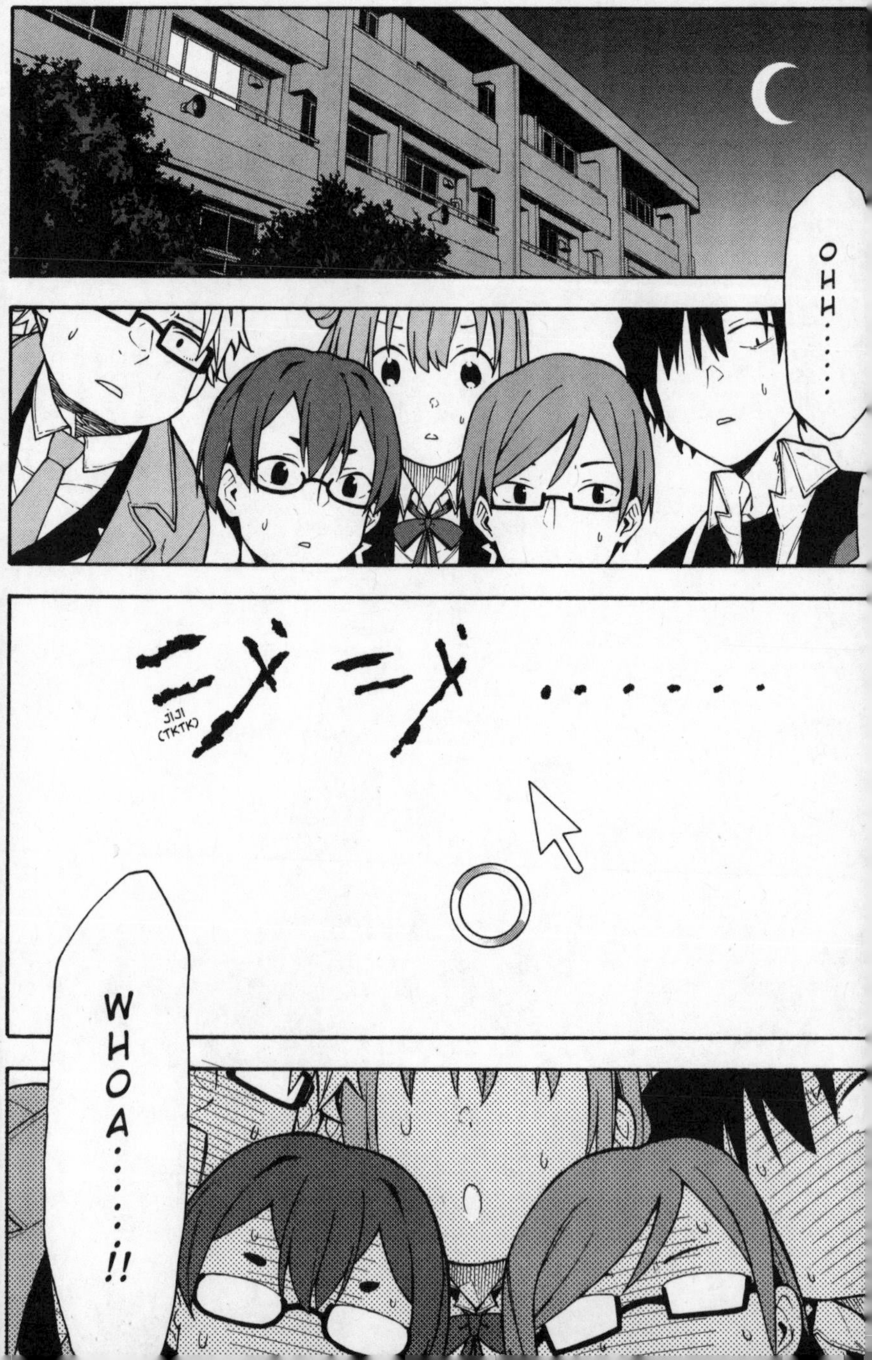
OHH......
ジジ......
JIJI (TKTK)
WHOA......!!

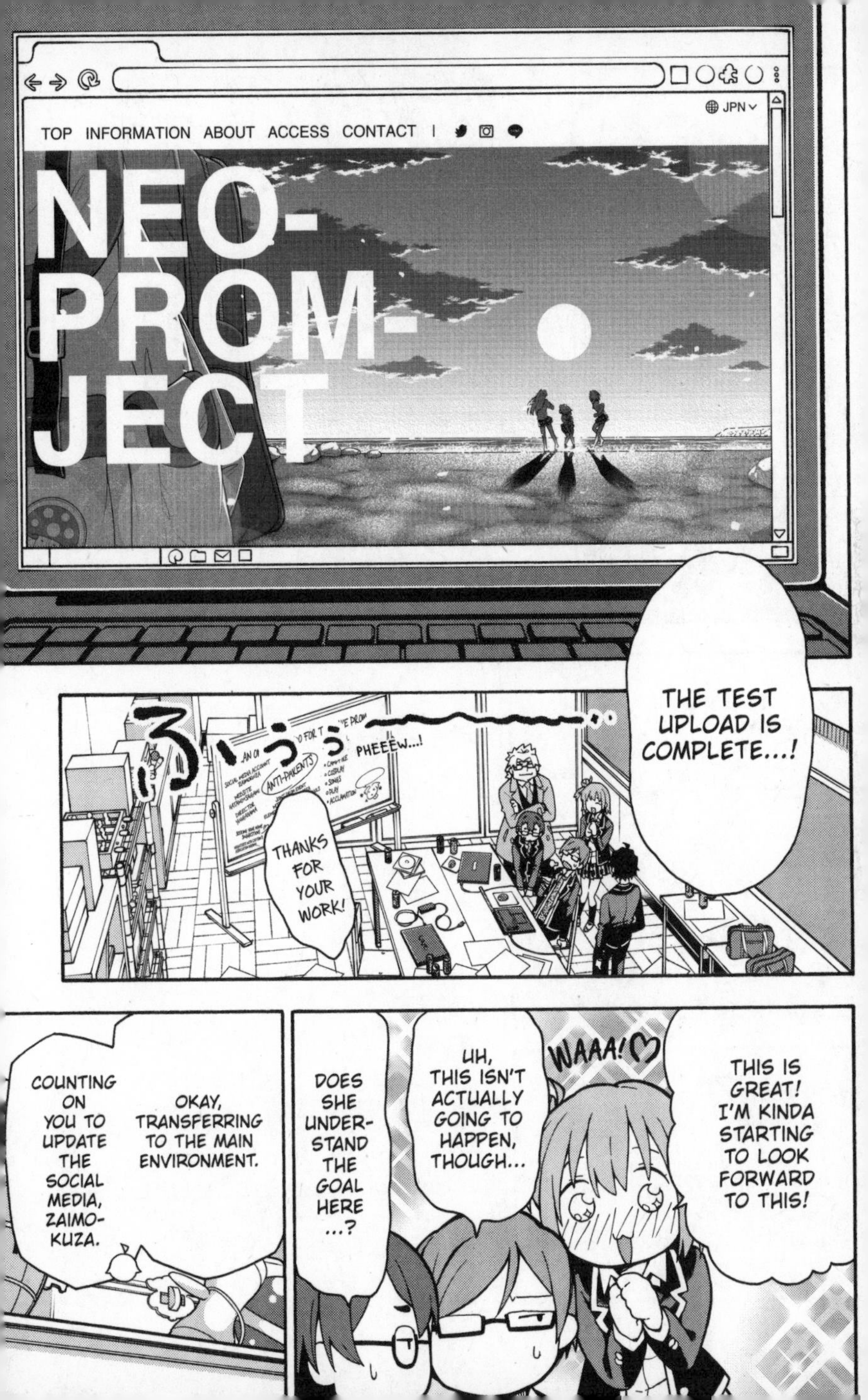
JPN
TOP INFORMATION ABOUT ACCESS CONTACT
NEO-PROM-JECT
THE TEST UPLOAD IS COMPLETE...!
ふぅ～
PHEEEW...!
ANTI-PARENTS
THANKS FOR YOUR WORK!
THIS IS GREAT! I'M KINDA STARTING TO LOOK FORWARD TO THIS!
WAAA!♡
UH, THIS ISN'T ACTUALLY GOING TO HAPPEN, THOUGH...
DOES SHE UNDERSTAND THE GOAL HERE...?
OKAY, TRANSFERRING TO THE MAIN ENVIRONMENT.
COUNTING ON YOU TO UPDATE THE SOCIAL MEDIA, ZAIMOKUZA.

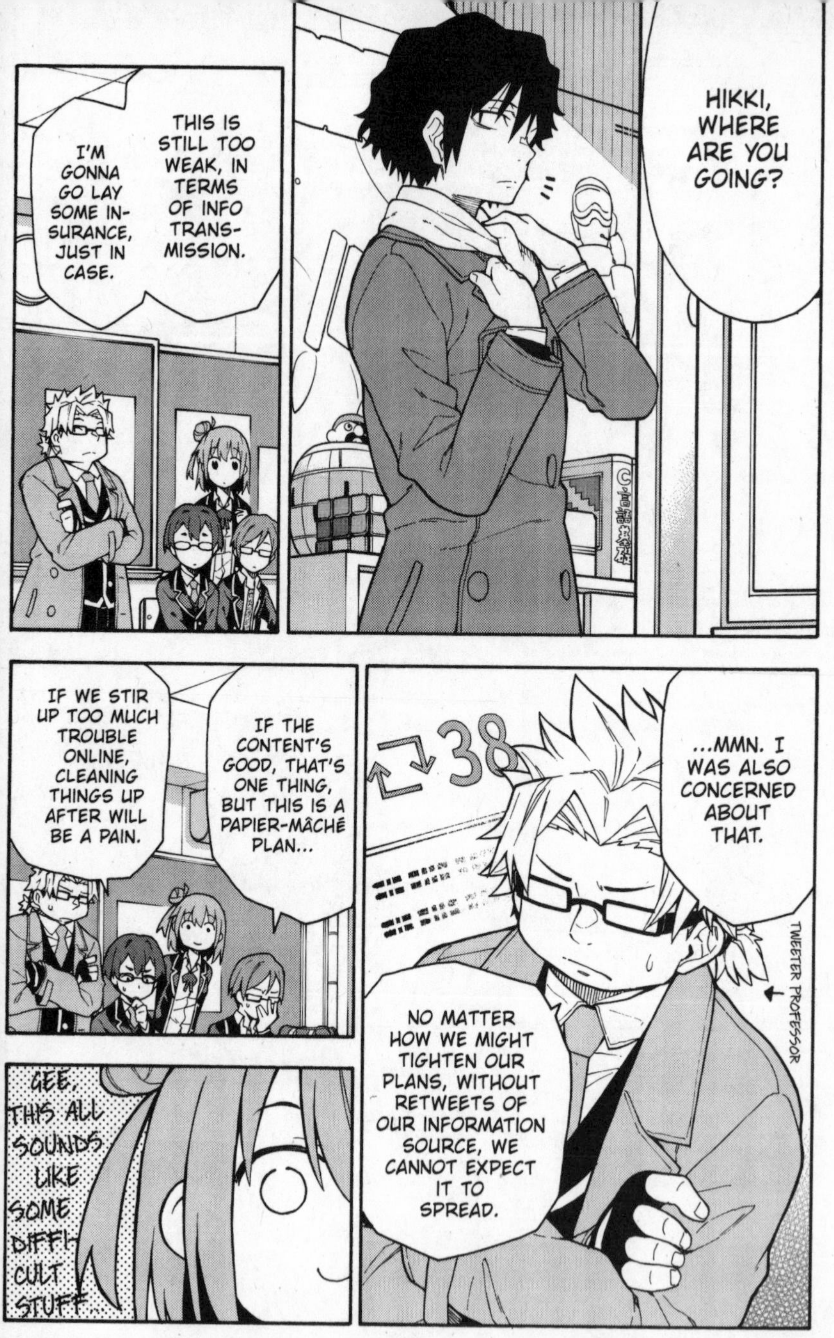
HIKKI, WHERE ARE YOU GOING?
THIS IS STILL TOO WEAK, IN TERMS OF INFO TRANS-MISSION.
I'M GONNA GO LAY SOME IN-SURANCE, JUST IN CASE.
38
...MMN. I WAS ALSO CONCERNED ABOUT THAT.
TWEETER PROFESSOR
NO MATTER HOW WE MIGHT TIGHTEN OUR PLANS, WITHOUT RETWEETS OF OUR INFORMATION SOURCE, WE CANNOT EXPECT IT TO SPREAD.
IF THE CONTENT'S GOOD, THAT'S ONE THING, BUT THIS IS A PAPIER-MÂCHÉ PLAN...
IF WE STIR UP TOO MUCH TROUBLE ONLINE, CLEANING THINGS UP AFTER WILL BE A PAIN.
GEE, THIS ALL SOUNDS LIKE SOME DIFFI-CULT STUFF...

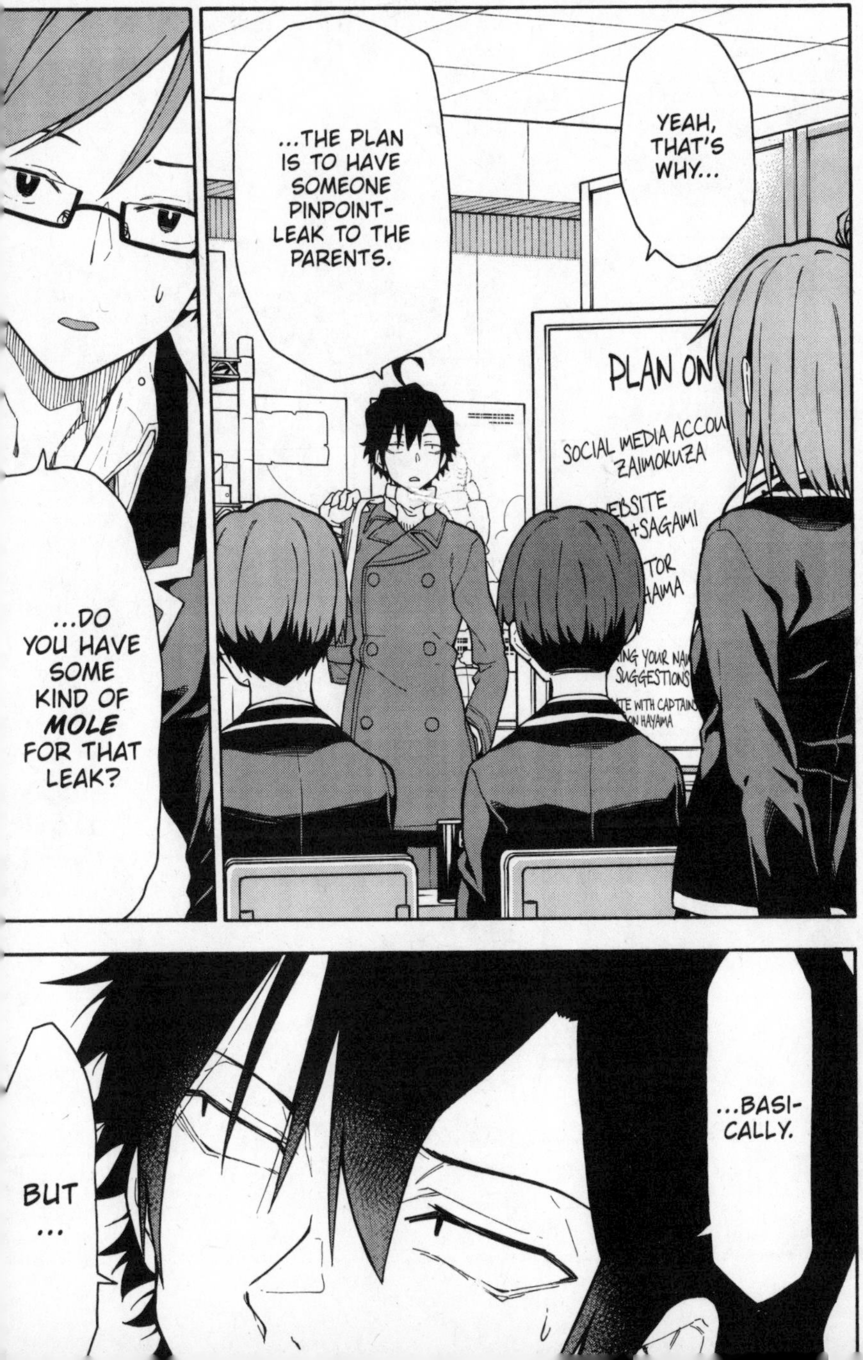
YEAH, THAT'S WHY...
...THE PLAN IS TO HAVE SOMEONE PINPOINT-LEAK TO THE PARENTS.
PLAN ON
SOCIAL MEDIA ACCOU
ZAIMOKUZA
SUGGESTIONS
...DO YOU HAVE SOME KIND OF *MOLE* FOR THAT LEAK?
...BASI-CALLY.
BUT ...

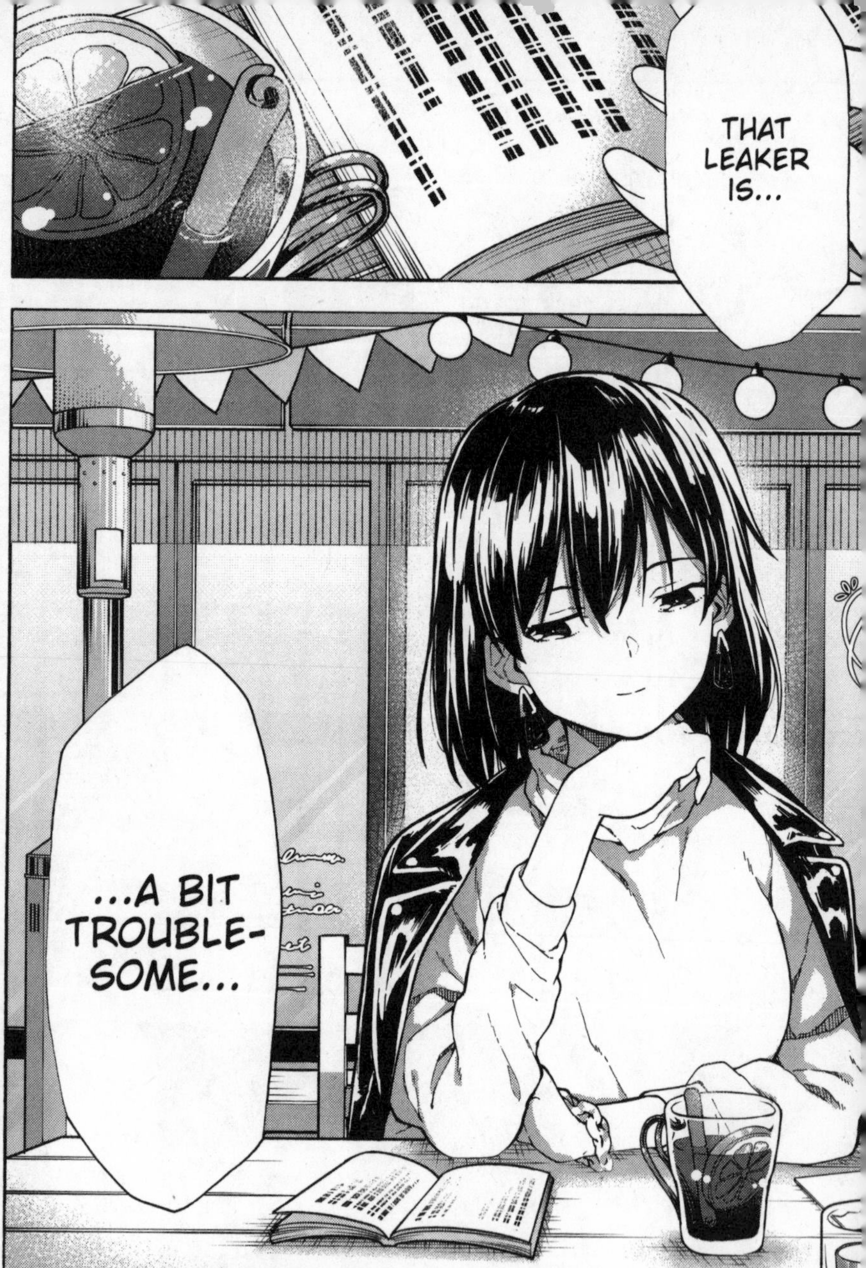
THAT LEAKER IS...
...A BIT TROUBLE-SOME...

TRANSLATION NOTES

Page 10
WAX Coffee is a parody of an actual brand called MAX Coffee.

Page 34
Saizeruya is a reference to the Italian-style family restaurant chain Saizeriya.

Page 37
M-2 Syndrome, or *chuunibyou* in Japanese, refers to the kind of cringey behavior one expects from a second-year middle school student and what someone that age would expect to sound cool and mysterious.

Page 53
Nishi-Chiba Lucky and **Numa Ace** are parody names of arcades in Chiba.

Page 54
"Wait! And hope!" is a line from the novel *The Count of Monte Cristo*, as well as the anime based on it, *Gankutsuou*.

Page 60
-shi is an impersonal honorific used in formal speech or writing, e.g. legal documents. It's another aspect of Zaimokuza's dorky manner of speaking.

Page 109
Destiny Land and **Destiny Sea** are parodies of the Japanese amusement parks Tokyo Disneyland and Tokyo DisneySea.

Page 110
In Japan, the school year typically starts in **April**.

Page 133
Katakana is one of the three writing systems used in the Japanese language and, in modern times, is mostly used for loanwords.

Page 147
"Hurr-hurr-hurr! Let it happen, let it happeeen!" is a stereotypical line in period dramas, often accompanied by the *"obi* spin," where a man yanks on a woman's sash, ripping it off to spin her like a top.

MY YOUTH ROMANTIC COMEDY IS WRONG, AS I EXPECTE

...To Be Continued

SPOT THE DIFFERENCES ANSWERS

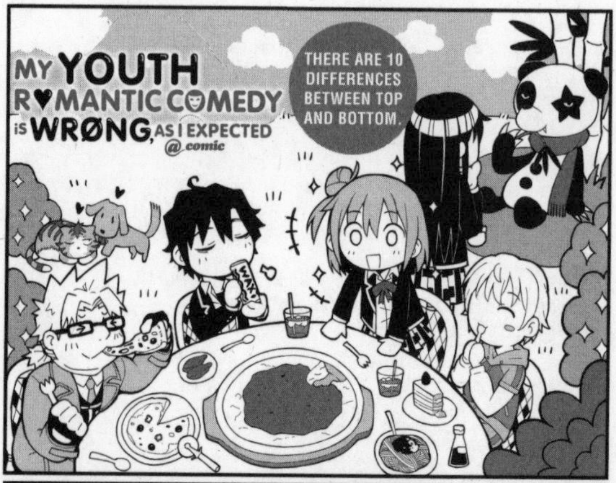
MY YOUTH ROMANTIC COMEDY is WRONG, AS I EXPECTED @comic
THERE ARE 10 DIFFERENCES BETWEEN TOP AND BOTTOM.
WAX

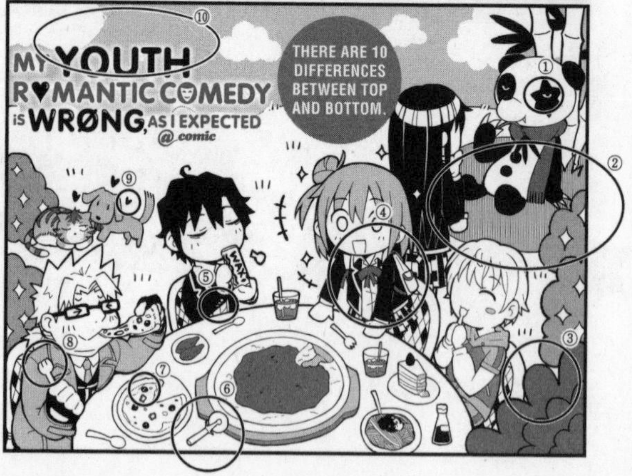
MY YOUTH ROMANTIC COMEDY is WRONG, AS I EXPECTED @comic
THERE ARE 10 DIFFERENCES BETWEEN TOP AND BOTTOM.
WAX

① The pattern in Pan-san's eyes is different.
② The pattern of the grass is different.
③ The angle of the grass is different.
④ Yui is wearing a backpack.
⑤ There's one extra button.
⑥ The pizza slicer is facing the other way.
⑦ There's an extra salami slice.
⑧ The shape of the fork is different.
⑨ Sablé's love is one heart stronger.
⑩ "Youth" isn't shiny enough.

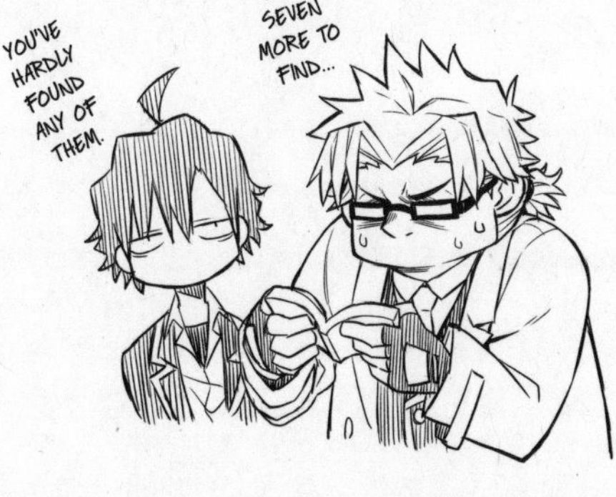
I HAVE ONLY SEVEN MORE TO FIND...
YOU'VE HARDLY FOUND ANY OF THEM.

MY YOUTH ROMANTIC COMEDY IS WRONG, AS I EXPECTED @COMIC ⑱

Original Story: Wataru Watari
Art: Naomichi Io
Character Design: Ponkan⑧
ORIGINAL COVER DESIGN/Hiroyuki KAWASOME (Graphio)

Translation: Jennifer Ward

Lettering: Bianca Pistillo

YAHARI ORE NO SEISHUN LOVE COME WA MACHIGATTEIRU.
@COMIC Vol. 18 by Wataru WATARI, Naomichi IO, PONKAN⑧
© 2013 Wataru WATARI, Naomichi IO, PONKAN⑧
All rights reserved.
Original Japanese edition published by SHOGAKUKAN.
English translation rights arranged with SHOGAKUKAN through Tuttle-Mori Agency, Inc., Tokyo.

English translation © 2022 by Yen Press, LLC

Yen Press
150 West 30th Street, 19th Floor
New York, NY 10001

Visit us at yenpress.com
facebook.com/yenpress
twitter.com/yenpress
yenpress.tumblr.com
instagram.com/yenpress

First Yen Press Edition: July 2022
Edited by Yen Press Editorial: Carl Li
Designed by Yen Press Design: Wendy Chan

Yen Press is an imprint of Yen Press, LLC.
The Yen Press name and logo are trademarks of Yen Press, LLC.

The publisher is not responsible for websites (or their content) that are not owned by the publisher.

Library of Congress Control Number: 2016931004

ISBNs: 978-1-9753-4789-5 (paperback)
       978-1-9753-4790-1 (ebook)

10 9 8 7 6 5 4 3 2 1

WOR

Printed in the United States of America